Cities and Growth

Cities and Growth

A Policy Handbook

Edited by ROGER L. KEMP

McFarland & Company, Inc., Publishers
Jefferson, North Carolina, and London

Library of Congress Cataloguing-in-Publication Data

Cities and growth : a policy handbook / edited by Roger L. Kemp.
p.   cm.
Includes bibliographical references and index.

ISBN-13: 978-0-7864-3197-7
softcover : 50# alkaline paper ∞

1. City planning — United States.   2. Cities and towns — United
States — Growth.   3. Sustainable development — United States.
I. Kemp, Roger L.
HT165.52.C58   2008   307.1'2160973 — dc22   2007037360

British Library cataloguing data are available

Cover image © 2007 Shutterstock

Manufactured in the United States of America

McFarland & Company, Inc., Publishers
Box 611, Jefferson, North Carolina 28640
www.mcfarlandpub.com

To Anika,
who will make the world a better place

Acknowledgments

Grateful acknowledgment is made to the following organizations and publishers for granting permission to reprint the material contained in this volume.

American Planning Association
Congressional Quarterly Inc.
Government Finance Officers Association
International City/County Management Association
League of California Cities
Missouri Municipal League
National Association of Regional Councils
National Center for Small Communities
National Civil League
New Hampshire Local Government Center
New Jersey State League of Municipalities
PRIMEDIA Business Magazines & Media
Prism Business Media
The Trust for Public Land
University of Baltimore
University of Georgia
Urban Land Institute
World Future Society

Table of Contents

Part III. The Future

Preface

Citizens, nonprofit organizations, and local public officials, in increasing numbers, are embracing growth management practices as a vehicle to facilitate positive growth in their downtowns, as well as enhance general planning practices within their communities. Public officials especially are learning that they have the municipal power to shape their environment, both in their downtowns and suburbs, in a positive manner to enhance the quality of life within their cities and towns. Not only can those involved in local government processes renew their neighborhoods and downtowns, they can have a profound influence on new growth patterns within their respective political jurisdictions. Contemporary growth management practices are quickly becoming a fact of life in our communities as our nation enters the 21st century.

The types of modern planning practices evolving in our communities now include measures that promote planning practices that relate to the creation, protection, preservation, and restoration of the man-made environment. The essence of the major contemporary planning projects and programs described in this volume in each of these categories is briefly highlighted below.

- "Creation" planning practices involve those land use and development regulations and techniques that will lead to the establishment of desirable downtowns, neighborhoods, and suburbs, including the protection and promotion of nature, during the coming years.

- "Protection" planning programs include those land use and development regulations and techniques that create measures to safeguard our downtowns, neighborhoods, and suburbs from further deterioration to either the man-made or natural environment, however limited it may be in some urban areas.

- "Preservation" planning projects encompass those land use and development regulations and techniques that impose requirements on the preservation of existing desirable qualities of the man-made and natural environments in our urban and suburban areas. Preservation techniques may focus on our suburban or rural areas of our cities and towns, due to past development patterns.

- "Restoration" planning initiatives focus on those land use and development laws that assist in the restoration of the deteriorated man-made and natural environment in our inner cities, their neighborhoods as well as their suburbs, and the more rural portions of land remaining in our communities.

This volume is broken down into four sections for ease of reference. The first section introduces the reader to the rapidly evolving field of "cities and growth." The second section and by design the longest, includes numerous case studies, or best practices, on how cities and towns (as well as their nonprofit organizations and public officials) are taking measures to create, protect, preserve, and restore

1

their urban, suburban, and especially their more rural areas. The next section focuses on the future of these contemporary, and evolving, planning practices. Several appendices are included in the last section of this volume to promote a greater understanding of this new field. Based on this conceptual schema, the four primary sections of this volume are explained in greater detail below.

- *Cities and Growth.* Chapters in this section describe the interrelationship of cities, land uses, and transportation; the impact of regulatory reform on redevelopment practices; and how cities are calculating their development impact fees. The last two chapters of this introductory section focus on contemporary county and state growth management practices. These chapters provide the framework and background against which the best growth management practices have emerged in America's cities in recent years.
- *The Best Practices.* The cities and towns examined in this volume, including the states in which they are located, as well as the best planning and redevelopment practices being utilized are listed below categorically in alphabetical order. These case studies represent *an important and significant* effort to obtain a body of knowledge on the best practices available in the dynamic, and still evolving, field of the best growth management practices in our nation's cities.

Cities —

Apopka	Colorado Springs
Athens	Concord
Austin	Cummings
Berea	Eastville
Bernards	Franklin
Boston	Hanover
Boulder	Hartford
Bozeman	Hoboken
Cape Coral	Irwindale
Cherry Hill	Las Vegas

Lowell	San Diego
Memphis	Santa Rosa
Minneapolis	Sarasota
Nashua	Seattle
Oakland	Silver Spring
Parkville	Stamford
Riverside	Taos
Rochester	Tulare
St. Louis	Vancouver
St. Maries	West Des Moines
St. Paul	

States —

Alaska	Missouri
California	Montana
Colorado	Nevada
Connecticut	New Hampshire
Florida	New Jersey
Georgia	New Mexico
Idaho	New York
Iowa	Tennessee
Kentucky	Texas
Maryland	Virginia
Massachusetts	Washington
Minnesota	

Best Practices —

Affordable housing and inner-city renewal

Air quality improvements and environmental protection

Citizen index, downtown renewal, and the quality of life

Colleges, cities, and neighborhood renewal

Community Development Corporations and urban renewal

Community visioning processes help plan for future growth

Development review process enhancements promote needed growth

Digital services, planning, and downtown renewal

Enhancing nature in downtown areas

Environmental controls and the protection of nature

Forest land preservation limits future growth

General Plan revisions and growth management practices

Global warming reductions protect the environment

Going "green" in the core promotes neighborhood renewal

"Green" practices and enhanced growth practices protect the environment

Heritage preservation promotes downtown renewal

Housing in the inner-city promotes downtown renewal

Inner city renewal through redevelopment practices

Inner-ring suburb improvements and neighborhood revitalization

Interactive growth model enhances urban planning

Land trusts, nonprofit organizations, and open space preservation

Main Street revitalization promotes inner-city renewal

Mixed commercial uses facilitate downtown renewal

Mixed land uses foster Main Street revitalization

Native lands preservation through nonprofit organizations

Neighborhood preservation enhances downtown renewal

Nonprofit organizations and environmental protection

Park improvements and inner-city revitalization

Redeveloping contaminated downtown areas promotes inner-city renewal

Redevelopment practices promote community safety

Redevelopment practices enhance the revitalization of downtown areas

Revenue distribution promotes development restrictions

Restorative development enhances downtown renewal

Revitalization practices improve inner-city neighborhoods

Safety improvements through enhanced urban design practices

Sustainable development promotes neighborhood renewal

Technology practices assist in controlling urban growth

Waterfront improvements facilitate downtown renewal

- **The Future.** The third, and final, section of this volume examines future trends in cities, societal changes taking place in them, as well as their urban growth patterns; cities and their infrastructure; and cities and their environment. The deterioration of our infrastructure and environment are two factors influencing the development of new urban planning practices. The final two chapters in this section examine and describe evolving "telecities" and their impact on future urban growth patterns, as well as the trend toward developing sustainable communities throughout our nation.

  These readings reflect that the various initiatives and best practices described in this volume related to the protection, restoration, and enhancement of our urban environment are here to stay. Modern planning and redevelopment practices that achieve this goal are being designed and implemented with greater frequency during the past few years. The various diseconomies associated with past planning and development practices, which have deteriorated our environment, have facilitated these positive planning practices.

- **Appendices.** Several appendices are included in this volume. They include a listing of all U.S. periodicals focusing on urban planning practices, a contemporary glossary of urban planning terms, and a comprehensive list of acronyms and abbreviations in the urban planning field. The last two appendices include a regional resource directory for those readers who wish to follow-up on any of the best practices mentioned in this volume, and a national resource directory that describes professional associations and research organizations serving local governments in the field of urban planning.

The various case studies in this volume represent state-of-the-art practices of how cities, nonprofit organizations, and local public officials alike are using new growth management practices to promote inner-city renewal, suburban planning, as well as restore and enhance the natural environment upon which our cities are based. All of these modern planning practices represent additional tools and techniques within the traditional field of city planning.

The various case studies contained in the best practices section of this volume are typically applied in a piecemeal and incremental fashion in cities and towns throughout America. For the most part, citizens, nonprofit organizations, and local public officials are preoccupied with projects within their respective communities. They do not have the time to find out what other neighboring cities and towns are doing in this area, let alone what other communities are doing throughout the nation. For this reason, the various case studies, or best practices, selected for this reference volume represent an important codification of knowledge in this new and rapidly evolving field.

This reference work assembles, for the first time, materials based on a national literature search, and makes this information available to citizens and public officials throughout the United States. The goal of this volume is to help educate citizens, as well as their public officials, on how to use these new planning and redevelopment practices to improve their own communities.

If additional information is desired to follow-up on any of the best practice case studies contained in this volume, every city and town listed in each chapter is included in the Regional Resource located in the appendix of this volume. Additional information can easily be obtained from this directory by contacting those individuals at the cities and towns included in this directory. Important state, regional, and natural resources are also brought together for the first time in the National Resource Directory to assist readers in becoming more informed about the evolving field of contemporary urban planning and growth management practices.

Roger L. Kemp
Meriden, Connecticut
October 2007

CHAPTER 1

Cities, Land Use, and Transportation

Curtis Johnson

I was riding along late last fall down a Maryland parkway with a good friend from college days, a former theology student who later became a developer. A very successful developer.

We were going to winterize his boat on the eastern shore, and had just made a couple of stops, in one of those suburban centers where, to look for something in a marine supply store, and then a hardware store, we had to get back into his car and drive a few hundred feet, even though we could see the second store from the first one.

Heading toward Annapolis, I decided to test his contemporary theology a bit by suggesting that our near-absolute dependence on automobiles had run its cultural course; that it might be good for civilization if we walked more; that if we got out of the cars which seemed to reduce our standards of personal encounter from friendly handshakes to obscene finger-gestures, we might solve some other problems as well.

My friend wasn't saying much, so I kept talking, rambling on about places I knew around the country where people were asking tough questions about the form of growth and development we've practiced over the past 40 years. I implied that big boxes and strip malls and monotonous subdivision residences don't always pay off economically these days, and besides, people were starting to talk again about whether the urban forms we choose — the way businesses and homes and streets and schools are related — might have some influence over whether we can act as a community.

"Wait a minute," said my friend, "you're missing the main point of this business, or maybe you're just forgetting how it works. I've done well as a developer because I'm building exactly what people want. If there were a market for something different, we'd be building it."

He went on lecturing me about the vagaries of working with municipal planning commissions, the costs of seeking variances, but most of all the feasibility of sprawl as an enduring American development strategy. "Even here in the east," he said, "we've still got lots of land. It's a big country, a prosperous, resilient economy. What's wrong with extending the roads and sewers and building more schools and retail? People want new places. They're pleased to pay for them."

Originally published as "Land Use, Transportation, and the Sustainable Region," *National Civic Review*, Vol. 85, No. 2, Spring-Summer 1996. Published by the National Civic League, Denver, CO. Reprinted with permission of the publisher.

The statistics do seem to back up my friend's argument. According to the U.S. Department of Transportation, in the 20 years ending in 1990, while overall population gained by 21 percent, the number of auto trips went up 50 percent, number of miles driven 82 percent, and the number of vehicles 128 percent. Cars are safer, fatalities are fewer, toxic emissions are trending down. Average vehicle occupancy slipped by 16 percent. During peak hours, cars average 1.6 persons, 1.1 overall, with each person making 3.5 trips a day.

From 1980 to 1992, transit's share of total trips dropped to 4 percent of work trips, 2 percent of all trips. Nine of every 10 persons over 16 years of age has a driver's license and owns or leases at least one vehicle. The average urban commuter spends 7 percent of daily wages on the work trip, compared with the 20 percent the turn-of-the-century worker shelled out to take the streetcar to work.

Fuel economy is up. Taxes on fuel remain flat. In the spring of 1996 a debate broke out in Washington over repealing the last 4.3 cents added in 1993, because the price at the pump had soared from 1950 to 1956 levels.

The picture one gets is a middle-aged baby-boomer executive driving to a Sierra Club meeting — alone — in his Jeep Grand Cherokee.

But even after this cold bath of realism, some of us still have suspicions that the affordability, the environmental sustainability, and the quality of community life in our region are threatened by extending the pattern of post–World War II America into the 21st century. What policies would have any effect on this pattern, and are they politically plausible?

If more communities were developed at higher densities with accessible transit, would it make any serious difference? Professional researchers, such as Reid Ewing of Florida International University, describe studies in search of a causal effect from higher densities on transportation behavior. Using fairly simple analysis of variance to compare communities in Palm Beach County (Florida), land use

effects appear not to significantly affect the number of trips, or the tendency to combine trips, or the much-observed modal split.

However, using more complex regression techniques, controlling for variables such as household size, income, and number of workers per unit, he did find that *accessibility* to transit made a powerful difference in travel times experienced. Accessibility and density also increased the prospects for "auto-shedding."

But headways — or the frequency of service — and the ratio of jobs to population in the community turn out to be the only reliable predictors of transit usage, along with the emergence of any truly serious charges for parking.

Just to give my friend the developer even more comfort, Genevieve Giuliano of the University of Southern California points to research showing the powerful appeal of "remote" living areas, where life is presumably safer and schools are believed better, which are factors far outranking accessibility or affordability.

She reminds us that Los Angeles' in-progress rail investment, pegged at $78.3 billion and counting, will raise the modal split there from 4.5 percent to a breath-taking 7 to 10 percent. Our in-place infrastructure around automotive travel is already so vast and likely to last so long, that nearly all changes come at the margin.

Even the celebrated LUTRAQ Project in the Portland area gets only 10 percent reduction in vehicle use and peak-hour vehicle travel from a major shift in land-use policy. And those effects are mostly traceable to a proposed transportation demand policy of making transit free while charging drivers a rate pegged to Portland's parking market.

My friend would admit one thing, though: automobile travel is subsidized every way we can think of. He conceded that car owners don't pay for the pollution they generate, or the consequences of road congestion, or emergency services, or even all road repairs.

Those costs are benignly buried in the property tax bills of fellow citizens. Direct fees for car ownership in America are the world's lowest, and parking remains free for most workers and shoppers. Small wonder that mostly the poor fear the decline of transit.

On the other hand, we Americans are a road-running, gas-guzzling pack of individuals who don't see much practical limit to the land we can consume or the energy it takes to do it. For those of us with suspicions about the sustainability of all this, what would it take to make a dent in our smug, sprawl-stuck car culture?

First, we should try some honesty in pricing. Whether it's fixing the problem on a congested local interstate or extending sewer interceptors to where growth is going, let's tell the truth about what it's going to cost and suggest a way to get the funding from the folks who're producing the demand. That means giving toll roads a try, mounting demonstrations of congestion pricing for high-demand corridors and peak times, and demanding realistic impact fees for new growth. (In some states, including Minnesota, these fees not only aren't common, they aren't even legal.)

While it makes obvious sense to confront our communities with the mounting costs of modern American forms of development and transportation, it strikes few people as politically realistic. Whose campaign for office wants to wonder aloud if our dominant form of development and its transportation consequences have degraded our environment, stretched the fabric of community to the breaking point, and created an infrastructure so vast that keeping it functional is producing costs people don't want to pay?

For a half century now, we have worshipped the notion of unfettered freedom to choose the location of our homes and businesses. The role of public policy has been to see that the bill gets sent to our neighbors.

We have consistently chased individual decisions about business and residential locations with new infrastructure. People, acting in rational self-interest, go to where the prices are lowest for the value they get. Developers work where regulations are the fewest. Then everybody turns to the public sector. If the roads are gravel-covered, we do a quick bow and pave them. If they're too narrow, we widen them. Someone shows up at a city council meeting and says they aren't safe, so we add shoulders and semaphores. We replicate the police stations, fire stations, retail centers, medical clinics, and schools, even if that leaves idle capacity — sometimes not yet paid for — behind.

At the same time, the most recent round of Clean Air Act amendments created pressure for metropolitan planning organizations (MPOs) to rip out of their twenty-year transportation improvement plans all the road improvements for which they don't have predictable revenues. In region after region, the emerging message, though not yet well heard, is: "The roads you see out there, folks, are the roads you're going to have for the next generation."

If we want more people to buy or build near the infrastructure we've already built, or have any choice about using public transportation, then let's create the right incentives.

For example, the Minnesota Legislature in 1995 offered a commercial industrial tax break to new businesses willing to locate within a quarter mile of a transit stop — a small step but in the right direction.

How about trying location-efficient mortgages for individuals, as they are doing around the revitalized Green Line transit service in Chicago — offering a lower interest rate, or lower down payments, or higher allowable house payments to people buying homes close to major transit investments? This policy recognizes and rewards the prospects of less reliance on the car. It institutionalizes confidence in transit.

If we were serious, other incentives spring to mind: How about cashing out hidden parking benefits, or charging the users what they actually cost? Or converting auto insurance to a pay-as-you-go system, collected at the pump?

Seeing that now occasional cost show up in the 50 to 70 cent per gallon range every time you fill up is estimated to have a 15 percent near-term and 40 percent long-term effect on vehicle miles traveled.

If "frequency" is the critical variable in building higher transit use, then let's get bold enough to try it. As federal funds for transit disappear, transit in most American regions is a terrible tale of higher prices and lower service. Let's put a radically different proposition to state legislatures: fund time-limited experiments, stepping up the frequency of bus service to neighborhoods in the urban core. Make it possible for anyone who's chosen an urban lifestyle to get to work and other daily destinations without using a car. Make service so frequent that no one has to learn a schedule. Keep fares affordable and measure the results. It would take a lot of money to try this ... almost as much as we might save in the long run.

For incentives to he really powerful, more choices are necessary.

How many business travelers would walk right by the car rental counter if there were real confidence in finding taxi service? In most American cities, taxis are a regulated scarcity. When Indianapolis Mayor Stephen Goldsmith set his sights on his city's taxi policies, he found that customers had to call or search out locations where taxis were stationed. It was actually illegal to hail a cab. No more. Now even some innovative jitney services are showing up along congested corridors.

Of course, along the dense corridors of the Atlantic seaboard, there are transit choices, but dark storm clouds hang over their fiscal future. And elsewhere around the country, the climate for higher quality transit has created its own clouds.

Over the past twenty years, some cities have launched or restored some rail service, in the hopes of guiding development and reducing congestion. Results are modest so far. But in most American regions the prospect for creating new choices has been squandered in an endless argument over light rail. In the Twin Cities we raised this squabble to the level of a civic art form.

It is now time to forget, in all our regional discussions, who was right or wrong. The realities are clear: if transit is to become a major factor in shaping a region's growth or serving more than the poor, it will come in a planned series of smaller steps.

The first step? Build demonstration transitways along corridors where there is day-long demand for transit. Connect high-traffic destinations. Pay for it with highway construction funds. After all, it'll be a real road, on which vehicles with rubber tires will travel. Make it bus-exclusive. The difference: people can see what it's like to take an express trip that doesn't compete with the traffic — without spending a fortune to find that out. As congestion mounts on roads, transit use will likely grow. When revenues and ridership make the case, rails can be put down and new rolling stock ordered. In Pittsburgh and Ottawa, corridors started out as busways and became railways.

In most regions, it doesn't take much searching to find some existing rail track not being fully used, and often this track is in right-of-ways that make sense for transit. Where track is available we should borrow from recent European development of "railbuses," transit cars designed to run on regular rail tracks, powered by efficient diesel engines — a system that costs a tenth of new light rail construction.

In most American regions, rail, as we've considered it and argued over it, is just too expensive for what it delivers. We can still have exclusive corridors for transit, though, at much lower prices, and have a powerful effect on the quality of the region's infrastructure.

Choices are already making a comeback in urban residential form, with a wave of neo-traditional communities showing up in both re-development and new development. Don't mistake this trend for a passing fancy in architectural design. The driving energy is social, and it's about reconnecting with each other.

That's why the lots are smaller and common spaces larger. It's the reason for seeing sidewalks again. It's the logic of having civic spaces in a neighborhood square, and the convenience of mixing in services and shops within footreach.

Not everybody wants a community with walkable destinations and transit accessibility, with smaller lots and larger parks, with narrow streets and shorter setbacks. But what's the case for making that choice largely illegal, as most *zoning* codes manage to do? Surely it's possible at least to remove the legal barriers to this form of community development.

While there is noticeable pressure to change the policy framework that shapes our communities — city by city, town by town — it is difficult to imagine much progress without success in redefining what the community is.

The most exciting recasting of the question is going on at the regional level. Whether it's the Twin Cities Metropolitan Council confronting its community with growth management strategies, or Atlanta reaching for 41 priorities developed through a multi-year consensus process, or Portland with its fifty-year reach into the next century with a regional commitment to the shape and quality of their community, it is becoming clear that the real drama is set on a regional "citistate" stage.

Few people are interested in a "government" answer to our problems. But most people who have tried new public processes are prepared to say that "governance" is the answer. We simply must find ways to make public commitments on difficult questions across entire regions.

Issues of land use and transportation are windows through which to see the challenge. And in most regions, the greatest successes in regional decisions have come in the process for deciding transportation improvement priorities under the Intermodal Surface Transportation Efficiency Act (ISTEA).

As the close of the century opens our minds to what the future holds for the American experiment, we can find good news in remembering how much we can do — region by region — if we have a consensus to act. Rediscovering the connections between land use and transportation and effective communities is local stuff. We don't have to change the world, just our community.

CHAPTER 2

Cities and Economic Development

Richard C. Feiock *and* Moon-Gi Jeong

Government regulations are often perceived as a barrier to economic growth. Local policymakers care about both the local environment and the economy, but they often confront choices between environmental protection and economic development (Brown 1992; 1994). This chapter critically evaluates the relationship between local regulation and economic development and presents an argument, based on transaction cost theories of governance, that development tradeoffs may not be inevitable.

We identify reforms designed to reduce uncertainty in the regulatory permitting process and examine whether such reforms might provide a means of protecting the local environment without imposing onerous burdens on industry or developers. Our empirical analysis reports enhanced economic growth in those communities that consolidate and coordinate regulatory permitting procedures. Although regulatory reforms are just one of many local actions that may impact development, regulation is unique in that it influences not just the costs of production, but also levels of uncertainty for investments. Thus, even stringent environmental regulation can reduce regulatory uncertainty and have the potential to promote economic growth while protecting the environment.

How Does Regulation Affect Development?

Questions regarding the economic implications of local government programs, policies, and regulations have interested scholars in several disciplines. To organize inquiry into the economic development consequences of local regulation, one first needs an analytical framework that provides a basis for explaining how regulatory costs influence the amount and location of new development. After elaborating upon this framework, we identify the ways in which local governments may be able to pursue regulatory goals without creating disincentives for development. One approach is to pursue regulatory reforms that lessen private-sector transaction costs by reducing regulatory uncertainty.

Competition for interjurisdictional development has led to numerous studies of business location decisions and of the economic consequences of local taxes, expenditures, and other programs on economic growth. It is clear that regulation can increase a firm's cost of producing goods. Local regulatory programs reduce the return on development investment if they increase firm-level production costs. In fact, critics of regulation point to

Originally published as "Regulatory Reform and Urban Economic Development," *State and Local Government Review*, Vol. 34, No. 3, Fall 2002. Published by the Carl Vinson Institute of Government, University of Georgia, Athens, GA. Reprinted with permission of the publisher.

state and local government regulations that exceed federal requirements and often result in costly delays (Conway Data Corporation 1981). Mounting empirical studies document increased production costs resulting from compliance with environmental regulation and provide evidence that these regulatory costs lead to reduced output, higher prices, and reduced income growth (Christiansen and Haveman 1981).

Related to the general question of whether costs imposed by government influence industrial investment are specific questions about how regulations affect the allocation of these developmental investments among communities. Attempts to answer these questions have focused on the relationship between local government policies and firm location decisions (Deurkson 1983; Yandle 1984; 1989; Gunther 1991) and on estimations of econometric models of local economic performance (Feiock 1994). Both of these literatures conclude that, although nongovernmental factors are more important in a firm's decision to locate to a particular state or region, taxes incentives and regulatory costs also influence not only which local jurisdiction is chosen, but also the resulting patterns of economic growth (Steines 1984; Warner 1987; Brace 1991; 1993; Bartik 1991). Econometric studies have not isolated regulatory costs but have established that overall business climate contributes to economic growth. This factor is particularly important because survey evidence suggests that perceptions of a jurisdiction's desirability as a location for investment are highly influenced by the friendliness of regulatory policy toward business (Wasylenko and McGuire 1985).

The development implications of regulatory costs are magnified by competition from neighboring states and communities. For this reason, competition among local governments may result in regulatory relief being used as a development incentive. Once a firm decides to locate in a particular region based on nongovernmental factors, local government policy becomes an important consideration in the choice among communities within a region (Wasylenko 1980; Kale 1984; Bartik 1991). Thus, local governments may use regulatory costs to gain an advantage (Feiock and Rowland 1991). Stringent regulation is costly because producers are free to "punish" local governments that impose regulatory costs on business by shifting resources to neighboring jurisdictions with more business-friendly regulations. The result may be tit-for-tat competition in reducing regulatory costs. Rowland and Marz (1981) describe this phenomenon as the regulatory equivalent to Gresham's Law, which holds that bad regulation pushes out good regulation, resulting in a "race to the bottom."

Regulating Without Economic Loss

The investment decisions of firms in certain industries are very sensitive to the costs of regulation (Feiock and Rowland 1991). It is the delay and uncertainty of regulatory processes that is often most objectionable and most costly. The burden of regulation is not just a function of its stringency; it also depends on the length and certainty of the development review and approval process (Feiock 2000). Reforms of regulatory processes to make property rights more secure and reduce regulatory uncertainty provide mechanisms to minimize disincentives. If these reforms effectively reduce uncertainty and delays, they provide a strategic advantage in competition for development. Effective economic development that emphasizes the structure rather than the stringency of regulation will promote adaptation of the private sector to more productive forms of organization and activity (Fosler 1992). Reforms, such as streamlined or "one-stop" permitting processes, seek to reduce risk and transaction costs for business by simplifying regulation.

Complex, unclear, or inconsistent regulation creates uncertainty for new investment. Variations in future regulatory directives that cannot be anticipated create a risky environment for investors that result in increased capital costs. Complex regulatory processes that create uncertainty regarding requirements and future expectations will therefore discourage new investment (Clingermayer 1989).

Regulation — even stringent regulation — if it is clear, stable, and certain, may diminish investment risk and reduce investment costs. Local governments with stable and certain patterns and processes of regulation may therefore be able to stringently regulate while promoting economic growth. Certain structures and processes of regulation, such as centralization of regulatory functions and strategic planning initiatives, have been demonstrated to reduce uncertainty in the regulatory environment (Feiock 2000; Feiock and Stream 2001).

Unified (rather than fragmented) organizational structures reduce coordination costs and ease the transmission of information. In particular, regulatory reforms such as one-stop facility permitting, which consolidates the process of gaining approval for new development and facility expansion, simplifies local regulatory processes (Council of State Governments 1975; Rabe 1986; 1995). Recent work at the state level demonstrates that economic growth is enhanced as transaction costs are lessened by administrative arrangements that reduce uncertainty regarding property rights (Feiock and Stream 2001). In the next section, we present our data and methods and then report an empirical test to evaluate the effects of regulatory reforms on local economic development.

Research Design

We first identified communities that have implemented one-stop permit issuance processes for new development. The effects of these reforms on the number of new businesses and capital investment are then estimated. We utilize data collected in a survey of local government economic development officials conducted by the International City Management Association (ICMA) in 1989. The survey collected information on local government economic development practices. In particular, the questionnaire identified communities that have implemented one-stop permit issuance processes for simplifying regulatory processes. The ICMA survey data provide useful information to understand changing reform activities in local governments. In addition, the survey collects information on form of municipal government, economic base of the community, and patterns of previous economic growth. These data were supplemented with U.S. census bureau population statistics.

Our intention is to explain patterns of new industrial development across cities. We therefore incorporated a longitudinal dimension by examining the consequent impact of regulatory reform on local industrial development between 1987 and 1992. Economic development is often conceptualized in terms of attracting both new firms and new investment. We utilized two indicators of economic development: total numbers of manufacture establishments and new capital investments in manufacture. The sources of these indicators come from Census of Manufactures, Geographic Area Series for 1987 and 1992. These two variables were collected for the 469 cities with populations of 10,000 or more that are included in the ICMA survey.

The relationship between regulatory reform and local economic performance was estimated using ordinary least squares (OLS) regression techniques. Regulatory reform effects were estimated for each indicator of local economic performance. To control for the communities' economic base, we identified a set of variables according to the ICMA survey. We constructed four dummy variables corresponding to the predominant economic base in a community: industrial, commercial, institutional, or residential. In addition, we controlled for the type of city and metropolitan status with dummy variables that measure whether or not a community is a central city and whether or not it is a suburb.

Findings

Table 1 reports those characteristics of the sample cities that were controlled for in the analysis of local economic development: metropolitan status, form of government, predominant economic base, and previous growth patterns. More than half of the cities are suburban communities; approximately two-thirds employ a council-manager form of government. Most cities have an industrial, commer-

Table 1. Characteristics of Sample Cities

	Total	
	Number	*Percent*
Metropolitan Status	147	31.34
Central city	241	51.39
Suburban	81	17.27
Independent[a]		
Form of Government		
Mayor-council	127	27.08
Council-manager	318	67.80
Town meeting	9	1.92
Representative	9	1.92
Town-commission	6	1.28
Predominant Economic Base[b]		
Agriculture	28	5.97
Industrial	142	30.28
Commercial	158	33.69
Institutional	41	8.74
Residential	100	21.32
Previous Growth Patterns		
Rapid expansion[c]	77	16.42
Moderate growth[d]	175	37.31
Slow growth[e]	131	27.93
Stable economic base[f]	50	10.66
Modest decline[g]	21	4.48
Significant decline[h]	15	3.20

[a] Independent = city is not in a metropolitan statistical area.
[b] Industrial municipality primarily has manufacturing firms as economic base; cities with mainly service-sector firms are classified as commercial community. As the main economic base, institutional municipality has a military base, state government, university, etc.
[c] Rapid expansion = more than 25 percent
[d] Moderate growth = 10 percent to 25 percent
[e] Slow growth = less than 10 percent
[f] Stable economic base = no real growth or decline
[g] Modest decline = less than 10 percent
[h] Significant decline = more than 10 percent

cial, or residential economic base. Previous growth patterns describe the approximate growth rate of communities' economies during the five years preceding the 1989 survey. Two-thirds of the cities report moderate or slow growth in the local economy.

The incidence of regulatory reform among these cities is reported in Table 2. This table reports the frequency and percentage of cities that have adopted consolidated one-stop regulatory permitting. By 1989 over 40 percent of the sample cities had adopted one-stop permitting practices.

The effect of regulatory reform on local economic performance is estimated in Tables 3 and 4. In each table, economic growth was estimated in terms of manufacturing activities in 1992. Economic performance outcomes for 1987 are included as lagged dependent variables to control for existing economic conditions. Inclusion of this variable allows us to estimate the marginal effects of regulatory policy on economic performance after taking into account previous economic conditions.

Table 3 estimates the total number of manufacture establishments. The model goodness of fit is about .99. Consolidated/one-stop permit issuance had a positive influence on manufacture establishments and was significant at the .05 level. The estimated coefficient suggests that a city's adoption and implementation of consolidated permit issuance resulted in an increase of six additional manufacture establishments in the five-year period. Table 3 also reports that, not surprisingly, a community with a predominantly industrial base is more likely to establish new manufactures. Population was also related to manufacturing firms, as expected.

Table 4 reports estimates of new capital investment. The model goodness of fit is more modest than in the first model (adjusted R^2 =

**Table 2.
Consolidated/One-Stop Permit Issuance**

Permitting Process	*Number*	*Percent*
Consolidated	190	40.51
Decentralized	279	59.49

Table 3. Regression Estimates (Manufacture Establishments)

Independent Variable	Estimated Coefficient (t score)
Total number of manufacture establishments in 1984	.88† (97.4)
Population in 1985	.00012† (5.5)
Form of government	1.75 (0.92)
Central city	2.53 (4.07)
Suburban	6.73* (1.71)
Industrial economic base	11.78† (2.04)
Commercial economic base	6.89 (1.18)
Institutional economic base	8.51 (1.26)
Residential economic base	1.68 (0.27)
One-stop permit issuance	6.02† (2.29)
Constant	-6.33 (-0.93)
N	469
Adjusted R2	0.99
F	9980

*p 0.1.   †p 0.05 (two-tailed test).
Note: t scores are in parentheses.

Table 4. Regression Estimates (New Capital Investments in Manufacture)

Independent Variable	Estimated Coefficient (t score)
Total number of manufacture establishments in 1984	.11† (3.24)
Population in 1985	.0002† (12.16)
Form of government	4.46 (1.13)
Central city	12.89 (1.55)
Suburban	6.91 (0.85)
Industrial economic base	26.26† (2.20)
Commercial economic base	5.76 (0.47)
Institutional economic base	4.37 (0.31)
Residential economic base	12.04 (0.93)
One-stop permit issuance	10.64* (1.96)
Constant	-18.03 (-1.28)
N	469
Adjusted R2	0.44
F	37.73

*p 0.1.   †p 0.05 (two-tailed test).
Note: t scores are in parentheses.

.43). Regulatory reform has a positive effect on economic development. Consolidated/one-stop permit issuance has a significant and positive influence on new capital investment. Cities that implemented consolidated permit processes were estimated to have new capital investments of $10.6 million more than cities lacking similar regulatory reform efforts. Municipalities that have an industrial base — like those that have manufacture establishments — have higher capital investment. Moreover, municipalities with larger populations are likely to experience greater industrial investment in manufactures. The OLS results support the predicted effects of simplified and consistent regulatory policy on activities of manufacturing firms. This finding lends sup-

ports to the argument that regulatory reform reduces uncertainty for potential investors.

Conclusions

We have examined the development impacts of regulatory reform in terms of total number of manufacture establishments and new capital investments. The empirical analysis provides evidence that regulatory policy can enhance rather than impede economic growth. These results suggest that cities may free themselves from choices between regulatory protections and economic development by reducing uncertainty over property rights through efforts to coordinate and consolidate regulatory decision making. By reducing uncertainty and delays, local governments may promote both regulatory goals and economic growth.

Implementing regulatory reform is just one of many local actions that may impact economic development. Furthermore, regulatory reforms are sometimes put in place as part of a more general effort to induce new development. Nevertheless, regulatory reform differs from an incentive approach because it is designed to influence levels of uncertainty or risk for investments, not just the costs of production. Even stringent environmental regulation can reduce regulatory uncertainty and therefore have the potential to promote economic growth while protecting the environment.

Administrative institutions and program design have been neglected in the development of policy research (Feiock and Kim 2001). The empirical results reported here as well as analysis at the state level (Feiock and Stream 2001) provide preliminary evidence to support the link between economic growth and institutions that enhance authority and centralize regulatory activities. These institutional arrangements may increase the certainty of regulatory environments, thereby obviating the environment vs. economy tradeoff, and therefore warrant greater attention from scholars of local economic development.

Although the results have important policy implications, we remain circumspect in our assertion that the tradeoff between economic development and economic growth is "false" because we did not directly measure the stringency of regulation in our empirical tests. The expressed purpose of these regulatory reforms is not to relax standards or to reduce the stringency of regulatory regimes but to assist business and industry in meeting regulatory requirements through coordinated regulatory processes that reduce uncertainty and delay (Rabe 1986). Nevertheless, it is not inconceivable that, in practice, streamlined permitting might result in a *de facto* relaxation of regulatory standards. Future research would benefit from the incorporation of more direct measures of regulatory stringency to address this possibility.

REFERENCES

Bartik, Timothy J. 1991. *Who benefits from economic development policies?* Kalamazoo: W. E. Upjohn Institute.

Brace, Paul. 1991. The changing context of state political economy. *Journal of Politics* 53: 297–317.

_____. 1993. *State government and economic performance.* Baltimore: Johns Hopkins University Press.

Brown, R. Steven. 1992. Environmental development: Merging environmental protection and economic development priorities. In *Book of the states 1992–93.* Lexington, Ky.: Council of State Governments.

_____. 1994. Emerging models for environmental management. In *Book of the states 1994–95.* Lexington, Ky.: Council of State Governments.

Christiansen, G. B., and R. H. Haveman. 1981. The contribution of environmental regulations to the slowdown in productivity growth. *Journal of Environmental Management* 8: 381–90.

Clingermayer, James. 1989. Regulatory uncertainty, investment climates, and state economic growth. Paper presented at the annual meeting of the Southeastern Conference on Public Administration, 3–5 October, Jackson, Miss.

Conway Data Corporation. 1981. Site selection handbook. Atlanta.

Council of State Governments 1975. *Integration and coordination of state environmental programs.* Lexington, Ky.: Council of State Governments.

Deurksen, Christopher J. 1983. *Environmental regulation and industrial plant siting.* Washington, D.C.: Conservation Foundation.

Feiock, Richard C. 1994. The political economy of growth management. *American Politics Quarterly* 22: 208–20.

_____. 2000. Regulatory reform, property rights, and economic development. *International Journal of Public Administration* 23: 1599–1620.

Feiock, Richard C., and Jaehoon Kim. 2001. Form of government, administrative organization, and local economic development policy. *Journal of Public Administration Research and Theory* 11: 29–49.

Feiock, Richard, and C. K. Rowland. 1991. Environmental regulation and economic development. *Western Political Quarterly* 44: 561–76.

Feiock, Richard C., and Christopher Stream. 2001. Environmental protection and economic development: A false tradeoff? *Public Administration Review* (May–June): 272–80.

Fosler, R. Scott. 1992. State economic policy: The emerging paradigm. *Economic Development Quarterly* 6: 3–13.

Gunther, William D. 1991. Plant location and environmental regulation. In *Energy, environment, and public policy,* edited by David L. McKee. New York: Praeger.

Kale, Steven R. 1984. U.S. industrial development incentives and manufacturing growth during the 1970s. *Growth and Change* 15: 26–34.

Rabe, Barry G. 1986. *Fragmentation and integration in state environmental management.* Washington, D.C.: Conservation Foundation.

_____. 1995. Integrated environmental permitting: Experience and innovation at the state level. *State and Local Government Review* 27: 209–20.

Rowland, C. K., and Roger Marz. 1981. Gresham's Law: The regulatory analogy. *Policy Studies Review* 1: 676–85.

Steines, Donald D. 1984. Business climate, tax incentives, and regional economic development. *Growth and Change* 15: 38–47.

Warner, Paul. 1987. Business climate, taxes and economic development. *Economic Development Quarterly* 1: 383–90.

Wasylenko, Michael. 1980. Evidence of fiscal differentials and intrametropolitan firm relocation. *Land Economics* 56: 339–49.

Wasylenko, Michael, and Theresa McGuire. 1985. Jobs and taxes: The effects of business climates on states' employment growth rates. *National Tax Journal* 38: 497–511.

Yandle, Bruce. 1984. Environmental control and regional growth. *Growth and Change* (July): 39–42.

_____. 1989. *Tracking the unicorn: The political limits of environmental regulation.* New York: Quorum.

CHAPTER 3

Cities and Development Impact Fees

Emil Malizia

Methods of calculating impact fees were developed and debated in the 1980s and early 1990s, in response to legal decisions that formulated the "rational nexus" test. Since then, methods have become simpler but less accurate. Some appear biased in favor of justifying higher impact fees for local governments, which are after all the clients paying for most impact fee studies, including regular updates.

Higher or Lower Fees?

Higher maximum impact fees give local governments more negotiating room with real estate developers and homebuilders. The higher the maximum fee, the greater the potential discount that developers may receive, to arrive at politically acceptable fee levels. Developers have rarely taken legal action, which would only delay the provision of needed public facilities and slow development. But many developers have called impact fees "pay to play" charges and have tried to win such compensatory concessions as higher densities.

In recent years, local governments have come under increasing pressure to find revenue sources beyond property taxes. Many have begun to charge impact fees at or near maximum levels. Developers have begun to push back, viewing the proposed fees as excessive and the methods on which they are based as suspect. In places where this confrontation occurs, local government managers and public officials need studies based on conservative methods that measure impact and benefit more carefully, even if the result is lower maximum fees.

In other local jurisdictions, developers remain willing to pay to play, perhaps because they can pass fees forward to space consumers or backward to landowners. In these places, managers and public officials may prefer aggressive methods, which result in higher maximum fees.

Impact Fee Methods

A general approach to estimating maximum impact fees — and one that is intended to meet the rational nexus test — is presented below. This approach involves one conservative and one aggressive alternative for conduct-

Originally published as "Best and Worst Methods for Calculating Impact Fees," *Public Management*, Vol. 88, No. 8, September 2006. Published by the International City/County Management Association, Washington, D.C. Reprinted with permission of the publisher.

ing each estimation task. For managers and public officials in jurisdictions with an adversarial development community, the conservative approach is better than the aggressive one. For those in jurisdictions with a cooperative and compliant development community, the opposite is the case.

Techniques presented below pertain to public facilities financed from the general fund (roads, open space, schools). Defensible impact fees for these facilities are more difficult to calculate, compared with those involving facilities for which special enterprise funds exist (water supply, sewage treatment, utilities). The relationships between demand/consumption and supply/capacity and the benefits received by fee payers are less clear. Thus, the rational nexus test is harder to meet.

Rational nexus requires evidence that new development causes a need for public facilities, is charged its fair and proportionate share of capital costs, and benefits from the public facilities provided. Rational nexus can be viewed as a continuum subject to broad or narrow legal interpretations. The aggressive methodology assumes a broad interpretation of rational nexus, whereas the conservative methodology assumes a narrow one. Under each task discussed below, "C" stands for the conservative method, and "A" is the aggressive alternative.

All methods driven by rational nexus involve estimating need/impact, capital cost, level of service, credits, and benefits.

1. Estimate need/impact.

C: Population, employment, and other growth forecasts over the next five- or 10-year horizon are translated into forecasts of new development (dwelling units, square footage of commercial space). These forecasts are disaggregated into the land use categories to be charged impact fees. The most appropriate demand indicator is determined (population, number of school-aged children, square footage of commercial space, and so forth) to connect the demand generated by new development to the needed public facilities.

Illustration: A county wants to charge school impact fees on new residential development. The forecast of dwelling units is disaggregated into single-family, multifamily, and possibly more refined categories. Next, census data or local surveys are used to estimate the number of school-aged children for each dwelling-unit type. The estimates are made for age cohorts that correspond to the ages of elementary, middle, and high school students. These data would, of course, be used to find the probable portion of elementary, middle, and high school students for each type of dwelling unit.

A: New development forecasts would not be necessary. The analysis would focus on the current use of existing facilities to estimate the units of demand now being served.

Illustration: The county determines the current average number of students in elementary, middle, and high school. Census data or local surveys are compiled to attribute the present number of students to the dwelling-unit types that will be charged impact fees.

2. Identify public facility costs.

C: The analysis should begin with a careful assessment of the comprehensive plan, the capital improvement plan (CIP) for the next five or 10 years, and the fiscal capacity of the local jurisdiction to assume debt. The results should indicate which public facilities are needed and their financial feasibility within the planning horizon.

A list, with the projected costs of the public facilities on which the impact fees are to be charged, is compiled. Any external funding (state, federal, and private contributions) for these facilities is deducted to find the local capital costs.

Finally, the plans are examined to determine whether standards for level of service (LOS) have been adopted.

Illustration: A city decides to charge impact fees for open space and park facilities. The open space and park facilities, their capital costs, and applicable standards are identified

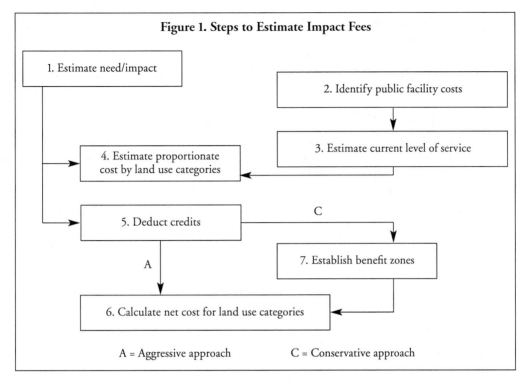

Figure 1. Steps to Estimate Impact Fees

1. Estimate need/impact

2. Identify public facility costs

3. Estimate current level of service

4. Estimate proportionate cost by land use categories

5. Deduct credits

C

7. Establish benefit zones

A

6. Calculate net cost for land use categories

A = Aggressive approach   C = Conservative approach

in the comprehensive plan and CIP. These facilities should be deemed financially feasible and necessary.

A: The analysis would not refer explicitly to the comprehensive plan or CIP. The method would simply assert that new development generates the need for public facilities. Recent capital outlays for this type of facility would be compiled to arrive at updated estimates of capital costs.

Next, the appropriate unit of demand to be served by this new facility (population, number of school-aged children, square footage of commercial space, and so on) would be determined to compute the capital cost per unit of demand. Again, expected external funding (state, federal, and private contributions) for the facility would be deducted to estimate local capital cost per unit.

Illustration: The city compiles recent capital outlays for open space and park facilities. The per-acre and improvement costs are applied to all existing open space and park facilities in the city. In effect, this aggregate value represents the total replacement cost of open space and park facilities. The current population or number of dwelling units in the city, when divided into this cost, gives the capital cost of parks per capita and per residential unit.

3. Establish current level of service (LOS).

C: The number of public facilities available to serve existing development must be carefully measured using demand indicators like population, school-aged children, vehicle-miles traveled, and so forth. The best approach is to disaggregate facilities to enhance the precision of LOS estimates (for such categories as elementary, middle, and high schools; neighborhood, community, regional, and special-purpose parks). Existing LOS should be compared with any adopted LOS standards identified in local plans. The lower LOS should be used in subsequent analysis.

The rationale for this approach goes something like this: If the adopted community standard is greater than the existing LOS, the latter should be used because impact fees cannot be used to raise the existing LOS. If existing LOS is greater than the adopted standard, excess capacity exists; charging impact fees at the adopted standard would generate sufficient fees to pay for planned facilities without generating excess fees.

Illustration: The city has neighborhood, community, regional, and special-purpose parks. For each type, the existing population served and the adopted standards for the population to be served are compared. The lower LOS is selected as the one to be applied to new residential development.

A: The LOS that exists throughout the jurisdiction for the category of public facility to be developed is considered the current LOS, which must be maintained. Therefore, any new development is expected to lower LOS through increased usage and therefore should pay impact fees.

Illustration: The analysis in the previous illustration produced an estimate of the acres of parks per capita or per residential unit. This estimate is considered the existing LOS in the city.

4. Connect need to capacity at the applicable LOS.

This task connects supply to demand and represents the application of the proportionality rule, or "prong," of the rational nexus test.

C: The objective is to connect planned public facilities to forecasted new development. The task begins with the detailed listing of public facilities to be built and their total cost over the planning horizon (see 2 above). Next, the amount of demand to be served by these facilities is estimated.

The careful estimate of current LOS is now applied to apportion these facilities and costs, either to address existing deficiencies or to serve new development. Only the latter figure can be funded with impact fees and represents the proportionate cost attributable to new development (that is, to all land use categories).

This task secondarily involves allocating demand to land use categories in order to translate units of demand (total population, total number of school-aged children, and so on) into development categories. First, the forecasted amount of new development is disaggregated into land use categories that will pay impact fees (see 1 above). Then, the corresponding demand indicator is used to estimate each land use category's relative demand for the public facilities.

Now, these estimates of supply and demand can be connected using the demand indicator. First, local capital costs are allocated to each land use category to reflect the demand from each category. Second, these costs per land use category are divided by the amount of new development in that category to estimate the local capital cost per land use category.

Illustration: A township wants to charge proportionate-share impact fees for arterial and collector roads financed from the general fund. An origin-destination study is conducted to assess current road use, and a related study examines road conditions.

The analysis determines that roads are now currently operated at LOS "C" and that certain roadway expenditures in the CIP would be used to maintain that service level. The results also show the percentage of through-traffic that could not be charged impact fees. Deduction of external funding expected for these improvements produces the estimate of local capital costs that can be assigned to new development, that is, its proportionate share.

New development is disaggregated into land use categories. ITE trip-generation data are used to estimate total trips expected from this new development. (Trip length could also be introduced.) New road capacity is needed to satisfy this trip demand, and the capacity is calculated at LOS "C." (The lower the LOS, the lower the amount of new capacity needed to satisfy a given amount of demand.)

Finally, the local capital cost for this capacity, divided by total new trips, gives the cost per trip. The average number of trips for each land use category is then multiplied by the per-trip cost to find the local capital costs attributed to each land use category (dwelling units, amounts of square footage of gross building area, etc.).

A: Local capital cost per unit of demand, multiplied by the portion of demand attributed to each land use category, gives the estimate of proportionate cost for each land use unit.

Illustration: The method proposed for the township in the previous example would apply. The standards, however, would be less rigorous. First, road improvements need not be based on any formal plan. Second, LOS calculations could be based on the overall number of trips generated by existing residents relative to existing capacity. This simple relationship could be treated as the existing LOS to be maintained.

Finally, the costs apportioned to each land use category (being charged impact fees) could be collected from new development without limit or reference to a schedule of planned capital improvements.

5. Estimate credits.

C: Proper calculation of credits requires identifying all sources of future payments to be made by occupants of new development for the public facilities in question. These payments may include taxes of all kinds, user fees, and/or special assessments. Payments for new facilities and for replacements needed to maintain existing LOS are allowed. Payments for operating expenses and routine maintenance are not.

Because public facilities last many years and are often financed with debt (GO bonds, revenue bonds, COP, etc.), payments are reckoned over a 20- or 25-year period. If payments are made to the general fund, the fraction of taxes devoted to the amortization of debt on these facilities must be estimated.

Present-value calculations usually match the term of the debt instrument used to finance the public facility (GO bonds: 20 to 25 years) and apply the local cost-of-funds rate as the discount rate. Present-value calculations are made per unit or in square footage for each land use category being charged impact fees.

An additional credit can be considered for land use categories that generate a true fiscal-impact surplus. The present value of this surplus would be estimated, and a prudent amount of this value (50 to 80 percent) could be treated as a credit available for capital outlays to fund the public facility in question.

Illustration: The county receives revenues from sales taxes to help pay for schools. The local expenditures of residential units paying impact fees are estimated to find the amount of annual sales tax payments. The present value of these payments over the next 25 years is the credit to be deducted from the local capital costs of schools.

Since residential development is not expected to generate a fiscal surplus, no additional credit would be recognized.

A: The logic and mechanics of credit calculations would be the same. The bias would be to ignore the fiscal-impact credit. Moreover, credits could be excluded entirely if they were not recognized in the state enabling legislation.

6. Calculate net cost for land use categories.

A: With the aggressive method, the net cost of public facilities for each land use category is equal to local capital costs less credits; net cost by land use units represents the maximum impact fee. The analysis ends here, and this schedule of maximum impact fees is presented to the local jurisdiction. This method assumes that the entire jurisdiction charging impact fees constitutes one benefit zone.

C: With the conservative method, an additional task is required: the consideration of benefit zones (see 7 below).

7. Demonstrate benefits.

Benefit zones spatially match the locations of planned public facilities with the pattern of new development. The purpose is explicit application of the benefit test, which requires that fee payers benefit directly from the public facility being provided.

Perhaps more than any other task, the establishment of benefit zones affects the schedule of impact fees. If these zones are strictly applied, new development in each benefit zone only pays for public facilities provided in that zone.

Illustrations: The entire jurisdiction charging impact fees may be an appropriate benefit district. For example, a township could be considered one district for road impact fees, and each land use category would pay the same impact fee regardless of location. A countywide school system, however, may be one school district but several subdistricts of the county could be established as distinct benefit zones.

If the jurisdiction takes this approach, residential units would only pay for schools to be built within their benefit zone. A city could charge all new development for special-purpose and regional parks but use benefit zones only for community and neighborhood parks.

Again, the program to expand neighborhood parks would first assign improvements to each benefit zone and then charge residential development in each benefit zone only for facilities in that zone. (For an illustration of the conservative method applied to impact fees for public schools, see E. Malizia and L. Gallo, "Reconsidering School Impact Fee Methodologies," Government Finance Officers Association Web site, 2005.)

Overview

It should be clear that the aggressive method will result in maximum impact fees that are likely to be higher than those arrived at with the conservative method. With the former method, local officials can negotiate either higher impact fees or steeper discounts, which may look to the development community like a "good deal."

With the conservative approach, local officials can be more confident that impact fees charged at or near the maximum levels will be legally defensible. As with other issues of local governance, which method is better or worse depends on your situation and perspective.

CHAPTER 4

Counties and Growth Management

Thomas Arrandale

Doris Fischer is just one of a thousand newcomers who've moved to Madison County, Montana, over the past decade.

Like the others, this Pennsylvania native was enticed westward by snow-capped mountains and blue-ribbon trout streams flowing down from Yellowstone National Park. As the county's only full-time planner, Fischer now helps community leaders figure out how to save the area's wide open spaces from being broken apart as more and more tenderfoots settle along secluded Rocky Mountains valleys.

Of all the region's spectacular places, Madison County may well have the best chance to hold onto the Old West's expansive and untamed character. Glitzy ski resort mansions already are cropping up on grizzly bear habitat along the county line. But down in the isolated valleys, pioneer families have begun working to preserve ranching as the county's most enduring way of life, in part by putting valuable rangelands under conservation easements.

Still, as in most rural western communities, Madison County residents hesitate about whether or not county government should step in and try to avert the hasty development that is already ruining other landscapes around old ranching and mining towns up and down the Rockies.

Madison County is still Marlboro Country. Cowboy individualism prevails. "People in urban areas are accustomed to living with limitations set by their governments," Fischer says. "Out here, old-timers still hold to the idea that the neighbors aren't going to do anything to make life more difficult."

That frontier sentiment makes Fischer's job a real challenge. Right now, Madison County has just 7,000 residents occupying 3,500 square miles, an expanse that's larger than Rhode Island and Delaware put together. But rugged mountains and forests take up half the county, and current residents live in far-flung ranches and four tiny towns scattered across sweeping valleys where the Madison and Jefferson rivers and their sparkling tributaries rush down from the wilderness.

The county's population grew more than 14 percent in the 1990s, and now hard economic times are tempting ranching families to cash in by subdividing the pricey acreage they own in a stunningly beautiful landscape.

Originally published as "Rocky Mountain Revamp," *Planning*, Vol. 70, No. 1, January 2004. Reprinted with permission from PLANNING, © January 2004 by the American Planning Association, Suite 1600, 122 South Michigan Avenue, Chicago, Illinois 60603, USA.

A recently completed build-out analysis suggests that growth will certainly match that rate in the current decade, and could possibly accelerate as more outsiders, who are buying vacation cabins and condominiums, decide to live there year-round.

If Not Now, When?

The county hired Fischer four years ago to help update its comprehensive plan. "We've been nibbling at it ever since," she says. "We're not doing enough." So far, independent-minded ranchers and small-town residents haven't been ready to let the county government use stricter land-use rules to direct where growth occurs. In the last couple of years, residents gave some thought to setting up zoning districts to protect parts of the Madison and Ruby River valleys, "but they didn't want to do it," says County Commission chairman Dave Schulz. "Not yet."

Fischer and the officials she works for acknowledge they've got to get ready for all the new residents that may be arriving in the county. Just since June 1999, the county has approved 53 new subdivisions that created 835 more lots; two-thirds of available tracts still remain available for new homes.

"The question I have is what are we going to do so growth does not eliminate the things that brought people here in the first place?" says Lane Adamson, a county planning board member who also directs the Madison Valley Ranchlands Group, an association that local ranching families have formed to keep economic change from overwhelming their way of life. The members have begun working with the Nature Conservancy to protect lands through easements, combat invading noxious rangeland weeds, and market local "conservation beef" at premium prices.

Ranchers are also watching uneasily as subdividers eye Madison Valley for potential development of more houses and cabins along one of the country's most prized fly fishing rivers. "At some point you say, okay, we're not going to allow that to happen," Adamson notes.

Helpers

Looking for ways to manage Madison's expected growth, Fischer, Schulz, and Adamson repaired with another county commissioner and two planning board members in October 2003 to Red Lodge, Montana. Along with counterparts from six other Montana, Wyoming, and Idaho counties, they spent three days rethinking how rural communities can accommodate growth without sacrificing the West's distinctive character. They'd all been invited by the National Association of Counties and the Sonoran Institute, a Tucson-based think tank.

The one-of-a-kind program, called the Western Community Stewardship Forum, brings rural counties together to talk over their options for managing the growth. Five of the counties whose representatives met in 2003 abut Yellowstone National Park, and the two others lie astride critical wildlife habitat that links the park to other Northern Rocky Mountain ecosystems.

They're all going through accelerating economic and social changes as newcomers flock into sparsely settled valleys that help sustain deer, elk, moose, wolves, grizzly bears, cutthroat trout, and the rest of the region's matchless wildlife populations. Yellowstone's threatened grizzly population has begun slowly expanding through mountain ranges and down into the valleys that surround the park, and conflicts between people and bears will inevitably increase if more and more subdivisions are built without regard to the bears' habitat.

The counties that gathered at Red Lodge "all share a commitment to deal with their growth," notes Randy Carpenter, a planner with the Sonoran Institute's northwest office in Bozeman, Montana. If their efforts keep privately owned landholdings from being completely carved up, he adds, "these counties will also play critical roles in linking the wilderness and keeping ecosystems intact."

As it is, the Yellowstone region is one of the last truly wild places in North America. That very wildness is one of the keys to its economic future. Demand for the West's timber, minerals, and beef has faded, but the Yellowstone region's population has grown by 131,000 since 1970 as retirees, engineers, accountants, and other service professionals have arrived. "The region's quality of life, including its natural amenities, is one distinct competitive advantage we have in today's marketplace," says Ben Alexander, the associate director of the Sonoran Institute's socioeconomics program.

About the Institute

The Sonoran Institute has been conducting community stewardship forums since 1999, advising 34 counties in eight Rocky Mountain states on their options for managing growth while maintaining their economic prospects. Planning and economic consultants from the institute's Tucson and Bozeman offices have helped counties build on growth management strategies their teams have crafted at the sessions.

Custer County, Colorado, used Sonoran's support to adopt a master plan, update zoning rules, and embrace privately funded conservation easements on 11,000 acres. Rio Arriba County, New Mexico, got help developing a comprehensive plan and conserving small-scale *acequia* farmlands along the Rio Grande and Rio Chama valleys.

After attending a previous forum, Sublette County, Wyoming, set up a program that will use oil and gas revenues to buy development rights to agricultural land. In Lemhi County, Idaho, where growth is spreading across private Salmon River ranchlands hemmed in by federally owned lands, the institute is advising a rancher-led working group

that is mapping parcels to help county officials determine where development will be least destructive and which lands they want to stay in agriculture.

Founded in 1991, the institute works with communities throughout the Rocky Mountain West, including those in southern Canada and northern Mexico. It operates with a staff of 32 economists, planners, and other experts and a $3 million annual budget with revenue raised from foundations, individual donors, and consulting contracts with the U.S. Department of the Interior.

Instead of providing top-down prescriptions, the institute provides advice and information to local communities. "Our goal is to help key decision-makers make better land-use decisions," says executive director Luther Probst, a former World Wildlife Fund official who founded the institute. "We're unique among environmental organizations because our objectives are not just preserving landscapes but also vibrant economies and livable communities."

Change of Heart?

County officials throughout the rural West are often leery of environmental agendas. But talking over growth management tools with similar counties at the Sonoran forums sits well with ranchers, farmers, and rural townspeople. In parts of Gallatin County, Montana, "if you mentioned the word 'zoning,' two years ago, they'd throw you out of the room," says Joe Skinner, a farmer who serves on the county planning board. "I came to the forum anti-zoning and anti–Sonoran, but when I got out of the forum, we realized that there are all different kinds" of tools for managing growth. "Sonoran is very honest about their goals, but what we want is very similar."

In follow-up work with Gallatin County, the institute helped organize workshops for county and local land trust officials to discuss tools for protecting agricultural lands. Located on Yellowstone's northwestern flank, Gallatin County contains some of Montana's richest farmlands. But in the last 30 years, 40,000 newcomers have moved into the county, and Bozeman, the county seat, began sprawling over the Gallatin River Valley.

Like local governments in places like Santa Fe, New Mexico; Aspen, Colorado; and Jackson, Wyoming, city and county officials are now locked in politically charged debates over banning big-box stores, charging development impact fees, buying development rights, and creating zoning districts to keep productive agricultural lands from being carved up and turned into more weed-choked, 20-acre home sites.

That's the fate that other counties in the Rockies hope to avoid. In organizing the 2003 community stewardship forum, NACO and the Sonoran Institute invited five other counties that border Yellowstone to sit down with two rapidly urbanizing Montana counties. Madison County sent a group to the forum three years ago, but commissioners decided to send Fischer and other leaders back once again to sharpen the focus on expanding the county's growth management options.

Not one of the seven counties yet has 60,000 residents, but they've all experienced the growth that's spread from Denver, Phoenix, and other large cities. Ennis, Madison County's biggest town, still has fewer than 900 residents, but at the Big Sky ski resort on the county's eastern border, developers are now sprinkling what Montana natives scornfully call "starter mansions" on steep forested slopes and Madison Range ridgelines.

The Big Sky complex already generates one-third of the county's tax base, and creates jobs for construction workers who commute 50 or so miles over a mountainous dirt road from Ennis and other towns. Not many will ever afford to live there, but Big Sky is giving Madison County residents a glimpse of how rapidly unplanned growth can occur.

Growth Pressures

All up and down the Rocky Mountains, from Mexico to Canada, retirees and footloose computer-era entrepreneurs are looking for new homes and vacation cabins where they can live under big western skies. In the last decade or so, new development has supplanted the Old West mainstays of boom-and-bust mining, logging, and agriculture as the Yellowstone region's economic workhorse.

Natural resource industries have been declining in the West since 1970. In the Greater Yellowstone region, mining employment has barely grown at all since then, and the region's farm and ranch income has dropped by two-thirds. In 2000, mining, logging, and agriculture provided less than 10 percent of the region's income, down by more than half 30 years earlier.

Meanwhile, the economy has boomed in the communities closest to the Rockies, according to the Sonoran Institute, with newcomers helping to fuel a population growth of 61 percent in the 20 counties surrounding Yellowstone National Park. The region has created 143,000 new jobs in the last three decades, more than 100,000 in the service and professional sectors. But investment and retirement returns are now the most important source of financial support for people in the area, accounting for 38 percent of personal income.

Television entrepreneur Ted Turner has bought two Madison Valley ranches, television network anchor Tom Brokaw and film star Dennis Quaid live part time in Park County, on the other side of the Bridger and Gallatin Mountains from Gallatin County. But not everyone shares in the prosperity. Average annual wages for workers have fallen in constant terms, from $27,262 in 1970 to $23,426 in 2000. In Madison County, 45 percent of the labor force is now self-employed, and those residents earn an average of $13,512 a year as farmhands, part-time construction workers, artists and artisans, and hunting and finishing outfitters. "That's a sign of stress" in the region's economy, Alexander says.

Meanwhile, the median price for a house in Teton County, Wyoming, has jumped to $365,000. One result is that the population of Teton County, Idaho, jumped nearly 75 percent in the 1990s, in part because resort workers began commuting through the sometimes treacherous Snake River Canyon to find affordable housing across the state border.

Moving On

Families who have worked the land for generations no longer make much of a living ranching or farming there. Now many are approaching retirement age, and their children are moving away instead of taking over the family homesteads. Now the pressure is on to sell to wealthy outsiders or to subdivide their holdings for new houses or vacation cabins. In many agricultural families, "they've worked their whole lives on that land, and that land is their whole IRA," says Jim Durgan, a Park County commissioner whose family has ranched along the Yellowstone River since the 1920s.

Durgan lives in the Paradise Valley, where the Yellowstone River flows down from the park through rangelands and irrigated fields lined by jagged mountains. He remembers nights when he could step out his back door and "all the lights you could see were the stars" above Montana's celebrated Big Sky Country. "Now you see lights all around you" up and down the valley from homes that have been built on what used to be nothing but farmland and pastures.

But like Madison County, Park County employs just one full-time planner. For years, politically influential Paradise Valley ranchers have dug in their heels against meaningful planning, contending that limits on how they can take profits from rising property values would unfairly rob them of their birthrights. Two years ago, they raised an uproar when the

Park County Environmental Council, a local environmental group, commissioned a build-out study of Paradise Valley.

Ellen Woodbury, the county's planner at the time, joined critics in challenging the study's validity. Back then, notes Jim Barrett, the council's director, county officials "perceived it as if we were singling Park County out as the worst place in the West when it comes to managing growth."

Durgan, who served on the county planning board for 16 years, was elected to the commission a year ago. Woodbury quit last year and was hired to help a Bozeman-based developer win county approval for a 38-unit subdivision on 900 acres of prime irrigated land right on the Yellowstone River.

Last fall, Durgan and fellow commissioner Ed Schilling traveled to the Sonoran forum in Red Lodge to take a fresh look at options for dealing with the consequences of future development pressures. Notably, they invited Barrett to sit on the county's delegation.

"With other counties there, and with a whole range of economic viewpoints represented, we could see that others are desperate for help in figuring out how they can respond to the same issues we're all facing," Barrett says. The way Schilling puts it, conferring with six other counties "shows that we're not the lone ranger here" in finally coming to terms with the challenges that growth creates for rural communities.

Resolutions

The Park County group left the forum last October with plans to conduct a county-wide build-out analysis, then ask the institute for help conducting public discussions on what tools the county could consider for managing development. Madison County officials headed back to the county courthouse in the old mining town of Virginia City with a more ambitious agenda. Along with a right-to-farm ordinance, county officials agreed to draft subdivision design guidelines including wildfire safety rules, outdoor lighting controls, and restrictions on ridgetop construction.

What's more, they agreed to push fees to cover the costs of extending county services. Later this year, the ranchlands group that Adamson heads may once more broach the idea of creating a zoning district to manage housing developments that are beginning to spread onto the Madison Valley.

Madison County remains wary about relying on government regulation. But after thinking the alternatives through at the Red Lodge forums, "we now feel that these are manageable things to accomplish," Fischer says. Working with Sonoran Institute advisers, and just talking with other counties that must deal with the same plight, "gave us a clarity and confidence that we're on the right track."

CHAPTER 5

States and Growth Management

Dennis Farney

Florida conservationists feared the worst when a real estate development firm entered into a contract to buy the 91,000-acre Babcock Ranch. They saw urban development spreading like a blob over an unspoiled area of cypress swamps and pinewoods, home to the endangered Florida panther and a host of other plant and animal species. But then the developer, Kitson and Partners, LLC, offered a deal. If Florida had the money, the developer would sell nearly 74,000 acres.

Florida had the money — and then some. Back in 1999, the legislature had passed Florida Forever, a $3 billion, 10-year land acquisition program financed by bond issues. Florida Forever, which bills itself as "the largest land-buying initiative in the nation," clinched the deal for $310 million, plus an additional $40 million from Lee County. The signing ceremony this June marked one of the largest land preservation purchases in state history. Governor Jeb Bush hailed the "massive endeavor" as a huge step toward establishing a southwest Florida conservation corridor stretching from Lake Okeechobee to the Gulf of Mexico.

Significantly, the federal government contributed no money toward the acquisition.

These days, that's usually the case. Congress is keeping Washington's flagship land acquisition program, the Land and Water Conservation Fund, on a short leash. Although the fund is authorized to spend $900 million per year, actual congressional appropriations have averaged only $100 million per year for the past decade. For fiscal years 1996 through 1999, Congress appropriated nothing at all.

The bottom line is clear: If environmentally sensitive land is to be saved and urban sprawl limited, the states are going to have to take the lead.

And they are doing just that. While Washington has been haggling over millions, states and localities have been spending billions. From 1994 to 2005, the states approved $12.1 billion in conservation spending and localities nearly $19 billion, according to the Trust for Public Land. (The totals reflect both large projects and small ones, such as urban parks and bike paths.) They, not Washington, have become the driving force in land preservation.

"States have kind of taken things into our own hands," sums up Bridgett Luther, director of California's Department of Conservation. Her boss, California Governor Arnold

Originally published as "Green Pieces," *Governing*, Vol. 19, No. 11, August 2006. Published by Congressional Quarterly Inc., Washington, D.C. Reprinted with permission of the publisher.

Schwarzenegger, made the same point in blunter terms when he recently discussed a broad range of environmental issues. "We cannot wait for the United States government to get its act together on the environment," he told *Newsweek* magazine. "We have to create our own leadership."

This state and local activism is coinciding with a fundamental shift in conservation thinking. An emerging school of thought, often referred to as "ecoregionalism," is increasingly influencing preservation projects across the nation. Ecoregionalism has conservationists thinking big.

The most spectacular example is Y2Y, which stands for "Yellowstone to Yukon." Y2Y envisions nothing less than a "wildlife corridor" nearly 2,000 miles long. It would start in west-central Wyoming and end just below the Arctic Circle, preserving a whole ecosystem, still largely intact, across the backbone of North America. *Audubon* magazine has called the idea "North America's environmental equivalent of the Great Wall of China."

Y2Y is more than a pipe dream — it is generating serious discussions among government officials in both the United States and Canada — but still far short of realization. Actually completing it, or even part of it, might well take decades. But Y2Y illustrates the central principle of ecoregionalism: Simply establishing isolated parks and refuges, even huge ones such as Yellowstone National Park, won't preserve biological diversity in the long run. Somehow, conservationists must find a way to stitch together existing parks and preserves with the privately owned connective tissue between them.

This means relying less on the traditional and sometimes controversial tool of outright acquisition. Conservationists can't possibly afford to buy all that connective tissue and political realities wouldn't allow it in any event. Thus, ecoregionalism relies more on such tools as easements and voluntary agreements with landowners. Identifying key tracts and protecting them, in turn, means working with state and local governments on an expanded scale.

The Big Picture

Ecoregionalism didn't just emerge full-blown, overnight. It has slowly grown out of the on-the-ground experiences of conservationists grappling with the basic problem of how to protect threatened species and open spaces in an era of urban sprawl.

Two decades ago, for example, freshly hired by the Nature Conservancy, Jora Young was assigned to manage a small preserve the organization had acquired on Big Darby Creek, near Columbus, Ohio. It was 50 acres in size and at its heart was a gravelly shoal harboring the rare Ohio Pigtoe mussel, along with 14 other mussel cousins.

Young looked the place over and had what she calls an "Oh, my gosh" moment. She murmured to herself, "This isn't going to work." Upstream from those unsuspecting mussels was a whole watershed, 560 square miles in size. With every downpour, pesticides and fertilizers washed into the creek. There were farming and gravel mining — "all going on above our little 50 acres."

Her recommendation to the Conservancy: Protect the whole watershed. The initial reaction was consternation. But today, the Conservancy is trying to do just that.

It hasn't used land acquisition as its primary tool, although the preserve has gradually expanded to 2,000 acres. Instead, it has worked with landowners and local governments. Earlier this summer, the Conservancy and 10 local jurisdictions unveiled the Big Darby Accord. It emphasizes open-space conservation, particularly along stream corridors, storm-water management and the restoration of natural stream flows. The accord is now in the public comment stage. The Conservancy hopes it will serve as a model for local governments elsewhere.

The ecoregionalism principles that the

Conservancy applied to one fairly small creek in Ohio are increasingly showing up in state and local projects, considerably larger and considerably more expensive, around the nation. Instead of the traditional preservation model of saving spectacular but isolated tracts — a mountain here, a waterfall there — these projects are preserving whole landscapes and sometimes entire watersheds.

Contiguous Tracts

In the process, conservationists have rediscovered ranches. Ranchers were once portrayed as villains in environmental literature, people who overgrazed the land and muddied the streams. But then conservationists had a collective "Oh, my gosh" moment. They realized that, for better or for worse, ranches have kept vast, contiguous tracts of land in one piece. Now, as economic conditions change, some big ranches are going up for sale. Other ranchers would like to keep their land in the family but don't know how to afford it, given rising taxes and tempting offers from developers. Conservationists realized that they themselves could buy these ranches or development rights to them — if, like Florida, they had the money.

Last year, a ranch and the money came together on a stunning one-of-a-kind property in California. It was the Hearst Ranch, once the home of legendary publishing magnate William Randolph Hearst, the man whose outsized life inspired the movie "Citizen Kane." But conservation of the 128-square-mile ranch, gateway to the Big Sur and overlooking the Pacific, didn't come easy.

For the past quarter-century, citizen groups had been fighting off development proposals by the owner, the Hearst Corp. At one point, the corporation hauled out an 1852 subdivision map to bolster its argument for developing 279 separate parcels. The state said no. Then, like Florida's Kitson and Partners, the corporation offered California a deal. It

would sell development rights to most of the ranch if, in turn, the state and local governments permitted development of a small part.

This led to six years of multi-party negotiations involving, among others, the corporation, the state, the American Land Conservancy, the San Luis Obispo Council of Governments, the California Coastal Commission and the California Transportation Commission. Finally, in February 2004, there was agreement on a price of $80 million, plus $15 million in state tax credits.

California, like Florida, had the money. In 2000, voters had approved Proposition 12, a $2.1 billion parkland bond issue, by a resounding 63 to 37 percent. Two years later, they approved Proposition 40, a $2.6 billion parkland measure, and Proposition 50, a $3.4 billion water-quality measure containing some land-acquisition funds.

After yet another year of hard bargaining, the land deal was consummated in February 2005. What Californians got was outright ownership of 13 miles of stunning coastline, as well as a conservation easement permanently barring development on most of the 82,000 acres. The state picked up the bulk of the tab, but its transportation commission, in an adroit move, found a way to apply about $23 million in federal transportation money to the purchase pot. What the corporation got, beyond the cash and tax credits, was the right to build a luxury development on a small piece of the ranch.

Not everyone was thrilled with the Hearst Ranch deal. Mark Massara, a Sierra Club official, complained that Hearst was "walking away with about $500 million in value" when the development rights it retained were factored in. "And what does the public get? The only thing we get for sure is a coastal trail that won't even follow the coast that closely." But former California Congressman Pete McCloskey, a moderate Republican who at the time was barnstorming the country to assail the Bush administration's environmental record, probably summed up majority opinion. "It's an incredible deal," he said.

Although such deals have protected hundreds of thousands of acres, they've also raised ethical questions. Some critics have accused developers of "environmental terrorism" — tactics analogous, perhaps, to a classic *National Lampoon* magazine cover, which pictured a dog with a gun to its head. The cover message read: "If you don't buy this magazine, we'll kill this dog."

Conservation organizations have taken heat as well. In 2003, a *Washington Post* series accused the Nature Conservancy of a too-cozy relationship with the corporations who sell or donate land to it. The articles also disclosed that in a few instances the Conservancy had sold back land (albeit with conservation easements attached) to its own trustees or employees. The Conservancy later acknowledged 19 such transactions. "We do not apologize for our partnerships with the corporate world," the organization said. But it also implemented the recommendations of an independent advisory panel that it ban sales to insiders and review more closely the appraisals of lands donated to it. Such appraisals determine the size of the tax deductions the donors get.

Shuttle Diplomacy

California and Florida have large and strong economies and healthy budgets. But the fact is that virtually every state is busily conserving land. A case in point is Michigan — economically troubled, yet still able in early 2005 to help pull off the largest single land-protection project in its history.

As in Florida, the catalyst was a development company, the Forestland Group, LLC. Forestland, having purchased huge tracts of land in Michigan's Upper Peninsula, offered to sell conservation easements on many of them. The Nature Conservancy began negotiating, and by late November 2003, the talks had reached a critical point.

That was when Michigan Governor Jennifer Granholm intervened with a round of shuttle diplomacy. On the day before Thanksgiving, she put the Conservancy in one room off the governor's office and Forestland in another. Then she went back and forth between them, relaying offers and counteroffers.

"It was, 'Would you accept this? Would you accept that?'" she recalls with a laugh. After a few hours, the framework of a grand compromise had come together.

By early last year, Michigan and the Conservancy could finally announce the purchase of easements on 248,000 acres, a swath of land sprawling across eight counties. The easements permanently prohibit all but minor development, but they do allow continued logging under sustainable forestry practices, thus preserving jobs and keeping the properties on local tax rolls. Capping the deal was the outright purchase of more than 23,000 acres in the watershed of the Big Two-Hearted River, a trout stream, "clear and smoothly fast in the early morning," celebrated in an early Ernest Hemingway story.

The Federal Land and Water Conservation Fund contributed nothing toward the $58 million agreement, although the Agriculture Department's Forest Legacy program pledged $5.4 million. Private foundations and the Michigan Natural Resources Trust Fund will pick up the bulk of the cost.

Community Support

The Florida, California and Michigan projects barely scratch the surface of what's going on around the country. Maryland, for example, points out that it has protected more land than it has developed for seven of the past 10 years. At the moment, it says, about 20 percent of the state is developed and about 19 percent protected. The state funds its Project Open Space through a real estate transfer tax.

In New Jersey, the Green Acres program boasts that it is "keeping the 'Garden' in the

Garden State." It has been around since 1961, financed by a series of bond issues. In 1999, the state committed itself to an additional decade-long effort that will spend about $1.2 billion.

In the West, excluding California, 13 states conserved 1.1 million acres from 1998 through 2002, according to the Trust for Public Land. This is particularly striking because the federal government also owns vast tracts in the West, and some of these states were home to the Sagebrush Rebellion in the 1970s that protested that ownership.

Ernest Cook, the Trust's national director of conservation finance and keeper of its LandVote database, says that since 1994 the Trust has helped states and communities draft and pass nearly 300 ballot measures, generating more than $19 billion in conservation funding. Cook thinks the most telling statistic is the consistent support for such measures at the community level. "Two out of three measures will always pass, baseline, but in most years, the percentage has been higher," he says. And those issues are passing in what might seem to be unlikely places.

Last year, voters in rural Routt County, in northwestern Colorado, approved a 20-year, $20.7 million ranchland preservation program. It passed by 18 votes — 59 to 41. In Texas, hardly a hotbed of environmentalism, San Antonio has spent $45 million to buy 7,000 acres in the scenic Hill Country west of the city. Austin, a liberal bastion, has passed $80 million in bonds and bought 20,000 acres in the Hill Country. It may buy more. Both cities are driven by hard practicality. San Antonio gets almost all its drinking water from the Edwards Aquifer, which underlies the Hill County, and Austin gets about 5 percent of its water there.

Connect the Plots

Informing and often inspiring such activity is the concept of ecoregionalism. Merely focusing on endangered species, one by one, isn't enough to ensure long-term biological diversity. By long term, conservationists mean centuries. Merely buying up isolated tracts won't work, either. Wildlife migrates in and out of public land, oblivious to political boundaries. If somehow confined and blocked from migrating, isolated populations become inbred and tend to fade away. Ecologists call this "the island effect."

The trouble is, just about every park and wildlife refuge is an island, some of them quite small and vulnerable. That was driven home to the Nature Conservancy a decade ago when it plotted its own hard-won protected areas on a national map.

For decades, Conservancy staffers could sum up their preservation strategy with an informal phrase, "the last of the best and the best of the rest." This resulted in a good number of preserves along the lines of Big Darby Creek — high in quality but small. On the vastness of the map, recalls Nature Conservancy biologist Jonathan Adams, the areas protected by the organization looked like "green measles."

It was a defining moment. Although known from the beginning for its non-adversarial approach, the Conservancy intensified its use of voluntary agreements and easements that kept the land in private hands. And, working with state and local governments, it began gravitating toward large-scale efforts such as Michigan's Upper Peninsula project. Today, the Conservancy has helped protect more than 15 million acres in the United States and an additional 102 million globally.

Adams elaborates on the voluntary emphasis of ecoregionalism in his new book, *The Future of the Wild: Conservation for a Crowded World*. He writes: "Conservation must come to grips with the human communities that surround parks.... Conservation has traditionally overlooked, intentionally or otherwise, the needs and values of those communities. Hence, a protected area becomes a line in the sand and an invitation to conflict."

Viewed in this light, some sweeping ecoregional proposals don't look quite as pie-in-the-sky. All of them would build on already-established parks and preserves. That said, the proposals are still mighty big — with the potential for mighty controversies.

The Southern Rockies Ecosystem Project proposes to link existing parks and refuges from Wyoming to northern New Mexico. The Sky Island Alliance wants to do the same thing in the deserts of New Mexico, Arizona and Mexico. The Northern Appalachians Project envisions the preservation and restoration of a Norway-sized forest stretching from northern New York, Vermont and New Hampshire into the Canadian provinces of Ontario, Quebec and Nova Scotia. The Heart of the West Wildlands Network focuses on the area where Idaho, Wyoming, Colorado and Utah meet.

Positive Momentum

But the biggest of them all is Yellowstone to Yukon. Ten major U.S. and Canadian parks already exist within the envisioned wildlife corridor. Again, the emphasis would be on gradually linking them together over what would be a very long time.

Y2Y has already drawn fire from the Forest Alliance, a Canadian timber industry group. The Alliance says Y2Y could cost 80,000 Canadian jobs. As an Alliance official has put it: "It's amazing to me that U.S.–based environmentalists have the nerve to come up here and propose that half the province [of British Columbia] be locked up."

Nevertheless, Y2Y has come a long way since originating as an idea in 1993. It has the support of some well-known environmental scientists and more than 100 environmental groups. Meanwhile, British Columbia is warming up to land conservation. In February, its provincial government announced a "new vision" for its long and rugged coastline. Years of contentious negotiations between timber companies, environmental groups and native aboriginal peoples had finally culminated in a sweeping agreement. If fully implemented, it will protect 4.4 million acres outright and establish an additional 11.6-acre preserve limited to logging that follows sustainable forestry practices. The area includes part of the Great Bear Rainforest, one of the largest intact temperate rainforests in the world. The areas covered are outside the contemplated boundaries of Y2Y, but the agreement raises hopes of applying the same approach in the Canadian Rockies and northern boreal forest.

So it seems a pretty good bet that at least fairly big pieces of Y2Y and other ecoregional proposals are going to happen sooner or later. Voter appetite for land conservation is strong and ecoregional thinking is deepening its roots.

The next few decades will witness a race between urban sprawl and large-scale preservation. "If it comes down to simply creating parks and defending them in a hostile environment, we're going to lose," Adams cautions in an interview. "Conservationists don't have the troops." But they do have an idea, a very big one — and it has momentum.

CHAPTER 6

Apopka Creates New Community Vision for Its Future

Robert B. Denhardt *and* Joseph E. Gray

One of the most difficult issues in community and economic development is to find a way to respect and extend what Robert D. Putnam[1] has called the "social capital" of the community: those "features of social organization such as networks, norms, and social trust that facilitate coordination and cooperation for mutual benefit." Obviously, this important need cannot be met by generic development strategies that treat all impoverished communities alike or top-down strategies that fail to involve local citizens. However, strategies that acknowledge the special character of each neighborhood, that promote a sense of community and responsibility with the neighborhood, and that generate specific interventions designed by and for the particular community can have a very positive effect. This chapter discusses the efforts of one local government in the United States to meet these goals.

Over the last several years, the government of Orange County, Florida (the county encompassing Orlando), has been experimenting with a Targeted Communities Initiative, an effort to use a citizen-based collaborative process to identify and address the needs of traditionally underserved communities. The initiative is taking place as part of the county's commitment to "putting Citizens First!"[2] The idea of "Citizens First!" is to promote active, involved, and responsible citizenship, as well as to increase local government's responsiveness to its citizens. The "Citizens First!" program goes beyond the efforts of many local governments to provide better "customer service." Indeed, the program is based on a distinction between persons acting as customers (typically self-interested and short-term in perspective) and those acting as citizens (in the public interest and longer-term in perspective). The idea is, on the one hand, to emphasize responsive government, but at the same time to encourage greater citizen understanding of government and other resources, and greater citizen responsibility for meeting their communities' most pressing needs.

The Planning and Implementation Process

The Targeted Communities Initiative seeks to encourage responsibility and commu-

Originally published as "Targeting Community Development in Orange County, Florida," *National Civic Review*, Vol. 87, No. 3, Fall 1998. Published by the National Civic League, Denver, CO. Reprinted with permission of the publisher.

nity through working with community residents to create a new vision for their community, develop action plans indicating how that vision might be realized, and implement programs that meet community needs. The county's first effort along these lines took place in South Apopka, a predominantly African American and highly disadvantaged community in northwest Orange County. At the time, South Apopka showed signs of considerable social and economic distress; it was especially characterized by high rates of juvenile crime, substance abuse, and poverty. The South Apopka project began with a series of public meetings in 1991 in which County Chairman Linda W. Chapin (the elected political leader of the county) encouraged residents to define community needs and priorities. The list ultimately included increased employment and training opportunities, affordable housing and code enforcement, drug awareness and enforcement, recreation and enrichment programs, health care, transportation, and education. Chapin pledged her support for many needed improvements, but she also challenged the community to organize its own resources to work collaboratively with county government on the various issues facing the community.

Soon residents created the Apopka Coalition to Improve our Neighborhood (ACTION), which brought together many different churches and community and civic organizations; it eventually became the parent organization charged with developing and implementing the South Apopka plan. ACTION developed working groups built around the various community needs that had been identified and then charged each group with developing specific goals and objectives, with time frames, measurable accomplishments, responsible parties, and estimated resources needed. The plan was approved by ACTION and submitted to the county, where staff from various departments refined the plan and identified service providers that could help meet the needs of the community. The pri-

mary focus of the South Apopka Project was to strengthen families through such efforts as Head Start, drug awareness, job fairs, parenting classes, preschool storytelling, and male mentoring. Orange County funded facility and infrastructure improvements; local businesses provided financial support either as corporate contributions or through in-kind donations; and community volunteers completed community service projects, raised money, and donated funds for special projects.

Chapin made a three-year commitment to provide needed resources, support, and technical assistance to the South Apopka project, but the primary focus of the county's support was to empower the residents and increase their ability to help themselves. The ultimate goal is to encourage ACTION and the citizens of South Apopka to stand as advocates for themselves. (The success of the project was recognized by President Clinton with one of twenty-one Points of Light Foundation President's Volunteer Action Awards in 1994.)

Since that time, the South Apopka Project has experienced significant improvements as a result of the partnership. Roads were paved, a major affordable housing project was completed, a new park was constructed, several older homes were rehabilitated, and a variety of new services were made available through a collaborative service network. The small community center was expanded into a state-of-the-art complex with four new buildings to supplement the original building, which was itself renovated. Extensive landscaping projects were completed throughout the community.

In spite of the many physical improvements that were made in the community, county staff felt that they had not completely succeeded in their major objective: to fully engage citizens in the decision-making and governance processes. ACTION began with a great deal of enthusiasm and momentum. However, the organization soon declined in terms of its active membership and came to rely almost completely on county staff to plan and implement its projects. Instead of being the umbrella organization that was originally intended, ACTION came to be viewed by other community groups as a competitor for resources and attention. Chapin found herself frequently mediating between the project staff and ACTION board members.

Although the county was encouraged by the South Apopka experience, there were clearly lessons to be learned, perhaps most importantly the importance of moving beyond leadership by narrow factions in the community, instead involving a broad range of citizens in the planning-and-implementation process. This lesson was central to the design of the next two Targeted Community Initiatives, in Bithlo (a predominantly white mobile home community in east Orange County) and in Winter Garden (a mostly African American community in the western part of the county). Although based on the same general strategy of citizen involvement and empowerment that occurred in South Apopka, in these cases the planning process — which was the same in the two communities — was somewhat more structured and more broad-based in terms of citizen participation.

The first formal step in Bithlo and Winter Garden was to conduct widely publicized town meetings to introduce the initiative and to obtain initial input from residents regarding community needs and concerns. The county chairman attended both meetings and talked with citizens about their current frustrations as well as their hopes for the future. In both cases, citizens voiced considerable distrust of government, based on their previous experiences; it was clear that this prohibitive level of distrust would have to be overcome. The chairman recognized this issue and explained that the county was ready to commit new resources to the communities and redirect existing resources so that they might be used more effectively and consistently with the resident's own needs and priorities. But she also pointed out the importance of having those in the community become involved and

active in the process. This was to be a partnership between the county government and citizens in the two communities.

During these initial sessions, citizens outlined a general list of needs and priorities. Based on these conversations, the county staff was able to remedy certain problems in the communities immediately by using existing resources and delivery systems. Other problems, however, required more extensive discussion and planning. This occurred over a period of about two months, again with the same pattern being followed in both Bithlo and Winter Garden and with each community maintaining an attendance of one hundred to one hundred twenty-five citizens.

At the first of a series of six biweekly meetings, citizens were asked to discuss the current image of their community, and then to construct a vision of what they wanted their community to be. Citizens worked in groups of about ten to twelve, facilitated by trained staff members from the county. Their images of current reality and the hoped-for future were both created as a series of drawings on flipcharts, a method that proved fun for the participants while addressing the potential issue posed by illiteracy.

More important, these discussions brought out some extremely important issues. The citizens first drew pictures that expressed all the problems and deficiencies they saw in their communities. Next they drew pictures expressing their vision for the future. The visions, which included playgrounds, a community center, places to shop, and decent housing, might have been considered modest by some standards. But to the residents of Bithlo and Winter Garden, the simple drawings with stick figures were an emotionally charged expression of their dreams. The session in Bithlo was particularly poignant, as the eyes of grown men welled with tears as they were reminded of their current situation of hopelessness and despair but also their dreams for their own and their children's future.

After the visioning exercise, the citizens

focused more on actually solving the problems they had identified. To accomplish this, at a second and a third meeting, attendees were asked to choose one of eight working groups defined by issues in the community:

1. Crime and safety
2. Code enforcement
3. Education
4. Health and social services
5. Housing
6. Parks, recreation, and youth programs
7. Public works
8. Planning and land use

Code enforcement and planning were ultimately combined, leaving seven groups.

Each working group or task force identified problems that needed to be addressed within its issue area and then developed a set of priorities for addressing those problems. For example, the public works group in Bithlo identified three major needs to receive attention in the next three years: road paving and sidewalks, traffic signal and intersection improvements at a particular location, and improved ditch maintenance. Similarly, the housing group in Winter Garden focused on housing rehabilitation and alternative uses for older structures, a home-ownership and down-payment assistance program, and elderly and rental housing assistance. In both communities, the need for a community center emerged as a major priority. Again, in all these cases, the community residents were the primary participants, with county staff acting as group facilitators and providing some technical assistance where necessary.

A final set of three meetings allowed the residents to bring their work group reports back to the larger community group and then begin discussing priorities across the various areas. At this point, the county staff offered information about available government resources and services and how they might be accessed. Obviously, the solution to many of the problems identified in this process lay outside of county government, involving other

local government jurisdictions or nonprofit organizations. But the strategy was to help empower residents to take action on their own, and with assistance from county staff to identify and enlist the help of whatever individuals and organizations were needed.

Based on these discussions, formal action plans were developed. They described the overall vision of the community that the residents themselves desire and then laid out the detailed action steps required to make the vision a reality For example, one crime-and-safety action item concerned installation of streetlights. A series of fourteen tasks were created, from streetlight site approval to funding identification and actual installation. For each task, an implementation schedule and projected budget were developed, and a responsible individual, either a county staff member or a resident of the community, was listed (with a phone number). The action plans were submitted to the county commission for approval, and work is now under way to implement the various ideas in the communities.

The Bithlo and Winter Garden projects were considered highly successful. Many physical and social improvements, including major capital projects in the communities, have already been completed and others are ongoing. In both communities, the level of interest and citizen involvement has been sustained, with residents forming advisory councils to monitor implementation of their plans. Watching the success of these efforts, other communities in Orange County became interested in implementing similar efforts. Indeed, the county began to receive requests, some even from fairly well-to-do communities that felt they could benefit from the planning process.

Although the county was open to working with other communities, it was decided that the same criteria used to select Bithlo and Winter Garden would be used to determine the next target area: the community would show significant signs of (1) economic and social distress, (2) a pattern of historic neglect in terms of allocation of county services and resources, and, most important, (3) willingness on behalf of the citizens to work in partnership with the county to solve problems. Based on these criteria, the community of Taft was selected as the next target area.

Taft is a small, semirural city in the southern part of the county, once the center of a booming turpentine industry that never recovered from the effects of the depression and consequently began to show the same symptoms of economic and social distress that were in evidence in Apopka, Bithlo, and Winter Garden. In the case of Taft, the same general planning process was employed. However, an effort was made to develop even more formal structures to achieve the kind of consistent citizen involvement necessary in building strong and stable communities. For example, the work teams became advisory teams, having a more permanent role in planning and implementation. The teams were also described in less bureaucratic language (instead of having titles on the order of "public works," teams were described using such language as *streets, sidewalks, and drainage; housing improvements;* and *landscaping and beautification*). The process in Taft actually moved more swiftly than in the other communities, in part because the residents of Taft recognized the sincerity of the county government and trusted in the planning process because of information they had gathered from the previously targeted communities.

The process in Taft was also formalized to include an overall advisory council with representatives of each of the teams. The advisory council was to meet monthly with county staff as well as representatives from various service agencies to discuss community issues and obtain assistance with specific projects. (Interestingly, following this development in Taft, similar ongoing structures were established in Bithlo and Winter Garden, and plans are under way to do the same in South Apopka.) After several months, the revised format appears to be working well in all three communities. Citizen involvement in the ad-

visory council and advisory team meetings is stronger than ever, new citizens join the teams regularly, citizens are engaged in a variety of service projects and community building efforts within their own communities, and those from the targeted communities are now in fact participating in significant numbers in countywide civic activities. Not only has the Targeted Communities Initiative been successful in improving physical and social services within the communities but there is also a heightened sense of civic interest and civic involvement, consistent with the county's overarching philosophy of "Citizens First!"

Lessons Learned

To this point, we have examined the efforts of Orange County, Florida, to revitalize several communities within the county through an extensive, detailed, and citizen-driven planning process. The process, which has now been applied in four communities, involves a series of community meetings resulting in a plan for action. The county made a commitment to respond to the needs identified by community residents, but it also established a process to ensure that citizens of the targeted communities would act to address many of their own problems. Throughout the planning effort, county staff members sought to raise citizens' awareness of existing opportunities to make a difference in their own communities through working in partnership with county government and other public, private, and nonprofit groups. Consistent with the goals of "Citizens First!" it is hoped that citizens gain a greater appreciation of their own responsibility in making improvements but also come to understand and trust their government more fully. Certainly the spirit of community or "social capital" has been improved, suggesting the long-term viability of these efforts. But lessons were learned along the way that might be of help to others engaged in similar activities.

First, community-based programs of development require strong political leadership. Elected political leaders may not initially be attracted to such programs, especially as they focus on areas with minimal political impact and potentially negative outcomes. In the case of Orange County, the leadership provided by Chairman Chapin seemed to be an authentic response to the plight of traditionally underserved communities. As Chapin visited the communities and talked with their residents, she came to understand clearly what kinds of needs citizens in the communities had. She also realized the importance of not merely "throwing dollars at the problem," but rather organizing citizens to act on their own behalf.

This latter notion is certainly in line with national shifts toward greater self-sufficiency and shared responsibility. Consequently, other elected leaders in the community, such as members of the county commission, were attracted to the program as well. Especially where it appeared that the Targeted Communities Initiative would enable citizens and administrators to work together to achieve desired outcomes, there was the possibility of really "getting things done" without pouring huge amounts of money into social programs. As a collaborative effort, targeted communities appeared quite different from the traditional pork-barrel programs that earlier politicians might have offered.

Finally, although the residents of the targeted communities did not provide the normal inducements that might spark interest by politicians, the planning process provided new ways for political leaders to meet with citizens and engage their interest. In a sense, the process allowed political leaders to build or extend their own base of support by shaping a newly activated constituency around them. Political leaders could certainly claim to be doing the right thing, but they were also attracted by the fact that building or strengthening their political base through work in these areas did not cost major dollars. Moreover, political leaders were photographed doing good work, appearing not with powerful interest groups but amid "real" people.

Certainly, the backing of the county chairman and members of the board of county commissioners helped stimulate private and nonprofit agencies to examine areas in which they might not seem to have a "constituent interest." For business leaders, the chairman offered the possibility of new markets and simply the opportunity to demonstrate good corporate citizenship; for those in nonprofit organizations, the opportunity to work more closely with citizens themselves in designing and delivering programs was extremely attractive.

Similarly, the support of the county's top political leadership also encouraged full participation of those throughout the county "bureaucracy," many of whom were initially reluctant to go outside their established ways of operating to engage citizens in meaningful dialogue and cooperative action. Indeed, some of those closest to the process have commented that getting the "bureaucrats" to go along was the hardest part of the effort.

From the standpoint of the citizens, the attraction was hope for physical improvements in their communities, as well as possibly learning how to play the political game to achieve even more in the future. At the early meetings in each community, citizens came to realize that if fifty or a hundred people got together, the top leaders of the county would pay attention. As they moved through the series of planning meetings, the citizens came to realize that by organizing effectively they had a voice where previously they had not. The Targeted Communities process taught citizens how to exert themselves within a system that previously had shut out many of them.

The process also stimulated and nurtured new leadership within the communities themselves. Many who had never held positions of leadership emerged in the process of leading work groups or advisory teams. For some, the possibility of having an audience on an equal plane with top elected officials and "partnering" rather than "begging for a handout" was an intriguing proposition. In some cases, the Targeted Communities process simply enabled people to be part of an organized effort in which their neighbors, friends, and families viewed them as leaders. Targeted communities gave people a platform, an opportunity to exert influence beyond their normal boundaries. For example, it gave many women a chance to take skills they had learned as wife and mother and exert them outside the walls of their homes. Remember that the people active in targeted communities were those whom government had left out — and those who had left government. In planning and implementing improvements in their communities, many became quite attuned to local politics and government. Indeed, early on the chairman confided that the Targeted Communities program ran the risk of creating "civic terrorists," those who might use their newfound constituency power as a kind of blackmail. (Chapin went on to say that this was a risk she was quite willing to take.) But the answer is to build relations of trust and confidence between the people and their government — and to make sure that power is indeed widely distributed. As one staff member pointed out, the more you distribute power, the less likely it is that any one person presumes to speak for everyone.

One result of the Targeted Communities effort has been substantial increase in political involvement in those communities. Citizens are now active in countywide meetings, they serve on boards and commissions, they come to county commission meetings and speak up, and they write letters to the editor — to the point that some indeed are now seen as "civic junkies."

Conclusion

Perhaps best advice to come out of the Targeted Communities Initiative in Orange County is simply to trust the citizens. Local governments often seem remote and detached (how much more so at the state and federal levels) — and uncaring. Indeed, part of this image is well-deserved, as few governments take the time to find out in detail exactly what citizens need and want and how they would prioritize their own needs and desires. Elected political leaders and those throughout government agencies seem to think they know what is best for citizens, when in fact their ideas may be quite off the mark. Involving citizens in a serious and detailed planning process allows government to find out exactly what citizens are thinking; more important, it expresses government's trust in its citizens. In line with the notion of "Citizens First!" people have to learn to trust in government; this can be greatly aided by government trusting in the people. According to those closest to the Targeted Communities Initiative, demonstrating real responsiveness is the most important thing government can do to rebuild the trust and confidence of citizens. That only occurs when you trust the citizens.

Notes

1. Putnam, R. D. "Bowling Alone: America's Declining Social Capital." *Journal of Democracy*, 1995, *6* (1), 65–78.

2. Chapin, L. W., and Denhardt, R. B. "Putting 'Citizens First!' in Orange County, Florida." *National Civic Review*, 1995, 82 (3), 210–217.

CHAPTER 7

Athens, Other Cities, Preserve Their Neighborhoods

John O'Looney

Recently the president of the university where I work suggested that the behavior of some residents has led to our town of Athens, Georgia, gaining a reputation for being antibusiness. As a member of a neighborhood that participated in two major efforts to stop certain developments — building an Eckerds mega-store in one in-town neighborhood and razing fifty-seven homes in another neighborhood to meet a hospital expansion plan — I am probably guilty of the behavior noted. I do not believe, however, that I or my neighbors are guilty of being antibusiness. I desire to refute this charge because I believe that, properly understood, neighborhood and business development can be complementary.

At the root of many existing conflicts between these two interests is the issue of scale. Our confusion about this issue stands in the way of local governments' crafting better development policies for both neighborhoods and the business community. By differentiating among three types of economy of scale, local governments may be able to facilitate achieving the seemingly contradictory goals held by business and residential communities. Let me explain.

The vigor of American business is the result of many factors. A key is the openness of our markets. As newer, more efficient businesses enter a local market, older and less efficient ones either improve their operations or go out of business. Corporate retail firms naturally seek opportunities to employ ever-more-refined logistics of production and distribution so as to gain market share. Some of the refinements in efficiency have been due to better use of technology, for which such firms should be applauded.

Other gains in market share, however, are not the result of corporate efforts alone. Rather, these gains occur through shifting the costs of distribution to consumers and to the community at large. This shifting occurs whenever firms choose a scale of operation and locations for new outlets that result in higher costs for citizens and taxpayers than is necessary. One indicator of higher-than-necessary cost is when consumers have to make additional trips over a long distance to consume the goods or services they need. Urban sprawl is the result. With people making more and longer trips, traffic congestion, transportation, and pollution costs soar. In nearby Atlanta,

Originally published as "Economies of Scale: Business, Neighborhood Development, and Local Government," *National Civic Review*, Vol. 89, No. 4, Winter 2000. Published by the National Civic League, Denver, CO. Reprinted with permission of the publisher.

the average commute is now one of the longest in the country, and the level of pollution has resulted in a moratorium on federal support for additional road construction.

A second indicator of higher-than-necessary costs is increased crime and law enforcement budgets. Large-scale retail contributes to these costs because it draws customers from multiple areas rather than from a single neighborhood area. The result is an increase in anonymity among shoppers and fewer social connections between shoppers and shop owners. The link between anonymity, weakened social bonds, and increased shoplifting and heightened need for law enforcement is well established in sociological and criminal justice research.

New roads, pollution controls, and social programs cost money, so taxes must be raised to pay for them. Additional transportation expense (for workers and shoppers) increases the true cost of production and consumption across the board. These costs are not typically calculated in a ledger as part of business decision making because they are hidden and appear to be a political abstraction ("some politician wants to raise my taxes") rather than as a result of a business decision. In truth, however, a business eventually pays these costs, through either taxes or loss of market. A market loss occurs when a whole area is written off owing to a high crime rate and general social disintegration.

With these additional costs, a business cannot expand as it might otherwise, nor can it be as competitive in a global marketplace. Unfortunately, without community or government restraint, the individual business has no incentive to act in ways that are ultimately good for business as a whole. An extreme version of this situation is at work in present-day Russia, where lack of restraint in the form of enforceable contracts and limits on unfair trade practices has undermined the health of business. In these areas, America stands as a shining example to the world.

However, in comparison to Western Eu-rope, we have a poor record of establishing the rule of law for business operations within the context of principles of urban economics or design. As such, even though we have stayed competitive with Western Europe with respect to the efficiency of energy inputs into production, our use of energy for transportation and distribution of goods is far less efficient than world-class standards. As long as energy costs remain low and our tolerance for pollution remains high, this weakness may not appear to be highly significant. However, if we experience a new energy crisis or if the number of Americans suffering from debilitating forms of asthma continues to climb, we may discover a business weakness that is hard to ignore.

Because of a variety of other factors, and because globalization is still a relatively minor factor in our economy, our business community has experienced success. But economic history suggests that such success is fragile and that weaknesses being glossed over do eventually show themselves. Just as the environmental movement has come to recognize the valuable concept of lifetime environmental costs, so too must we begin to recognize and address the total costs of business.

Local governments have generally been reluctant to regulate business. In addition, the increased economic power and legal expertise of the global corporation is likely to erode further local government's willingness to make needed reforms. Nevertheless, it is local government that may be best positioned to put in place the necessary incentives for individual businesses to act in the interests of business as a whole. To make the case for local government action, however, it is necessary to understand the roots of a particular kind of business efficiency and inefficiency: that related to economy of scale.

A key way in which the choices of individual business are undermining the viability of business as a whole relates to scale. I believe that we are being led astray by our inability to distinguish among three types of economy of scale: (1) classic or physical-law economy of scale; (2) situational economy of scale; and (3) urban, regional, or system economy of scale.

Classic or Physical-Law Economy of Scale

It is an economic maxim that business operations must be of a certain size to be efficient. This is so because the specialization and division of labor that can make production more efficient also demand that operations involve a larger number of people (and more machinery and space) than is the case under craft production. However, economy of scale has its limits as the cost of coordinating ever-larger entities can lower the overall efficiency of the operation. At an efficient size, a company's cost of production cannot be lowered by increasing or decreasing the scale of the operation. As such, all else being equal, a firm typically discovers upper and lower limits to a competitive operational scale. For example, an economist might be able to study a particular industry and determine that one can efficiently produce Good A with an operation that involves thirty-five people and one thousand square feet of workspace. If all else were equal, we would probably see all industries producing Good A establish operations of this size.

Situational Economy of Scale

But all else is not equal. Rather, there are numerous factors specific to the local environment: variation in location and lot size, availability of customers, routine purchasing minimums set by suppliers, the strength and offerings of local competitors, and so on. These factors contribute to what I call situational economy of scale, or economy that occurs at a certain scale of operation that is not derived from any law of time and motion or organizational efficiency, but rather from man-made or haphazard circumstances.

For example, inequality in consumer purchasing power and in crime rates among different areas means that some market areas are much more attractive than others. As such, a business may choose to forgo building in a less attractive area but compensate by building a superstore in a more attractive area. Also, large transportation arteries, which are built by governments, create an overly rich market opportunity in one area while draining the market in another.

The impact of these man-made opportunities on business decisions about scale can be seen in the sprouting of factory retail outlet centers at interstate highway junctions — in areas that are nearly devoid of population. Finally, if a transportation artery is combined with a facility of sufficient size to be market making rather than market taking, the stage is set for that firm's suppliers or codependent firms to locate in the same area and at the same scale.

A situational economy of scale often creates a vicious cycle of ever-increasing scale. Where I live, for example, there are indications that two national drugstore chains wish to build superstores in an area that was shunned in years past. This desire can be traced to increased daily traffic count on the newly expanded transportation artery through the area, movement of more middle- and upper-middle-income families into the area, and continued expansion of a regional medical center and codependent physician offices. The scale of this medical complex, as the term *regional medical center* suggests, is designed to serve not just a single neighborhood or community but an entire region. As a result of these changes, the area is now attractive to large-scale, corporate pharmaceutical services even though there are already a sufficient, if not excessive, number of pharmacies located there.

Unfortunately for the neighborhood, the most economical facility size for a corporate-level pharmacy is not the same as for a mom-and-pop operation. This is the case because these corporate operations actually compete in a number of areas, including foodstuffs and other convenience items. Having opted to compete in multiple product lines, a megastore developer can spread start-up and transaction costs across a number of business areas. Hence, although the operational or classic economy of scale for a megastore may be no better than a small-scale operation, the situational start-up economy for a megastore firm is lower.

Additional situational economy can be achieved in an instance where local zoning allows a megastore developer to follow standardized large-scale footprints and facility design. Not only do these usually not mesh well with the unique designs of historical neighborhoods, but they are often chosen or built for the short run on the understanding that markets are likely to change. Hence, our urban landscape is dotted with hundreds of abandoned strip malls located in what were, ten years ago, the area of choice for corporate firms. Once abandoned, the scale and isolation of these facilities tend to make them less desirable as a location for a start-up firm. For communities that want to establish a healthy business climate for the long run, constructing such a facility is often counterproductive.

Urban or Regional Economy of Scale

Classic economy of scale needs to be given consideration in developing urban design policy. Without such consideration, American business may be unable to compete globally. Situational economy of scale, or the economy that exists because of government-made transportation and development policies, deserves no such consideration. Instead of rubber-stamping an existing situational economy of scale, we must be guided by a third type of economy of scale: regional or urban. This is the economy that all businesses share (through lower transportation, utility, and social costs) as a result of good urban design. Such design typically involves compact, multiuse, small-scale development that reduces overall transportation needs while saving open space.

By-products of such design are minimized pollution and the improved economic feasibility and convenience of alternative forms of transportation.

Once the chain reaction of scale begins, it is difficult to stop. As a substantial purchaser of water and electricity, a megastore can sometimes take advantage of column price breaks that a smaller firm cannot. The economy of scale in this case is operational, but it is often based on market power rather than any real competitive advantage in delivering goods and services. Public policies that promote or allow volume discounts (which deplete natural resources) rather than standard unit pricing create an artificial advantage for a large-scale enterprise. Furthering the advantages of scale in this instance can actually undermine true competitiveness since small business, which provides better customer service but has higher overhead, may be unable to compete with a larger business that gives poorer service but has lower overhead.

The juggernaut of scale is also difficult to stop because of the impact on property value. An area that attracts large-scale business experiences increased property values because of the added consumers who patronize a large-scale business. Other businesses want to tap this consumer base and therefore offer higher payment for property in the same area. As property values rise, it becomes difficult for anyone whose business is not well capitalized to afford to start on operation in the area. The typical outcome is clustering of businesses of the same sort in the area (both because of capitalization and the desire for similar customers).

This may make for short-term prosperity, but as observers of urban life have noted for years, multiple use of properties in an area is what makes for vitality and sustainability in the long run. We have all visited tourist areas where nearly all of the shops sell T-shirts and trinkets. These uses obviously do a good job of attempting to capture the money of the transient consumer, but they simultaneously make the area as a whole less attractive to the majority of tourists who are seeking a place of beauty and quality. Similarly, in my neighborhood, if bike shops, dry cleaners, shoe stores, bakeries, and restaurants cannot afford to locate in the area because all the properties have been purchased by more profitable medical services firms, neighborhood folks will then be forced to drive to other areas for these goods and services — increasing sprawl and its associated costs to business while undermining the natural neighborhood cohesiveness that comes from the serendipity of neighbors meeting neighbors at local stores, shops, and restaurants.

Regulating the scale of firms and ensuring diverse land use in an area is not antibusiness. Rather, like the rule of law, it is the foundation for real business competition and for business behavior that supports rather than supplants community. Because they lack this foundation, downtowns throughout the South and Midwest have been decimated as megastores arrive on the outskirts of town. In most of these communities, the government leaders who were there at the time the new stores were built saw only the gold mine of a new business in the community. Few realized that in return for a short-term increase in tax revenue, many people would experience the consequences of property tax shortfall as the value of once highly valued downtown property shrank from loss of business in the area, while the ability of the new stores to generate property tax revenue was not as great since they were typically built on lower-valued property using low-cost, low-quality construction.

In many cases, the gold mine of the megastore was found to be peppered with only fool's gold. Unfortunately, for many the communities the chance to create real neighborhoods where one can work, live, plan, and shop all in one place appears an unrealistic dream. The typical middle-class resident in these communities is likely resigned to multiple daily trips to malls, schools, offices, and convenience stores. Living in such places

probably makes it difficult to understand that it is not antibusiness for people who live in neighborhoods where these functions are combined to want to have rules that make the continued existence of their neighborhoods possible.

The cry of being antibusiness should not be used to cut off needed debate about what makes for a sustainable community — including the business community. In my mind, unbridled growth in the scale of operations and rote standardization of megascale facilities — outside of any consideration of the system impacts on real economic growth and community viability — is at the root of the sustainability problem. This stance is not the same as that of people who protest the influence of global corporations. While I may prefer a local business to the likes of Wal-Mart, Eckerds, Starbucks, or the Gap, I am (and I believe most of my neighbors are) more than willing to welcome these global businesses on equal terms if they are willing to respect the human scale on which we hope to live our lives.

Although the issue of scale may appear at first glance to be beyond the power of local government to address within the scope of traditional police powers to protect health, welfare, and safety, this may not be the case. When one combines traditional zoning ordinances with others on height and placement of buildings that have been upheld by the courts, many of the needed regulatory powers are typically available. Moreover, in many communities it is possible to negotiate for better development through planned development ordinances. The key to passing the needed ordinances is to develop political will at the local level. Here, the coincidence of a number of political and social movements (antiglobalization, smart growth, and promotion of existing business-based local economic development) should make passage of the necessary ordinances politically feasible in many communities.

CHAPTER 8

Atlanta Takes Measures to Revive Its Inner-City

Dan E. Sweat *and* Jacquelyn A. Anthony

In the bustling Olympic city of Atlanta, a new paradigm of corporate involvement in urban revitalization is taking root. Initiated by former President Jimmy Carter, partnerships of local neighborhoods and major corporations, working through The Atlanta Project (TAP), are connecting resources with residents to implement community goals and priorities on a scale and ways never before attempted in an American city. The result: a collaborative process rejecting the traditional "top-down" corporate philanthropy approach to community revitalization in favor of an empowerment model vesting ownership, decision making and responsibility at the community level.

A number of corporate CEOs encouraged Mr. Carter to apply his skills and energies to problems of the urban poor in Atlanta. They wanted the former president to bring to Atlanta the same kinds of tools of collaboration and facilitation that The Carter Center had applied so successfully in countries around the world. If you take a close look at Atlanta and most urban centers in the United States today, they said, you will likely find many problems of human suffering and decay even more over-whelming than those you see in many Third World nations.

The former President took their advice. He went into the neighborhood around The Carter Center and other inner-city neighborhoods and was shocked at what he saw: Families being torn apart and crippled by unstable homes, violence, drug abuse, teen pregnancy, substandard housing and homelessness, lack of access to quality health care, rising school drop-out rates, an over-crowded juvenile justice system, joblessness, and a lack of quality education. He wanted to do something to remedy the situation.

The encouragement President Carter received from his friends and supporters came with substantial financial support. While visiting Marriott Corporation CEO William Marriott, Jr. at the company's Washington, D.C. corporate headquarters, Mr. Carter received an interesting proposal. "We will give you $500,000 to support TAP," Bill Marriott stated, "but we need to do more than that. We have more than 40 hotel properties in metro Atlanta, more than in any other city in which we operate. The economic and social health of the city directly impacts our financial bottom line."

Originally published as "The Role of Corporations in Urban Revitalization," *National Civic Review*, Vol. 84, No. 3, Summer-Fall 1995. Published by the National Civic League, Denver, CO. Reprinted with permission of the publisher.

Marriott further stated that "a great number of our employees live in TAP neighborhoods. They are the workers who keep our hotels running. If they do not perform their jobs, we do not run a good hotel. Yet, we don't really know what happens to them after they leave work. Do they go home to decent housing? Are their children getting a decent education? Are they safe in their neighborhoods? We would like to get involved in TAP in such a way that we can involve our entire corporation in a direct relationship with the people in the community."

That meeting triggered the corporate partnership model that emerged in the early development of TAP. Upon returning to Atlanta, Mr. Carter enlisted McKinsey & Company, a worldwide management consulting firm, to work with the Marriott Corporation and community leaders to develop the corporate partnership model further. That model was used to recruit other corporations.

Impressed by Mr. Carter's vision, corporations decided to partner with TAP to rebuild some of Atlanta's poorer neighborhoods. "In every case, the decision to partner was made by the CEO and the company's board," says Fred DeMent, vice president of Georgia Power Company, and on full-time loan as TAP's partnership and economic development coordinator. A corporate partnership advisory board was assembled with the presidents and CEOs of the following companies: A.W. Dahlberg of The Southern Company, Donald Keough of The Coca-Cola Company, Arthur Blank of Home Depot, Kenneth Lewis of NationsBank, and Kent C. Nelson of United Parcel Service. They assisted Mr. Carter in planning his initial corporate strategy. Today, more than two dozen companies are TAP partners.

The unprecedented corporate commitment to the empowerment partnership approach to urban revitalization at work in Atlanta is a clear signal that corporate America is eagerly searching for new ways to have a positive and meaningful impact on improving the lives of the urban poor. This approach to community building is an exciting and courageous challenge to corporate America. Traditionally, corporations have avoided becoming involved in the inner city. The scale of problems seemed too large for corporations to successfully solve, and the drain on resources, both human and financial, was immense. However, many corporations are joining with government, community groups, and neighborhood residents as partners in rebuilding strategies.[1] Their participation comes at a critical societal juncture when crime is escalating among youth, the education system is in crisis, and the urban economy is crippled. Even though corporations have long been involved in the communities where they have headquarters or branch operations, direct partnerships with poor neighborhoods have been virtually non-existent.[2] Now it appears that no discussion of urban renewal can take place without the voice, leadership, resources, and commitment of corporations. Once on the periphery of revitalization, corporations are now a major partner in community building.

The Atlanta Project

The Atlanta Project, created in late 1991, has as its mission "to unite Atlanta as a community working to improve the quality of life in our neighborhoods." TAP seeks to empower citizens to develop and implement solutions to the problems they identify in their neighborhoods. TAP also fosters collaboration among government agencies, service providers, community organizations, people who want to help, and those who need help. TAP also accesses the resources needed to implement solutions.

This pioneering grass-roots initiative has brought together thousands of individuals to identify the needs and create the avenues for change in education, housing, community redevelopment, economic development, public safety, and health. The guiding principles of TAP — empowerment, collaboration, volunteerism, and partnerships — are the driving forces behind everything TAP attempts to accomplish. Instead of tackling each problem individually, the initiative employs a holistic approach.

TAP's service area embraces approximately 500,000 residents in Atlanta and Decatur, and parts of Fulton, DeKalb and Clayton Counties. "Clusters" are coordinated around high schools and the elementary schools that feed into them. Approximately 25,000 people live in a cluster area. There are 20 clusters, each with a coordinator (who must reside in the area) and an assistant. Coordinators work with residents to develop a strategic plan that includes initiatives residents want to implement. A team of resource coordinators assist residents in their efforts to strengthen their communities. Resource coordinators are paid professionals or loaned executives from various corporations, agencies, health organizations, and colleges and universities with expertise in TAP's focus areas.[3]

Corporate Involvement in TAP

"One of the most unique and promising aspects of TAP is the extensive involvement of private corporations" and academic institutions.[4] This partnership component is one that other cities and communities find especially interesting and compelling. Corporate involvement takes a variety of forms. Corporate partners generally make a cash contribution to support TAP's overall administration and supply an executive to work full-time with a specific cluster for a specified period of time. Most of the companies directly involved in TAP are headquartered in Atlanta. All have major facilities in the area. They include Georgia Power Company, The Coca-Cola Company, Home Depot, United Parcel Service, Delta Air Lines, AT&T, Ford Motor Company, Andersen Consulting, Turner Broadcasting Systems, Sprint, and major financial institutions (Figure 1).

Each of these corporate partners makes a unique contribution. According to James Jennings of the *Boston Review*, "The gathering of so many corporations under one tent to fight poverty in partnership with the poor is unique among community-building initiatives.[5]

The activities of TAP's corporate partners may be grouped into four broad categories: The first includes corporate activities that are supportive of the initiative TAP-wide; the second includes corporate support for the cluster organization and programs; the third includes instances where the corporate partner has provided support, financial or in-kind, to organizations operating within clusters; and the fourth includes what may be broadly defined as corporate initiatives.[6]

Partnerships are unique to the clusters, for each community has different needs and partners have varying resources. For example, Marriott Corporation encouraged the entrepreneurial spirit of 16 teenagers when the company donated used furniture for a signature initiative, Simply Furniture. The teenagers' corporation turned a profit of $7,000 from selling furniture during its first year of operation. The youngsters donated some of the items to churches and social service agencies in the area. AT&T and SunTrust Bank have paired 20 students with some of their executives to share real-world work experiences and foster career awareness. Georgia State University refurbished a high school's in-school day care center in another cluster. Georgia Power Company established a program resulting in 13 residents' receiving commercial drivers licenses. Graduates have been successful in obtaining employment. Additionally, an $11.5 million Entrepreneurial Development Loan Fund was established in collaboration with six banks and the Atlanta Chamber of Commerce. The fund enables entrepreneurs who otherwise would not be eligible for a conventional loan to qualify for financial assistance. Because the effort is directed at economic development, there is a special but non-exclu-

---

Figure 1
The Atlanta Project

CORPORATE PARTNERSHIPS

Arthur Andersen & Company	John H. Harland Company
Atlanta Gas Light Company	Marriott Corporation
BankSouth Corporation	NationsBank
BellSouth Corporation	Nortel
Cox Enterprises	Prudential
Delta Air Lines	Scottish Rite Children's Medical Center
First Union National Bank	SouthTrust Bank of Georgia
Ford Motor Company	SunTrust Bank
Equifax	Sprint
Equitable Real Estate	The Coca-Cola Company
Georgia Power Company	Turner Broadcasting Company
Harry's Farmer's Market	United Parcel Service
Home Depot	Wachovia Bank of Georgia
IBM	

ACADEMIC PARTNERSHIPS

Agnes Scott College	Interdenominational Theological Seminary
Atlanta Area Technical College	Kennesaw State College
Atlanta Metropolitan College	Mercer University
Clark Atlanta University	Morehouse College
Clayton State College	Morehouse School of Medicine
Columbia Theological Seminary	Morris Brown College
DeKalb College	Oglethorpe University
DeKalb Technical College	Southern College of Technology
Emory University	Spelman College
Georgia Technical University	University of Georgia
Georgia State University	

---

sive focus on working with companies operating within TAP's boundaries.

In addition to their relationships with specific communities, corporations also support TAP on a project-wide basis. IBM contributed approximately 150 computers and a technical support team that has given the project a technological capacity comparable to most corporations. Home Depot provides home-improvement training and maintenance, and has established a fund to provide building materials to each cluster. The Kroger Company, a supermarket chain, is involved with children's issues and nutrition. Cox Enterprises, a privately held communications company, assists in the area of communications. Feasibility studies are supported by Equitable Real Estate. Scottish Rite Children's Medical Center loaned a nationally certified family-life educator to provide leadership and

facilitation for parenting-skills classes. As stated earlier, corporate involvement varies according to the available resources of the corporation. The potential benefits and challenges presented by managing the delicate relationships are enormous, varied, unpredictable, and difficult to measure.

A large proportion of the corporate initiatives are directed both toward accomplishing the goals of TAP and other, longer-term effects. At least five of the corporate partners are working or have worked through Habitat for Humanity to develop housing in the clusters. Most notably, Equifax, a credit services corporation, and Wachovia Bank have entered into an agreement with Habitat that will result in the construction of several houses over the next five years. The corporate partners are listening and responding to the communities. They are working with the communities, rather than merely imposing their own problem definitions and solutions.[7]

The Rationale for Corporate Involvement

The economic distress of America's inner cities may be the most challenging issue facing the nation. The lack of businesses and jobs in disadvantaged urban areas sustains a crushing cycle of poverty and crippling social problems. The myriad problems maiming inner cities — crime, crises in education, drug abuse, illiteracy, homelessness, joblessness, and the economy — encourage the deterioration of cities. And, as inner cities continue to decline, the debate over ways to aid them grows more polarized.

For many years, the burden of sustaining and rebuilding inner-city areas in the United States rested with government subsidized programs and projects established in an effort to spur economic development. Past efforts — relief programs, such as in home maintenance, housing subsidies, food stamps, etc. — have been guided by a social model built around the mere satisfaction of immediate human needs. Such programs were not as successful as anticipated. Additionally, "programs aimed more directly at economic development were fragmented and ineffective."[8] In short, the social intervention model may at one time have been the ideal solution, but today is outmoded. The time has come to recognize that revitalizing the inner city requires a radically different and multi-faceted approach.[9]

One of the "facets" must be the private sector. Corporations are getting involved in urban initiatives for a number of reasons. In addition to financial aid and public good will, many corporate boards want their companies and employees directly involved in community development. Some of the reasons are self-serving: to preserve economic stability and thereby protect their own investments; to ensure that a competent, healthy and educated work force will be available to them in the future; and to have a more directed outlet for their philanthropic dollars. Today however, most corporations making commitments to community building, whether direct or indirect, have community service as part of their corporate mission statements. The key for corporations is to make profit maximization and community building compatible.[10]

The problems of urban areas have caused alarm among executives and community leaders alike. One effect of entrenched urban problems has been a re-examination of corporate philanthropy and a shift toward innovative corporate philanthropy programs. Business is refocusing its philanthropic goals, funding or teaming up with local groups to take on many problems simultaneously. Unlike past efforts, corporate America is not trying to impose its own solutions. Private sector companies are targeting inner cities as profit centers, helping to rebuild communities — and perhaps more importantly, they are working in partnership with community residents. The only fundamental, lasting solution to inner-city problems must be developed with the input and direct participation of residents.[11] And the corporate-community partnership, even with little documented empirical data for support, seems to be achieving results.

Linden Longino, senior vice president of SunTrust Bank, a TAP corporate advisor and a member of the Prince of Wales Business Leaders Forum's International Partnership Advisory Group, has commented, "These valuable experiences support our conclusions that the private sector must play an increasing leadership role because government cannot solve the problems. It makes good business sense for companies to lead the way in partnerships with community organizations and local governments. I have met dedicated people in business, community and government from many countries who sincerely want to help, and who understand the need to work together. All agree that money alone will not get the job done."

While financial support of the business community is critical, there are other areas where the contributions of the corporations are just as important. Corporations are suited to bring their own industry-unique services and human resources — loaned executives, volunteers, training, and specific skills in management, strategic planning, administration, and technical expertise to community efforts. Corporations also are able to exert "peer pressure" to help galvanize the participation of other companies.

The America Project

Since TAP's high-profile inception, there has been an overwhelming response from other communities and cities across the United States and the world for information about the initiative. Because of this response, The America Project was developed by The Carter Center to share the principles, methodology and experiences of TAP. It provides opportunities for representatives from other cities to experience TAP and serves as a resource in specific programmatic areas in which TAP has experienced particular success. The America Project does not replicate TAP, but rather highlights components of the corporate-community partnership model. Through tools like publications, videos and computerized communications technology, The America Project seeks ways to broadly share the TAP experience with other communities.

Conclusion

All has not been easy for TAP. We do not have all the answers, and we do not claim to be the solution to urban decay. We have not solved the problem of unemployment. Instead, we are working to introduce the conditions necessary for economic development, entrepreneurship and job generation. We have not solved the problems of juvenile violence, but we are looking at ways to involve youth in constructive and productive programs. We have not solved the homelessness problem, but we are working with housing providers to keep some residents in structurally sound, clean, safe, and affordable housing. What we have done is come to understand that community involvement is a critical component to solving these problems. Residents must take responsibility for the community's growth, development and vitality.

The involvement of corporate America in urban revitalization is just beginning. As TAP has seen, the corporate partner is emerging as a major force in community development. Although corporations cannot replace government or community-based nonprofit organizations, they can bring special capabilities to the partnership. The roles of the public, private and civic sectors are being redefined with regard to urban renewal. Even though companies bring vast resources to community development, they must recognize that comprehensive renewal requires a long-term commitment of at least a decade. The current urban situation did not develop overnight; therefore, resolving inner-city problems will not be accomplished overnight. However, in the words of former President Carter, "The real failure would be not to try."

NOTES

1. The Conference Board, *Corporations as Partners in Strengthening Urban Communities*, Research Report No. 1079-94-RR (New York: The Conference Board, 1994), p. 7.
2. The Conference Board, *Corporations as Partners in Strengthening Urban Communities*, Research Report No. 1079-94-RR (New York: The Conference Board, 1994), p. 14.
3. For more information on the structure of The Atlanta Project, see, Michael W. Giles, "The Atlanta Project: A Community-Based Approach to Solving Urban Problems," *National Civic Review*, 82:4, Fall 1993, pp. 354–362.
4. Michael Giles, *The Atlanta Project Evaluation* (Atlanta, Ga.: The Carter Center, 1994), p. 54.
5. James Jennings, "The New War on Poverty," *Boston Review*, June–September 1994, p. 4.
6. Michael Giles, *The Atlanta Project Evaluation* (Atlanta, Ga.: The Carter Center, 1994), p. 56.
7. Michael Giles, *The Atlanta Project Evaluation* (Atlanta, Ga.: The Carter Center, 1994), p. 58.
8. Michael E. Porter, "The Competitive Edge of the Inner City," *Harvard Business Review*, May-June 1995, p. 55.

9. Michael E. Porter, "The Competitive Edge of the Inner City," *Harvard Business Review,* May-June 1995, p. 55.

10. The Conference Board, *Corporations as Partners in Strengthening Urban Communities,* Research Report No. 1079–94-RR (New York: The Conference Board, 1994), p. 12.

11. Michael Galen, "How Business is Linking Hands in the Inner Cities," *Business Week*, 26 September 1994, p. 81.

CHAPTER 9

Austin, Other Cities, Go "Green" in Their Core

Matt Stansberry

Cities are overcoming the barriers to creating energy-efficient buildings.

Local governments face a host of challenges — from interdepartmental wrangling to budgetary restrictions — when applying green building practices across their communities. Nonetheless, cities such as Austin, Texas; Eugene, Ore.; and Chicago have pursued green initiatives using the Leadership in Energy and Environmental Design (LEED) green building rating system developed by the Washington-based U.S. Green Building Council (USGBC) and are helping set the standards for municipal construction projects.

Public officials can take a variety of actions to bring their green building goals to fruition, including using cool or green roofs, photovoltaics (solar power), daylighting, energy management and cogeneration. Also, local governments can use a community-owned electric utility to encourage green building projects.

For example, Austin Energy, a city department, began its energy conservation programs — energy efficiency, renewable energy and distributed generation — in the early 1980s. "Austin is a progressive city, so we're a progressive utility," says Richard Morgan, manager of the city's green building program.

In June 2000, Austin's City Council required all municipal buildings built with city funds to meet LEED criteria.

According to Morgan, the city has completed two green projects. City Hall opened in November 2004, and a $50 million mixed-use emergency services facility — the Combined Transportation Emergency and Communications Center — opened in October.

Working with the Salvation Army, the city also constructed the Austin Resource Center for the Homeless, a $5 million, 26,820-square-foot, three-story building with a parking area. The facility was designed using LEED guidelines to maximize natural light, ventilation and views through openings in the building, courtyards and terraces.

One major challenge for Morgan was educating the public about the lifecycle cost of green buildings vs. traditional construction. According to Morgan, too many public officials over-emphasize the initial cost of a project and overlook the building's total cost of ownership.

Even when a city wants to build green, implementing those practices across local government agencies can be difficult. In Austin, each city department is considered the building's owner and allocates the budget for its

Originally published as "It's Not Easy Being Green," *American City & County*, Vol. 120, No. 3, March 2005. Published by Prism Business Media, Overland Park, KS. Reprinted with permission of the publisher.

building project. Construction costs are a frequent target of cuts.

"Each department has its own project manager," Morgan says. "Some do an exceptional job [executing projects under green guidelines], and some don't. That's why we went to the city council [to develop a green standard], because we were getting mixed results from project managers. By imposing an outside standard, it is easier to enforce, and it puts interdepartmental wrangling aside. Since [the city's] resolution, standards are defined by the USGBC, and project managers can't say that Austin Energy is being unreasonable."

A Consolidated Approach

In the early 1990s, every department in Eugene had its own design and operation standards. But that did not work very well, according to Ron Sutton, the city's facility operations and maintenance manager. By the mid 1990s, Eugene had created a consolidated facility department. "We have a set of [green building] standards that everyone in the organization works towards," Sutton says. "Individual departments are focused on their programs, not the buildings, which is why a consolidated facility unit is important. It lets departments focus on their core missions."

Eugene uses LEED standards for its construction and major remodeling projects and for existing buildings (LEED-EB) to evaluate its overall operations program. "Eugene [has] about 100 buildings, ranging from park restrooms to performing arts centers, [each presenting] its own set of challenges in cleaning chemicals, operation policies and procedures," Sutton says.

Using LEED-EB gives the city a consistent, third-party way to evaluate Eugene's operations and maintenance program. "We summarized all that we had done and learned [using the green building guidelines] into a presentation to our city council, which was very well received," he says.

As a result of the emphasis on green buildings, Eugene expanded its recycling program, increased indoor air quality diagnostics, improved refrigerant monitoring/reporting, adopted standards for cleaning chemicals created by Washington-based Green Seal, reviewed service contracts and added sustainable procedures. "If you're putting the money in the building, you need to know what you're getting for your money," Sutton says. "The only way to see if that performance is following through is to certify the building. [While many] private companies have the resources to pursue LEED, there are ways people in the public sector can do this within their budgets." Sutton says that building green could initially cost more, but "if it is truly an organizational priority, there may be opportunities to request additional funding, over and above your baseline budget for the LEED certification process."

A Mayor with a Plan

Chicago has a clear rationale for building green, according to Sadhu Johnston, assistant to Chicago's mayor for green initiatives. "Over the total lifecycle of a building, operating the facility is 80 percent to 90 percent of the total cost of ownership. People ask how we can afford to construct buildings in this way. I ask how we can afford not to," Johnston says.

According to Johnston, Mayor Richard Daley is committed to making Chicago one of the greenest cities in the country in terms of sustainable design. In 2001, the city began its first green building project: a major renovation on a brownfield site. The site previously had served a variety of purposes but most recently was used by a construction and demolition debris recycler.

Completed in January 2003, the facility was named the Chicago Center for Green Technology. The 40,000-square-foot building uses solar and geothermal energy, and includes a rooftop garden and a natural habitat to filter stormwater. The city invested $9 million in cleanup costs and another $5.4 million toward construction and renovation.

Today, the city uses the facility to test sustainable design processes and gauge costs for green construction, and to teach the public about green buildings. The facility's Green Building Resource Center is designed for builders, developers, architects and homeowners looking to incorporate sustainable design practices and green materials into their next building projects.

The center's resources include green building standards and construction guides; reference books; recycled, reused and renewable building material samples; a public-access workstation with links to green technology Web sites; and staff and volunteers to guide visitors through the research process. Workshops are conducted on topics such as solar electricity, native landscaping and green roofs. The center also hosts seminars designed specifically for building industry professionals that address issues such as boiler efficiency.

"Following that project, the city [built more green buildings]—three libraries and a police station—and with each successive project we saw costs going down," Johnston says. He says the first certified building had a 6 percent construction premium. As project managers, engineers and architects learned to optimize green construction practices, by 2004 the city's police station premium was less than 2 percent.

"In June 2004, the city mandated all new buildings would be certified under LEED-NC [for new construction], and we have 12 projects under way. We also require all projects that receive any city funding to pursue green initiatives," Johnston says. Target is building two stores in Chicago, and it is receiving tax increment financing from the city because of its commitment to build green.

Securing the commitment from city officials, private companies and construction professionals to build green has been the city's biggest challenge, Johnston says. Learning new techniques and strategies to make the entire process more efficient is a large part of the effort, and the city conducts extensive training in the private sector.

"Chicago is learning the processes and then reaching out to the private sector through these types of incentives," Johnston says. "We're also creating a green building permit process and a green building code which will expedite green building projects."

And if towns the size of Eugene, Austin and Chicago can go green, other local governments can as well. Though different methods, municipal structures and philosophies exist, the local governments can have one goal: to achieve sustainability in the built environment.

LEEDING the Way to Building Green

The Leadership in Energy and Environmental Design (LEED) Green Building Rating System is a voluntary, consensus-based national standard for developing high-performance, sustainable buildings. Members of the Washington-based U.S. Green Building Council, representing all segments of the building industry, developed LEED and continue to update the system.

LEED standards currently are available or under development for:

- New commercial construction and major renovation projects (LEED-NC),
- Existing building operations (LEED-EB),
- Commercial interiors projects (LEED-CI),
- Core and shell projects (LEED-CS),
- Homes (LEED-H), and
- Neighborhood development (LEED-ND).

LEED provides a framework for assessing building performance and meeting sustainability goals. It emphasizes strategies for sustainable site development, water savings, energy efficiency, materials selection and indoor environmental quality. LEED offers project certification, professional accreditation, training and practical resources.

CHAPTER 10

Berea, Other Cities, Manage Growth through Environmental Controls

Nancy Stark *and* Hamilton Brown

A national task force, after examining the environmental needs of rural America, concluded that, "Small towns are not just smaller than large ones, they are different." The small town and rural economic development strategies presented in *Harvesting Hometown Jobs* are different too, in scale and in the level of commitment expected from the communities which will benefit. In contrast to many urban dwellers, rural people do not commute to work from a place they live, to a place in which they have no personal investment. Because work and personal life are located in the same general setting, small town economic development involves preserving the people and the place, as well as the livelihood of current and future residents.

When rural communities were largely agricultural, or dependent on single industries such as timber, mining or manufacturing, there was little discussion or public disagreement that what was good for the core industry was good for the entire community. With fewer people, more expanses of undeveloped land, less pollution of the land, air and water and less knowledge of the future impact of current practices, many town accepted without question the course of the community's future.

Times have changed. For most small town and rural governments, the decline of key industries and/or the pressure for unplanned growth from metropolitan areas have brought large and controversial issues, such as the size and type of development and land use planning, to center stage.

In examining how to manage development, these issues need to be addressed:

- The distinction between sustaining and depleting essential community resources;
- The tools to achieve shared community goals; and
- The procedures to reconcile differences among competing interests and distribute benefits across the spectrum of those who contribute to community life.

To Preserve and Sustain

Even when rural communities were dependent on a single industry, business interests

Originally published as "Managing Development," Chapter 7 of *Harvesting Hometown Jobs*, 1997. Published by the National Association of Towns and Townships, Washington, D.C. Reprinted with permission of the publisher.

and conservation interests often seemed to work at cross purposes. In recent years, the debate has sharpened in many communities where the traditional economy has simply collapsed; or where there are immediate financial returns for residential and commercial development driven by the expanding collar surrounding major population centers. The U.S. Department of Agriculture now classifies only 556 of America's 2,276 rural counties as primarily dependent on agriculture, and even within these counties, only one of 10 residents, on the average, lives on a farm.

Nationwide, nearly one million acres of agricultural land are lost each year to some form of development. If a small community is to remain one that still feels like home, then the key is to manage growth or development in a way that is consistent with the will of the community and assures that resources remain for the future.

There is now a national, even international, movement to reconcile necessary economic development with the preservation of environmental resources in a way that serves the needs of the whole community. Perhaps the best known phrase to describe the dynamic relationship among these concerns is "sustainable development." [We use a number of other terms in this chapter, should "sustainable development" acquire a limited or negative connotation.]

One of the first explanations of sustainable development is among the most balanced and useful. In 1987, the World Commission on Environment and Development offered this definition: "to meet the needs of the present without compromising the ability of future generations to meet their own needs." It does not say "no growth," and it does not say all new industry must be "green," or have zero environmental impact. At the same time, it challenges present-day businesses and individuals to look at the definition of need, in light of what we now recognize as limited resources. As many a planner has observed, "they're not making any more land, air or water." And, as

experience shows, the cost of reclamation or cleanup far exceeds the cost of initial protection.

Strategies for managing growth, compatible development and sustainable industries are essential approaches for any community anticipating change. They may be especially important tools for making decisions in those towns faced with extraordinary pressure for development or job creation. For example, when a major entertainment conglomerate proposed construction of a multi-million dollar theme park near tiny Plains, Va., there was plenty of sentiment that "any job was a good job."

Local authorities approved many of the procedures which would have cleared the way to bring up to 30,000 visitors a week to an area where the central town's population was 300. While elected leaders generally side with the developers, citizens circulated and publicized traffic studies which suggested that the existing interstate virtually would have to be renamed as "the corporate parking lot" when the predicted gridlock occurred. Other projections seemed to confirm that the minimum wage jobs created at the theme park would never generate the revenues to pay for the required expansion of local services.

The corporation backed off when faced with such fierce opposition from people whom it considered a primary target audience for its theme park. Would this proposed project have been all bad? No one will know, but it would have radically changed the face of an area, even a region, that satisfies its citizens and attracts a manageable flow of tourists through its unspoiled rural atmosphere.

Likewise, a number of economically depressed communities and chronically poor states have welcomed large scale chicken, pork and beef producers and processors. Many of those small communities now wrestle with what are known collectively as Confined Animal Feedlot Issues (CAFI), which include odors; animal waste products contaminating surface and ground water; and the overuse of gravel roads by heavy vehicles carrying livestock.

Also, food processing plants often place a huge strain on existing waste treatment facilities. The waters of the Potomac River near Washington, D.C., show signs of contamination from chicken rendering operations hundreds of miles upstream in West Virginia.

Should all meat producing activities be avoided when considering how to strengthen the local economy? Like any other option, there should be some community criteria or benchmarks that establish the nature and size of what is acceptable and a decision, upfront, of certain activities that simply will not meet these future goals.

According to a study by Anthony Downs, cited in the Lincoln Institute for Land Policy's *Managing Growth and Change*, 90 percent of the population want to own a detached, single family house. Virtually every adult and teenager wants to own a vehicle in which they can reach major sources of goods, services and entertainment in 20 minutes or less of congestion-free driving. [Between 1975 and 1990, vehicle ownership increased 30 percent, vehicle miles driven rose 62 percent while the population rose only 15 percent.] Many newcomers to rural areas, who still commute to an urban workplace, will push for access roads and four-lane highways to the city, providing yet another push for out-of-control development.

When faced with the need for or inevitability of economic change, the first challenge is to incorporate the often competing interests of business and the environment into a vision that shares common goals. The second challenge is to find the tools that will enable these goals to be achieved locally.

What Is Sustainable Community Development?

In its guide, *Communities by Choice*, the Mountain Association for Community Economic Development of Berea, Ky., says there are three Es that help build prosperous communities over the long term: Economy, Ecology and Equity. The *economy* involves the management and use of resources to meet individual and community needs. *Ecology* concerns the interaction between living things and the environment — primarily the relationship of human beings to their surroundings, *Equity* involves fairness in the way in which communities make decisions and distribute benefits from common efforts and shared resources. Keeping these forces in balance is what characterizes a community that can weather difficult times and keep its citizens committed to common goals.

Local governments can play a critical leadership role in these fields individually, as well as in managing the competing or conflicting goals that can cause tensions within the community. Particularly in rural areas, local land use management practices have a profound impact on: the local economy; the prudent use and protection of natural resources; and the equitable assignment of the costs and benefits related to development.

Certainly, development is a responsibility of many parties, private and public, individual and organizational, if it is to truly be community-owned. But where large tracts of private land are yet to be developed, local governments usually must take the lead because of the unique powers they may exercise over future land use. The reluctance to act because some in the community may actively resist must be measured against the consequences of not acting at all. In looking at how government may carry out this role, it is critical to come to agreement on the terms "manage" and "development."

There are few times when local economic conditions are so consistently favorable that the best policy is to leave well enough alone. Small and rural communities generally find that they are experiencing either economic decline, economic stagnation or economic growth, all of which are likely to have some unintended or undesirable consequences. While each of these circumstances calls for active local management, the strategies chosen are going to be very different. The authors of the Lincoln Institute's *Managing Growth and Change* offer some observations on the local government management of land that are applicable to the thinking for rural economic development, in general.

> In this nation, ... the overwhelming majority of development decisions are private ones. Given this inherent right to develop, the intent of government intervention is to alter how private and public investments are made in order to produce a more socially acceptable result. Often, this is by specifying the end result an owner must achieve if he or she chooses to develop a property (i.e., single-family homes, construct a place for neighborhood retail activities, etc.) More recently, the focus has been shifting from the specified end result of development to the transaction itself, as in impact fees or performance systems. In either approach, when markets are strong, regulation or market restraint is the normal mode of intervention and when markets are weak, public incentives or inducements are employed.

This quotation points up three key considerations when a community moves from merely reacting to economic change, to structuring long-term economic activities in a dynamic relationship with shared environmental and social goals. First, the recent publicity given to the property rights movement is a reminder that many long-time property owners — particularly of large, family held lands — believe that governments should have a very limited say in how land is used by current or future owners. Second, however, government has the right, and often the responsibility, to restrict certain activities on private land that would harm others who are affected by how local land, air and water are used; or, to promote activities which serve a general public good. Land use restrictions on hazardous waste disposal, for example, would fall in the first category; a requirement that developers set aside a certain percentage of property for park and recreation land would fall

into the second. Finally, whether intervention is in the form of restrictions or incentives, economic goals should be directed towards the creation of lasting jobs that do not deplete community resources; and land use decisions should, ideally, benefit the many, rather than the few.

There is a town, famous throughout New England, that has two motor speedways within its corporate limits. The predictable traffic, public safety and litter problems materialized as soon as the first track opened for business. As a result, the town now has relatively strict zoning laws governing its commercial and residential development, which never enjoyed public support in the past.

Other small cities have passed ordinances requiring a minimum of 40 acres for a residential lot, that, in effect, hold farm families hostage from selling smaller parcels of land, even if agriculture can no longer support full time farming operations. Other towns have passed such strict limits on commercial development that they preclude the business community from contributing to a reasonable expansion of the local economy.

Neither extreme of too loose or too strict an approach to zoning seems a good model to follow. Like land use planning, development strategies may polarize communities, if they are only presented as a choice between extremes. There are the champions of "no growth," who see each new resident or business enterprise as threatening community character or draining the public budget. On the other end of the spectrum are advocates of "all growth is good growth." Often, pro-growth leaders maintain that they are advocates only for small, clean, well-paying industries or for residential development that will pay its way. But a number of people who have studied economic development trends suggest there are new ways to view economic development and to assess its true costs and benefits to your community.

Michael Kinsley of the Rocky Mountain Institute in Snowmass, Colo., says in the Institute's *Economic Renewal Guide*: "The assumption that economic prosperity requires growth seems so reasonable that most of us don't think much about it. The trouble is, the work 'growth' has two fundamentally different meanings: 'expansion' and 'development.' Expansion means getting bigger; development means getting better, which may or may not involve expansion."

Even within smaller communities, it is easy to think of examples where growing bigger resulted in the loss of something special: The move of the main street diner to a modern new building with three times the seating; or the purchase of the family-owned hardware store by a national chain that doubled sales volume with deep discounts and that replaced knowledgeable sales people with a computerized inventory system.

The *Guidelines for Sustainable Development*, reprinted here, are drawn from Kinsley's book and offer some general rules for implementing sustainable development in your town or region. They may help local community and business leaders recognize actions that are already underway or which could be easily added to current efforts.

Links to Other Efforts

The principles of managing growth in a sustainable manner introduce another dimension, both to the planning process and to the consideration of actual economic development strategies. This way of thinking may be incorporated into visioning or other long-term approaches to planning. It may be used to refine the way that a community carries out specific job creation or infrastructure projects. Many of the development strategies discussed in other chapters reflect a sustainable development approach.

For example, recreational and eco-tourism at manageable levels do not require or exhaust resources to the same degree that permanent manufacturing facilities or residential development are likely to. Stopping retail leakages and adding value to homegrown products before they are shipped to market keep dollars circulating for local benefit and enable local jobs to grow in dollars earned — but not necessarily in number. Business visitation programs and the encouragement of entrepreneurs may lead to more and better jobs in the future, while drawing upon community resources at approximately current levels.

Even business attraction can be gauged according to a standard that renewable resources cannot be used at a rate faster than they can be renewed. [The lumber and fishing industries are two examples where the widespread exhaustion of resources in the past has finally prompted efforts to assure that demand does not exceed the exhaustible supply.] As a flexible and adaptable process, the sustainable management of growth allows for its incorporation into virtually all small town job creation strategies.

But managing resources in a sustainable manner is not exclusively associated with economic development decisions. Of equal importance, local governments have major responsibilities for the protection of public health and the preservation of land and water resources where concerns about sustainability also must be aggressively pursued.

Water is perhaps rural America's most precious natural resource, critical to agriculture, current and future business and residential development, recreation and general public well-being. In many parts of the country, however, water has become contaminated, more costly to provide and increasingly scarce. Contaminants from industry — past and present — agriculture, underground storage tanks and numerous other sources have been found in a number of the nation's surface and underground water supplies.

Often, these contaminants are colorless, odorless and tasteless, giving no evidence of their harmful presence without sophisticated testing. The monitoring requirements in the Safe Drinking Water Act of the federal government, and its recent 1996 amendments, assign major responsibilities to public water systems for the identification and removal of both chemical and bacteriological contaminants to levels posing no threat to human health.

There are ways that local governments can manage natural resources, just as they would economic development, which are better, but not necessarily bigger. If drinking water contamination is expected to increase in the future, the problem could be handled by building a bigger treatment facility. Yet many water systems are developing source water protection programs that focus on the prevention of pollution in the first place and the wise use of water in homes, business and agriculture.

Source water protection programs typically identify actual and potential sources of contamination and then develop mandatory and voluntary strategies to remove or control the causes. A gallon of petroleum can make a million gallons or more of water undrinkable. Therefore, many communities now identify all abandoned underground storage tanks and have them removed by the owners; or with public dollars when an owner cannot be located.

Runoff from agricultural chemicals and animal waste products is the single largest contributor to rural non-point source pollution [that type of pollution which does not originate from a identifiable point, such as a sewage treatment plant]. Local government leaders and farmers now meet in many areas of the country to work out voluntary best-management practices to minimize the impact of runoff from agricultural sources on streams, rivers, lakes and underground water supplies.

Preservation Strategies

Another key area of growth management in which rural governments can work with community partners is the preservation of farm land and open spaces. Statistics on the annual loss of farm land to development and the overwhelming home owner preference for single family houses with a yard would seem to place agricultural interests and new residential development on a collision course. But there are several promising approaches that do not stop development altogether, and locate growth on nonagricultural lands where public services can be provided at the least cost and with the least impact on the environment.

Many smaller governments, such as Washington Township in Berks County, Penn., have recently discovered a zoning tool that allows landowners in preservation areas to permanently sell or transfer their development rights to landowners in development area — a concept known as the transfer of development rights (TDR). A common thread can be found in successful programs across the nation: a concerted effort to induce developers in the private real estate market to purchase development rights from landowners in a preservation area, or sending area, and transfer them, and the potential development they represent, to a development area, or receiving area.

By using the TDR concept, small and rural governments have a powerful incentive to preserve and protect virtually any natural resource the community has identified as invaluable and irreplaceable, including agricultural land, forest land, park land, and recreation and conservation areas, and simultaneously increase development densities. A locality interested in incorporating TDR into its zoning ordinance must begin by first identifying the priority preservation and development areas of its jurisdiction.

With the sending and receiving areas identified, a township must then allocate to landowners in the preservation area a predetermined number of development rights, which they can sell to landowners who want to develop their own land. But to provide an incentive to sell these rights, landowners in the preservation area must normally be allocated rights for more dwelling units than they would be permitted to build under the township's current zoning.

Washington Township proved to be one such "natural fit" for a transferable development rights program. A largely rural community of 2,800 residents near the eastern tip of Berks County, Washington Township surrounds the small Pennsylvania boroughs of Bally and Bechtelsville. The township managed to escape the development boom of the 1980s, but the board of supervisors realized early on that their rural community lay directly in the middle of an area ripe for development. The board also agreed that just sitting back and waiting for development to hit would quickly lead to disaster.

According to Sandy Moser, who has served Washington Township for 21 years as secretary, the supervisors felt they could better facilitate cooperation among the farming interests, members of the planning commission, other township residents, and the township's planning consultant by taking the lead role in the revision of the comprehensive plan and update of the township's zoning ordinance.

In response to concerns regarding the cost of infrastructure to support the high-density development created by the TDR program, the board argued that villages in the township were already in need of sewerage and that sewers would be more affordable for everyone if the villages were the core of the TDR receiving area. More development to share the costs would eventually lead to lower sewer bills for many township residents. And, lastly, in response to reservations voiced about the impact of higher-density development on the township's rural roads, the supervisors reasoned that a successful TDR program would deflect development pressure away from the most rural areas of the township, thus providing the only hope of preventing unmanageable traffic levels.

These and many other concerns were expressed time and time again throughout the process by both supporters and opponents, explained Moser. The board questioned every-

thing as it proceeded cautiously through the project. Under the direction of the board of supervisors, the township's planning consultant delineated endless possibilities of sending and receiving areas and considered several different development densities before the TDR concept was written into the township's zoning ordinance. John Weller, planner for Systems Design Engineering, the township's planning consultant, noted that the endless hours of research and planning eventually paid off for the township.

The resulting zoning ordinance outlines a number of procedures and tools to implement the TDR concept, including provisions for a high-density residential and village district as the receiving area for development rights. Single-family, detached dwellings and two-family dwellings with traditional lot sizes and densities are allowed in the district, but smaller lot sizes and higher building densities are allowed with the purchase of TDRs. The number of development rights required for other uses varies.

The zoning ordinance specifies that transfers of development rights must be approved by the township board of supervisors and the rights must be officially transferred by a deed recorded in the Berks County Office of the Recorder. Purchasers of development rights must also pay any municipal real estate transfer tax due to the township. Ninety-five development rights have been proposed recently using TDRs. "The township is reviewing those subdivision plans now," said Moser, "and public sewer and water service is going into the receiving areas outlined in the zoning ordinance. These improvements and the availability of the development rights from the agricultural district should begin to attract more developers who are interested in building higher-density housing in Washington Township's TDR receiving area."

Weller, the township's consultant, warns that townships should thoroughly investigate the TDR concept before proceeding with any significant zoning ordinance changes that incorporate the concept: "Any growth management concept must be specifically appropriate for the community." And TDR is very community-specific — above everything else, you must have the support of a project before being perceived as being in pursuit of their own agenda.

"In Washington Township's experience and the experience of other communities that have implemented TDR," notes Weller, "I am convinced that TDR would never have been adopted without the constant support of all of the groups who faithfully attended the many work sessions and participated in the process of planning and zoning."

The Washington Township case study was documented in a series of articles on "Preserving Open Space" which appeared in the *Pennsylvania Township News*, in the July, August and September 1995 issues. The series also described several other local and state initiatives to protect farm land. They include: agricultural protective zoning; the outright purchase of farm land by local, state or non-profit entities; agricultural easement purchase programs [a public sector version of the transfer of development rights program]; and open space, which clusters development in a way that minimizes the land required for homes and infrastructure, but which provides home owners with visual and physical access to the land which remains undisturbed.

Inclusion and Resolution

In this guide, economic decisions are presented as deliberate choices that are consistent with the wise use of community resources and with future community goals. Virtually all resources can renew themselves — given time and use which do not exhaust or irreversibly contaminate them. Of the three Es involved in building a sustainable community, there remains the issue of equity. It is a word that should cast a wide net. If used in a restrictive or self-serving way, equity can be a divisive, rather than inclusive, process.

Equity at its core is about fairness. It involves the distribution of economic and social benefits across the community. It recognizes the range of economic needs within the community and allows affected parties to be heard, as choices on development initiatives are presented, debated and made. If consensus cannot be reached on issues such as the line between the use and misuse of local resources, then an equitable solution may require establishment of an independent dispute resolution process or an outside mediator.

An equitable view for sustaining the community, for example, will recognize that jobs must be available for young people graduating from high school or risk that many of the community's future taxpayers and leaders will settle elsewhere. As another example, the transferable development rights ordinance adapted by Washington Township enables farmers to receive some of the financial benefits that their land would bring, if developed for business or residential purposes. But in exchange for selling these rights to a developer who can use them on non-agricultural property, the farmer is legally bound to keep the land in agriculture, as a sustainable community resource.

Equity involves looking out for more than just a worker's paycheck. In Vermont's Mad River Valley, town leaders from Warren, Waitsfield and Fayston have worked successfully in partnership with the Sugarbush ski resort since the 1970s to make development compatible with town life and the environment. Yet the popularity of the area steadily drove up the cost of housing to the point that many young families who staffed the resort could not afford to live in the area. When approached about the problem, the owners of Sugarbush donated a parcel of land located off the mountain slopes, which is being developed by a volunteer, nonprofit community group, as a site for affordable housing.

Efforts are underway to attract tourists

to the resort on a year-round basis, so that many of the seasonal jobs will become year round jobs.

Equity provides everyone a place during the discussion of decisions that affect them. If a controversial facility such as a prison or landfill is to be located in your town, make certain that its placement is not imposed on a group or area that is unable to mount effective resistance. If the project is a good one for the community, then open discussion should make people stakeholders, not opponents.

In some small towns, there may be strong traditions or incentives not to open up the decision-making process. Often a small, recognized group has, over the years, taken the lead for determining the community's future. The leadership group is familiar, if not always content, with the way its members conduct business. In some communities, citizens are content to let those willing to serve take all responsibility.

Yet when decisions will affect current and future residents, their livelihood and the quality of community life for years to come, these decisions must be made by as broad a base of citizens as possible. Inclusiveness is one of the benchmarks of sustainable communities and one of the keys to success.

To Avoid or Accept

When issues are as all-encompassing as how land will be used for generations to come and what kinds of jobs and businesses may or may not meet community criteria, conflict is almost inevitable and this fact is better faced early on in the process.

History demonstrates that the cost of avoiding conflict is high. In the late 1930s, Neville Chamberlain, Prime Minister of England, was known as the Great Compromiser, who averted conflict with Hitler's Germany though a series of appeasements that sacrificed many a nation's freedom. Chamberlain is now recalled with disgrace, however, for not forcing an early diplomatic showdown that might have led Germany to seek a political rather than a military solution to territorial disputes.

At a more local level, while unnecessary arguments expend time, energy and people's ability to work with one another, on many issues, conflict is inevitable and must be recognized and worked through. Rather than dreading conflict, local leaders should utilize the opportunity to fully examine and resolve issues that may fester and resurface if ignored. Volumes have been written on conflict or dispute resolution. There are some general rules, however, that apply to most public conflict, including those involving sustainable growth decisions.

- *Define the issue.* Often, conflict is over a choice of words or emphasis within a generally acceptable solution. Norman Mailer once observed that two people meeting face to face are still looking in opposite directions. When opposing views of a contentious issue are first verbalized, they frequently are full of inflammatory language. Generally, it is good to let people speak as forthrightly as they want in order to clear the air. The moderator may want to record each position on a flip chart, but also restate the key points in less loaded language. "I hear you saying this...," or "You seem most concerned about this..." are two ways of introducing such restatements without putting words in the mouth of the original speaker or passing judgment on what was said initially. Sometimes the issue itself cannot be agreed upon and discussion may move on to other dimensions of the resolution process.
- *Determine if information, emotion or personality is at the root of the conflict.* A lack of convincing information is often the basis for conflict, and its presence is also the key to resolution. The impact of eco-

nomic development, positive or negative, on property values and quality of life concerns most citizens. Additional study, or reassurances from towns which have had parallel experiences, may resolve the issue. Some issues are argued on purely an emotional basis. Landfills and low-level nuclear waste sites, for example, generate almost immediate opposition. Sometimes, emotional resistance to a local issue cannot be resolved to everyone's satisfaction, although it may help to identify the consequences of not landfilling solid waste. A possible resolution would be for the community to undertake a large-scale effort to recycle and to collect household hazardous waste for separate disposal outside the community.

Personality conflicts may be the hardest public disputes to resolve, because both parties are often willing participants. The root cause may have little to do with the issue under discussion and much to do with family or business transactions in the far past. If a member of the decision-making body, such as the town council, becomes embroiled in the dispute, he or she should not serve as the moderator, for example, and should perhaps be asked to be excused from a role in making the decision itself. If a real issue lies behind the public conflict of personalities, local leaders may move discussion ahead by asking both parties what they would choose as a general outcome. This question forces people to refocus on the issues. This same approach may work when a group or public forum is having problems defining the issue. Occasionally, it helps to work backward from where you hope to end up.

- *Allow all sides a chance to be heard and to be heard seriously.* Many individuals or organizations will press their position in a disruptive way if they believe they have been ignored or disrespected. Public

meetings should be well-publicized and different interests encouraged to schedule an appearance. Groups representing minorities, smaller constituencies or disadvantaged residents should not purposely be scheduled when few are in attendance or attention spans have grown short. Most people and organizations are willing to accept that dispute resolution involves giving up some goals to achieve others that are shared with the rest of the community. But first, all parties who will be committed to what emerges as the common good must sense that their views have been heard and weighed in the final decision.

- *See if a consensus is emerging.* In full and open discussions, a combination of information, logic, cross fertilization of ideas and respect for others' viewpoints often opens the way for consensus. It is best for one of the parties in dispute to suggest initially the outline for a resolution since some people will not move from their original position until they see movement from the other side. Group leaders may try to structure the suggestions that come from different interests in ways that appear to be equitable, but that remain consistent with overall community economic development goals. Most people are willing to work towards and accept consensus, if they have been included from the beginning and do not feel they are being conspired against when choices are made.

- *Engage an outside mediator for complex, highly divisive and legally high-risk situations.* Some conflicts either start or become so charged with implications that they are best handled by an experienced, outside, neutral party. There is no check list to determine when this type of situation has arrived. But if most of the decision-makers feel overwhelmed with the prospect of peacefully resolving an issue, or the financial and legal consequences of the decision are substantial, then a professional mediator may be the best option. It is important before the mediator is chosen to have the different parties agree that they will accept the outcome of the mediator and that they will have some input into determining the skills which the mediator should bring to the negotiating table.

Ideally, managing growth in a way that is consistent with community concerns for the environment and with the equitable involvement of all citizens should bring the community together, not apart. It may prove to be an important part of your community's unfolding history when job creation is linked directly to quality of life issues; and when land use planning preserves the century-old view of croplands free from development into the foreseeable future. With sustainable development as a goal for growth, we can be more certain that what we value from the past will live on, and in our ability "to meet the needs of the present without compromising the ability of future generations to meet their own needs."

CHAPTER 11

Bernards Embraces Nature to Enhance Its Downtown

Peter A. Messina

Bernards Township was chartered in 1760 and presently encompasses the areas of Basking Ridge, Lyons, Liberty Corner and West Millington. The 24.5 square-mile township in northern Somerset County has grown over 100 percent in the last 25 years — from 4,700 homes and 12,920 people in 1980 to 10,250 homes and approximately 27,650 people in 2005. The township is now a mature community with minor small-scale growth. However, the concept of continuing the small town character of the historic township was ever present in the minds of the governing officials and residents.

In the late 1990s, in concert with the Garden Club, the township's engineering department investigated the conversion of the township's many traffic islands to landscape gardens. After the initial investigation, the costs appeared to be prohibitive on a township wide basis. We then proceeded to look at individual islands one at a time.

The first traffic island was massive, over 500 feet long and 200 feet wide. The island was a large crater with guide rail all around. The engineering department proceeded to work with an area developer to truck in over

40,000 cubic yards of fill dirt to berm the island. After the hole was filled the perimeter guide rail was unnecessary and was removed. A township resident then volunteered to re-seed the area with wildflowers.

A second traffic island made of concrete was jack hammered and the debris removed by public works and community service crews. A local landscaper donated the labor to install tulips and carpet roses.

The next traffic island started with just a grass lawn and was converted with 2,000 daffodils, black-eyed susans, grasses, butterfly bushes and catmint.

The main gateway to the Basking Ridge Village on North Maple Avenue had a traffic island that was overgrown with many old bushes. This island was transformed with three specimen magnolia trees, 1,000 daffodils, grasses and many ornamental perennials.

This landscape movement was not just limited to traffic islands. The township reconstructed Somerville Road which is a main collector road from a large planned development. A large bridge over the Dead River was designed with stone parapet walls and wood guide rail. The shoulders of the one mile road-

Originally published as "Beautification: Bernards Township in Bloom," *New Jersey Municipalities*, Vol. 83, No. 4, April 2006. Published by the New Jersey State League of Municipalities, Trenton, NJ. Reprinted with permission of the publisher.

way were lined with white horse fence and planted with wildflowers such as purple coneflowers and black-eyed susans.

After a new traffic signal was installed at the intersection of South Finley Avenue and Cross Road, the township engaged the services of a landscape architect to design plantings for all four corners to soften the effects of the signal poles, hardware and electrical cabinets. The installation included numerous maple, cherry and dogwood trees, ornamental grasses, daffodils and numerous perennials.

In 2002 the township's engineering department designed a municipal parking lot in the center of the Basking Ridge Village. The 50 space parking lot included 20 sugar maple trees, 2,000 daffodils, grasses, perennials, and a flowering spirea hedge row along the street frontage to hide the car bumpers from view. A pedestrian alleyway was constructed from the parking lot to Henry Street, which included cherry trees, grasses and perennials. Landscaped sitting areas were also constructed within the parking lot.

In 2004 the township designed a "traffic calming" measure known as curb extensions in the center of the Basking Ridge Village. The design eliminated over 2,500 square feet of asphalt and created an outdoor dining area for an adjacent restaurant.

The Department of Public Works has created a landscape division which now maintains these landscaped islands. Summer seasonal employees as well as community service crews help with maintenance. The landscaping became so infectious even the Public Works garage entrances were enhanced with a flag pole and plantings.

After the intense growth and then maturing of the township, the "livability" issues became of utmost importance. The residents of Bernards Township greatly appreciate the beauty of these landscape areas and look forward to the changing seasons as they travel through the township.

CHAPTER 12

Boston, Other Cities, Use CDCs for Urban Renewal

Alexander von Hoffman

It was the early 1980s, the dawn of the public-private partnership era and the twilight of Mayor Kevin White's administration in Boston. After a terrible decline, the city's inner-city neighborhoods were in dire need of help. Houses were abandoned and burned, and crime was rampant.

Paul Grogan, the young deputy director of the city's Neighborhood Development and Employment Agency, had just been placed in charge of the department and a novel program for developing low-income housing. Grogan's boss had abruptly resigned, but not before coming up with the idea of working with corporations and community development organizations to fight poverty and rebuild troubled neighborhoods. The program, called the Boston Housing Partnership, was designed in part to compensate for Ronald Reagan's drastic cutbacks in federal social programs.

Agency Under Fire

Unfortunately, however, the Neighborhood Development and Employment Agency was in trouble. The residents of Boston's neighborhoods did not trust the agency — it had a reputation of being ineffective, political, or both — and the U.S. Department of Housing and Urban Development (HUD) was investigating the agency's administration of federal funds. And, to top it all off, Grogan, the agency's neophyte director, knew nothing about nonprofit community development, the heart of the new partnership.

Grogan was not alone in his ignorance of nonprofit community development; the concept was unknown to most Americans in the early 1980s. Yet in the next 20 years, it would produce a revolution in urban revitalization, converting the most infamous neighborhoods in the country into healthy communities.

Led by small nonprofit groups, often known as community development corporations (CDCs), the broad-based movement has developed new homes and retail businesses, and instituted job training classes, day care programs, health care centers and anti-crime efforts. Unlike the federal urban renewal program of the 1950s and 1960s that was run for downtown business interests, community development takes a bottom-up approach, with

Originally published as "Communities Born Again," *American City & County*, Vol. 118, No. 9, August 2003. Published by PRIMEDIA Business Magazines & Media Inc., Overland Park, KS. Reprinted with permission of the publisher.

the local nonprofit CDCs setting the agenda and carrying out the efforts.

Today the results of the community development movement can be found all over the United States. From Newark, N.J., to San Francisco, empty buildings have been rebuilt, and real estate developers are constructing new homes and stores. Crime rates have fallen to levels not seen in 40 years. The fire engine houses are quiet where arson fires once burned almost incessantly.

People used to worry that inner-city neighborhoods might never be saved. Now, in many places, they worry whether those same neighborhoods will have room for families of modest means.

As effective as grass-roots CDCs have been, they would not have gone far on their own. Fortunately, governmental agencies and private institutions stepped forward to assist the small groups at the forefront of the community development movement. Philanthropies and nonprofit financial institutions — including such national powerhouses as the New York City–based Local Initiatives Support Corp., the Washington, D.C.–based Neighborhood Reinvestment Corp. and the Columbia, Md.–based Enterprise Foundation — proffered loans and grants and technical advice.

No group has been more essential to the revitalization revolution than local government. Local elected officials, department heads, and rank-and-file staff helped bring back inner-city neighborhoods in countless ways — by donating land or supplying funds for housing development, clearing projects through regulatory hurdles and sending policemen to shut down the haunts of criminals. In many states and cities, local governments disbursed the monies for federal programs, such as community development block grants, that allowed community development organizations to operate.

The revitalization efforts of local governments ranged in size from the mammoth — the largest by far was the $5 billion, 10-Year Plan created by Mayor Ed Koch to redevelop tens of thousands of housing units in New York City — to the modest cooperation of the local inspection or zoning departments.

Boston Creates Model

In Boston, for example, the city government — the Neighborhood Development and Employment Agency and its novice director Grogan — created a new model for urban revitalization efforts when it led the Boston Housing Partnership in the 1980s.

The basic idea of the Boston Housing Partnership was that the city government and the corporate sector would assist local CDCs to identify, acquire and redevelop the deteriorated and abandoned apartment buildings that were blighting the city.

The Partnership was headed by William Edgerly, CEO of Boston's State Street Bank, who enlisted representatives of banks, insurance companies and state government departments, such as the Massachusetts Housing Finance Agency, to serve on the board of directors. Yet when he called the first meeting of the Partnership in 1983, Edgerly had no money or staff to plan, let alone develop, housing. At the start, the private sector partners looked to local government to launch the new program.

Thus it fell to Grogan, who found himself at the helm of the unpopular agency beset by corruption charges, to send city funds to the CDCs. It was not that Grogan particularly believed in the CDCs or even knew anything about them. It was more that he needed to buy some time to solve the agency's problems and hoped that supporting the local CDCs might win back some of the trust of neighborhood residents.

First, Grogan had to make sure that no hint of interference would further damage the reputation of his agency. He convinced Mayor White to keep political operatives out of the housing program, threatening at one point to resign.

Then, Grogan learned that his agency was not corrupt, but merely woefully inefficient, having failed to carry out a number of programs for which it had received funds. With a windfall of close to $50 million, almost double his yearly budget, Grogan got the Boston Housing Partnership rolling.

Under the first Boston Housing Partnership program, 10 CDCs developed 700 dwelling units in 69 derelict buildings throughout Boston at a cost of $40 million. The experimental program had its trying moments but in the end demonstrated how local government could collaborate with nonprofit CDCs and corporate leaders to rebuild the city.

A few years later, with Grogan now enjoying the support of Mayor Raymond Flynn, the Boston Housing Partnership carried out a second program, in which CDCs restored almost 1,000 units in 51 apartment buildings that had become the most dangerous slums in the city.

Those community development projects transformed the image of inner-city Boston and paved the way for still more innovative programs either spearheaded by or done in close cooperation with the city government.

Chicago's Direct Approach

Like local administrations around the country, Chicago's city government supports CDCs in a number of ways. Under Mayor Richard M. Daley, Chicago has taken a distinctive approach to community development by building and improving its public facilities to encourage neighborhood revitalization.

For example, the city decided to bolster redevelopment on the South Side, the city's historic African-American district, by replacing an infamous motel — mocked by locals as the "ho hotel" — with a new central police department headquarters. The state-of-the-art, high-tech building was completed in 2000 at a cost of about $65 million. By counteracting the neighborhood's unsafe reputation, the presence of the police command center improved the marketability of nearby real estate in what had been a severely depressed market.

It also had another positive effect. Officials of the Illinois Institute of Technology, one of the most important private institutions in the area, had been debating whether to close their central campus in the middle of the South Side and move it to the suburbs. But once the city agreed to build the police headquarters, as well as a new entrance to a nearby elevated train station, the college officials changed their minds, upgraded the campus, and for the first time, constructed student dormitories. The city, in turn, rebuilt and landscaped the public streets that ran through the campus.

Chicago also has been in the forefront of the effort to rebuild its public housing projects, which, until demolition began, included the largest concentration of public housing in the country, a four-mile wall of high-rise buildings along South State Street.

For the infamous Cabrini-Green project near the city's Gold Coast, Mayor Daley pushed through a $1 billion development project that included demolition of the old buildings, construction of a new school and development of hundreds of new homes. In February 2000, the mayor, HUD and the Chicago Housing Authority (CHA) signed a five-year, $1.5 billion plan that called for CHA to develop or rehabilitate more than 25,000 public housing units and destroy 51 high-rises containing more than 18,000 apartments. The program provides all residents of the high-rises with either a low-rise home in new mixed-income developments on the same site or a housing voucher to use for private housing elsewhere. The demolition and placement of public housing residents is well underway, and Chicago's sense of the potential for future growth in its neighborhoods has transformed.

L.A. Takes Care of Business

Los Angeles is another city that supports community development by many methods, but its economic development program has a particular West Coast flair that has put Los Angeles in the forefront of a national movement to help inner-city businesses multiply and grow.

In the wake of the violence sparked by the verdicts in the Rodney King trial, leaders in the private and public sector launched a massive effort to "Rebuild L.A." Only after the crusade was drastically scaled back, however, did a few perceptive leaders realize that, contrary to its notorious image, South Central Los Angeles was a powerful economic generator. Looking beyond the image, the area contained an astounding array of food processors, clothing makers, toy distribution companies, furniture builders, metalworking and plastics manufacturers, as well as lucrative biomedical, entertainment and electronics firms that operated in and around the district. The community development leaders devised an innovative strategy of assisting mom-and-pop manufacturers to benefit the area's low-income workers.

Inspired by that innovative work, Los Angeles began to emphasize inner-city economic development. Mayor Richard Riordan and Rocky Delgadillo, a lawyer and deputy mayor for economic development, created

Genesis L.A. to assist communities where low-to-moderate income households predominate or where unemployment rates are higher than average.

Genesis L.A. combined the government's resources with funds from large banks; its five-member board included the CEO of Washington Mutual and retired basketball star and entrepreneur "Magic" Johnson. Its first order of business was to redevelop 15 — later the number rose to 22 — large blighted industrial and commercial sites.

Besides the usual business of trying to lure companies, the city's economic development office, under Delgadillo, also sponsored trade associations for the small manufacturers and helped start roundtables, including one for new entertainment media. Today, the city continues to place inner-city, small-scale manufacturing at the center of its economic development policy. And this spring, the Genesis L.A. Economic Growth Corp. created a real estate fund to develop approximately 3,000 homes and apartments.

Those are just a few cases of local governments pushing community development forward. All across the country, state and local government officials have supported and led community development efforts and contributed to one of the greatest domestic policy triumphs in recent American history: the revival of the inner-city.

CHAPTER 13

Boulder Metro Area Shares Revenues to Restrict New Development

Richard M. Sheehan

Colorado has been experiencing enormous growth throughout the state and particularly in the Denver-metro area. In 1994, the governor started his "Smart Growth Initiative"; this program included organizing a summit of more than 1,000 people who discussed the creation of local councils to develop regional plans to deal with this growth. The group assigned to the Denver-metro region joined with the Denver Regional Council of Governments (DRCOG) plan, which was already in progress. DRCOG, consisting of eight counties and 41 municipalities, was developing a plan to face the anticipated population growth of nearly 700,000 over the next two decades. DRCOG's *Metro Vision 2020* is a 25-year comprehensive plan designed to guide the development in these jurisdictions and examine issues such as transportation, air quality, water quality, and urban sprawl.[1] It was in this environment that the issues of urban planning crossed paths with the existence of local government competition for retail sales revenues.

In Colorado, urban sprawl has financially impacted local governments. To meet growth-financing needs and infrastructure demands, municipalities and counties often "face off" against one another to get more revenue into their own operating budgets. Local government revenues are collected at the local level in Colorado to allow for more autonomous decisions regarding the use of these resources. In contrast, in some state systems, the state government acts as a central collection source that distributes revenues based upon a formula or population base.

Colorado's revenue collection structure does not automatically encourage cooperation among jurisdictions and often results in a struggle to gain revenue share. For the Denver-metro area, this struggle can produce inconsistent "flagpole" annexation (an attempt by municipal government to annex around residential development in the shape of a flagpole in order to gain property having retail sales) and undesirable urban planning as cities fight for a piece of the revenue pie. Inspired by

Reprinted from *Government Finance Review*, Vol. 14, No. 2, April 1998. Reprinted with permission of the Government Finance Officers Association, publisher of *Government Finance Review*, 203 N. LaSalle St., Suite 2700, Chicago, IL 60601-1210. (312/977-9700; fax 312/977-4806; e-mail: GFR@gfoa@org; Web: www.gfoa.org.) Annual subscriptions: $35.

"Smart Growth" and *Metro Vision 2020* planning, the Metro Mayors' Caucus initiated a task force to seek and study alternative solutions. The task force's goal is to identify tools that have been successfully employed in the past and to create models for voluntary agreements that reduce competition and increase cooperation between local governments around retail development. One common tool used by governments in the Denver-metro area has been a number of revenue-sharing agreements; other tools include county planning restrictions, comprehensive planning agreements including "development phasing," and creative alternatives such as transferring development rights.

Metro Mayors' Task Force

In an effort to seek out methods used to discourage competition between cities, the task force examined several regional revenue-sharing efforts as well as other methods used to increase cooperation and control the type of development in growing surrounding areas. Among these were:

• The Boulder Chamber of Commerce was encouraging the City of Boulder to consider an intergovernmental agreement (IGA) with its outlying cities. This agreement, although unsuccessful, would turn revenues over to adjacent cities in hopes of encouraging growth outside of Boulder's boundary. It was also the goal of Boulder to control development along its central access road of US 36 and to slow the growth of inner-city traffic congestion.

• Two cities outside Boulder, Superior and Louisville, recently achieved success in creating an IGA to share revenues and avoid a legal entanglement. The goal of the IGA is to discuss the determination of 80 acres based upon land-use and serviceability issues rather than solely on revenue sharing.

• To control unincorporated development, Adams County, just northeast of Denver, is negotiating intergovernmental agreements to encourage development within municipal boundaries. The county hopes that by having an IGA it will not be forced into providing expensive infrastructure before its time.

• Thornton and Westminster, cities on the northern border of Denver, in 1986 developed an IGA designed to define a "sphere of influence" related to revenues generated on the Interstate 25 corridor.

• During what was called the "annexation wars" of the 1980s, officials of Brighton and Commerce City developed an IGA, which defined the boundaries of two cities along a major access road that the cities believe will one day be a thriving commercial district generated by development around Denver International Airport.

These models represent the Denver-metro area's effort to meet urban growth financing needs and attempts at minimizing urban sprawl before the infrastructure and municipal government are there to support it.

The Metro Mayors' Caucus Task Force, while exploring these projects, has stirred up a debate centered on sales tax collection policy and its impact on development: Is the current sales tax collection policy of Colorado creating uneven urban sprawl and encouraging unincorporated municipal-like communities, or would such haphazard development occur anyway? Should revenue-sharing agreements be used to curb the cost to local governments as they attempt to meet financing and infrastructure needs or should a more comprehensive approach be initiated to limit urban area growth in counties altogether?

The following sections of this chapter summarize five studies by the Metro Mayors' Revenue Sharing Task Force, providing examples of attempts by local government leaders to avoid a centralized state collection system with the use of revenue-sharing agreements and comprehensive land-use planning. These models have proven effective in developing cooperative approaches to what might otherwise be a divisive situation between local government entities. It is in these trenches that the battle will be won or lost to preserve autonomy and keep local sales tax control.

Boulder Regional Tax-sharing Plan

In 1995, the Boulder Chamber of Commerce recommended a regional sharing effort. After determining a base-year level of revenues, each city would share in the incremental growth of sales tax revenues based upon an allocation formula of population or existing retail share. Large cities might receive less sales tax than previously but still increase revenues based on their population. Smaller cities would have substantial gains, which would allow them time to develop income from market sources other than retail, such as manufacturing, tourism, service firms, or construction.

In theory, by equalizing sales tax revenue distribution, policy decisions would shift towards planning that focuses on neighborhood characteristics, land-use decisions, and environmental concerns rather than on the struggle to gain retail market share to meet short-term budgetary needs.[2] This attempt to create a revenue-sharing agreement was abandoned in 1997, as it became too difficult to gain a consensus in the political climate of the time. As growth continued, outlying cities around Boulder saw enough development in their jurisdictions to discourage continued dialogue of the IGA.

Tax Sharing for Two Cities

As a result of territorial battles around Boulder, the cities of Superior and Louisville entered into a revenue-sharing agreement. This agreement, ratified by citizens in the November 1997 election, concentrated more on land-use issues and serviceability than on urban growth. Superior and Louisville are separated by US 36, which forms a natural boundary; however, because 80 acres on the south (Superior side) of US 36 were included in the Louisville city limit, property owners of this region made two attempts to file with the court to disconnect from the City of Louisville. Rather than battle it out in court, the two communities entered into a revenue-sharing agreement through which the property would become a part of Superior, and Superior would collect any retail taxes generated from any development. In return, the City of Louisville would receive 50 percent of the retail sales tax revenues, and Superior allowed Louisville to include an additional parcel in its natural boundary north of US 36. Superior experienced some complication in implementing the agreement, as it had to accommodate three special districts inside its borders that also were counting on future revenues generated from any retail development. The agreement was careful to include specific provisions dealing with utility sales tax, tax rate changes, and how the collection process would work within statewide law. Although forced by legal concerns, this model emphasizes the need to take a proactive posture when competitive issues arise.

Adams County: Growth Policies

The Adams County approach to revenue equalization is tied to its comprehensive planning process. Adams County and its constituent cities — Arvada, Aurora, Bennett, Brighton, Broomfield, Commerce City, Federal Heights, Northglenn, Thornton, and Westminster — are developing growth-related policies within a countywide comprehensive plan which uses a tiered system designed to phase in urban-level development in three tiers: the next five years, by the year 2020, and post–2020. The goal for these local governments is to promote contiguity, infrastructure compatibility, and formal integration of their comprehensive plan. This effort is supported by government officials in the area who generally believe that urban-level growth belongs in municipalities where services can be provided in a more cost-effective manner. Adams County officials hope to achieve this goal by a series of intergovernmental agreements.

If the comprehensive plan is adopted in Adams County, urban development during the next five years that occurs in unincorporated areas would be required to meet city development efforts that historically have played cities and counties off against one another. With this policy, cities must annex development within their individual urban growth boundaries. By the year 2020, comprehensive planning will be done in concert with urban centers and the county to insure consistency between individual plans. These are lofty goals, but if the spirit to cooperate remains, Adams County might have a model other local area governments can adapt rather than "duking it out" over limited resources.

Westminster-Thornton IGA

Another case in point is the "sphere of influence" revenue-sharing agreement between Thornton and Westminster, two cities just north of Denver. For Thornton and Westminster the issue was boundaries.[3] The city of Thornton was considering the annexation of land west of I-25. The City of Westminster, however, viewed that same territory as "sacred ground" that it expected to annex one day. The two city managers met to discuss the development of an agreement that would outline boundaries and set the stage for future development in the area. The discussion evolved into a 10-page IGA that included a requirement for a cooperative master plan, outlined consistency in building codes, and suggested the kinds of public services to be provided. Most importantly, a revenue-sharing formula was agreed upon. This agreement, believed by

some to have curtailed development in the I-25 corridor, has yet to reach fruition, as build-out has not occurred. The city manager stated that the reason development has not occurred is not the existence of the intergovernmental agreement, but rather because there is "a lack of roof tops" in the area — once there is more housing, retail development will follow. Both mayors felt that this agreement allowed the governments to retain control over development in the area, and they believe that it removed the pressure from the two cities to compete for sales revenues. As a model to potentially follow, other cities — Commerce City and Brighton, for example — were influenced by the Thornton/Westminster agreement.

Boundary Line Agreement

In February of 1989, Brighton and Commerce City both wanted to stake claim to certain potential annexation areas. Some property owners were petitioning one city to be included in its boundary while the other city was concerned that if it did not act quickly, it might miss out on an opportunity to expand its borders and achieve potential sales tax revenue from what looked to be an area of future retail development as an outgrowth of Denver International Airport.

A good line of communication existed between the two municipalities, and avenues existed for increased cooperation — the Adams County Council of Governments (ADCOG), for example. With a cooperative environment in place, and a willingness of both parties to seek a "win-win" scenario, Brighton and Commerce City developed a revenue-sharing agreement that included land-use issues and boundary specifications. This agreement carefully described the use of debt for infrastructure and the pledging of revenues.

With the state legislature closely watching these "annexation wars," the two cities developed a model that other municipalities could follow. One of the terms of the agreement required that a joint plan be prepared as a guide for the development of land and the provision of public services and that it include design standards and land-use criteria. A truly cooperative venture now gives both cities the ability to control development and insure a steady proportionate revenue stream. In addition, their government officials do not have to concern themselves with developers trying to pit one city against the other to gain tax advantages.

Future of Revenue Sharing

The next areas of study for the Revenue Sharing Task Force include investigating a regional agreement to limit urban-level development to municipalities and promoting a dialogue between cities and counties. Cooperative agreements of this type are being explored by Boulder, Adams, and Larimer Counties.

Other alternatives to development phasing include encouraging developers to build in a city. To encourage density in the city rather than in potentially agricultural or unincorporated areas, in Boulder County a property owner can sell his/her right to build at a certain density level and grant that right to an owner of a parcel of land inside the city. The opportunity to sell this right (like a mineral right) encourages the owner not to sell to developers and to keep the land rural in nature; yet the owner may "profit" by not selling. In turn, property owners inside the city boundary, who cannot build high-density property due to historical zoning restrictions, now can purchase this right and increase their profit margin by developing more units and therefore selling more units.[4]

Jefferson County, also concerned about this urban sprawl into unincorporated areas, recently put together a task force to address this issue. This task force will examine the need for a tax increase or new taxes, cutbacks in services, and incorporation or annexation of incorporated areas. The commissioners have seen financial forecasts that suggest the county's tax base cannot support what are essentially municipal services that are incurred by the unincorporated areas and to which the rest of the county is contributing financially. Whether statewide law changes are necessary or a spirit of brotherhood among local governments must continue, solutions to this issue are not easily found.

Whether these models work or lead to statewide policy changes, the issue behind these cooperative plans and revenue-sharing models is clear: Philosophically, economic development in a community needs to be based on desired characteristics and local community needs, rather than on short-term revenue gains; in practice, however, sales tax policy in Colorado in one of the driving forces that often prevents this type of development from happening. The communities in the Denver-metro area have seen the result of this retail competition and redistribution of wealth in the financial misfortunes of two major shopping malls in the region.

Local communities like Adams County, nevertheless, have found ways and created models to benefit the citizens through comprehensive land-use planning. Local governments have kept their autonomy and avoided a centralized state collection system with the use of revenue-sharing agreements, in the case of Louisville/Superior and Westminster/ Thornton. Competition, although healthy to an economy, can be crippling to a community government that relies on retail sales taxes. Cooperation between communities continues to hold the key; if answers cannot be found at the local level, state-wide solutions may become the only alternative.

Notes

1. Metro Vision 2020 Implementation Strategy: Economic Development/Regional Tax Policy, DRCOG, May 1996.

2. Clark, Tom, *Colorado Real Estate Journal*, "Regional Tax Sharing," July 1995.

3. Intergovernmental Agreement between The City of Thornton and The City of Westminster, January 1996.

4. Boulder County Transferred Development Rights, April 1995.

CHAPTER 14

Bozeman, Other Cities, Use Nonprofits to Protect Nature

Todd Wilkinson

On a glorious Sunday morning just past dawn, Alex Diekmann walks with his eight-year-old son, Logan, and a hiking companion up a treeless hill shaped like a camel's hump. From this skyscraping vantage, Diekmann, who manages The Trust for Public Land's work in the greater Yellowstone ecosystem, lifts his binoculars to spy the rugged panorama along the Taylor Fork of the Gallatin River in the remote central reaches of the Madison Mountain Range southwest of Bozeman, Montana.

Below him lie scores of narrow, barely discernible lines etched into the earth. These lines funnel into larger tracks that could easily be mistaken for well-worn footpaths or possibly off-road vehicle trails. They are in fact wildlife highways, fragile passages between Yellowstone National Park to the east and the verdant Madison Valley on the other side of the western horizon.

Only days earlier, Montana state biologists conducting an aerial census in this area counted 11 grizzly bears (including four sows with cubs); a huge scattering of elk (including mothers and newborn calves); moose wading through swampy bottomlands; mule deer grazing across sagebrush-coated uplands; and even a few wolves.

"Isn't this place great?" Diekmann says to his son. "We're standing at the spot where it all comes together."

"Who owns this land, Dad?" the boy asks.

"You do," Diekmann replies. "We do. We all do."

Ten years ago the Taylor Fork drainage was in imminent jeopardy of being developed and fragmented, many of its wildlife corridors blocked forever. While some of the land was protected national forest, there were many private, developable in holdings left over from frontier times when railroad companies were given vast tracts of land by the federal government. Hundreds of 20-acre home sites had been platted. A network of roads was being bulldozed. Prefabricated guest cabins were beginning to pepper the hills. Farther upstream, a timber company planned to fell old-growth trees.

This prospect was particularly troubling to bear biologists such as Chuck Schwartz, who oversees the Yellowstone Interagency Grizzly Bear Study Team, headquartered in Bozeman. "The Taylor Fork has the highest density of bears in the northern half of the greater Yellowstone ecosystem," Schwartz says.

Originally published as "Making Way for Wildlife," *Land & People*, Vol. 18, No. 1, Spring 2006. Reprinted with permission from The Trust for Public Land. To learn more about TPL, please visit www.tpl.org.

With plenty of elk calves, rodents, and a wide variety of native plants to eat, some grizzly bear sows have given birth to as many as four cubs in a litter, twice the usual number. "It's not just incredibly productive for grizzly bears," Schwartz says, "the Taylor Fork is a rich piece of real estate for a whole array of species." But carve it up with development and the Taylor Fork, instead of being a natural factory for bears, could have quickly become a "black hole" for bears, where their numbers would have dwindled.

In 2001, TPL began working with private landowners, local conservationists, citizen stakeholders, government leaders, and Congress to protect the land, eventually transferring more than 3,400 acres to the Gallatin National Forest. "The Taylor Fork is one of the most precious wildlife areas in the entire Yellowstone area," says Kurt Alt, regional wildlife manager for Montana Fish, Wildlife and Parks. "Losing it would have been tragic. Saving it was a close call. TPL stepped forward at a critical moment."

National Parks Are Not Enough

But the Taylor Fork is just one critical piece in a much larger jigsaw puzzle that must be assembled to protect wildlife in the 18-million-acre Yellowstone ecosystem, the largest intact bioregion in the lower 48 states. Encompassing northwestern Wyoming, southwestern Montana, and southeastern Idaho, this area the size of New England is best known for Yellowstone and Grand Teton National Parks — home during much of the year to the nation's most diverse assemblage of large wild mammals outside Alaska.

Yet ecologists have long recognized that the national parks alone cannot protect the region's abundant wildlife. As autumn advances and the park interiors are blanketed by several feet of snow, animals instinctively go on the move, following age-old pathways to lower-elevation valleys. Public and private lands outside the parks provide vital linkages to winter habitat elsewhere in the ecosystem. Should these lands be developed, the parks would become biological islands. Such isolated places, no matter how vast, suffer restricted and weakened gene pools and higher rates of species extinctions.

In addition, development is consuming more and more land in the ecosystem, according to an analysis by the Sonoran Institute. Over the last three decades the human footprint in the greater Yellowstone has expanded disproportionately faster than in other regions experiencing similar growth. Not only are greater numbers of people moving here, but they are building homes on increasingly larger tracts of land.

Over the last decade scientists, conservation groups, and government wildlife managers have begun focusing on the protection of habitat linkages between parks and wildlife refuges, says Rob Ament, former executive director of American Wildlands, which promotes the protection of wildlife corridors throughout the Rockies. He describes this as "stringing together the pearls of protected areas by focusing on the common threads that stitch them together."

Together, TPL, the Montana congressional delegation, the U.S. Forest Service, the Rocky Mountain Elk Foundation, The Nature Conservancy, the Montana Land Reliance (a nonprofit land trust), and local leaders have protected hundreds of thousands of acres of key wildlife habitat in the greater Yellowstone region that were in danger of being lost. TPL has protected more than 200,000 acres across the three-state northern Rockies region since 1998.

This work has been bolstered by the Doris Duke Charitable Foundation, which in 2001 awarded $8.2 million to groups working on conservation within the Yellowstone region, including $1.8 million to TPL. It also has relied heavily on support from Congress through the federal Land and Water Conservation Fund (LWCF) and the USDA Farm and Ranch Lands Protection Program (FRPP). In recent years budget pressures have taken a toll on these federal funding programs. Despite this, Congress has continued to invest millions of dollars in Montana conservation efforts — a credit to Montana's congressional delegation and in particular to U.S. Senator Conrad Burns, who chairs the Interior Appropriations Subcommittee that dispenses these funds.

Years ago Senator Burns served as a county commissioner in the Yellowstone region, and he recognizes that the stakes here are high. Senator Burns and a network of supporters (including senior administration officials, fellow Montana senator Max Baucus, and the staff of the USDA and other federal natural resource agencies) are working to safeguard local economies, opportunities for outdoor recreation, and the natural values of this unique region. Taylor Fork is only the latest victory in a lengthy list of conservation successes, including many TPL projects, that Senator Burns's work in Washington has made possible back home in Montana.

Besides protecting land for wildlife, these conservation projects have created better access for hunters and guides, anglers, skiers, horseback riders, snowmobilers, and family recreationists — all part of a natural-amenity economy worth more than $1 billion a year to local communities. "There's a balance you have to strike," says Senator Burns. "It is important to protect and preserve our natural areas and ensure we have habitat for our wildlife and recreational opportunities. That said, we have to guard against locking away our public lands to the detriment of the folks who live and work in the area."

"We've come a long way, but we've still got a ways to go," notes Diekmann. "We've been given a second chance to save the best that's left by applying better thinking and better tools to modern problems. But we only have a limited amount of time to do it right because the clock is ticking."

Elk Tracks

Farther south, near the western border of Yellowstone National Park, Diekmann pulls off the road and strolls to the sparkling meander of Duck Creek. A tributary to the Madison River system, Duck Creek isn't a large waterway, but it nurtures a wide riparian floodplain thick with willow. Grizzly bears use the corridor in their secretive travels from the park to nearby Hebgen Lake. So, too, do moose, elk, and bison. Brown, brook, and rainbow trout spawn in the creek's cobble bottom.

A few years ago a developer sought to build an 18-hole golf course and almost 1,000 homes on 320 acres overlooking Duck Creek, adjacent to the park and Gallatin National Forest. The plan drew red flags from wildlife biologists, park officials, and conservationists, who worried that it would pose a gauntlet for migrating wildlife and pollute the stream. No sooner had that project been stopped by a district court judge than another development, of 71 homes, was proposed on an adjacent tract. TPL acquired this parcel in 2004 and transferred it to the Forest Service. Today a new picnic area and fishing site sit on the creek's banks, and wildlife moves through the area unimpeded.

"These pieces of property might seem relatively insignificant compared to the millions of acres of public land surrounding them," Alex Diekmann says. "But their location is what makes their protection crucial. Even a small amount of development within this corridor would jeopardize its ecological function and block access for anglers and people interested in viewing wildlife."

Dennis Glick, director of the Sonoran Institute's Northwest Office, agrees. "Protecting Duck Creek has been long recognized as a high priority by the conservation community and residents of the Hebgen Basin," he says. "This purchase will help conserve critical wildlife habitat and support the land use goals of local residents. It's a win-win for wildlife and people."

Facts About Bears

Acreage required by the typical female grizzly bear: **32,000 to 192,000**

Acreage required by the typical male grizzly: **128,000 to 320,000**

Estimated population of grizzly bears nationwide in 1800: **50,000**

Estimated populations in 1975, when the grizzly bear was placed on the Endangered Species List: **fewer than 1,000**

Estimated population today: **1,100**

Estimated percent of the grizzly's historic habitat in the lower 48 states still inhabited by grizzlies: **1 to 2**

Number of ecosystems in the lower 48 judged by the U.S. Fish and Wildlife Service to be suitable habitat for grizzly bears: **6**

Rank of Yellowstone Ecosystem among these habitats in current grizzly bear population: **1**

Human satisfaction in knowing that land is being protected for grizzlies and other wildlife: **incalculable**

Sources: U.S. Fish and Wildlife Service, Greater Yellowstone Coalition (www.greateryellowstone.org)

Duck Creek and Taylor Fork straddle an ancient fall migration path for elk moving out of Yellowstone National Park. After moving through these areas and then navigating the spine of the Madison Range, the elk enter the open expanse of the Madison Valley, ford the Madison River (internationally famous for its blue-ribbon trout fishery), and head farther west onto the lower flanks of the Gravelly Mountains, where they spend the winter on the windblown grasslands of the Wall Creek Wildlife Management Area, administered by Montana Fish, Wildlife and Parks. The migration takes them 50 miles across a mosaic of public and private land.

"The dramatic journey that these wapiti take underlines the impact on wildlife of the mixed ownership pattern that has arisen since the era of frontier settlement," says Rob Ament. "If any segment is compromised by development, the ecological integrity of the whole corridor can fall apart." (Wapiti, another name for the American elk, is a Shawnee word.)

For this reason conservation groups have been working to assemble protected habitat in the Madison Valley along the elk's route. In 2002, The Nature Conservancy helped protect 6,800 acres of the 18,000-acre Sun Ranch,

in the upper Madison Valley, with a conservation easement. The ranch is home to 8,000 elk—the second-largest elk herd in the ecosystem—and also offers habitat for wolves, grizzlies, lynx, fisher, martens, and wolverines.

Until 2005, however, there remained a troubling and difficult-to-close gap in conservation on private land just south of the Sun Ranch and next to the Lee Metcalf Wilderness. In that year TPL brokered a pair of agreements conserving nearly 1,700 additional acres by purchase or easement, ensuring that one of the most important wildlife corridors in the upper Madison area remains free of subdivision. The transactions included permanent public hunting rights, a trail easement that guarantees public fishing access to almost four miles of the Madison River, and a new trailhead for hikers and hunters entering the Beaverhead-Deerlodge National Forest and the Lee Metcalf Wilderness Area.

Striking such deals depends on the right circumstances and combinations of personalities, says Kurt Alt of Montana Fish, Wildlife and Parks. "Thanks to the perseverance of Alex Diekmann and TPL, some very difficult land deals were put together that nobody thought had a chance of getting accomplished. Future managers are going to have some wonderful opportunities to conserve wildlife—opportunities that easily could have been lost."

For their part, in addition to funds they might receive for land or easements, landowners get the satisfaction of protecting the land and safeguarding a primordial passage of animals that has been going on since the time of the glaciers.

"So often you read about intractable environmental problems," says Alex Diekmann. "But what's happening with protection of wildlife corridors in the greater Yellowstone region is about finding win-win solutions. We still have a lot of work to do, but I'm optimistic. You have to be optimistic if you want to accomplish anything worthwhile."

CHAPTER 15

Cape Coral Uses Interactive Growth Model to Plot Its Future

Paul Van Buskirk, Carleton Ryffel, *and* Darryl Clare

Many communities across the nation are facing extreme growth, great pressure for services — and a drop in tax dollars.

To address these realities, a first-of-its-kind interactive growth model was developed for the city of Cape Coral, Florida, that can be adapted for other government agencies to weigh different scenarios and the positive and negative impacts of planning decisions.

Typical growth models only allow planners to look at growth in a static way. They don't account for change over time, new trends, or community and regional expansions and contractions. In contrast, Cape Coral's model allows new data to be input over time, thus producing better, more accurate projections.

The city's Interactive Growth Model was developed by planning and population consultant Paul Van Buskirk, AICP, who first used this type of model in the early 1980s to test the effects of developments of regional impact in the state of Florida, and in cities with rapid growth.

Cape Coral is one such city. It has experienced extraordinary growth, increasing in population from 10,930 in 1970 to 102,286 in 2000, a 10-fold jump over 30 years. The ultimate population is projected to exceed 400,000. Moreover, at 114 square miles, Cape Coral is Florida's second largest city in land area. Almost three-quarters of Florida's residents live within 150 miles of the city.

Looking Back

Cape Coral is a peninsula that is part of Lee County, and includes the cities of Fort Myers, Fort Myers Beach, Sanibel, Bonita Springs, and several unincorporated areas. Cape Coral and Fort Myers are separated by the Caloosahatchee River.

Cape Coral was pre-platted and incorporated as a city in 1970. The area resulted from one of the largest dredge-and-fill projects in history. When the dredging was completed, what remained was an extraordinary 400-mile network of navigable salt and freshwater canals. The designers then platted residential areas, commercial zones, industrial parks, streets, canals, parks, public areas, and transportation corridors.

About one-third of the city is currently

Originally published as "Cape Coral, Florida, Uses an Interactive Growth Model to Plot its Future Intelligently," *Planning*, Vol. 69, No. 7, July 2003. Reprinted with permission from PLANNING, copyright July 2003 by the American Planning Association, Suite 1600, 122 South Michigan Avenue, Chicago, Illinois 60603, USA.

built out; it has one of the largest operating reverse osmosis plants in the country and introduced one of the nation's first and largest residential dual water systems, which reclaims and recycles domestic wastewater for irrigation and fire fighting.

Carleton Ryffel, AICP, the city's recently retired planning director, knew that in a city that approves 200 to 300 building permits per month, there was a critical need to accurately forecast total population. Of equal importance was knowing the short- and long-term distribution of the total population over time. Old methods used to project Cape Coral's population growth could easily over- or underestimate anticipated population at given points in time.

In order to determine the best population projection methodology for Cape Coral, the city retained consultant Paul Van Buskirk in 2001. He was asked to develop and apply a population projection system that could accurately forecast the city's population over the short- and long-term. This initial work led to the development of the Interactive Growth Model, which became a comprehensive tool for planning, and went into full operation in Cape Coral in 2002.

Forecasting Methods

Van Buskirk examined four different models: a cohort survival component model, an extrapolation model (simple curve fitting), an exponential model, and a sigmoid model.

The cohort survival component model "ages" the various age groups or cohorts in the population into the future and applies the appropriate birth and death rates, usually found at state vital statistics offices. This model is sophisticated and expensive but does not accurately forecast long-term growth for rapidly growing cities experiencing large immigration.

The extrapolation model plots past population levels in a time series and then extends the line or curve into the future by regression analysis. This method has the weakness of over- or underestimating future population. Another shortcoming is that long-term limits to growth (such as build-out) are not factored in.

The exponential model assumes the population is increasing at a constant rate of change each year. This compounding effect can result in astronomical increases in forecasted population over the long term.

Basically, the sigmoid model is a complex variation of an extrapolation model and is more accurate than other methods for a forecasting short- and long-term growth for cities experiencing extraordinary growth and an estimated build-out population.

Many biological populations, including cities, tend to grow at a rate that simulates the sigmoid curve (or S-shaped curve). Population growth increases at an accelerating rate over time until it reaches an inflection point. Then, the rate of increase slows down until it reaches an upper growth limit.

One of the key variables in this growth equation is its upper limit or build-out. The upper limit for large-scale communities such as Cape Coral can be defined by calculating the total number of housing units that can be built by type and intensity. Then the housing units can be translated to population.

Cape Coral decided to use the sigmoid model for two reasons. First, it incorporates numerous variables that affect growth, and secondly, it has historically proven to be the most accurate growth curve for built-out incorporated cities, including Tampa, St. Petersburg, and Miami.

In 1982, using 1980 census data, Van Buskirk applied a sigmoid model to forecast the future population of Palm Bay, a large, growing community on Florida's east coast. The model predicted a population of 82,331 in 2000. That number was not far off. The U.S. census conducted in 2000 counted 79,413 residents — a mere 3.5 percent lower than the 1982 estimate.

Van Buskirk developed another sigmoid model in Lehigh Acres, Florida, using 1990 data. The model forecasted a 2000 population of 33,098. That year, the U.S. Census Bureau recorded a population of 33,430, a difference of 0.1 percent.

Most recently, the Cape Coral Planning Division used building permits, vacancy rates, and household size to estimate a current population of 117,676. The sigmoid curve had predicted a 2003 population of 117,559 — another difference of only 0.1 percent.

How to Use the Model

Accurate forecasting is important. Overestimates of population growth may lead to premature expenditure of public funds. Underestimates can have the opposite effect: infrastructure lagging behind needs. The cost to catch up on infrastructure needs far exceeds the cost to meet demands as they occur.

Three basic steps were employed to apply the sigmoid model in Cape Coral: First, an upper limit of growth was set as a key variable in developing Cape Coral's growth curve. The Cape Coral Interactive Growth Model team (Paul Van Buskirk plus staff from various city departments) estimated the permanent population at build-out to be 413,713, based on the city's future land-use map. Next came a sigmoid curve with regression analysis. Finally, the forecasted results for Cape Coral were validated by comparing the values of its regression analysis formula with that of similar cities in Florida that were already, or nearly, built out.

Typically in south Florida, most of the earliest residents are retirees in small households. A service population moves in to provide retail, financial, and medical services. The city then becomes more diverse in age, income, and household size. Next the construction industry grows, and so does the demand for public services. Eventually, the community begins to represent more traditional demographics. The sigmoid growth curve captures these characteristics of growth and incorporates them over time.

On August 26, 2002 the Cape Coral mayor and city council adopted the forecasted population estimates based on the sigmoid curve, and authorized the application of the Interactive Growth Model for planning purposes.

Creating the Interactive Model

Under the leadership of consultant Paul Van Buskirk, the city of Cape Coral put together a staff team to help with data and geographic information system (GIS) mapping. Team members included a broad cross section of various departments such as planning, GIS, economic development, fire and police, public works, transportation, and utilities. By using this staff team, the city spent less than $50,000 in consultant fees to put together its interactive growth model.

For the next nine months, between October 2001 and July 2002, the team met bimonthly for two hours. At those meetings work assignments from the previous meeting were reviewed and new work was assigned. On average, each staff member worked on parts of the model for about eight hours a month, including the bimonthly meetings. This approach kept the consultant fees low and was educational for the staff because it showed them how to deal with a highly complex issue in an innovative way.

In total, some 50 variables were built into the interactive growth model. These included: the city's comprehensive plan, future land-use map, parks and recreation master plan, transportation plan, fire station plan, utilities master plan, school data, GIS information, and census data.

Here's how the model works. Suppose the location and timing of roads and water and sewer lines are delayed or advanced in a particular location. The result would be overall development of that area as well as other parts of the community. When this happens, community leaders have a better understanding of the implications of their decisions and can get the most from the investment of public and private funds.

Because Cape Coral has a huge land area, the data had to be managed and mapped in smaller segments. When the original developer, Gulf American Corporation, first created Cape Coral in the 1960s, the city was pre-platted into 158 numbered areas called GACs (named for the developer). The GACs became the fundamental unit for the interactive growth model and are also used for comprehensive planning, real estate legal descriptions, and local data generation.

To further manage the data, the staff team created 20 planning districts, which consisted of roughly seven contiguous GACs each. The city's GIS division established the base map for the GACs and planning districts.

April 1 was chosen as the start date of the model to coincide with the release of U.S. census data. That date is also used as a benchmark date to test and validate the model annually and every 10 years when the census is updated. Several sub-models were developed as a regression model of key indices over time. The sub-models were:

- Demand for housing units
- Enrolled school population by grades
- School plants by type of facility, enrollment, and employment
- Demand for acres for parks
- Demand for fire stations and emergency facilities
- Demand for gross leasable area of floor space for retail trade and number of employees
- Demand for office service space and number of employees
- Demand for hotel and motel rooms
- Demand for gross leasable area of floor space for manufacturing and wholesale trade and number of employees.

The building department provided data for the current number of housing units by type for each GAC. City GIS staff then presented data from the current tax rolls on the amount of existing square footage of building area for retail, office-services, manufacturing, and wholesale trade. GIS staff also received data for current areas of developed recreation lands, and the county school system provided current data on school facilities, enrollment, and employees.

The build-out development data for housing, acres of retail trade, office-services, manufacturing, and wholesale trade came from the planning staff and were based on the future land-use map. Information on the location and size of future park and recreation sites also came from the planning staff. Regional research studies, as well as Urban Land Institute guidelines, were used to calculate the number of employees for retail trade, office-service, manufacturing, and wholesale trade.

Current, forecasted, and build-out data were generated for each GAC and put into an Excel spreadsheet. The challenge was to translate the data by GAC so that the information would coincide with U.S. census block groups and traffic analysis zones. This was a job for GIS staff, because they had established the base map for the GACs and planning districts.

GIS to the Rescue

Nearly all GIS practitioners require data from multiple sources. It is important to build and share data that can be used by any organization. The city of Cape Coral's GIS division uses the Federal Geographic Data Committee's suggested guidelines, which encourage the use, sharing, and distribution of geospatial data.

One of the goals of the FGDC is to provide standards to help create common definitions for geospatial metadata. GIS data management, by its very nature, is disaggregated, but it fundamentally involves the integration of data from multiple sources. To address the need to build and share geographic information in concert with the interactive growth model, ESRI, of Redlands, California, is helping to develop common content standards (i.e., common data model designs).

The city of Cape Coral's GIS division, headed by Darryl Clare, compiled digital data from various sources, including the U.S. census, Lee County land data, the metropolitan planning organization, traffic analysis zones, and the city's GIS database. These different sources comply with "standards" so data can be referenced to fit together seamlessly.

ArcView was the software package chosen as the building block of the interactive growth model, because it is easy to use. The model had to be more than a conceptual framework; it had to support real GIS work, including the update and maintenance of data.

For starters, data from the Cape Coral database needed to be translated to U.S. census block data. Different layers were combined to make that happen, depending on the particular application and information requirements. Each layer would involve a specific data type, such as tables, relationships, and feature classes.

For example, the street network data used for traffic analysis are contained in the traffic analysis zones within the metropolitan planning organization's database map. These traffic analysis zones contain information about traffic loads. The growth model incorporates information about development into the traffic analysis zones in order to forecast future traffic loading.

Much of the parcel and land-use data were extracted from the city-county parcel database with data attributes of the characteristics of each parcel, in accordance with the state of Florida land-use codes. This base map data set consists of 17 data layers related to the themes of parcel characteristics such as roads, utilities, drainage, land cover, cultural land marks, and transportation structures. The interactive growth model now had a tool to translate data from the GAC polygons to census blocks and traffic analysis zones for their respective forecast.

A Tool for Interpretation

Cape Coral's interactive growth model is a systems approach that is population driven. When one variable changes, it proportionately changes the other 50 variables in the model. In the past, this function involved separate software packages not well integrated with GIS.

Fortunately, the linking strategies used in Cape Coral are wholly compatible with one another, so that the interactive growth model, though built for one GIS system, will accept data from another. This tightly coupled system allows modeling information to exist as specially coded modules (objects) within the framework of GIS. Such modules could be written in various languages provided by the GIS (for example, the Avenue Language for ArcView).

The combination of Excel and ArcView enabled GIS staff to produce maps that the public could readily grasp. For example, a particular spreadsheet held data that would help the city decide how much development could occur in each GAC in five-year periods until build-out. That data had to be translated into a graphic — and that is where ArcView's mapping tools came into play.

One series of maps shows the population growth of the city in five-year increments by the progressive darkening of colors on a city map. As the color darkens, the population grows in a given area.

Another series of maps shows commercial development demand over time in square feet. These maps show larger and larger red circles at five-year increments, representing the amount of square feet of commercial floor area needed to serve the projected population in a given area. The larger the red circle in a given year, the greater the commercial demand.

Similarly, this type of map series can be used to show the demand for all land uses and the timing of such facilities as utilities, transportation corridors, fire stations, parklands, and schools through buildout.

Bottom Line

Data output from the interactive growth model demonstrated a demand for 6.243 million square feet of gross leasable retail area and a supply of only 4.054 million in the year 2001. The residents of Cape Coral were shopping outside the city.

Judging by the model, Cape Coral would be able to support a regional facility between 2005 and 2010, when the population is expected to reach 150,000. In other words, the interactive growth model has alerted the economic development office when to start recruiting developers for a regional shopping center.

The model can also help ensure that the right parcels are available to meet the current and future demands for neighborhood, community, and regional shopping centers. This is smart growth: People should not have to travel great distances outside their neighborhoods in order to shop. To do otherwise increases demands on roadways, the infrastructure, and travel costs.

School facility planning is greatly enhanced by use of the interactive growth model as well. Output data indicate when and where the school district will run out of school sites. The school board can then identify parcels large enough to support future demands for new school facilities.

Cape Coral's interactive growth model is being used across city department lines. Users include Community Development (comprehensive plan update and commercial corridor studies), Parks and Recreation (timing and location of parks), Public Works (water and sewer timing), Fire (station timing), and Police.

The city is also using the growth model to update its transportation model, a basis of state and federal transportation funding. The public, electricity providers, real estate and the development community, and the county school board have expressed strong interest in the model as well.

With this level of interest, the city established an interactive growth model information function to update the model and provide tailored information to those diverse groups.

We believe the interactive growth model, in combination with GIS, will revolutionize how communities plan and use their resources for the maximum benefit of its citizens.

CHAPTER 16

Cherry Hill Embraces Mixed Uses for Its Commercial Center

Bernie Platt

Headline performers? Luxury shopping and fine dining? In the 60s, Cherry Hill was the place to go.

Today, thanks to the opportunities presented by the sale and redevelopment of the Garden State Park raceway, the township is planning to lure visitors and residents with the same types of amenities.

A Legendary Past

The 1960s proved to be the township's heyday for entertainment, with crowds from the entire South Jersey and Philadelphia region streaming in to see acts like Frank Sinatra at the Latin Casino, enjoy fine dining at the Hawaiian Cottage, experience the finest indoor shopping at the Cherry Hill Mall, and go to the races at Garden State Park. Cherry Hill was the entertainment capital of Southern New Jersey.

With the Cherry Hill Mall as the sole remaining ambassador of the 1960s, we decided it was time to embrace a new era of economic prosperity, with the crowning jewel being the redevelopment of the Garden State Park.

A New Era

The sale of the 223-acre Garden State Park to Turnberry Associates in 2000 for $30 million marked the beginning of this new era. In partnership with M & M Realty, one of the largest real estate development firms on the East Coast, Turnberry Cherry Hill, LLC conceptualized the state's most appealing example of Smart Growth.

My vision for this property — a community where residents could live, work, play and raise a family — was identical to that of the developer. I envisioned a community where residents and visitors of the Garden State Park would be able to walk from a day of shopping at the *Market Place* to *Plaza Grande* without having to leave the Park. This shared vision will enable Cherry Hill Township to have the downtown "Main Street" feel that our otherwise desirable municipality has always sought.

This landmark partnership between my administration and renowned developers will make the reconstructed Garden State Park a place for entertainment, professional services, dining, shopping and luxury living.

Originally published as "Bringing the Sizzle Back to Cherry Hill," *New Jersey Municipalities*, Vol. 83, No. 4, April 2006. Published by the New Jersey State League of Municipalities. Reprinted with permission of the publisher.

A New Era for Business Expansion

The *Marketplace* and *Towne Center* sections of the Garden State Park will provide residents of the tri-state area with dining and entertainment options that have never been available in our region, recalling Cherry Hill's heritage as a recreation mecca. More than 30 new businesses will relocate to Cherry Hill to join the excitement at the corner of Route 70 and Haddonfield Road.

Business relocation equals job creation for the region. We expect to add roughly 2,000 new jobs over the next five years. These workers will not only be the friendly faces greeting patrons at the area's first Cheesecake Factory or Wegmans, but they will also be the new patrons for the township's existing businesses. Everyday, I receive word from the greater township business community saying how eager they are to welcome the influx of customers to their stores. Cherry Hill will once again be a regional destination.

A New Era for Luxury Living

The residential sections of Garden State Park offer living accommodations for active senior citizens, professionals working in Philadelphia, and anyone looking to raise a family in a good neighborhood.

The *Plaza Grande*, the active senior citizen condominium community by D.R. Horton, has many buildings near completion. Seniors from the township and surrounding communities are buying these luxury condominiums and look forward to the countless planned amenities.

The townhouse section of Garden States Park, *Park Place*, has already sold over 90 units, totaling more than $40 million, to young families and professionals who are eager to live in a community that offers everything — shopping, dining, entertainment and leisure — within walking distance of their front doors. Groundbreaking has already taken place with first occupancy expected in late 2006.

A Brilliant Future

This redevelopment will have a positive impact on all of our neighborhoods and existing businesses through increased tourism to Cherry Hill. Residents from the surrounding area will once again make Cherry Hill a destination for fine dining, premier shopping at *Towne Centre*, Cherry Hill Mall and other fine shops. Families will gather at the township's 48 parks and playgrounds.

Everyone who participated in shaping this project should be congratulated for a superb job in what is a truly collaborative effort. We are fortunate to have a developer who shared my vision of a "Main Street" community and to have planning officials who saw this vision as a new model for Smart Growth for the state and entire nation to follow.

As we often say, "You Couldn't Pick a Better Place" than Cherry Hill for living, shopping and entertainment! By 2010, the township will have successfully reinvented itself once again as the entertainment, dining and shopping capital of southern New Jersey.

CHAPTER 17

Colorado Springs Focuses on Nature to Revive Its Downtown

Mark A. Nuszer

Colorado ranked third in the United States in population growth from 1990 to 2000, according to the U.S. Census. Spurred by the state's technology and telecom opportunities, abundant recreational amenities, and overall quality of life, the leap in the number of new residents resulted in a plethora of new master-planned communities. Despite the state's economic difficulties over the past few years — triggered by the burst of the high-tech bubble — Colorado's level of residential development continues to rise, especially on the fringe of the state's metropolitan areas, where the majority of the greenfield sites await.

Nestled where the High Plains border the Rocky Mountains, Colorado's Front Range — a ten-county area stretching from Colorado Springs to Fort Collins — is home to approximately 850 new communities. While some contend these natural settings are being sacrificed by relentless development at "the edge," others maintain that these areas can be preserved and even enhanced through smart planning principles. "Greenfield development offers the most practical, affordable, and achievable chance to build without sprawl, given its potential to create large-scale, conserved open lands and sustainable modern in-

frastructure," argues Urban Green founder Jim Heid's *Greenfield Development Without Sprawl: The Role of Planned Communities.*

Since 1990, the greater Denver area has seen an influx of more than 1 million people. Weld County, on the northern edge of the Front Range, for example, has doubled in new-home sales the last three years. While not all of Colorado's new developments are situated at the edge of the metropolitan area, many are located in parts that were once home to short-grass prairies and free-roaming wildlife. With the passing of the FasTracks initiative — a 12-year comprehensive plan to deliver high-speed and light rail to metropolitan Denver that will be at least as extensive as the networks in Chicago and the Bay Area — commuting may become less of a deterrent for expansion in some of these areas.

While greenfield development runs rampant throughout the country, there are several characteristics unique to Colorado. For example, the state's landscape recovery cycle is much longer than in other, more humid environments. The arid climate found in Colorado and much of the West poses challenges to those trying to rebuild disturbed landscapes. Accordingly, incorporating sustainable design

Originally published as "Communities in Context," by Mark A. Nuszer, *Urban Land*, Vol. 64, No. 5, May 2005. Published by the Urban Land Institute, Washington, D.C. Reprinted with permission of the publisher.

practices to preserve and integrate the natural landscape into community development is seen as vital to creating successful, harmonious greenfield developments there.

Because of limited natural tree coverage, the Front Range is known for its seemingly unlimited horizon and sense of open space. Other natural elements particular to the region include foothills, the gray-green textures of the high prairie, and the transection of wildlife corridors from mountain to plain via watersheds and drainages — regarded by some as possibly the most important component of this natural system. To integrate this landscape into any greenfield development in Colorado, it is necessary to preserve and enhance the drainages, no matter how minor, and the existing plant and wildlife.

"Edge" developments along the Front Range that are regarded as successful have embraced the aesthetic of the Great Plains and blended it with traditional landscape practices. This kind of scenic stewardship needs to go hand in hand with the smart growth practices and urban design principles of identifying and protecting vistas and views, rather than building them out in the development process.

Site planning that is sensitive to the existing plant- and wildlife located on these edge properties is essential since such efforts inevitably safeguard, or promote the return of, indigenous plant and animal species. Leaving untouched open space for habitat corridors, and bending trails with heavy pedestrian traffic away from them, enables animals to move through the areas with minimal conflict. For the first time in more than 100 years, for example, elk are foraging year round in the high plains range despite the considerable population growth in the nearby Interstate 25 (I-25) corridor.

An example of a development that integrates the state's natural resources is Village Homes' 685-acre master-planned community, Idyllwilde. Located 20 miles south of Denver's urban core in Parker, the project is designed to preserve two major drainages, dozens of large cottonwoods and Ponderosa pines, and several native animal species. "We believe it's critical to maintain the most significant physical attributes of the site while planning the development," emphasizes Gary Ryan, Village Homes' senior vice president of community development. "Preservation of the existing drainages was a prime goal of the town, and one we endorsed," he notes.

The town of Parker's ordinance specified the inclusion or preservation of wildlife corridors, open space linking to trail systems, steep slopes, and riparian areas as parameters for all developers of new communities. "From our perspective, we viewed these as requirements," says Garner Stoll, community development director for the town of Parker. "The developer and planner viewed them as an opportunity to add value to their development. The outcome was a win-win situation." Stoll goes on to note that the shared "big picture" vision and existing ecological palette both contributed to the success of the project. He also mentions that the town did not have to enforce its regulatory document citing tree preservation because the Idyllwilde plat was laid out to preserve major clusters of trees.

More than 50 percent of the site is dedicated to open space. "When we bought the property, it was annexed to the town of Parker," explains Ron Hettinger, vice president of development operations for Village Homes. "It's been a unique property from day one," alluding to the 300 acres of open space weaving through the site. "It's all about being a partner with the land and incorporating the special beauty that's already there," he adds, such as including vast areas of open space and natural habitats, supported with "educational" trails and multiple nonintrusive outdoor recreational amenities.

Village Homes retained a naturalist to identify and re-create habitats respective of indigenous plant materials and animal life within Idyllwilde. More than ten interpretive trails, named for native flora and fauna, meander among the development's 900 residences and are identified by a variety of environmental graphics. Trails eventually will link Idyllwilde's high school site with a nearby junior high school, creating a virtual laboratory for viewing wildlife species, including antelope, mule, deer, coyote, and horned owl. The open spaces not only pay tribute to the native environment, but also provide a functional amenity to the community.

Idyllwilde's initial development footprint was reduced by 40 acres to allow for more meaningful open space. This was achieved by decreasing the minimum lot size from 6,000 to 3,250 square feet, as well as by reevaluating the hierarchy of streets. Overall, infrastructure costs to the builder were significantly lessened.

The end result of the two-year planning and design process is what many perceive as an eco-sensitive development that embodies the essence of Colorado without sacrificing the density needed to achieve the short- and long-range goals of the Idyllwilde pro forma.

Although located in a vastly different setting, the 2,000-acre Wolf Ranch, 60 miles south of Denver in Colorado Springs, provides another example of a greenfield development integrated into the existing landscape.

The site is home to views of the legendary Pikes Peak and rural Cottonwood Creek. "Essentially, we're celebrating what is already there," notes Ralph Braden, vice president of Colorado Springs–based Norwood Development Group, who is responsible for developing the master-planned community, which will comprise 7,500 residences, a mixed-use village core, 20 additional acres of commercial development, and an estimated 250 acres of open space.

The existing site conditions and topography have been incorporated into the development at every opportunity, he says. Accommodating a 400-foot elevation change from the northern to the southern end respected the site's natural slope and provided an opportunity to showcase views of Pikes Peak and to capture the greater context of the landscape.

Major arterials and collector streets were oriented toward the mountains in a subtle radial pattern — a slight variation on a traditional grid pattern — rotated in minor degrees to achieve direct views of Pikes Peak. These broad boulevards were designed to mimic the historic downtown parkways of Colorado Springs. Their medians will be planted with low-profile plants that will respect and, ideally, preserve the view.

The collector and arterial street network was also narrowed throughout the site using roundabouts that eliminated the need for signals and acceleration/deceleration lanes. This design allowed for more frequent intersections and thus increased access and connectivity to adjacent neighborhoods.

The "village area," sited on a broad plain at the southeast portion of the site, lent itself to a traditional urban grid street pattern with lot sizes measuring less than 4,500 square feet. Its design and the parkways allowed for more density overall, in turn increasing the project-wide amount of open space and recreational amenities that will be developed along the major drainage in the form of a 120-acre central park.

The water-smart design for this community amenity involves a wider stream channel than would be expected for a development of this magnitude and density. This allows for the uninterrupted natural flow of Cottonwood Creek. Rather than "channeling" the stream and using rebutment walls, it will be left to meander and flood in its natural state. The landscape surrounding the creek eroded over the years, due to what experts agree was overgrazing by nearby cattle, leaving a desertlike environment along the banks of the creek. The introduction of additional irrigation runoff to the stream is expected to return the area to its native context.

The demand for communities on the urban periphery seems to be inevitable. How developers, planners, and designers choose to respond to the growing demand for more housing is the crux of the sprawl debate. New residential developments can be planned and designed using sustainable practices and systems that embrace rather than destroy natural landscapes. These well-planned, connected, and diverse developments that promote a sense of community and take their natural surroundings into careful consideration are necessary to preserving the natural settings in Colorado and other locales.

CHAPTER 18

Concord Emphasizes Restorative Development for Its Downtown

Storm Cunningham

At last, some good economic news: There's a mushrooming new global economic sector that already exceeds a trillion dollars per year — and even restores natural resources. It's called *restorative development*, defined as socioeconomic revitalization based on the restoration of our natural and built environments. And it will dramatically reshape our economies, communities, and environments throughout the twenty-first century.

Turning an old-growth forest into a farm, or demolishing a historic building for a shopping mall, is the kind of development we're most familiar with: new development. Decontaminating abandoned industrial property and turning old factories into apartments and stores is another kind of development, one that builds without destroying: restorative development. Returning a distressed old farm to productivity by rebuilding topsoil, removing accumulated salts, and restoring surrounding watersheds is another example of restorative development.

Nations around the globe have accumulated backlogs of needed restoration projects worth trillions of dollars. Meanwhile, hundreds of billions of dollars of new restoration needs are added annually, creating perhaps the largest new growth sector of the world economy. What's more, most of the other so-called "new economies," suck as hydrogen, biotech, nanotech, and digital, are either a direct outgrowth of the restoration economy, or will find their greatest markets in restorative development.

Restoration Industries

Our current restoration economy comprises eight industries. Four involve the natural environment: ecosystem restoration, fisheries restoration, watershed restoration, and agricultural restoration/rural development. The other four industries, which restore the built environment, are:

- **Brownfields remediation and redevelopment.** Brownfields are lands that are not being used productively as a result of real or perceived contamination. The U.S. Environmental Protection Agency's Brown-

Originally published as "Restorative Development: Economic Growth without Destruction," The Futurist, Vol. 37, No. 4, July-August 2003. Used with permission from the World Future Society, 7910 Woodmont Avenue, Suite 450, Bethesda, Maryland 20814. Telephone: 301/656-8274, Fax: 301/951-0394; http://www.wfs.org. Reprinted with permission of the publisher.

fields Initiative has awarded more than $140 million in nationwide grants to help communities clean up abandoned, lightly contaminated sites and restore them to productive community use. For example, in Concord, New Hampshire, officials are working to identify contamination in a 440-acre (178-hectare) industrial corridor and develop a remediation and redevelopment plan with the potential to create more than 2,500 new jobs — or 8% of the city's total unemployment.

- **Infrastructure refurbishment and reconstruction.** This aspect of restorative development deals with the flows that connect our built environment: power, sewerage, traffic, water, even garbage. One major infrastructure refurbishment project is the London Underground with an estimated budget of $42 million (£27 million).
- **Heritage restoration.** A community's physical heritage comprises aspects of the built environment that lasted long enough to be a source of community attachment — or where an event occurred that the community considers intrinsic to its identity. Heritage can also be environmental (fisheries) or cultural (indigenous languages).
- **Disaster/war restoration and rebuilding.** Three categories of disasters make up this restoration industry: war, manmade disasters (such as oil spills, nuclear power accidents, and even mudslides due to deforestation), and natural disasters (such as volcanic eruptions and earthquakes). The cost of rebuilding war-torn Afghanistan is estimated at $15 billion. The cost of restoring worldwide disasters is roughly $52 billion per year.

Some of these industries, such as disaster and war restoration, have been around for millennia. Others, such as brownfields restoration, just appeared in the past decade. (New regulations in 1990 made it possible for business people to buy contaminated lands.) But the sudden growth of restorative development and its emergence as a collective economic force can be traced to the convergence of three global crises:

1. The Constraint Crisis: We are out of room. This doesn't mean there are no more wide-open spaces fit to develop, but rather that virtually every developable acre of land — whether it's a farm, a historic battlefield, or a recreational greenspace — already serves a vital purpose that people will fight to protect from developers.

2. The Contamination Crisis. Chemical, organic, and radiological contamination from industrial, agricultural, and military activities have affected ecosystems and supplies of water, food, and air.

3. The Corrosion Crisis. We've been building practically nonstop since the beginning of the Industrial Revolution, and many of the world's cities are getting very old. In the United States, much of the infrastructure is decrepit: The American Society of Civil Engineers has documented a $1.3 trillion backlog for restoring infrastructure.

These are the same three crises that have brought down civilizations throughout history — and that have sometimes triggered their renaissance. However, we now face all three crises simultaneously on a global scale.

Beyond Sustainability

Restorative development, while benefiting the environment, is not an "environmental message" per se. Rather, restorative development is a strategic path for leaders of businesses, nonprofits, and government agencies that wish to grow economically, or that want to revitalize themselves.

Since the beginning of the Industrial Revolution, our growth assumptions have been based on exploring new geographic frontiers and exploiting new natural resources. Now that the greatest new growth frontier is behind us, we need to reexamine what devel-

---

Figure 1. The Money in Restoration

The following selected initiatives come with a hefty — and worthy — price tag, author Cunningham notes. Total projects exceed $1 trillion in expenditures to revive environments, economies, and aesthetics. Here are 10 current (or recently completed) restorative projects worldwide.

1. **$100 million** in dam restoration or removal worldwide.
2. **$225 million** to restore site around Stonehenge.
3. **$450 million** to restore Reagan National Airport in Washington, D.C.
4. **$500 million** to restore Istanbul's Golden Horn Waterfront.
5. **$700 million** rebuilding of a single highway interchange in Springfield, Virginia.
6. **$2.5 billion** to replace the Washington, D.C., area's Wilson Bridge.
7. **$3.1 billion** to launch first phase of Russian railway rehabilitation.
8. **$12 billion** restoration of a single watershed in China.
9. **$15 billion** to rebuild and restore Afghanistan.
10. **$52 billion** per year to restore natural disasters, not including human-caused disasters or terrorism.

Source: *The Restoration Economy* by Storm Cunningham.

---

oped in the past three centuries — and all the natural places we've damaged in the process.

For instance, many cities have no remaining greenfield areas (i.e., land that has never been developed) that they can use for expansion. Some cities, such as Niagara Falls, New York, have discovered that 100% of the buildable land they still possess is contaminated. Meanwhile, cities that do have greenfields are finding increasing resistance to developing them. To grow economically, both types of architecturally challenged cities must redevelop their brownfields instead.

In fact, some of the largest opportunities for restoration industries involve revitalizing the cities we've created during the past 300 years of unfettered growth. That's why developers worldwide are shifting their focus to restorative development. Now when they propose to restore ugly, abandoned property that generates no tax revenues, the same citizens' groups, historic preservation societies, and en-

vironmental agencies that used to fight their new developments are instead supporting them.

However, restorative development should not be confused with sustainable development. Sustainable development — which has yet to be properly defined or measured — usually requires a decade or more to produce an attractive bottom line. Restorative development pays off big, and pays off now.

What's more, the field of sustainable development emerged in reaction to uncontrolled new development, but it doesn't solve the problem. Sustainable development is simply a greener form of new development; it can't repair the accumulated corrosion and contamination, which will only exacerbate the Constraint Crisis. Sustainability is a great concept, but the world needs restoration first. After all, who really wants to sustain the mess we're living in now?

Restorative development should also not be confused with the maintenance/conservation mode of development. Though highly essential, conservation has largely lost the battle against new development. This is why most of the largest conservation groups, such as The Nature Conservancy, have embraced ecological restoration. They're not just preserving our last few pristine ecosystems; they're buying and restoring the damaged land around them so they can actually *expand*.

We've moved from an unsuccessful attempt to slow the decrease of wildlife habitat to a successful strategy of *increasing* wildlife habitat. That's a very different, and much more hopeful, dynamic. Of course, as with any new field, standards are still being set, and not all early attempts are successful. But that, too, is part of the opportunity for academics, engineers, and scientists.

Tomorrow's Restoration Economy

Restorative development is fully capable of replacing new development as the dominant economic growth mode. It's every bit as profitable as new development (often more so), so it offers an attractive path, a natural evolution, away from the old model. In a corporate world that demands dramatic quarterly profits, and a political world that demands results during an election cycle, only restorative development can deliver the goods with bipartisan support.

Integrated partnerships among the public sector, private industry, and nongovernmental organizations may be the best long-term vehicles for complex, large scale restoration

---

Figure 2. The Truth about Brownfields

In the early 1990s, few people had heard of brownfields. Now they're in the dictionary — and already widely misunderstood. Here is the truth about five common brownfield misconceptions.

1. The purpose of brownfields remediation is not simply to clean the environment. Unlike Superfund sites — the largest, most-contaminated sites in the United States, selected for cleanup by the Environmental Protection Agency to keep the public safe — the chief goal of brownfields remediation is turning a profit.

2. Brownfields comprise more than just ground and groundwater. Buildings can also be highly toxic with contaminants such as lead paint, asbestos insulation, and mercury that fall under the "hard costs" of brownfields cleanup.

3. Most brownfields are not heavily contaminated. Contamination is often minimal, yet perceived as serious. Abandoned industrial sites, for example, have sat idle for decades because the public falsely assumes they're toxic.

4. Most brownfields are not abandoned. Many contaminated sites are in use, but their contamination has not been assessed. When 30% of industrial acreage in Hartford, Connecticut, was abandoned between 1986 and 1997, much of it was found to be contaminated — which means workers toiled in toxic environs.

5. Brownfields are not restricted to large industrial sites in urban locations. Many are small and rural, such as rural gas stations (abandoned and operational) with leaky underground storage tanks. Further, in 27 states, the EPA cannot prevent a company from putting fuel or chemicals into underground storage tanks that are known to be leaking.

Source: *The Restoration Economy* by Storm Cunningham

---

projects. They will also likely be the entities that restore nations in decades to come.

With a new economic sector that delivers strong economic, aesthetic, and environmental returns, many new legal tools and investment products will emerge. This will likely include a broad spectrum of restorative real estate, investment trusts (REITs). What's more, the opportunities for inventors, entrepreneurs, programmers, and consultants are virtually unlimited: Almost any industry or profession that existed in the dying new development economy will have its analog in the restoration economy.

This is the greatest new frontier for hardware, software, the sciences, economics, art, philosophy, architecture, engineering, academia, and policy makers: Nothing is more urgent, nothing is more important, and nothing is more economically productive than restoring our world. Virtually every major trend and discipline of this century either will be rooted in restorative development or will converge with it in a way that will transform and revitalize it.

Every city that is currently being touted as a model of rebirth, sustainability, or economic health has already embraced restorative development projects in their new model. For most of them, this was an intuitive, emergent transition: Until recently, they didn't possess the terminology or theoretical structure to talk about or plan for restorative development in a coherent manner.

Now, the dialogue has begun, and this first phase of the restoration economy is about to enter a period of maturation. The concepts and lessons of the past decade must start to be formally incorporated into public policy, university curricula, and business strategies.

Restorative development has already reversed several trends that are taken as gospel by many futurists. Desertification is a good example: We all know that the Sahara has been expanding for decades, right? *Wrong.* Recent analysis of satellite images shows it's been

**Figure 3. The Sudden Rise of
Restorative Development**

Technology, business, politics, and academic study are all being affected by the restoration economy — yet this dramatic and lucrative shift in development focus has gone largely unreported. How could an economic sector possibly grow to over a trillion dollars annually without being noticed? Four reasons:

1. It has emerged very quickly (some of its component industries didn't even exist in 1990).
2. Rather than putting old companies out of business (which would be newsworthy), existing firms — many of which used to earn most of their money from new development — have quietly moved into the new markets of restoration.
3. Restorative development is not being measured or reported as a discrete economic sector. Planning and budgeting processes are still based on the old "frontier" model of growth, so they only address new development and maintenance/conservation, largely ignoring the critical third phase of all natural development life cycles: restoration.
4. Lack of standardized terminology: Government reports use a bewildering number of synonyms for restoration, including modernization, capital improvement, regeneration, retrofit, reclamation, and many other terms.

Source: *The Restoration Economy* by Storm Cunningham

shrinking for about 15 years. Why? The primary mechanism has been restorative agriculture, which was taught to farmers 15 to 20 years ago in about a dozen nations on the edge of the Sahara.

Restorative development already accounts for a major portion of the good economic news on the planet, yet it seldom gets the credit, because we don't measure it. Within the next five to 10 years, it will dominate most development budgets, and will continue to do so for the rest of the twenty-first century.

CHAPTER 19

Cumming Focuses on Its Neighborhoods for Sustainable Development

Stella Tarnay

Twenty years ago, the concept of sustainable development, with its emphasis on the interplay among economic, social, and environmental dynamics in communities, suggested a different framework for thinking about planning and development. Progressive policy makers and international agencies embraced it as the future of development. However, many questions from the mainstream remained, such as what is meant, exactly, by sustainable development, what it looks like on the ground, and whether it can it be a part of successful business practice.

More recently, a diverging set of currents in design, policy, and building have also been changing development practice. New urbanism, smart growth, low-impact and conservation development, transit-oriented development, and green building have all contributed tools and practices that are now available to private developers and public officials alike. Yet, each can only contribute to — not create — sustainable communities or regions because the scale of intervention is usually too limited, such as a single green building, or too broad and strategy specific, such as a metropolitan transportation network.

Now, some leading-edge developers are bringing together many of the best practices and tools from green building, smart growth, and related movements to create innovative communities with lasting value, at a scale where it matters most — the neighborhood. With an intersecting network of buildings, infrastructure, and human and natural systems, neighborhoods provide unique opportunities for realizing sustainable development.

Green Neighborhoods in the Suburban Sprawl Ring

The most compelling example of a green neighborhood currently under development may be Vickery — a mixed-use project in Cumming, Georgia, outside of Atlanta. With 100 homes occupied and the village center underway, the project will have 600 homes and a commercial and civic core at completion in 2010. Homes are sited to take advantage of the terrain and solar gain; sidewalks and paths move easily between housing, parks, and the denser mixed-use core; preserved natural trees

Originally published as "Green Neighborhoods," by Stella Tarnay, *Urban Land*, Vol. 64, No. 5, May 2005. Published by the Urban Land Institute, Washington, D.C. Reprinted with permission of the publisher.

and landscape are integrated throughout the project.

Vickery is located on 214 acres of former agricultural land 30 miles north of Atlanta in the city's sprawl ring. It is being developed by Hedgewood Properties, a custom homebuilding and development company known for high-end, infill housing and conservation development in the suburbs. Rather than building large houses on one-third-acre lots as is common in Atlanta's suburban ring, Hedgewood partners Pam Sessions and Don Donnelly have chosen instead to build a green neighborhood clustered around a mixed-use village core.

The Vickery plan grew out of recognition by Sessions and Donnelly of unmet demand for sustainably developed neighborhoods, as well as their personal frustrations with housing and neighborhood options. The husband-and-wife team initially owned 20 acres of the Vickery site and had made it their family home. "We had bought this piece of farmland in the 1980s, and now, with two children in school, found ourselves driving them everywhere. We wanted to create an environmentally responsible, walkable community that we ourselves would want to live in and where our kids could feel free to meet friends and explore," explains Sessions.

Sessions and Donnelly worked with master planning and design firm Duany Plater-Zyberk & Company to create a plan for the neighborhood and its connectivity to its surroundings. Vickery's narrow streets and traditional architecture embody a new urbanist design vocabulary reminiscent of historic Atlanta neighborhoods, relates Sessions. A network of sidewalks and paths connects residents within the neighborhood to conservation land and parks, active recreation areas, the village core, and two local schools. The design team planned the project so that all residents are within a five-minute walk of a community amenity.

The village center, with its community green, will have small shops, restaurants, offices, a new YMCA, and 125 housing units ranging from townhouses, to condominiums above retail space, to live/work spaces. Single-family homes in the surrounding medium- and low-density tiers are planned at densities of two to six homes per acre. One-third of the land on the site is being preserved for green space and recreation areas. Parks are located around old-growth trees and natural features, such as the site's two ponds, and a creek and its wetlands form the spine of Vickery's conservation area, located a safe distance from the commercial core.

Sessions jokes that suburban homebuyers at Vickery are "trading large lots for lots of community amenities." The smaller craftsman-quality homes are earning a 30 percent premium over comparable housing in the region, with 90 percent of the customized homes selling before the start of construction. All of Vickery's homes meet EarthCraft Home standards for energy efficiency, indoor air quality, and human and environmental health. Hedgewood's builders have employed techniques to minimize the impact of construction. For example, leftover gypsum was ground up and returned to the soil as an additive to improve its quality; wood chips from trees cut down on the site were incorporated into erosion control efforts; and an innovative grading technique and machinery were used to help Hedgewood save three additional acres of land.

While Vickery is a greenfield suburban development, Hedgewood Properties and its planning team are creating a neighborhood that provides alternatives to automobile use. Residents are closely connected to schools, parks, restaurants, shopping — and to one another — so that walking and bicycling are options.

Green Neighborhoods on the Urban Edge

In Colorado and several other western states, developer Jim Leach is building green neighborhoods in direct partnership with homebuyers. Leach, president of Boulder-based Wonderland Hill Development, so far has completed 15 cohousing neighborhoods with his resident partners. The cohousing community model typically combines compact clustered homes, a pedestrian-based orientation, commonly held community amenities, and resident social participation, all in small neighborhood settings of 15 to 40 homes. Residents typically partner with a developer in developing a cohousing community, and sometimes develop it themselves. A leader in the creation of Built Green Colorado standards for residential construction, Leach has made the intimate neighborhood scale of cohousing a foundation of environmentally sustainable development.

Wonderland's Hearthstone cohousing project, developed on the urban edge of Denver, illustrates the potential for environmental and social innovation through cohousing. Some 33 townhouses are clustered on a 1.6-acre site around a linear common green and a neighborhood common house.

The cohousing neighborhood model offered Hearthstone residents an opportunity to make environmentally friendly choices they probably would not have been able to make as individual homebuyers, points out Leach, including use of green building technologies such as hydronic radiant heat and high-end, ecologically friendly finishes. Already a Built Green Colorado participant, Leach was able to take the project further environmentally because he had committed buyers who had made green features a priority and were willing to pay for them. The neighborhood's green features include xeriscaping and water conservation, and a social organization to support environmental stewardship. Leach presold 50 percent of the units by the time of construction, and sold the remainder within several months of the project's completion.

Hearthstone is unusual for cohousing neighborhoods in that it is located within the larger mixed-use, new urbanist neighborhood of Highland's Garden Village, developed on a former brownfield site. When Highland's Garden Village is completed, Hearthstone will be a three-block walk from a grocery store, restaurants, and community amenities. Leach says he is convinced that many of his resident partners were attracted by Hearthstone's context in a walkable new urbanist neighborhood. Hearthstone residents are now the main organizers of the Highland's Garden Village community garden and make their common house open to that community's association meetings.

Neighborhoods such as Hearthstone and Highland's Garden Village have important implications for communities on the urban edge. Although the site is within the city boundaries of Denver, its surroundings are typical of outer-edge urban areas dominated by commercial strips and aging post–World War II housing. Few of Denver's city amenities are readily available to area residents without a car. By bringing urbanity and a healthier living environment to the city's edge, Hearthstone and Highland's Garden Village should not only help to improve the quality of life for surrounding neighborhoods, but also help reduce vehicle miles traveled within the city's limits.

Recognizing the Green Neighborhood Market

Some 25 years ago, Judy and Michael Corbett's pioneering Village Homes project in Davis, California, integrated conservation development, permaculture, and solar-powered homes in a walkable, socially innovative neighborhood. Turnover in the popular 240-unit neighborhood is so low that most homes are sold by word of mouth. Homes resell at an estimated 30 percent premium over surrounding Davis housing.

Today, Sessions and Leach are responding to what has been identified as the "cultural creatives" demographic, identified by Paul H. Ray and Sherry Ruth Anderson in their 2001 book *The Cultural Creatives: How 50 Million People Are Changing the World*. These homebuyers and residents value authenticity, community, creativity, and environmental stewardship. Most feel alienated from the conventional market and tend to purchase older homes. The real estate and market research polling firm American LIVES estimates that 22 percent of the American population identifies with cultural creative values. "It's really a lifestyle choice," says Sessions, "and green building and land conservation are part of that."

When given an opportunity, many homebuyers who would not label themselves as cultural creatives may choose to purchase homes in green neighborhoods. Recent surveys by the Cahners Residential Group and *Professional Builder* magazine found that 80 to 90 percent of homebuyers interviewed say new homes do not meet their expectations for environmental conservation. Well-designed, environmentally sensitive developments have the power to persuade homebuyers. Homes at Prairie Crossing, the conservation development west of Chicago, initially sold at a 15 percent premium over housing in the surrounding area. Ten years after the first homes were completed, the premium is now 33 percent. Vickery's high premium of 30 percent only one year into sales suggests that well-executed green neighborhoods that integrate pedestrian-based connections to community services and shopping may command even higher premiums over the long term.

Master Planning for Green Neighborhoods

Developers with an understanding of sustainable development and green building have made it possible for those with less green building experience to get involved in building environmentally friendly neigh-

borhoods. In Playa Vista, a 1,100-acre mixed-use redevelopment project in Los Angeles, the Playa Vista corporation created development and green building standards for commercial development and neighborhood residential clusters that incorporate 3,200 housing units. The western division of Standard Pacific Homes, builder of five green condominium projects at Playa Vista, has gone on to make green building a standard practice. Stapleton Development Corporation and its primary developer, Forest City Stapleton, Inc., created green building and development, standards for mixed-use neighborhoods that eventually will accommodate 30,000 residents and 35,000 jobs on the site of Denver's old Stapleton International Airport.

Like the site-specific plan for Vickery, these master plans develop with and around natural systems, make environmental conservation a foundation for community amenities, and create a convenient network of pedestrian connections. Green building standards tied to a competitive request for proposals (RFP) process can help to motivate builders to participate.

Green Neighborhood Standards

A half dozen nonprofit organizations, building associations, and public agencies are in the process of developing or piloting national and regional guidelines for green neighborhoods. The goal is for these guidelines, incorporating third-party certification, to provide developers with measurable standards and a certification process to brand and market their projects.

Among the most anticipated guidelines are Leadership in Energy and Environmental Design (LEED) standards for neighborhood development, being developed by the U.S. Green Building Council in collaboration with the Congress for the New Urbanism, the National Resources Defense Council, and other organizations, including the Urban Land Institute. Southface Institute and the Greater Atlanta Homebuilders Association are collaborating with ULI Atlanta on EarthCraft Community standards, which are being piloted at Vickery and three other Atlanta developments. In addition, Audubon International is partnering with and certifying developers of environmentally sustainable communities through the Audubon Signature program. The Enterprise Foundation has made the largest investment in green neighborhoods to date with $550 million in grants, loans, and equity investment. Its Green Communities Initiative, launched last fall, defines green neighborhood standards for developers of affordable housing.

Green City Neighborhoods

Nonprofit developers in poor urban neighborhoods have understood the connection between environmental sustainability and neighborhood-scale development for years. In Chicago, Bethel New Life (BNL), a faith-based community development corporation on the city's west side, has made green neighborhood development part of its overall community and economic development strategy. The initiative dates to the 1980s when, as BNL founder and president Mary Nelson says, "We started bumping into brownfields just about everywhere we wanted to do housing." Since then, BNL has built infill housing and rehabilitated commercial properties on former brownfields, created jobs through environmental remediation, helped to save a historic park conservatory, collaborated with the city to plant trees and develop five parks, and worked to create safe and attractive pedestrian connections. More recently, BNL has integrated green building into its practices and focused on transit-oriented development.

BNL's constituency neighborhood, West Garfield Park, with 20,000 residents, is far

larger than the 33-unit Hearthstone neighborhood or even the 600-unit Vickery. But BNL's approach shares with them an understanding of the neighborhood as a network of natural and built systems that offer opportunities for sustainable development. By working with these systems in a creative and thoughtful way, the developer has the opportunity to create projects that are far more innovative environmentally, socially, and even economically than conventional developments or a single green building.

What may be the country's most ambitious green neighborhood project is being developed at Manhattan's Battery Park City. Five years ago, Battery Park City Authority (BPCA) chief executive Tim Carey and his staff released green standards for residential — and later commercial — development on the 92-acre landfill site. These are being integrated with BPCA's master plan for a walkable, bikeable neighborhood along 1.2 miles of the Hudson River waterfront. The first green residential high-rise project has been developed at the site, the Solaire, with 293 environmentally friendly units. With their natural wood floors and green materials, triple-filtered air, concierge service, rooftop garden, and views of the Hudson, apartments at the Solaire are renting at a 10 percent premium over comparable units in lower Manhattan — in what is still considered a recovery zone after the terrorist attacks of September 11, 2001.

The Solaire's rooftop garden, irrigated with collected rainwater, helps to counteract the heat island effect, and the building's graywater recycling plant provides water for the city's Teardrop Park being built next door. The Solaire, developed by the Garden City, New York–based Albanese Organization, connects to the walking and bike path in Rockefeller Park, and its residents are within walking distance of restaurants, grocery stores, public schools, the subway, and bus systems.

The scale of the project enabled the Albanese Organization to order innovative green materials and technologies at an attractive price, with suppliers willing to cut a deal because of the project's scale and high profile. Several manufacturers even refined products to suit the project's needs.

Is It Green?

The Epicenter building, a 130-unit apartment building in the Fremont Avenue arts district of Seattle, is an interesting case in the evolving understanding of green neighborhoods. Its style of contemporary architecture does not suggest conservation development or green design. Its target tenant would probably be more aptly described as "metrosexual" than cultural creative. So, is it green?

Epicenter's developer, Seattle-based SP Multifamily, LLC, a division of Security Properties, Inc., did not go out of its way to make the building green, except for including a modest green roof and meeting Seattle's stringent energy-efficiency and stormwater-mitigation codes. But these codes take the building 20 percent beyond the energy performance of new structures in most municipalities. The developer saved and moved the beloved local 19th-century Red Door Alehouse to a new location across the street, where it was restored, and used recycled timber from the site to build an outdoor pedestrian canopy. The building is located on a major bus route and next to a popular walking and biking path. Except for some missed opportunities for green construction and occupant health, the answer to the question whether it is green is probably yes.

The Neighborhood as Building Block for Sustainable Development

If sustainable development is the goal, then understanding neighborhood-scale de-

velopment for environmental innovation is key. Developers who have made sustainable development a priority are finding that they have a new and evolving set of tools available to them to make project decisions. Public agencies are finding ways to support green neighborhood development through integrated standards based on green building, low-impact practices, and the tools of smart growth, transit-oriented development, and new urbanism. National standards may soon make green neighborhood development a state-of-the-art, rather than cutting-edge, practice.

The advantages of green innovation at the neighborhood scale go beyond competitive pricing. Clustering of buildings and multifamily structures by their nature conserve energy. Neighborhood-scale developments can support graywater recycling plants such as the Solaire's, or community-based energy production plants such as wind farms and solar arrays. Mixed-use green neighborhoods reduce auto pollution and support community and economic life. Social organization at the neighborhood level creates opportunities for community and environmental stewardship, such as that developed in cohousing neighborhoods.

Developers who have invested their resources and imagination in the development of green neighborhoods are earning handsome rewards. The market acceptance — and enthusiasm — for homes in well-executed green neighborhoods suggests that there is an underestimated demand and market for projects that integrate environmental sustainability with community-oriented design.

CHAPTER 20

Eastville Enhances Its Economy through Environmental Protection

Lance Metzler, Mary Lechner, *and* Timothy Hayes

Economic development and environmental protection often are viewed as competing interests at best and mutually exclusive at worst. Clean air and water, protection of wildlife, and resource conservation often are pitted against jobs and business expansion. Proposals for new industry may be met with cries of "not in my backyard" because of fears of pollution and negative community impacts.

Despite this seeming incompatibility, Northampton County, Virginia, has opened the first phase of a new kind of industrial park in which waste streams are cycled into revenue streams and industrial processes are based on the designs of natural systems. This "ecological industrial park" is part of an innovative county strategy whereby economic development is protecting valuable environmental assets and environmental protection is fostering development of a sustainable economy.

The Land Between Two Waters

Venture across the Chesapeake Bay from the mainland of Virginia to the southern tip of the slender finger of land known as Virginia's Eastern Shore and you will find Northampton County. With the Chesapeake on the west and the Atlantic on the east, Native Americans referred to this Virginia treasure as "the land between two waters." Northampton County is a place rich in natural and historic resources, including miles of pristine beaches, a string of preserved barrier islands, thriving marshes and tidal creeks, fish and shellfish, birds and wildlife, open land and clean water, small towns and historic villages, woodlands, and farms. Recognizing the global importance of this ecosystem, the United Nations has designated much of Northampton County and the surrounding region as a World Biosphere Reserve.

In sharp contrast to the county's natural and historic wealth, many of its people live in

Originally published as "Economic Development and Environmental Protection: The Northampton County, Virginia, Experience," *Government Finance Review*, Vol. 18, No. 1, February 2002. Reprinted with permission of the Government Finance Officers Association, publisher of *Government Finance Review*, 203 N. LaSalle St., Suite 2700, Chicago, IL 60601-1210. (312/977-9700; fax: 312/977-4806; e-mail: GFR@gfoa@org; Web: www.gfoa.org). Annual subscriptions: $35.

severe economic poverty. The closure of nearly all of the area's seafood and agricultural processing plants during the 1980s resulted in the loss of more than 1,500 jobs. By the early 1990s, 28 percent of the population was living in poverty, while 10 percent of the county's homes lacked plumbing and 12 percent lacked adequate sanitary facilities.

Having declined economically to become one of the poorest communities in Virginia and in the nation, the county began to wrestle with difficult, seemingly contradictory questions. Should the environment be sacrificed for economic development? Should a stagnant economy, lack of jobs, and poverty be accepted as the price of protecting a unique environment? Should the county try to strike a balance between economic development and environmental protection that would provide for "manageable" levels of both poverty and pollution? None of these scenarios was acceptable.

Triple Bottom Line

Rather than compromising the local economy for the environment or vice versa, the county instead decided to pursue a strategy that would simultaneously maximize both the economy and the environment for the benefit of the entire community. As one member of the Northampton County Board of Supervisors put it: "We must do business today in a way that won't put us out of business tomorrow."

The community and its elected governing body came to understand that they were trustees of a valuable portfolio of natural, cultural, and human assets. Consequently, they began to explore ways to invest in and protect these assets in order to build a strong and lasting economy and to preserve one of the last truly exceptional unspoiled environments on America's Atlantic coast. Success would be measured in terms of a triple bottom line: economy, environment, and equity.

Sustainable Development Action Strategy

In 1993, the county formally began its sustainable development initiative with a mission to "build a strong and lasting economy by capitalizing on and protecting Northampton's rich natural, cultural, and human assets." The commitment was to develop in a manner that would simultaneously benefit business, the environment, and all of the county's people both now and in the future.

Through a partnership with the National Oceanic Atmospheric Administration and the Virginia Coastal Program, the county hired the nation's first local director of sustainable development. With funding from the NOAA, VCP, and other partners, this individual organized the Department of Sustainable Development and led Northampton in formulating a vision for the county's future and a strategy to achieve that vision.

What came to be known as the Sustainable Development Ac 101 Strategy was developed through an intensive, collaborative process involving community workshops, task forces, meetings, and events. The county involved a broad cross section of its diverse citizenry in the strategy development process, leveraging their combined experience to identify industries with realistic, significant, immediate, and ongoing potential for development. As a result of this process, Northampton decided to target the following industry sectors: agriculture, seafood/aquaculture, heritage tourism, research/education, arts/crafts, local products, and sustainable technologies. The community also identified the vital natural, historic, and community assets that would need to be preserved and capitalized on to develop and sustain these targeted industries. The final step in the process was the formulation of an action plan for implementing the strategy. In June 1994, the Board of Supervisors adopted the strategy as the county's official development policy and immediately kicked off its implementation.

One of the keys of the Sustainable Development Action Strategy was to leverage private investment in the county in ways that would achieve the integral goals of building an economic base and protecting natural and cultural assets. It was clear that public financial resources would have to be carefully focused to achieve the greatest possible return for each dollar invested. It was also clear that Northampton's strategy would need to be phased in over time using major impact projects as long-term building blocks. As such, county officials had to determine which course of action would yield the highest economic and environmental return in the shortest period of time. The decision: an ecological industrial park to be known as the Sustainable Technology Park and to be located in the Town of Cape Charles.

America's First Ecological Industrial Park

As it began planning the infrastructure to facilitate business and industrial development, Northampton set its sights on an industrial park that would truly be world class. The goal was to provide an "environment for excellence" that would attract and produce companies that would share the county's high business, environmental, and human equity standards. The vision was for a "green" industrial park — green as in the color of the environment and green as in the color of money.

Economically, the consensus vision was for a park that would help build a strong and diversified economic base by attracting and growing new companies and by retaining and expanding existing companies. The companies in the park would provide quality jobs with competitive wages and benefits and opportunities for training and advancement.

Environmentally, the park would preserve natural and cultural resources, protect habitat and water quality, and strive to eliminate waste and pollution. It would showcase green technology companies and maximize efficient use of resources through "industrial symbiosis." Industrial symbiosis is the notion that the byproducts of one industrial process or company can serve as the raw material for another industrial process or company.

Funding

Northampton County and its Department of Sustainable Development raised more than $8 million of local, state, and federal funding to develop the first phase of the eco-industrial park. This funding included a $2.5 million bond issue approved by local voters. To date, this public investment has leveraged another $8 million from private companies locating in the first phase of the park. This funding provided the means to achieve the initial objectives of the county's Sustainable Development Action Strategy.

The public funding covered everything necessary to open the facility as a world-class eco-industrial park, including master planning, community involvement, covenants and sustainability standards, environmental assessments, land purchase, engineering, permits and approvals, infrastructure construction, multi-tenant green building construction, a solar electricity system, natural area purchase, construction of lakes and wetlands, trails, amenities, marketing, legal costs, and the leasing of initial corporate tenants.

Private investment accomplished tenant improvements for office, research/development, and manufacturing space, as well as partial funding for the solar energy system. In addition, $7.8 million has been committed for development of a wind farm within the park that will produce more electricity than used by the entire county. The county has contracted to export this wind electricity to utilities within the northeastern United States energy grid.

Master Plan

A master plan for the park was created through an intensive three-day community design workshop known by architects as a "charette." The plan carefully integrated the park with the historic town of Cape Charles and the natural landscape adjacent to the Chesapeake Bay. The site centered on redevelopment of former industrial land surrounding the town's harbor. The specifics of the plan included roads, utilities, water, sewers, water and stormwater management, and wetland tertiary treatment for water recycling. Fully half of the site was reserved for "ecological infrastructure," including the Chesapeake Bay Coastal Dune Habitat Preserve, natural and created wetlands, and historic/archaeological sites. As an ecological industrial park, its facilities are based on the designs of natural systems. Electricity is generated from sunlight. A water reuse and recovery system is planned to recycle water for industrial use. Porous paving reduces stormwater runoff, which is collected and filtered by constructed wetlands.

Management Structure

The community formed its own development company to manage the park. Known as the Sustainable Technology Park Authority, the entity's legal name is the Joint Industrial Development Authority of Northampton County and Towns. The Authority is a political subdivision of the Commonwealth of Virginia. Its seven-member board of directors is appointed by the governing bodies of Northampton County and the towns of Cape Charles, Cheriton, and Exmore.

Land Assembly

Slightly more than 200 acres of land was acquired in five transactions between 1995 and 1998. This included 30 acres adjacent to the Chesapeake Bay to be permanently preserved as a Coastal Dune Natural Area Preserve within the park. The land also included 45 acres of brownfields, including a former town dump and abandoned industrial land adjacent to Cape Charles Harbor. The United States Environmental Protection Agency funded environmental assessments that documented the lack of any hazardous materials or pollution problems associated with the site.

Infrastructure

Detailed engineering designs were created based on the vision and plans of the original community charette. Construction documents were subsequently prepared for the first phase of roads, utilities, and other infrastructure to serve the park. Local, state, and federal permits and approvals were obtained through a streamlined process, as representatives of most of the agencies involved had participated in the community design charette. Ground was broken on October 17, 1996, in a ceremony during the second national ecoindustrial roundtable in Cape Charles. The first phase of roads and utilities was completed in 1998.

Sustainable Technology Incubator

Completed in January 2000, the showpiece of the Sustainable Technology Park's first phase is a 31,000-square-feet multi-tenant manufacturing/office building. The building meets the U.S. Green Building Council's standards as a "green" building. It features an integrated solar photovoltaic roof system that converts sunlight into 42,000 watts of electricity. With the building operating at full capacity, this will provide up to half of the building's total annual electrical demand.

Other sustainability features include skylights for natural-day lighting, a common meeting and conference center, enhanced insulation, interior environmental sensing, carbon monoxide sensors and alarms, low-energy lighting, low-water fixtures, porous parking lot paving, and native non-irrigated landscaping. The building, which was constructed primarily from local materials, has enhanced structural strength and a longer life span than typical designs. Interior space can be divided flexibly to accommodate up to eight companies for the purposes of manufacturing, research and development, office space, and other uses.

The building's features are designed to not only reduce energy and resource demands, but also to reduce operating costs and to increase occupant productivity and health. As such, the building is expected to be superior economically as well as environmentally.

Ecological Infrastructure

In addition to the more traditional infrastructure of roads, utilities, and buildings, Northampton County and its partners integrated key natural resources into the Sustainable Technology Park. A local/state/federal funding package of more than $727,000 was used to fund the park's "ecological infrastructure." Included is a natural preserve, beaches and dunes, a critical migratory bird habitat, constructed wetlands and ponds, a system of trails and boardwalks, more than 4,000 new trees, and a total of 90 acres of protected natural area.

This ecological infrastructure created a win-win-win synergy among the economic development, environmental protection, and community improvement objectives of the park. The natural amenities have enhanced economic development efforts by helping to attract the corporate tenants the county has targeted. Without the projected financial income produced by the corporate tenants of the technology park, it would not have been possible to fund protection of the natural areas or construction of the trails, wetlands, and ponds. The community, meanwhile, has gained a new natural area park, which has proven to be popular among joggers, birdwatchers, and families alike.

Economic Results

The sustainable technology strategy already has attracted several diverse companies to Northampton County and its eco-industrial park. The Norwegian-based company, Hauge Technologies, develops and manufactures "pressure exchanger" equipment that significantly reduced the cost and energy demands of converting sea water to fresh water. This technology promises to make safe drinking water more affordable and available to more people worldwide. Transforming Technologies is another start-up company in the park. It is developing computer security and identification devices. ProVento America, Inc., is a subsidiary of a German wind energy developer that has initially leased offices for 12 employees and expects to grow to 50 employees within five years. ProVento also has leased sites for six wind turbines that will produce 7.8 megawatts of electricity to be sold into the national power grid. The park also has provided land for the expansion of the county's largest manufacturer, Bayshore Concrete Products Corporation, which employs more than 400 people.

In addition to the companies on site in the park, Northampton's sustainable development efforts have attracted several companies that have located throughout the county and its towns. One of these companies, Atlantis Energy Systems, is the successor of a Swiss firm that produces "architecturally integrated photo-voltaics." These are commercial and residential roofing, siding, windows, and skylights that generate electricity from the sun. Scientific and Environmental Associates is a consulting firm that provides coastal resources management services to government and corporate clients the world over. The company moved its headquarters to Northampton because of its commitment to sustainable development. Delisheries is a homegrown company using space in the park's incubator to produce gourmet cookie mixes.

A total of 800,000 square feet of building area is planned for future phases of the park, which will provide space for 200 or more companies and 1,200 to 1,500 jobs. The park's first incubator building includes 31,000 square feet of space to accommodate its first four to six companies and as many as 100 employees. Depending on market conditions, buildout of the park will occur over the next two or three decades, providing a long-term public framework for private investment.

In the year since the park opened, these companies have combined to create more than 50 new jobs, a significant impact given Northampton's rural economy. Over the next two years, they are expected to create an additional 50 jobs and to bring $15 million in direct real estate and equipment investment to the county. Cape Charles Wind Farm alone is valued at $7.8 million and will generate $120,000 annually in business personal property, machinery, and tools taxes.

Annual debt service for the park is approximately $200,000, with annual operating and maintenance expenses of about $100,000. As soon as the first building is fully leased it will generate an annual rental income of $180,000. Combined with annual tax revenues of $120,000, the park's direct revenues and expenditures are balanced for the first phase. The financial sustainability of the park will remain a key measure of success as development continues.

Toward a Sustainable Future

Building on the success of the eco-industrial park, Northampton already is aggressively moving forward with the next phase of its sustainable development strategy. One key project is the reclamation of the county sanitary landfill as a "seaside ecological farm." The goal is to turn trash into treasure by transforming an economic and environmental challenge into a valuable community asset. The county landfill will reach capacity within two years, at which time it will have to be closed

and capped. It forms the highest point in the county and affords breathtaking views of the Atlantic Ocean, coastal wilderness marshlands, and a string of barrier islands. Conceptual development plans include a network of hiking trails, a high-point observation platform, and the restoration of ponds, wetlands, forest, and other bird habitat.

The seaside ecological farm project already has been selected as a Brownfield Redevelopment Showcase by the United States Environmental Protection Agency, which has committed $400,000 to support the project. In addition, the National Oceanic and Atmospheric Administration has committed $10,000 to fund partner workshops for project planning. The county also has entered into a Rebuild America partnership with the United States Department of Energy to develop the renewable energy components.

The county is investigating the potential of a renewable energy farm that would harvest methane from the landfill, bio-fuels from soybeans grown on the county's farms, and wind energy from the strong coastal winds. The six wind energy turbines planned for the landfill property will produce 7.8 megawatts of clean renewable electricity to be exported to the northeastern United States power grid. Early financial projections indicate that tax revenue from these turbines will offset a significant portion of the debt service required to fund the multi-million dollar landfill closure costs. The county has applied for a grant/loan from the United States Department of Agriculture for construction of a waste transfer station.

Northampton's strategic plan also focuses on ways to further support the county's growing aquaculture industry, which involves cultivating fish and shellfish for harvest. The most profitable specie being grown in Northampton's aquaculture farms is the famous Cherrystone Clam, which has grown from less than a $1 million dollar industry in 1990 to more than $20 million in 2001. Other fish and shellfish species also are being developed for commercial aquaculture farming. And by integrating aquaculture with agriculture, the county hopes to create eco-industrial synergies whereby soy-diesel byproducts serve as fish food and fish farm effluent provides nutrient-rich agricultural fertilizer. Virginia Tech, The Nature Conservancy, and Cornell University's Work and Environment Initiative have provided initial support for this work.

Conclusion

Northampton's Sustainable Technology Park is living proof that economic development and environmental protection are not mutually exclusive and that these goals can be pursued simultaneously to enhance a community's overall quality of life. Although the county has a long way to go to completely overcome its severe poverty and to rebuild a healthy economic base, its experience demonstrates that integrating asset development and protection in an action-oriented, community-based plan is a powerful strategy for success. An extensive local, state, and federal partnership for project financing has been key to leveraging private investment in Northampton's development strategy thus far and will continue to be relied upon as the county continues its course toward a sustainable future.

CHAPTER 21

Franklin, Other Cities, Revitalize Main Streets to Improve Their Inner Core

Kim A. O'Connell

With increasing frequency, small-town preservation principles are being applied to urban revitalization.

A hundred years ago, Franklin, Tenn., was a small country town that still bore reminders of the Civil War battle that took place there in November 1864. Complete with churches and plantation houses, Franklin was determined to preserve its down-home charm, even as the construction of Interstate 65 brought it headlong into the latter half of the 20th century. By the 1980s, however, the historic city was in serious danger of being swallowed up by Nashville, less than 20 miles away.

Fearing their big-city neighbor would consume the community, local officials sprang into action. In 1984, the city became an official National Main Street Town, after applying for and receiving designation from the National Main Street Center, established in 1980 by the Washington-based National Trust for Historic Preservation. Under the Main Street program, which grew out of an experiment in three small Midwest cities, historic preservation and downtown development are used as an eco-nomic driver and an antidote to suburban sprawl.

Today, Franklin serves as a model of how a city can revitalize its urban core and maintain its unique character, while boosting the local economy and preparing for growth. Government officials have crafted plans that work together to preserve and enhance the city's downtown area, while establishing public-private partnerships with nonprofit groups and local residents.

Using a four-pronged approach that includes design, economic restructuring, promotion and organization, 1,800 communities in 42 states also have adopted the Main Street program. Efforts range from small-town projects and county programs to larger efforts in such metropolises as Boston, Baltimore, Washington and Milwaukee. Although it is just one method that cities employ for urban revitalization, the Main Street approach has had tangible results by focusing both public and private resources on targeted areas.

Originally published as "Core Values," *American City & County*, Vol. 120, No. 12, November 2005. Published by Prism Business Media Inc., Overland Park, KS. Reprinted with permission of the publisher.

A Future for Franklin

The Main Street idea has paid off for Franklin. In 2004, the city's downtown hosted the world premiere of "Friday Night Lights," and this fall Cameron Crowe's "Elizabethtown" had a premiere there as well. That is just one example of the success of the city's urban revitalization program, says Franklin's City Administrator Jay Johnson.

Although the city's population more than tripled between 1980 and 2000 and now stands at about 42,000, the central Franklin area had grown at a slower pace. With about 10 percent of the central area vacant, and the core city housing more lower-income residents than surrounding areas, Franklin was in danger of losing more than its identity. Suburban development around Franklin exacerbated the problem, siphoning away dollars and development from the core area.

"We began to experience a lot of growth as a suburban area to Nashville," Johnson says. "A lot of people saw the charm and uniqueness of downtown Franklin and helped form the debate on how to preserve and enhance it. No matter where you live in the community, there seems to be a real attachment to the physical downtown of Franklin, or 'the Square,' as we call it."

In the 1980s, approximately $3 million in both public and private funds was invested to improve facades and add trees, parking, lighting and new businesses to the Square — an effort that continues today. In 1995, Franklin received a Great American Main Street award from the National Trust for its revitalization efforts.

In recent years, city planners have worked with residents, consultants and local groups to craft plans that focus on land use, urban redevelopment and historic preservation. Goals include keeping important government functions downtown, such as the new judicial center and parking structures, both designed in a traditional style that mimics the historic square, and maintaining the city's character

through a series of festivals. "The festivals help create the ambience of downtown," Johnson says. "We've used it to attract people to come back."

Franklin's downtown renaissance has raised other concerns for city officials, however. As the retail shops become more successful, rents are increasing. "There has been a gradual evolution from local ownership of almost everything downtown to several national or regional chains," Johnson says. "The success of the retail has caused the rents to rise, so you have the challenge of the small business person's ability to pay the rents compared to a national or regional chain. One business will go out and another will come in, so some of your marketing can be difficult as well."

The city hopes to develop policies, ordinances and building codes that continue to encourage downtown rehabilitation and development. One goal is to fill the upper floors of downtown buildings with residential units to ensure that the downtown area remains active, even into the evening. "We want to level the playing field for historic buildings and infill in historic districts when compared to new greenfield development," says Shanon Wasielewski, Franklin's preservation planner. "We also want to capitalize on the wealth of historic resources through increased heritage tourism and better way–finding, promotion and interpretation of city-owned resources."

City officials also plan to keep an eye on the continuing growth of the region. "The mayor and I both serve on a number of regional planning organizations, and we are very aware of our role within the region," Johnson says.

Boston Commons

The Main Street concept also is working well in the large and diverse communities of Boston, which became the first citywide participant in the program in the mid–1990s. Today, Boston's program spreads across 19 business districts, with each district receiving technical assistance and training from the city's six full-time employees working in its Boston Main Streets office. Using a funding package from the city that includes Community Development Block Grants, each district can hire an executive director and secure matching private funds for redevelopment. In addition, the city provides local districts with design assistance from local architecture firms, which are contracted through the city's Office of Business Development.

The seeds of the citywide program were planted in 1983, when Mayor Thomas Menino, then serving on the City Council, launched a Main Street initiative in Boston's Roslindale Village neighborhood, which had become rundown and underused. Using the Main Street framework, local merchants, business owners and residents created a nonprofit organization to manage revitalization efforts. In three years, the neighborhood had benefited from more than $5 million in investments.

By 1995, when Menino had become mayor, he worked with the National Trust to establish the nation's first multi-district Main Street program. Following a citywide competition, 10 neighborhood commercial districts were designated as Boston Main Streets that year, with four more selected in 1997 and four more in 1999, in addition to Roslindale.

Since the program's inception, Boston Main Streets has charted significant results, including a net increase of 540 new businesses and more than 3,600 new jobs, 443 storefront improvement projects and total physical improvement grants of more than $1.2 million, which have been further leveraged to bring in more than $9.1 million in private investment.

"For the amount of money we provide to these programs, you get a lot of bang for your buck," says Boston Main Streets Director Emily Haber. "Each district had challenges — some were stable and vibrant and wanted to be better, and some had suffered from disinvestment. Today, there is a level of vibrancy in our commercial districts that just wasn't there 10 years ago."

The perennial challenges, Haber says, are recruiting volunteers and fundraising. But the city is working to keep business owners, volunteers and residents interested in the Main Street program. This year, for example, the city created the Boston Main Streets Foundation. Because each local Main Street district might have only one employee, the foundation's role is to seek funds from national, regional or local foundations and companies, which can be distributed among districts.

Milwaukee's Best

In February, Milwaukee followed Boston's lead by launching a citywide approach to urban revitalization by adopting the Main Street program in four districts. Main Street Milwaukee is operated through a public-private partnership between the Milwaukee Department of City Development (DCD) and the Milwaukee office of the New York–based Local Initiatives Support Corporation (LISC). Milwaukee DCD coordinates the program and oversees the management and designation of the districts, while LISC uses funds and resources raised from private organizations to provide the designated districts with consulting, grants and technical assistance.

Each Main Street Milwaukee district receives $70,000 yearly for three years in Community Development Block Grants to offset the cost of the district's operations and projects. The yearly grant must be matched by at least $10,000 in private funds, to be raised by the districts themselves. Each Main Street Milwaukee district also receives $70,000 worth of technical assistance administered by LISC each year for three years.

Nicole Robben, director of the Main Street Milwaukee program, says that she appreciates the fact that Main Street works from the ground up. "With Main Street, you are concentrating resources and you're building capacity [within each district]," she says. "We wanted to see how that would work in our central-city neighborhoods."

Two years ago, the city held a series of workshops to determine how city residents and businesses viewed urban revitalization and the Main Street program. Participants emphasized the need for a coordinated approach to neighborhood economic development, technical assistance to small businesses to encourage entrepreneurship, and a public-private partnership between DCD and LISC, Robben says.

"We wanted that hands-on, community-driven effort," she adds. "Our Main Street is a partnership between us, the city and the private corporation LISC. They bring in dollar to dollar what we bring in with public dollars."

Each designated district — Burleigh Street, West National Avenue, Lincoln Avenue, and North 27th Street — has a distinct urban character and a diverse population. Before being designated as Main Street districts, the low- to moderate-income neighborhoods were each centered on commercial strips that had vacant or underused buildings. They all needed an economic booster shot, as well as some old-fashioned cleanup and renovation.

To that end, over the next three years, each Main Street district will create four committees focusing on design, organization, promotion and economic restructuring. "Design is going to improve the physical environment of the street, organization is going to continue to bring people to the table, promotion is going to work on promoting those assets, and economic restructuring is going to make sure that the businesses that come in are the businesses the districts want," Robben says.

Looking ahead, Robben has secured the pro bono assistance of four local architectural firms to help the districts with their redevelopment efforts. "There's a purpose to this program, and the private sector is very excited about it," Robben says. "The end result will be revitalized commercial districts where we feel safe and comfortable. This program allows us to accomplish those kinds of things."

CHAPTER 22

Hanover Uses "Civic Index" to Improve Its Downtown

David A. Bloom

Something exciting is happening in the state of New Hampshire. For more than ten years, it has been engaged in a process to strengthen citizen democracy and promote civic renewal. This process, called the Community Profile, has its roots in the National Civic League's (NCL) Civic Index and developed out of two community forums and a statewide visioning process facilitated by the National Civic League in 1989. This chapter documents the history of efforts in New Hampshire to strengthen communities statewide. It also records my observations and learning as a member of the National Civic League; I traveled to New Hampshire to witness the state's fifty-first Community Profile in the town of Lisbon.

In 1989, New Hampshire launched an effort to protect and preserve those characteristics and qualities that the people living in New Hampshire deemed most important to the quality of life. The Governor's Commission on the Twenty-First Century, initiated by then–Governor Judd Gregg, was developed to identify, protect, and promote these qualities and characteristics. A statewide citizen survey identified citizen engagement and the living landscape as the two most important and overarching themes for residents of the state. To address these two themes, Gregg and hundreds of individuals and organizations began developing and implementing multiple statewide initiatives. One of them was called the Civic Profile.

The Civil Profile initiative was developed to give communities the opportunity and technical support to assess what they do well and to take action to improve the quality of life. To assist in designing and implementing this initiative, the NCL was invited to New Hampshire. The Granite State Civic Index, introduced by NCL and the Governor's Commission, was developed to identify a statewide vision for New Hampshire and to allow every citizen to contribute to the vision. To do this, ten individual Civic Profiles — one in each county of the state — were scheduled. The results from the ten Civic Profiles were compiled by a group of stakeholders from across the state and presented in a statement of vision for New Hampshire and a "living report" on New Hampshire's communities. Using the *Civic Index*, a tool for communities to assess their civic infrastructure and level of social capital,

Originally published as "The Civic Profile: A Case Study of Community Building in New Hampshire," *National Civic Review*, Vol. 89, No. 4, Winter 2000. Published by the National Civic League, Denver, CO. Reprinted with permission of the publisher.

NCL conducted the first two Civic Profiles in Exeter and Lancaster and extended training and technical support to members of the Governor's Commission for future profiles.

In 1990, when the ten Civic Profiles for the Granite State Civic Profile were completed, the results were compiled into the final report of the Governor's Commission, *New Hampshire: My Responsibility*. This report served as a guide to communities, suggesting the next steps in preserving and promoting citizen engagement and the living landscape. The report included a section titled "Book of Ideas," a comprehensive listing of all of the ideas and projects that were produced in the ten Civic Profiles. The "Book of Ideas" and word of mouth from profile participants were enough to excite other communities around New Hampshire about hosting their own Civic Profiles and to encourage the Governor's Commission to pass official responsibility for the Civic Profile process to the University of New Hampshire Cooperative Extension, the outreach organization of the University of New Hampshire (UNH). Ten years later, UNH Cooperative Extension has facilitated and provided technical support for more than thirty-six profiles across the state.

The Civic Index *and the Community Profile*

Between 1989 and 1995, the Governor's Commission and UNH Cooperative Extension conducted twenty-four Civic Profiles. After NCL and the Governor's Commission completed the first ten in 1989 and 1990, other communities viewed the profile process as an excellent opportunity to bring residents together and create a vision for the future. Some of these communities used the process to bring citizens together to update their community master plan, a document defining the community's vision, goals, local regulations, and codes of conduct for achieving these goals. Other communities used the process to gather citizen input on pressing local issues or to set up action groups to pursue community projects. Regardless of the intent behind convening a Civic Profile, members in each community used the ten components of NCL's *Civic Index* (the first column in Figure 1) as a primary guide in identifying their strengths and weaknesses, measuring civic infrastructure and social capital, and addressing their most pressing challenges.

In 1995, the Upper Valley (a region along the border between Vermont and New Hampshire) initiated the first significant changes in the Civic Profile process and the ten components identified in the *Civic Index*. The League of Women Voters in the Upper Valley collaborated with cooperative extensions from UNH and the University of Vermont to spearhead an effort to host a new kind of Civic Profile in Hanover, New Hampshire, which sits at the border with Vermont. The collaboration gave birth to the Community Profile and a revitalized set of ten components (the middle column in Figure 1) that better represented the issues and challenges facing communities in New Hampshire and Vermont. The new components were designed to improve an individual community's opportunities to address a broader set of issues of regional and cross-community concern while retaining the ability to address local issues.

The strength of the new components had an immediate influence on the quality and quantity of the ideas and projects that resulted from Community Profiles. Two significant changes in the components are apparent from Figure 1: the language used to name the components and redefinition of components that better reflected the issues important to people in New Hampshire. Because the components were written in language easily understood by profile participants (for instance, "Civic Education" became "Education and Social Services: Meeting Our Citizens' Needs") and redefined to reflect real issues in New Hampshire (for example, "Community Vision and Pride" became "Cultural Heritage: Arts, Fes-

Figure 1
Evolution of the Profile Components, 1989–1999

Civic Index (First Edition), National Civic League, 1989	UNH Cooperative Extension/ League of Women Voters in the Upper Valley/University of Vermont Cooperative Extension, 1995	UNH Cooperative Extension Community Profile Implementation Team, 1999
Citizen participation	Effective community leadership: A broader definition	Effective community leadership
Community leadership	Informed citizen participation: More than voter turnout	Informed citizen participation
Government performance	Intergroup relations: Celebrating diversity within the community	Sense of community
Volunteerism and philanthropy	Cultural heritage: Arts, festivals, and celebrations	Fostering healthy families, individuals, and youth
Intergroup relations	Education and social services: Meeting our citizens' needs	Lifelong education and learning
Civic education	Community infrastructure: The basics that serve our needs	Community services, facilities, and utilities
Community information sharing	Natural resource base: Water, energy, and materials	Recreation and cultural heritage
Capacity for cooperation and consensus building	Our working landscape: Village, farm, and forest	Working landscape and the natural environment
Community vision and pride	Economic vitality: Stability through diversity	Economic vitality
Intercommunity cooperation	Local business, local wealth: Recirculating money within the community	Growth and development

tivals, and Celebrations"), communities were able to focus their small-group discussions effectively and identify issues of significance. Thus, with a change in the category of "Civic Education" to "Education and Social Services," increased quality and focus of the small groups and their outcomes would be observable if one compared the final reports of Lebanon (1990) and Hanover (1995), two neighboring and interdependent communities.

After another fours years and fourteen more Community Profiles, the ten components were modified a second time. In 1999, members of the UNH Cooperative Extension evaluated the final reports from ten years of Community and Civic Profiles and identified several areas that could be improved in the profile process (the third column of Figure 1). For example, there was a lack of focus on and participation by families and youth, which resulted in creating a new component, "Fostering Healthy Families, Individuals, and Youth." The 1995 components "Natural Resource Base: Water, Energy, and Materials" and "Our Working Landscape: Village, Farm, and Forest" consistently received similar responses and parallel discussions, so they were combined into a single component: "Working Landscape and the Natural Environment." "Sense of Community" a new component, was added, and "Education and Social Services: Meeting Our Citizens' Needs" was expanded into "Lifelong Education and Learning." The social services portion of the 1995 education component was combined with "Community Infrastructure" and renamed "Community Services, Facilities, and Utilities."

The strength of the new components was demonstrated at an initial meeting between members of the Community Profile Implementation Team (CPIT) of the UNH Cooperative Extension; county extension educators; and a community leader from West Ossipee, New Hampshire, in March 2000. The village of West Ossipee is experiencing several changes at once: more residents (year round and seasonal), decisions made by the state to extend Route 25 into Ossipee, and the need to revitalize the downtown area. Proposed plans would add several miles of bike paths, a transportation hub (bus and train station) with adjoining one-hundred-room hotel, a transportation museum (Ossipee is the home of the snowmobile), and new pedestrian access routes into and around the downtown area. The challenge for the town and the developers was to find a way to improve community services and infrastructure while retaining the sense of a small-town community. Because this project is so large and influences every resident, backers of the proposed development plan were looking for a way to gather input from the village. They agreed that the Community Profile was the best way to do it.

The discussion between extension educators and a representative of the West Ossipee community began with a dialogue of the issues facing Ossipee and the proposed plan to address these issues. It was agreed that the Community Profile process would meet the needs of the community and the developers, but how to use the process was still unclear. Initially the extension educator suggested that a single-day conversation using a customized version of the profile would focus the community discussion on only a few of the profile components ("Recreation and Cultural Heritage," "Community Services, Facilities, and Utilities," and "Growth and Development"). These targeted discussions would be enough to collect the necessary input for the project. As the conversation progressed, however, the strength of the connections and links among the profile components became apparent. It was clear that for a balanced conversation on "Recreation and Cultural Heritage" to occur, the "Sense

of Community" would also have to be discussed. If West Ossipee chose to discuss "Community Services, Facilities, and Utilities," the townsfolk would also require a parallel conversation on "Fostering Healthy Families, Individuals, and Youth." Finally, it was agreed that the full day-and-a-half Community Profile, using all ten of the components, would be both appropriate and helpful.

For West Ossipee, this meeting was just the beginning of the Community Profile process. From completion of the initial meeting with the Cooperative Extension in February 2000 until the Community Profile scheduled for late October 2000, West Ossipee and UNH Cooperative Extension will engage in an intensive effort to plan and promote the profile, encourage citizen participation, and develop the support structures to implement and use the results of the process. These actions are explained in greater detail in the following case study of the town of Lisbon.

Lisbon, New Hampshire: A Case Study

Lisbon, population approximately fifteen hundred, is located in northern Grafton County, eleven miles southwest of Littleton and northwest of the White Mountain. Tucked into the valley cut by the Ammonoosuc River, Lisbon is a picture-perfect New England village whose economic base is predominantly industrial and dependent on three major companies: an institutional furniture manufacturer, a shoe distribution company, and New England Electrical Wire. Two neighboring communities, Lyman and Landaff, depend on Lisbon for jobs, fire and emergency services, and schools. As described by Lisbon residents, the community is "youth oriented," as shown by the primary source of pride, the recently constructed K–12 school.

In recent years, Lisbon has been struggling. A growing industrial and service park, including a Wal-Mart and a Staples office supply store in neighboring Littleton, has steadily led to the closing of Lisbon's gas stations, mom-and-pop retail stores, and eateries. A drive down Lisbon's main street does little to reflect the economic boom being experienced across most of the United States. As in other towns in many of New Hampshire's northern counties, Lisbon is experiencing much migration of young people (aged eighteen to thirty-five) because there are few jobs for college graduates and few cultural and social opportunities (few operas, theaters, nightclubs, and so on).

Despite its challenges, Lisbon has a variety of active social groups, including the Lion's Club, Women's Club, and Chamber of Commerce. Although many of these groups make regular contributions to the town, there is little collaboration between groups and individuals. This lack of teamwork, coupled with the with on the part of many residents to revitalize Lisbon, was enough reason for residents to host their own Community Profile.

On a cool spring afternoon, 125 residents assembled in the cafeteria of the Lisbon Regional School to share a lasagna dinner. Attendees ranged from executive councilor to blue-collar worker, junior high school student to retiree, and newcomer to resident of sixty years. For the next day and a half, these residents shared their visions and concerns for Lisbon, discussed possible plans for action, and ultimately committed to making four to six community projects a reality.

Pieces of the Profile. Before the residents of Lisbon met in the school cafeteria, much time and energy was spent in planning and preparing for the event. At an initial meeting between extension staff and community members it was agreed that a Community Profile was the best way to proceed, as demonstrated by the example of West Ossipee. The community then put together a steering committee to ensure the success of the profile.

Built-in Support Structures. As early as six months before the profile date, public announcements (television, radio, press releases,

fliers, posters, and so on) were used to inform citizens of the meeting and to encourage their participation. The location was set and arrangements for food and other refreshments made. As a community-building effort, UNH Cooperative Extension encouraged every community to have a potluck dinner for the first meal. Local businesses, organizations, and restaurants were encouraged to donate food or other resources on behalf of the community effort. (Extension staff recommended using a local school to hold the meetings because all the members of a community generally recognize a school as a neutral and safe venue.) A small amount of community research is also required for a Community Profile, so a historian was selected to give a report during the opening session of the profile; other community members accepted responsibility for researching additional funding sources and neutral locations prior to the event.

After the preliminary work was begun and once a date and location were set, the steering committee was asked to identify residents who fully represented the diversity of the community; invitations to the profile were extended. The combination of personal invitation and public announcement is generally adequate to encourage a good turnout at these events. Finally, a group of residents were chosen to serve as facilitators and scribes; these people, including youths from the community, were to facilitate and record all that would be said in the small-group discussions. Several weeks before the profile was to convene, a member of the CPIT — a group of thirteen extension staff from across the state — held an evening training for the facilitators and scribes. The CPIT member also conducted training before and even during the profile event.

After the profile event was held, the steering committee turned to final evaluation of the process and coordination of the action groups that had been identified. In some cases, steering committees may choose to add members, change their membership, or break into multiple groups to focus on individual tasks. In most cases, the county extension educator and members of the CPIT worked with the steering committee and the community work groups to offer technical assistance and guidance at the request of the community.

Discussion Tools. As a part of the 1999 evolution of the Community Profile components, UNH Cooperative Extension changed all of the discussion questions for each component into statements (Figure 2). The questions, as used in the *Civic Index* and the Civic Profile, are designed to engage citizens in meaningful and directed discussion regarding a specific issue and its relation to the component at hand. The shift to statement form stemmed from an observation by extension staff that when discussion groups were presented with a question, they tended to deliberate with the purpose of answering that question. Group discussion during the profile is held not to answer questions but to share ideas, concerns, and potential solutions. So using a statement format gave discussion groups the opportunity to talk freely, without limitation, and with less tendency to seek answers to a single question.

The component discussion statements, the names and descriptions of each component, and the component areas were all developed carefully by UNH Cooperative Extension staff to incorporate simple, easy-to-understand language. Rather than use such terms as *civic infrastructure* or *social capital*, the profile components reflect these ideas using terms of the sort *services* or *networks*. Giving names to the components on the order of "lifelong education and learning" rather than "civic education" has allowed profile participants to begin their discussion quickly, with little or no need for clarification or redefinition of the component area or what specific terminology means.

Lessons from Lisbon. As the Lisbon Community Profile began, many residents were both excited and cautious. "We've had town meetings before," said one resident, "and little

has ever come from those meetings except a lot of complaining. I've heard that these Community Profiles have worked in other communities. We'll just have to see if it can work here."

Many of Lisbon's residents echoed this sentiment of skepticism, yet 125 residents attended on Friday and 80 returned on Saturday (the decline on Saturday was attributable to a combination of the first sunny weekend of the spring season and a donkey-riding basketball tournament in neighboring Landaff). Despite their challenges, residents of Lisbon have visible pride in their community and believe in the need to make it a better place to live, work, and play.

Citizens arrived prepared to discuss the future of their community. Their expectations for outcomes varied widely. Community leaders came looking for a new infusion of ideas for directing Lisbon's future. Others had specific issues, such as taxes or their children's education, that they wished to bring to the floor. Many residents declined to share any expectations until they could see how the process would work, stressing that if it turned into another "gripe session," they would not likely contribute to the conversation or return the next day.

The strength of the process, and the wisdom of the facilitators, was evident from the beginning. After a few icebreaking activities and a brief description of the profile process and the ten small discussion groups, and immediate immersion into the process began.

Safe Space and Ownership. Much of the success of the Community Profile rested on the ability of UNH Cooperative Extension and the steering committee to create a safe space, where people could come together and share their ideas and concerns without fear or concern of personal attack, negative criticism, or unannounced agenda items. In four very practical ways, the success of the process was ensured from the beginning. First, by using the local school, the variety of participants perceived the space to be neutral, giving them one less reason to keep their defenses up.

Figure 2
Questions Versus Statements for the "Effective Community Leadership" Component

The UNH Cooperative Extension shifted from questions to statements to avoid discussions that were directed toward answering a specific question or addressing narrow issues. The use of statements has provided discussion groups with the opportunity to talk freely without any limitation and with a reduced tendency to create answers to a single question.

Question Form

- Is there active leadership in all three sectors of the community — public, private, and nonprofit?
- Do leaders seek out the interests and ideas of local citizens?
- Do they represent diverse community interests (age and gender groups, length of time resided in the community, and so on)?
- Do leaders demonstrate knowledge, accountability, professionalism, and innovation?
- Is leadership results-oriented?
- Are leaders willing to take appropriate risks?
- Do leaders demonstrate long-range thinking (more than twenty years)?
- Do they understand the impact their actions have on the long-term health and vitality of the community?
- Are leaders willing to consider and use alternative methods for delivering services, and to undertake regional solutions where appropriate?
- Do all three sectors actively recruit, train, and empower new leaders?
- Do leaders have a common forum to discuss issues with other leaders in the region? How are regionwide policy conflicts resolved?

Statement Form

- Our leadership actively recruits, trains, and empowers new leaders.
- Leadership represents diverse community interests (age and gender groups, length of time they have resided in the community, culture, and so on).
- Community leadership demonstrates knowledge, accountability, professionalism, and innovation; it is results-oriented.
- Leaders involve local citizens in identifying community goals and resolving community issues.
- Leadership seeks out opportunities to exchange information with citizens about community issues.
- Community leadership is proactive, dealing with critical issues before they become a crisis.
- Leaders demonstrate long-range thinking (more than twenty years). They understand the impact their actions have on the long-term health and vitality of the community.
- Leaders share community responsibilities with members and empower others to help find solutions.
- Leaders are willing to consider and use creative methods for addressing challenges, and to look for regional solutions where appropriate.
- Leaders discuss issues with other leaders in the region.

Second, residents of Lisbon planned Lisbon's Community Profile for residents of Lisbon. Extension staff provided training for the facilitators and technical assistance and guidance when asked, but the profile itself— from the coffee to the invitations — was a community effort, not a third-party intervention. Third, using Lisbon residents to facilitate and record the small-group discussions, instead of third-party facilitators, maintained community ownership and the sense that the community is doing the work for its own benefit.

Finally, the process itself was designed to keep the discussion safe. The agenda was simple, with the time for each session carefully controlled and driven by a clear and specific set of goals. The clarity and focus of the process discouraged any one person or issue from dominating the conversation. Judith Bush, the profile facilitator and chair of the CPIT, noted, "The process is safe because people can see what's happening at any given moment. There are not surprises."

Access to the Power of Discussion. Lisbon and extension staff successfully created a safe space for people to assemble and take ownership of the process from the onset of the planning. As a result, a strong foundation was laid for people to come together to discuss their community openly. Discussion is an effective way to reach consensus and to create new ideas or solutions, but it is not commonly regarded as a means to generate excitement and enthusiasm. But in Lisbon, this is exactly what happened. Each consecutive discussion session, both large and small, generated a consistently higher level of interest and enthusiasm for the future of Lisbon among profile participants. Walter Johnson, Lisbon's town administrator, went into the process hoping that citizens would propose some new ideas and share enthusiasm for the future of Lisbon. "It happened," explained Johnson. "I definitely got what I needed, and what Lisbon needed."

Safe space and ownership were, in large part, credited with the open and frank quality of Friday's small-group discussions. Donna Northrop, a local business owner and treasurer of the Lisbon Chamber of Commerce, described this safe space in an interview with the local paper, the *Littleton Courier*. "Everyone was open," said Northrop; "[Everyone] shared their concerns and there was a spirit of cooperation among the participants." Noticeably strong facilitation also contributed, as facilitators kept their small groups on task and kept the discussion moving forward, not allowing individual participants or issues to slow the pace. Also of importance to the discussion was the language used to name and describe the ten components. In every discussion, the language of the component was the same as the language participants used. Because the language and component description required little explanation, both the process and the discussion were easily accessible to participants. As a result, essentially every individual contributed to the discussion.

Lisbon's enthusiasm was clearly evident during the large-group sessions. These are used in the process for the entire group of participants to make decisions about the issues they would like to discuss and the direction of the process. According to extension staff, the large-group sessions in many communities are usually very focused, and discussion is generally minimal. Lisbon was an exception. The excitement and momentum generated in the small-group sessions carried over into the large group, and participants continued to discuss the issues. This demonstrated the townspeople's high level of commitment to the process, and especially to Lisbon itself.

Community Courage: One Person Can Change a Community. Discussion alone does not change a community. Action — and the commitment, energy, and resources necessary to support action — are also necessary. At the end of the process, Lisbon made a final decision to develop and implement four projects. (Generally, depending on the size and enthusiasm of the community, the number of projects selected varies. Larger communities are likely to select more projects because they have the resources to be successful. Also, communities with a high level of enthusiasm often select more projects, although communities with high enthusiasm but a small population are encouraged to combine projects or to prioritize to avoid community fatigue and depletion of limited resources.) After the projects were selected, Lisbon's profile participants had the opportunity to self-select the work group to which they wanted to contribute; then they broke into small groups and began their project planning.

Extension staff have observed distinct differences among these work groups, compared to the previous small-group and large-group sessions. The general feeling was more reserved; participants spoke less frequently and in subdued tones. It was unclear why the group dynamics changed so significantly until one member stepped forward and claimed responsibility for the process, the ideas, and the results. By taking responsibility for action, this individual directly and immediately changed the dynamics of the group, and the earlier enthusiasm returned.

Discussion is easy; people love to talk, share ideas, and dream about what they might become. But taking action is something different. To act means to address the challenges that confront you, to accept responsibility for your thoughts and ideas, your relationships with people around you, and the results of your endeavor. For many people (and communities), making the leap from idea to action can be excruciating. In Lisbon, participants noted that each work group faced this challenge, yet when one person found the courage to say "I will..." the other participants comfortably fell in, ready to act on the challenges of their community. Once this occurred, the enthusiasm that had built up from the start of the process reappeared, and participants found themselves reinvigorated and ready to make a change.

Lessons from UNH Cooperative Extension

UNH Cooperative Extension has constructed a process that gives every community the means to face its issues and improve itself. Built on more than ten years of experience, the Community Profile is an inspiring example of uniting hands-on experience, keen observation, and determination to help communities become better places. It is particularly important to acknowledge three parts of the process.

First, flexibility is the key to the success of the process in many communities. Communities of any size, economy, and composition use the process. It can also be used for many purposes. Communities may wish to gather data and encourage citizen input to a community process, to develop work groups to tackle the challenges in their community (as Lisbon did), or (as West Ossipee did) to engage the process to do both. The process is flexible in another important way: it may be taken apart to allow a community to address a single component or a small cluster of them. Although the strength of the components as a single unit may encourage communities to use the entire set, it is not necessary to do so. In fact, extension staff developed an eleventh component, to help communities address transportation issues; it is introduced when an individual community identifies this as a significant issue.

Second, the process is accessible to every community in New Hampshire. To conduct a profile, the cost for UNH Cooperative Extension — work hours, materials, transportation, communication, and so on — well exceeds $7,000, yet the cost to any community is significantly less than $1,000. No community in New Hampshire is unable to use the Community Profile process for lack of funding.

Finally, the strength of the profile is due in large part to continuous assessment and review of the process itself. No process — especially one designed for communities — can be highly effective if it is not regularly updated and reviewed. Communities change, as do their needs, challenges, and concerns. Because communities are not static, the processes that they use to improve themselves must also avoid rigidity. The Community Profile is an excellent example of how a process can be maintained and updated to meet the needs of the communities that use it.

Community Success: Building Civic Infrastructure and Social Capital

Ongoing evolution of the profile process is an important part of UNH Cooperative Extension's work in New Hampshire. Improving the process, however, is not the only important piece of their work. It is extremely important to develop ways to measure and document the success of the process. For every individual profile completed, reports and media articles are released listing the successes of the profile process in the form of decisions made and actions undertaken. These successes range in scope from hiring a new town manager to creating a community center or updating a local master plan.

Successes like these often do not clearly reflect success in building the level of a community's civic infrastructure and social capital. For example, the town of Hillsborough conducted a Community Profile in 1998. A sixty-three-page report documenting all of the ideas, goals, and successes to come out of the profile was written, and numerous media articles celebrating the community's efforts have been published over the past few years. Hillsborough's greatest success, however, is not clearly stated anywhere in all that text. Prior to the Hillsborough Community Profile, the community was attempting to confront some serious issues surrounding an economically depressed Main Street. Local business owners and members of the local select board were constantly at odds over how to address the problems on Main Street. Much of this animosity stemmed from the business owners' perception that the select board was attempting to destroy them.

During the Hillsborough profile, common ground was discovered: the desire to revitalize Main Street with a strong economic base and thriving local businesses. Since the profile was completed, Hillsborough's business owners and select board, with the help of many citizens, have directed a successful collaborative effort to revitalize their main street, including hiring a new town planner and submitting an application to the Main Street USA project. It cannot be suggested with certainty that business owners and the select board member could have found common ground on issues of contention without the Community Profile. Fortunately, because they used it, they were successful in raising the level of social capacity, and Hillsborough has begun to reap the rewards of building new community collaboration.

Another success in capacity building can be found in the town of Pittsfield. That Community Profile, held in 1997, was in part to address growing unrest among the community's residents. Taxes were on the rise, the select board was in turmoil and experiencing turnover, and the town administrator had just been fired. "We really needed the profile to build community," explained Susan Muenzinger, a Pittsfield resident. She attributes the town's current success to the Community Profile. "It takes time for things to develop in a stagnant community," she said, describing Pittsfield's past.

The Beautification Committee, started three years earlier at the profile, learned that the newly revived Pittsfield Conservation Commission (also a result of the profile) was proposing a large community planting of trees and the like — an activity generally perceived to be the responsibility of the Beautification Committee. In times past, citizens and groups would have simple clashed and attempted to block each other's progress and success. This time, however, the lessons on discussion and collaboration learned at the profile prevailed, and a collaborative effort resulted.

Even Lisbon, only one month after the profile, is experiencing improved social capital and civic infrastructure. In a postevent interview, town administrator Johnson commented, "I see new people working together ... to partner on some of the big projects." Johnson even expressed his pleasure in the development of new leadership in the community. "[New] leaders have surfaced in each [work] group," he said. but he was careful to preface his comments with words that mirrored Muenzinger's observations in Pittsfield: "It's going to take some time."

As the Hillsborough and Pittsfield examples demonstrate, it will take time in Lisbon for the lessons of the Community Profile to become part of the everyday interaction of citizens. The opportunity for success, however, is very real.

Representatives of UNH Cooperative Extension know that identifying and documenting the results, especially the successes, from the Community Profile process is the key to maintaining the program. A project is currently being developed by extension staff to begin documenting the success stories of communities such as Hillsborough, Pittsfield, and Lisbon, and the ways in which civic infrastructure and social capacity are augmented as a result of the profile process. This is certainly no simple task, but the potential lessons that can come of this kind of research are well worth the effort.

Conclusion

The Community Profile process facilitated by the University of New Hampshire's Cooperative Extension is an inspirational effort in community building in America. The profile process is an excellent example of how community members can come together to face their challenges and create a better future for their communities. UNH Cooperative Extension has developed a remarkable ability to keep the process useful and accessible to all communities; it has maintained awareness that New Hampshire's communities need to keep the process relevant to the state's citizens.

The Community Profile is a resource in community building for individuals and organizations alike that are focused on helping a community become a better place to live, work, and play. The NCL is proud to have been involved in New Hampshire, recognizes the outstanding efforts of UNH Cooperative Extension, and wishes New Hampshire many more years of positive community-building efforts.

CHAPTER 23

Hartford Works with Local College to Renew Its Inner-City Neighborhoods

Rob Gurwitt

From the perspective of Zion Street, a mile or so from the state capitol in Hartford, Connecticut, the notion that cities are riding the crest of a comeback seems ill-considered. The area Zion runs through, known as Behind The Rocks, is faltering. It's nothing obvious yet: The streets aren't littered with broken glass, the houses aren't boarded up, there are no gangs hanging around on street corners. But you can tell that hard times are coming. Most of the neighborhood's shops — a couple of restaurants, a liquor store, a barber shop — have the faintly woebegone look of establishments that can't spare a dime to spruce themselves up. The houses running down the side streets need new coats of paint, porches shored up, gutters repaired. It is a neighborhood whose residents obviously care about it — there are plenty of blocks not too far away where the windows *are* boarded up — but events are just as obviously passing it by.

And that galls Marilyn Rossetti, who lives in Behind The Rocks and is a long-time neighborhood activist. Because next door is another neighborhood, Frog Hollow, that events most definitely are *not* passing by. There

are three new schools about to go up in Frog Hollow, and a boys' and girls' club. New housing is on the drawing board, and older housing is due to be renovated. All told, several hundred million dollars' worth of investment is flowing into Frog Hollow. And Rossetti can only watch with envy. "They are not addressing Behind The Rocks with the same enthusiasm," she says. "And this strip, Zion Street, is on the cusp. It doesn't even have a year left. It's still a great neighborhood, but it's dog-eared, and it needs that boost. If it doesn't get one, it isn't strong enough to make it."

What is most striking about Rossetti's comment is not so much the frustration, it's who she wished were paying attention. For the "they" in this case, the engine behind Frog Hollow's revitalization, is not the local redevelopment agency or the city of Hartford or the state of Connecticut. It is the private institution on the other side of the rocks, Trinity College. For people such as Marilyn Rossetti, who have spent years struggling to ward off the forces tearing at Hartford's neighborhoods, this is the form that deliverance now takes: the

Originally published as "Town, Gown And Survival," *Governing*, Vol. 12, No. 8, May 1999. Published by Congressional Quarterly Inc., Washington, D.C. Reprinted with permission of the publisher.

hope that her neighborhood will be noticed by a small liberal arts college.

But then, the same is true a 90-minute drive to the north, in Worcester, Massachusetts. The small Kilby/Hammond neighborhood there, a bit south of downtown, already look like Marilyn Rossetti's worst fears for Behind The Rocks. At one end stretches the hulk of an abandoned factory, its red bricks dark with age, surrounded by tangles of barbed wire. The streets are lined with decrepit houses and empty lots where decrepit houses stood before they were torched. The lots these days are filled with scraggly maple trees. As one local puts it, "It's going back to what it was: woods."

Or at least, it would be if nearby Clark University and its partner in local development, the Main South Community Development Corp., weren't about to intervene. Within a few years, Kilby/Hammond's 30 acres will see at least a hundred units of new housing, a boys' and girls' club, and a set of new athletic playing fields to be shared between Clark students and kids from surrounding neighborhoods. It is perhaps the single most ambitious project that Main South has undertaken in the 13 years since it was formed by Clark and nearby St. Peter's Catholic Church, and without a doubt the most concerted effort in Worcester to revitalize a blighted neighborhood.

Urban revitalization is "in" right now on campus, all across America. The University of Pennsylvania has set out to build a new public elementary school and to improve existing schools in its West Philadelphia neighborhood, and has committed $130 million to creating a new hotel and retail space in an area that has been devoid of commercial development of housing and planning to build up to 1,500 affordable and market-rate units nearby. Schools from Marquette, in Milwaukee, to USC, in Los Angeles, to Yale, in New Haven, Connecticut, are putting their money into neighborhood development efforts, and other colleges and universities are trying their hand

at everything from neighborhood health centers to education programs tailored to public housing residents.

They are motivated, in many cases, by what Richard Traina, the president of Clark, calls "altruistic self-interest"—that is, a commitment driven by the realization that if they *don't* act, the neighborhoods they sit in could drag them under. As Fran Reale, a Hartford restaurateur and community activist, puts it, "A college is a business, and they can't stay in business in a hole." Encouraging as it seems, in other words, the move by institutions of higher learning into urban revitalization is a conspicuous comment on how deep the plight of central city neighborhoods remains.

It might seem an odd moment to suggest this. The press, after all, is filled with word of falling crime rates and dropping urban unemployment, new downtown stadiums and colossal urban entertainment complexes, returning flocks of empty-nesters and hordes of young professionals chasing thrills and jollity. Cities, we have concluded, are hot once again.

Except that demographic and economic trends don't entirely bear this out. "At the rhetorical level, cities are coming back," says Bruce Katz, who directs the Center on Urban and Metropolitan Policy at the Brookings Institution in Washington, D.C. "But the reality on the ground is more stark: In many cases, the economy is decentralizing—jobs and people are moving to the suburbs—and poverty is centralizing. If this is as good as it gets in the larger economic picture, that's a fairly dire picture." Scholars such as Katz believe not only that colleges and universities can play a vital role in reviving urban areas but that they—along with hospitals, the other major private institutions that can't just pick up and leave—may, in fact, be indispensable in revitalizing some cities.

So as college presidents such as Traina and Trinity's Evan Dobelle rewrite traditional notions of their place in the community, efforts are growing to encourage more institutions to join them. The federal Department of Housing and Urban Development has an Office of University Partnerships, which this year is giving out about $7 million in grants to 18 colleges and universities for community-focused activities. In Massachusetts, at the behest of U.S. Senator Edward M. Kennedy, a small group of the state's institutions of higher education have formed the Massachusetts University Community Partnership to offer technical assistance and advice to such efforts. "More than a dozen institutions in or near seriously needy communities," Katz and Dobelle wrote last year, "have endowments of more than $1 billion. And yet many have not tapped their wealth to benefit their communities. Their endowments are untouchable rainy-day reserves. Well, just outside the campus gates, it *is* raining."

This is an opportunity for cities to jump on — a chance to cultivate institutions with major endowments, vibrant intellectual resources and the capacity to provide strong civic leadership, and to enlist them in restoring urban vitality. The problem is, it's not clear that city governments recognize it yet. Indeed, if anything is going to get done — judging from the experience of Hartford and Worcester — it's the people in the ivory towers who are going to have to do the conscripting.

If there is any community that has begun to reap the fruits of town-gown cooperation, it's Hartford. When Evan Dobelle was appointed president of Trinity late in 1994, it wasn't just Frog Hollow that was ailing, it was the city as a whole. As late as the early 1980s, Hartford had been enjoying a small renaissance as the insurance industry grew, but then came a downturn. The local government began struggling with gangs and deteriorating neighborhoods, and mainstay companies such as Aetna, Travelers and Phoenix began turning their attention away from the city and toward surviving globalization.

The result wasn't just the usual litany of urban ills, it was a dearth of strong private leadership. Not long after Dobelle's appointment, he was asked to lunch by the retired CEO of one of the city's leading insurance companies. "He said, 'Let me give you some advice,'" Dobelle recalls. "'We are a city of actuaries. We are very good at what we do, but we're not visionaries about the community. Give us a plan and we'll fund it. But if you ask us our opinion, we'll have to make believe we have an opinion and know what to do. We *don't* know what to do. That's your job.'"

To be sure, Dobelle had not stepped into a complete vacuum. Community groups had been working for years to marshal resources at a neighborhood level, and had found a few willing institutional partners. But until Dobelle came along, there was no one at a prominent level — other than Mayor Mike Peters, who'd taken office earlier in 1994 — who seemed convinced that dramatic improvement was possible. "Dobelle came at a good time," says Jim Boucher, who directs an umbrella group of south Hartford neighborhood organizations known as HART, or Hartford Areas Rally Together. "Morale was low, and people were wondering whether the neighborhoods in this area were beyond the tipping point where even an infusion of resources wouldn't make a difference. He set that question to rest."

What Dobelle did, essentially, was to set out with the other Frog Hollow institutions — most notably Hartford Hospital and the Institute of Living, a psychiatric hospital — to remake the neighborhood's support structure. He first persuaded the Trinity board of trustees to spend some money tearing down six crack houses — "We had to make a difference right from the beginning," he says — and then to pony up another $6 million to $8 million of the college's endowment. With a similar commitment from Hartford Hospital, that was enough to bring in heavy money from elsewhere, most notably a pledge by Republican Governor John Rowland for $82 million in school construction money, $75 million from Fannie Mae for low-interest home-ownership loans, and millions more from a variety of corporations and foundations.

"There is no great genius involved here," says Dobelle. "There is no need for any more urine samples or blood tests or X-rays — this is not a complicated diagnosis. Are the schools good? Are the parks safe? Do people have a job? Is there home ownership? Do kids have hope? You don't have to sit around figuring out what to do. You *know* what to do. *Everybody* knows what to do. They just don't do it."

The centerpiece of all the efforts is the "Learning Corridor," a nine-acre site across the street from Trinity that will hold a new public Montessori school — which Dobelle and his vice president for community relations, Eddie Perez, snagged after other neighborhoods balked at hosting it — a 600-student middle school, and a high school resources center that will house a science, math and technology academy and an arts academy, both of them designed for students from all over the city to use as a supplement to — not a replacement for — their own high schools. Less visible, but quite significant in terms of its long-term impact on the city as a whole, is the Trinity Center for Neighborhoods, which is becoming perhaps the premier source of technical support for neighborhood groups in the city, and which has played a central role in enlisting Trinity faculty to do research on concrete problems facing particular neighborhoods.

In all of this, Trinity has worked closely with the city, and not just in securing land. Perez meets weekly with the city manager's office, and whenever the college's efforts have needed political endorsement — in Washington or at the state capitol — Peters, a weak mayor structurally, though not politically, has done everything he could to help out. "There has been not one bump in the road," says Dobelle. "The mayor, the city council, the school committee, the speaker of the House, the president of the Senate, the governor — I have had absolutely no one be an obstacle in this project."

His use of words is telling, though: Maybe the government wasn't an obstacle, but

it wasn't leading the charge, either. There is no doubt in anyone's mind where the driving force for change lies, and it is not in City Hall. "Maybe in the '60s you would have expected the city to be in the lead," says Jim Boucher. "But today, HUD dollars are scarce, the state is rebuilding its budget, the corporate presence on the property-tax list has collapsed, the city has scarce resources it has to figure out where to put."

These are, of course, precisely the circumstance that "public-private partnerships" were designed for, and in that regard, Frog Hollow is deservedly a national model. But because the city's resources are so limited, its ability to institutionalize neighborhood redevelopment, and so to build on what is happening in Frog Hollow, depends on the willingness of other private institutions to put their money and prestige on the line. There are not many college presidents with Dobelle's combination of charisma and political ability in the U.S., let alone in Hartford, and the city's window of opportunity may be closing. With the state's decision to spend $374 million on a new downtown football stadium for the New England Patriots, and a high-profile move to construct a new office and retail complex known as Adriaen's Landing, both public and private attention is shifting toward downtown. And that makes people working on neighborhood issues nervous.

"The Patriots and Adriaen's Landing will make Hartford a regional center and will bring people to Hartford from outside, but they will not make Hartford a *livable* city," says Alta Lash, director of the Trinity Center for Neighborhoods. "What you need is an equally legitimate development track that talks about increasing home ownership in the neighborhoods, securing public safety, dealing with quality of life issues, dealing with job creation and keeping the commercial strips vibrant. That agenda should not be neglected because it's less sexy than having some football yahoo running around downtown." She worries that the city will shift its planners and other scarce resources, leaving Trinity and its partner institutions as the *only* force for neighborhood revitalization. So does Linda Bayer, the assistance city manager responsible for the city's neighborhood development efforts. "There is this huge political pressure to make all this happen downtown," says Bayer. "So when push comes to shove, I'm not sure what the policy will look like."

If you wander around the area of Worcester known as Main South, you see no signs of renewal as dramatic as the cranes and exposed rebars that will eventually become Hartford's Learning Corridor. What you see instead is a vibrant, working class neighborhood, its modest Vietnamese restaurants, small bodegas and well-worn Irish bar testifying to the canopy of immigrants that has taken root there. It is a much quieter accomplishment than the one in Hartford, but no less impressive.

The three-deckers of Main South used to be filled with Irish and French-Canadian families whose fathers worked at one of the nearby foundries or at the Brown Shoe Co., immigrants struggling to gain a toehold on American life. They worshiped at St. Peter's, drank at Moynihan's, and pretty much ignored the well-appointed Clark campus at the neighborhood's heart. For its part, while it never erected the physical walls found on some urban campuses, Clark didn't much concern itself with the humble community around it, except when it acquired and tore down housing to make way for a new basketball arena or other campus project.

This standoffishness was fine until the mid–1970s, when the shuttering of the factories forced a lot of families to pick up and leave, to be replaced either by poorer families moving in or, in the case of buildings whose absentee landlords couldn't stomach the plummeting value, the arsonist's match. In one three-block area, some 60 buildings burned down during the '70s and '80s. Drug-dealing, prostitution and simple urban decay quickly turned Main South into one of Worcester's shabbiest neighborhoods.

That was the situation Dick Traina found when he took over Clark in 1984, and it did not please him. "It's pretty hard to have in your mission statement that you want to graduate imaginative and contributing citizens of the world and then turn your back on the neighborhood in which you live," he says. "What kind of hypocrisy is that if the institution itself is not a good citizen?" Traina began by patching up relations with the neighborhood, meeting with the heads of local social agencies and the priests at St. Peter's, putting up housing on campus to keep students from driving up rents in the neighborhood, buying up shops and apartments to keep them out of the hand of a notorious slumlord. But far and away the most important step Clark took was to accept the help offered by SEEDCO, a Ford Foundation affiliate that helps urban institutions pursue community development, in setting up a CDC.

In the 13 years since the Main South CDC got off the ground, it has renovated about $10 million worth of housing, helped local home owners get low-interest loans to fix up their own property, and evolved from a tiny outfit in the attic of the Clark administration building to become the leading housing developer and landlord in the area.

In all of this, Clark and the CDC have been close partners, with the university serving as an associate rather than an overseer. Clark, which has only one representative on the CDC's 15-member board, has given Main South unsecured loans and guaranteed others. As Steve Teasdale, a city planner who is Main South's director, puts it, "the beauty is that the real cost to the university is very low: If we don't screw up on the loan guarantee, it doesn't cost them anything. But for us, the university is a credible partner at the state and federal level — it gives our funding applications more credibility."

Clark's commitment, though, goes beyond the CDC. "Rehabbing scores of properties was great," says Jack Foley, Traina's assistant, "but we recognized we weren't winning the battle in the neighborhood. We needed good schools, jobs and programs for kids." Clark took two especially far-reaching steps in that regard. One was to offer free tuition — currently $21,000 a year — to any neighborhood kid who meets the college's entrance requirements. The other was to help set up a neighborhood public school, the University Park Campus School.

The school, housed in a former elementary school that is now owned by the university, will eventually run from seventh through 12th grade; it is only in its second year, and so at the moment has only seventh and eighth graders. It is the brainchild of schools Superintendent James Garvey, who saw in Clark an opportunity to set up the equivalent of a charter school within the public school system. Its students use university facilities, they are tutored by Clark students and faculty, and a few Clark professors teach classes there. Its focus is determinedly academic: The school day runs from 8 in the morning until 4 in the afternoon.

"I had a strong vision of the school not being an inner-city school," says Donna Rodrigues, who taught in the Worcester public schools for 30 years before being tapped by Garvey to be the campus school's principal. "'Inner city' means you have to apologize for performance. Well, if Clark was offering free tuition, kids had to be ready to take them up on it." Drawn by the school, Clark's tuition guarantee and Main South's rehabilitation of the neighborhood, working families are finally moving back in significant numbers.

In Traina's mind, the close partnership between the university and the school system in dreaming up an entirely new joint venture is the ideal for how universities and local governments ought to relate. It is not one that the university and Worcester have been able to match otherwise. "I do think there is some level of concern at the university that too much of the load is falling on us as an institution rather than being distributed over other kinds of institutions, mainly city government," he says.

Traina and Foley *are* quick to point out — as is city manager Thomas Hoover, who says that he and Traina "somewhat differ" on this score — that the city has come forward with grants and loans, and that the police department has set up a community service branch right by the campus. But, argues Foley, it could have been more creative. The city side, he says, has gone through traditional models of block-grant funding and police support, rather than becoming directly involved in planning with the community.

In the end, of course, Worcester and Hartford will benefit from the new academic engagement regardless of how fully they move to take advantage of it. And they will do so in ways that go well beyond simple bricks and mortar. "The one activity that is hardest to quantify but may be the most critical down the line," says Bruce Katz, "is the reengagement of leadership in the urban governing class. Many of these cities are really bereft of leadership: Their corporations have merged or downsized or are caught in a very dynamic environment. So the engagement of a university president and faculty as civic leaders is fundamentally important."

It may also only be a matter of time before it spreads. Dobelle argues that colleges and universities don't just have an immediate interest in the health of their neighborhoods. In an era in which the limits of government at all levels have been made abundantly clear, they will inevitably come under the same kind of pressure to contribute to their communities as any other wealthy institution.

"Higher education," he says, "has long been looked at as so arrogant, so pretentious about going at community situations saying, 'It's your problem, not my problem.' Well, someday, someone's going to say, 'Excuse me, you have what, six billion dollars, fifteen billion in your endowment? You invest in all kinds of high-end projects, hotels and shopping centers and golf courses, but you redline your own neighborhood just like banks? So what makes you different from a bank?'"

CHAPTER 24

Hoboken, Other Cities, Focus on Affordable Housing for Inner-City Renewal

Susan Bass Levin

At the New Jersey Department of Community Affairs (DCA), we are committed to investing in our communities for a better New Jersey, and we work to achieve that goal through a variety of innovative programs. To ensure a great quality of life for residents, we know we must provide jobs, housing and economic growth — while at the same time preserving and protecting our natural resources. In short, we must strike a balance between economic growth and environmental preservation. Green design and construction can accomplish both.

In 1998, DCA launched the state's first sustainable development pilot program to test the viability of building energy efficient, environmentally friendly affordable housing. The program required all units in the pilot to meet the standards of the PSE&G Energy Efficient Home (EEH) 5-Star Program; the precursor to what is now known as the national EPA/DOE Energy Star Program. In an effort to promote a market transforming approach to energy and resource efficient design, construction and methodologies, 367 units were designed and built. The success of the pilot resulted in the creation of DCA's Green Homes Office (GHO) two years later.

Capitalizing on the opportunity to change energy use habits and further explore energy efficiency through the lens of green building, the GHO developed the New Jersey Affordable Green Program (NJAG). The only statewide green affordable housing program in the country, NJAG has become a national model for green affordable housing and has inspired architects and construction officials across the state to "go green."

NJAG collaborates with DCA's affordable housing subsidy program, Balanced Housing, to fund "green" affordable housing. In addition to the substantial subsidy that Balanced Housing puts into a project to write down the cost of development, up to $7,500 per unit is made available to a developer incorporating green materials and technologies. As project designs come to fruition, this subsidy is allocated to pay for the incremental cost of upgrades from conventional materials to high performance green features.

Originally published as "Green Construction: Affordable and Environmental Friendly," *New Jersey Municipalities*, Vol. 83, No. 4, April 2006. Published by the New Jersey State League of Municipalities, Trenton, NJ. Reprinted with permission of the publisher.

In the last five years, incorporating a blend of Balanced Housing and Green subsidies, the GHO has worked to increase the use of innovative green materials, design and high performance building technologies in over 2,400 homeownership and rental units across the state — including those in Hoboken and East Orange in the north to Bridgeton and Atlantic City further south.

Housing units developed through the Green Homes Office are among the most energy efficient homes in New Jersey. All units, at a minimum, must meet NJ Energy Star Certification requirements, which is 30 percent more efficient than required by the Uniform Construction Code.

In addition to the heavy emphasis on achieving energy efficiency through fundamental building science strategies, NJAG aggressively addresses indoor air quality issues. By requiring the integration of low VOC materials, and insisting on advanced ventilation systems and healthy and durable flooring including hardwood, ceramic, bamboo, linoleum, recycled rubber and cork, New Jersey renters and homeowners are provided with excellent indoor air quality. We are also reducing water usage through the use of duel flush toilet and low flow fixtures.

Looking into the future, the Green Homes Office has two exciting initiatives on the drawing board. The first is the development of a Microload Project in the City of Camden, which is undertaking a number of initiatives to improve its economic vitality and provide quality, affordable housing to residents. The Camden Microload Project will use high performance design principles and passive and active solar strategies to construct 25 housing units, which will have a near net-zero use of grid provided electrical power. DCA, with the assistance of nationally recognized experts, will demonstrate that zero energy principles can apply to affordable urban housing.

The second program is the New Jersey High Performance Homes Plus, which is designed to support the green efforts of market rate builders and promote the benefits of high performance home building and renovation. High Performance Homes Plus will establish a state green building standard, advance whole system, energy efficient building practices among builders and educate consumers about the advantages of the features in their homes. The program will coordinate with other national green building programs to address bioregional issues, and provide New Jersey builders and residents with a one of a kind program tailored to the specific needs of the state. We hope to have the program up and running by the end of 2006.

DCA's affiliate agencies are also thinking green. We are collaborating with the New Jersey Housing & Mortgage Finance Agency to promote and incorporate energy efficiency, indoor air quality and other green building strategies into units that serve as homes for residents with special needs. This green building emphasis on Special Needs projects is a unique plan to create the healthiest and most durable housing units possible for New Jersey's most vulnerable and underprivileged population.

In North Jersey, the New Jersey Meadowlands Commission's 10,000-square-foot expansion of the Meadowlands Environment Center educational facility will aim for a LEED certified level of gold. The LEED (Leadership in Energy and Environmental Design) Green Building Rating System is a voluntary, consensus-based national standard for developing high-performance, sustainable buildings. If achieved, the Meadowlands Environment Center will be the first state-owned building to earn the gold rating. With a project completion date for summer 2007, this would be the first step in upgrading the entire NJMC Lyndhurst campus of buildings to green building status.

The NJMC has also entered into an agreement with Ramapo College of New Jersey to create a Sustainable Meadowlands Resource Institute. The goal of the SMRI is to increase green building redevelopment and retrofitting in the Meadowlands District through a partnership-based model with business leaders. The SMRI will help develop cost-effective green design guidelines, host workshops on green design, and find resources, such as grant applications for developers and the public sector.

Green buildings are cleaner, healthier, brighter and more livable. They represent the housing we need today to ensure a better tomorrow. Working together with local officials, architects and builders, we are one step closer to preserving our future through the use of innovative green design and building technologies across the state.

For more information, please contact the New Jersey Green Homes Office at 609-292-3931, by email at njgreenhome@dca.state.nj.us, or visit us on the web at www.nj.gov/dca/dh/gho/index.shtml.

CHAPTER 25

Irwindale Uses Redevelopment to Revitalize Its Downtown

John F. Shirey

Redevelopment agencies generated $31.84 billion in total economic activity for California in fiscal year 2002–03. This economic activity suggests a story worth telling from the rooftops — rooftops that redevelopment helped to build. It's a story about the retail shops attracted to an underserved neighborhood, the housing for residents who revitalize a downtown, and the commercial buildings and industrial parks bringing new permanent jobs into a community.

Two years ago, the California Redevelopment Association (CRA) contracted with the California State University, Chico, Center for Economic Development (CED) to perform an analysis of the economic impact of California's redevelopment agencies. CED recently released its findings.

This chapter describes the study and reports the findings. It also includes examples of projects illustrating how redevelopment supports economic development. Three of the 2005 CRA Award of Excellence winners tell how they used redevelopment in their projects, the lessons they learned and tips for other cities to follow.

The Report on Redevelopment's Economic Impact

At the end of 2004, CED completed its second analysis of the economic impact of redevelopment on California's economy. Examining only redevelopment-related construction activity, CED collected data from residential, commercial, industrial and public infrastructure projects representing a sample of redevelopment agencies throughout the state.

An established computer model was used to calculate the direct, indirect and induced economic output of redevelopment agency construction in order to determine the statewide economic impacts. CED identified the economic flows associated with construction in redevelopment project areas, including those involving agency funds outside project areas during FY 2002–03.

The study's key findings are startling. Redevelopment agencies generated $31.84 billion in total economic activity in California. Furthermore, redevelopment-related construction activity created 310,000 full- and part-time jobs in one year through its multiplier effect on the state's various industries. In FY 2002-03, redevelopment construction activity generated an increase in California state income of $16.56 billion (state income is defined as the sum of wages and salaries, proprietor income, corporate profits, property income and indirect business taxes).

Tax revenues for state and local governments grew by $1.58 billion during the same period because of redevelopment construction activity.

The impact on the construction industry stands out. Of the 310,000 jobs produced, 158,000 were construction sector jobs, or 14.6 percent of all construction industry jobs in California. Construction output totaled $16.42 billion, of which redevelopment activities generated 12.6 percent in 2003.

The study was not intended to be a cost-benefit analysis of redevelopment programs. Nevertheless, it did show that the economic impact of these programs justifies the current levels of funding and expenditures. Every $1 that a redevelopment agency spends results in nearly $14 in state sales of goods and services. Furthermore, the average dollar of redevelopment spending increases state income by $7.22.

Irwindale Business Center

A mining town for more than 100 years, Irwindale was at one point the largest aggregate mining district in the nation. Nearly seven years ago, the city identified 120 acres of developable land situated in a gravel pit in the middle of the city. The upside was that the pit could be developed without filling it to street level.

By moving a lot of dirt around (called "over excavation") and bringing more in as well as addressing drainage issues, a commercial development became possible. The resulting Irwindale Business Center includes commercial and industrial spaces surrounded by retail and greenbelts. It is now the city's showpiece.

Walking paths and meandering sidewalks invite city residents and workers to explore the area. A four-acre community park will open soon. The center includes the first retail development in the city since 1988, including a coffee shop, a bank facility and a variety of restaurants. The center's industrial park retains existing tenants and attracts new ones. The buildings and unit sizes range from 2,000 square feet to 325,000 square feet and include features to accommodate manufacturing, high-tech and warehousing uses. The buildings appeal to a diverse mix of commercial tenants: major corporations, established local firms and start-up businesses.

The assessed value of the former quarry site was $3.06 million prior to the development. When the center was completed, assessed value for the site rose to $63.5 million. The center hosts 37 businesses employing 2,300 people. Sales tax revenues since the center opened have been estimated at $593,000 a year.

By partnering with a major developer, the city transformed this former mining quarry into a successful business center. The redevelopment agency played an important role providing funds at critical junctures, including intersection treatments. Because the agency understood the problems faced by developers as well as the vision of the Irwindale City Council, its involvement facilitated problem resolution. The redevelopment agency also coordinated the different agencies and entities involved in reclaiming the site.

"The city councils over the past decade have remained committed to the redevelopment of Irwindale, despite the knowledge that they will not get credit for its success," commented City Attorney David Aleshire. The council members' commitment to a vision for their town enabled them to work through the obstacles that emerged.

In addition to its 1,500 residents, the city's daytime population was more than 40,000. The city needed to bring in retail to serve this population and make Irwindale more attractive for new businesses to locate there. To make it appealing to new employers and retailers, citywide design standard guidelines had to be adopted.

Flexibility came in handy during the resolution of a drainage problem that came with transforming a gravel pit into an industrial park. The drainage issue was resolved without having the entire pit reclaimed to street level. The design of the flood control system, pump station and retention basin received support from the county flood control district. This complex drainage solution pushed the financial limits of the developer as well as the regulatory demands of the local county flood control staff; however, it paid off when the pump station was built and the center could move forward.

Irwindale is a big winner due to the redevelopment agency's investment of nearly $620,000. "Economic development and redevelopment go hand in hand. They may serve separate functions and roles, yet this project proved a winner for both," said Irwindale's Economic Development Manager Elaine Cullen.

Alhambra's Downtown Main Street

Alhambra began the process of transforming Main Street into a vibrant commercial corridor in 1994. "Twelve and a half years ago, you could have shot a missile down Main Street and not hit anyone," commented City Manager Julio Fuentes. "Today, 1.3 million people annually enjoy downtown Alhambra. Our weekend Summer Jubilee events regularly attract 10,000 people downtown. We added 1,000 parking spaces, and we still need more."

From 1994 to 2003, redevelopment along downtown Main Street led to the rehabilitation of 28 buildings, the opening of more than 45 new businesses, and the creation of 314 housing units and 1,487 new jobs. Following the completion of the Alhambra Renaissance

Plaza, Alhambra celebrated its centennial in 2003. Since then, additional retail shops and restaurants have opened — or are about to open — and the much anticipated Alhambra Regency Plaza, a large-scale mixed-use project, was completed. The city estimates its annual sales tax revenues at $538,000 and property tax revenues at $553,000.

The City of Alhambra and its redevelopment agency included downtown in a redevelopment project area. Thus, the agency was able to acquire land and hold master leases. It fostered public-private partnerships through owner participation agreements and business improvement loans. The agency instituted a facade improvement program and acted as ombudsman to shepherd new businesses and developers through the city's permitting process.

By acting as developer and master leaseholder, the city could control the downtown revitalization. In this way, the agency can purchase or lease properties, make tenant improvements to them and then sublease the properties to the desired tenants. Through tax increment financing and leveraging federal development grant funds, it was possible for the city and agency to make the standard improvements that retailers expect when they move into a property — fresh paint, plumbing and electrical upgrades, bathrooms, roofs that don't leak and adequate air conditioning. "These buildings were in bad shape," Fuentes recalled. "Many of these property owners didn't have the resources to improve their properties so they could attract and retain the tenants that enable them to keep their property in good shape."

The city kept its goals for downtown Main Street broad and all the tools of redevelopment available so it had the flexibility to respond as opportunities arose. The city and agency urge others not to lock themselves into programs with strict parameters.

Recent opinion surveys show continued community support for Alhambra's redevelopment efforts with a 93 percent approval rating. The dedicated city council, city manager and agency staff created an environment in Alhambra's downtown Main Street that attracts businesses and people to be a part of a proud and vibrant community.

West Hollywood Gateway

The City of West Hollywood celebrated the completion of the West Hollywood Gateway in March 2004. The eastern entrance to this diverse community had become run down and put a damper on the city's economic revitalization. With the gateway, the city has created a plaza for community gathering and public art, provided retail to meet community needs, cleaned up a contaminated site and saved a historic restaurant.

When West Hollywood officials determined that redevelopment was necessary to turn the area around, they engaged in a series of in-depth community workshops and dialogues on redevelopment. With their core group of neighborhood members, they took "walkabouts" through the area to determine where redevelopment could be used. The group agreed on the gateway site. This community group became the Project Advisory Committee (PAC) for the project and grew to 35 people. The agency and the city decided it was important that anyone who wanted to be involved should be.

The PAC worked with redevelopment staff on drafting the request for qualifications to ensure that it reflected community needs, concerns and visions. The PAC also was a part of the team selecting the project's developer. The community's extensive involvement and the sensitivity of both the developer and the architect helped gain community acceptance when changes had to be made.

This 257,000 square foot retail and restaurant complex has created 800 permanent jobs. Target, one of the anchors, was the number one performing store for the chain nationwide for two weeks. The store continues to be among the top 10 performing Target stores. Allyne Winderman, deputy executive director of the redevelopment agency, commented, "The success of this center shows the great need in the area for this type of retail." Its success has had a ripple effect; the stores across the street have had improved business as well.

To assist with site acquisition, the agency entered into a disposition and development agreement (DDA) with the developer. The agency leveraged its contribution to the project with a $2 million Brownfields Economic Development Initiative grant and an $8 million HUD Section 108 loan. The DDA also included provisions for equity participation by the agency in the operations of the gateway and upon its sale. The city estimates that the project will generate approximately $1.5 million in various taxes and fees.

Redevelopment: Serving Communities and the Economy

Throughout the years, there have been plenty of examples of redevelopment's impact on the quality of life in California's cities. The CED study shows that redevelopment activities also have a powerful economic impact. The three cities showcased in this article illustrate the many stories behind the numbers CED found in its analysis of redevelopment-related construction activity in California. The more we document the successes, track permanent and construction-related job gains and report on the dollars infusing communities because of redevelopment, the more compelling our story will be about how well redevelopment serves the California economy and our communities.

Elements of Successful Redevelopment Projects

• Provide committed leadership. Because Irwindale's city council remained committed to its long-term vision, all their goals were achieved with the Irwindale Business Center project.

- Maintain flexibility. Alhambra kept its goals for downtown Main Street broad and all the tools of redevelopment available so that it could respond as opportunities arose.

- Engage the community. The West Hollywood community's extensive involvement and the sensitivity of the developer and architect helped gain community acceptance when changes had to be made.

CHAPTER 26

Las Vegas, Other Cities, Use State-of-the-Art Digital Practices in Their Downtowns

David Gales

"Public space is dead," Dutch architect Rem Koolhaas proclaimed during a conference at the Harvard University Graduate School of Design in spring 1999. His observation was based on the rapidly increasing allure of cyberspace, which he termed a "universal city that exists wherever we are in the world." Seven years later, the powerful draw of the Internet and other forms of digital media intensifies with every new technological advance, putting the world at our fingertips through an array of miniaturized devices.

No one would deny that the public realm has been profoundly altered by the ubiquity of technology that allows people to shift time and place and absent themselves from the public moment, not only in their homes and offices, but also in cars and on the street corner. As younger generations — those technology natives who have grown up with dual citizenship in actual and virtual communities — enter more fully into public life, this reality will continue to reshape notions of public and private space.

Yet, Koolhaas's remarks have proved premature because champions of civic life have begun to co-opt the very technologies that threatened to keep people in front of their private screens and out of the agora.

What is happening in a select number of public gathering places reflects the predictions of media artist and researcher Michael Naimark, presented in the Van Alen Institute's November 1999 report Digital Dilemma: Where Is the "Public" in E-topia? "At best," he wrote, "bold new forms of the virtual and actual community will appear: Imagine actual public spaces wired together by ultra-high-bandwidth network connections, where actual neighbors are co-present with virtual ones. Imagine a public space for 100 people tapping 100 times the bandwidth available to the home. Imagine an Imax-meets-the-Web immersive, interactive space."

Welcome to the advent of urban media — the integration of media and technology that is creating new forms of communication designed specifically for public places. Urban screens that identify, entertain, or educate are being networked to form communication systems that capture the public imagination with multimedia narratives. With the maturation

Originally published as "Design and the Digital Age," by David Gales, Urban Land, Vol. 65, No. 3, March 2006. Published by the Urban Land Institute, Washington, D.C. Reprinted with permission of the publisher.

and convergence of multiple forms of media technology, sophisticated digital displays are now a programming option for museums and parks, as well as retail and entertainment districts. Improved affordability allows designers to combine architecture, digital sound, visual imagery, and lighting to create communications platforms that can be leveraged to build a sense of community, as well as used for commercial purposes.

If Times Square or the Las Vegas Strip comes to mind, think again. In those bright, media-packed environments "every sign is screaming for itself," says Don Richards, principal of Foghorn Creative in San Francisco. "The new environments replace the simple signage model with one that borrows from broadcast, where there is a constant stream of complex but controlled programming to create a media model with a juxtaposition of program elements that allow for multiple, coordinated messages."

What these environments do share with other bright, sign-saturated locales from Broadway to Tokyo's Ginza district is that they are at high-density crossroads. The people coming together or passing through provide a large audience for a constant flow of information, whether for commercial or not-for-profit purposes. The challenge for developers of the physical environment from the buildings to the screens, as well as for the content developers who create the digital messages, is to keep the message from becoming virtual clutter or another piece of video wallpaper. Giving primacy to the content is a prerequisite to coalesce communities, whether citizens or shoppers.

"We need to think in four dimensions to create a meaningful experience," explains Richard Orne, president of Orne + Associates Inc. in Los Angeles and a pioneer in the design of these environments. "We have to take a holistic approach that will allow for change rather than a linear one that ends when the project is built. Digital media are fluid and instantly refreshable for the needs of context over time."

While the marriage of digital media and architecture presents a loss of control for the architect at one level, it opens up new possibilities for extending the influence of the design into the public realm. As Orne notes, "The integration of architecture and digital media makes it possible for us to create new value — artistic, cultural, educational, and commercial."

Early adopters of the new technologies include retailers who have seized the opportunity to build brand awareness with media-saturated environments. Randy Byrd, principal at Sensory Interactive in Pasadena, Maryland, predicts the rise of "multimedia campaigns based not on point-of-purchase advertising, but on sharing corporate philosophy and goals with potential buyers. Nike is one of the best examples of this." By incorporating digital media in their stores and offices, companies like Apple, the Gap, and Bloomberg help to establish a shared culture among buyers. Byrd cites the advantages of this approach. "When you create a marketing platform that runs through an entire project, the media are scalable to the needs of the environment or the event," he says.

The larger the project, the greater the opportunity to develop a dynamic narrative on multiple screens for multiple purposes. One of the first large-scale explorations of the synergy of new media, architecture, and communication strategy occurred with the redesign and expansion of Fashion Show, a regional mall located on the Las Vegas Strip amid the glare of competing commercial messages. The Rouse Company, which built its reputation on creating retail centers with a strong sense of connection to community, searched for a way to make the project belong to this most transitory of environments.

Deciding to build a campaign on the existing name of the center, the company pursued a makeover that integrated a sleek, modern, architectural aesthetic with an equally state-of-the-art communication platform. Instead of using a volcano or pirate ship, the mall entices shoppers off Las Vegas Boulevard with a media-enhanced public plaza. Suspended 150 feet above the street is a 500-foot-long "cloud" with aluminum skin that functions as a sunshade by day and a canopy of projected images at night. Five projectors located in glass cubes on the plaza are each capable of projecting a 70-foot-square image on the underside of the cloud. In addition, there are four 24-by-43-foot light-emitting-diode (LED) monitors on an elevated track, or "media curve," capable of displaying individual images or creating a 172-foot-long digital canvas.

Inside the mall, multiple displays are capable of broadcasting events and content from the fashion runway and from around the fashion world. Orne, who designed the project in conjunction with Los Angeles–based Altoon + Porter Architects, sought an interplay between the media and the physical environment to leverage the developer's ability to provide sponsorship opportunities for tenants, retail brands, and others, which in turn would generate additional revenue streams for the project. With the sale of the Rouse Company to General Growth Properties of Chicago, the concept lost a champion; time will tell how the new owner adapts the media platform to its own business model and messages.

The success of sponsorship sales and advertising at the American Airlines Center at Victory Park in Dallas spurred Hillwood Capital, based in Dallas, to investigate the potential for a large-scale media platform for Victory Plaza, an open-air entertainment and retail district located at the heart of the project. The result is the Victory Media Network, a technologically sophisticated combination of static, digital, broadcast, and interactive media elements to be integrated throughout the property. The scale and scope of this undertaking are unprecedented and could elevate public expectations and understanding of urban media in many ways.

Rescaling the new media model for a much larger public space ups the ante for the infrastructure investment, which in turn requires a business model that will create value in multiple ways for developers. "We are developing a revenue model built on sponsorship sales to forward-thinking companies that want to be a part of this exciting new form of communication," explains Kristin Gray, director of business development for Victory Media Network, which is part of Hillwood, a Perot Company. "We also understand that there has to be a mix of programming — commercial and not-for-profit — for the media platform to win a strong following. Hillwood is in this development for the long haul; we want to create not only differentiation for ourselves, but to provide a legacy for the city of Dallas."

Hillwood has been intimately involved with all aspects of the development of the media network, from infrastructure to content development. "We are helping to define a whole new media category that is immersive, entertaining, and educational," notes Gray. "We want to be sure that all the content is high quality and high definition, whether it comes from a sponsor or from a community agency, so we are working with outside agencies to develop material."

The extensive network will create all-day demand. It is "a lifestyle-magazine approach to the screens with intriguing and engaging content — digital art from local and national artists, cause promotion, community events, visual candy, as well as sponsorship programming that underwrites the platform," Gray says. "The ebb and flow of the programming should reflect changes in the traffic throughout the day, moving from news to culture to entertainment."

To achieve this, 11 individual LED screens, totaling over 4,600 square feet, will be constructed at Victory Park, offering potential sponsors an innovative platform to communicate messages to consumers. The Victory Media Network will comprise a multimillion-dollar collection of design and technology components, including two fixed 20-foot-square tower displays, a digital portal, and eight movable 15-by-26-foot LED walls installed in two four-panel groups that will face each other across the 100-foot wide Victory Plaza.

Digital kiosks will be located across the entire development, disbursed media hydrants will provide ready access to power and high-speed data connections, and wireless data connectivity will provide network access throughout the district. Supporting the entire platform will be a network infrastructure with a fiber-optic backbone connected to a network head end located adjacent to the plaza.

Scheduled to open late this year, Victory is keeping a number of creative organizations busy. Kevin and David Goddess, creative directors at Spark, a New York City–based agency, say they are migrating with their clients from small screens to larger ones as they work to extend brand identity into the architectural realm. "We are working on details like the use of color palettes and logos and the look and feel of the visuals that subtly let visitors know where they are, to the creation of a five-minute spectacular that will be a signature moment for the space," they say.

Still others, like Foghorn Creative's Richards, are busy adapting the technologies that have been used for years in purely commercial ventures to fit the new media mix. He hopes to see "the first great digital gallery" at Victory, he says. Meanwhile Sensory Interactive's Byrd delves into the commercial possibilities, seeking to determine how many sponsors it takes to create a successful platform.

Other projects also are paving the way, albeit in a less ambitious fashion. While small in size, Spanish artist Jaume Plensa's Crown Fountain in Millennium Park in Chicago, which combines glass bricks, LED display technology, and flowing water, has had a major impact on the concept of public art. In Vienna, local architects and engineers Nau-

mann + Partner recently completed the design of a new headquarters tower for UNIQA Group with a shimmering glass facade that at night turns into a venue for a light show — a digital performance that combines public art with a subtle reinforcement of the UNIQA brand identity. In September, the Institute of Contemporary Art is scheduled to move to its new home on the Boston waterfront. Designed by New York City–based Diller Scofidio + Renfro, the building not only will include a digital media center where patrons can get access to digital artworks, interpretive material, and the Internet, but also its translucent walls will be illuminated at night, providing outside space for performances and digital projections.

The timing is considered auspicious for the ascendancy of urban media. A confluence of factors points toward a newly digital public realm. Social factors include the widespread public acceptance of digital media and technology in everyday life, coupled with the resurgent popularity of public spaces. Economic factors include the decreasing costs of the hardware and software needed for large-scale presentations, advertiser thirst for new and innovative promotional opportunities, and the developers' need to differentiate their offerings. Finally, technology has established media and production standards, and created high-capacity digital media storage capability, high-speed data networking and wireless communication, high-definition video production and imaging, and high-quality video display screens that are bright enough for daylight applications.

The future of urban media seems far less like *Blade Runner* or the empty space described by Koolhaas, and a lot more like the energized, connected public realm envisioned by the creators of today's new venues. Stay wired.

CHAPTER 27

Lowell, Other Cities, Preserve Their Heritage

Edward T. McMahon

What did you do on your last vacation? Would you recommend the place you visited to a friend? Or were you disappointed? Did dirty air, traffic congestion, crowded beaches, slipshod service, or excessive commercialism leave you feeling frustrated and cheated? Americans spend almost $800 billion a year on travel and recreational pursuits away from home. One out of every 8.4 jobs — or 11 percent of total U.S. employment — is related to the travel/tourism industry. Some 37 states claim it as their leading industry and in 2004 alone it generated over $250 billion in federal, state, and local tax revenues.

Tourism provides American communities with many benefits, including new jobs, an expanded tax base, enhanced infrastructure, improved facilities, and a market for local products, art, and handicrafts. It can also create burdens such as crowding, traffic, noise, more crime, haphazard development, cost-of-living increases, and degraded resources.

Sustainable tourism, on the other hand, helps maximize the benefits of tourism while minimizing the downsides. It differs from the mass-market brand of tourism because tangible benefits are measured rather than sheer heads counted.

American cities and towns spend millions of dollars on tourism marketing to entice visitors. This, in turn, helps create demand or expand a market. This is critical in a competitive marketplace.

Yet, tourism involves much more than marketing. It also involves making destinations more appealing. This means conserving and enhancing a destination's natural tourism assets; in short, protecting the environment. The unique heritage, culture, wildlife, or natural beauty of a community or region is really what attracts visitors in the first place.

In today's tourism marketplace, competition for tourists' dollars can be fierce. If a destination is too crowded, too commercial, or too much like every other place, then why go there? It is for this reason that local planning, land development, and urban design standards are so important to communities with tourism resources. Communities get the message that they are in trouble when new development shapes the character of the community — instead of the character of the community shaping new development.

There are significant differences between tourists' and residents' perceptions of a community. Tourists tend to be open and recep-

Originally published as "Sustainable Destinations," by Edward T. McMahon, *Urban Land*, Vol. 64, No. 8, August 2005. Published by the Urban Land Institute, Washington, D.C. Reprinted with permission of the publisher.

tive to everything they see, while residents tend to tune out the familiar environment along the roads they travel day in and day out. This suggests that local tourism officials need to become much more aware of the overall character of their community.

If the character of a destination is at odds with its description in advertising and promotional literature, for example, the tourist will feel cheated. Creation of a false image — beautifully photographed uncrowded beaches when the more realistic picture is standing room only — can spoil a vacation. What is more, it can reduce the likelihood of repeat visitation: tourists may come once, but they will not come back. Alternatively, fond memories and word of mouth can be a destination's best public relations.

Tourism is a voluntary activity — which means that tourists can choose from a wide range of competing destinations. Given a variety of choices, where will they end up? According to heritage tourism expert Amy Webb, virtually every study of traveler motivations has shown that, along with rest and recreation, visiting scenic areas and historic sites are the top reasons why people travel. In a speech, travel writer Arthur Frommer noted, "Among cities with no particular recreational appeal, those that have preserved their past continue to enjoy tourism. Those that haven't, receive almost no tourism at all. Tourism simply doesn't go to a city that has lost its soul."

So how can a community attract tourists — and their dollars — without losing its soul? First, a community needs to recognize that sustainable tourism is a long-term strategy, not a quick fix. Second, a community needs to understand that people become tourists in order to visit a specific, special place. As economic development expert Don Rypkema says, "Nobody goes anywhere to go down a waterslide or buy a T-shirt. They may do both of these things, but that isn't the reason they went there." People travel to see places, especially those that are special, unusual, and unique. In short, any place can create a tourist attraction, but it is those places that are attractions in and of themselves that people most want to visit.

Preservation-minded cities like Annapolis, Maryland; Savannah, Georgia; Charleston, South Carolina; New Orleans, Louisiana; Santa Fe, New Mexico; Quebec City, Canada; and San Miguel de Allende, Mexico, are among North America's leading tourism destinations precisely because they have protected their unique architectural heritage. By contrast, cities that have obliterated their past attract hardly any tourists at all, except for the highly competitive and notoriously fickle convention business.

Not every community is blessed with a great natural wonder or a rich legacy of historic buildings, but most communities have tourism potential. Realizing this potential begins by inventorying a community's assets — both existing and potential. What natural, cultural, or historic resources does a community have to offer? What features give a community its special character and identity? This is how Lowell, Massachusetts, began its transformation from a gritty, industrial city, with an unemployment rate of 23 percent, to a city that now receives over 800,000 visitors a year, has restored 250 historic buildings, and has seen over $1 billion in new investments. It all began by recognizing the potential that existed in the abandoned mill buildings that characterized the city, and then planning to realize that potential.

Sustainable tourism means preserving and protecting resources. The more a community does to conserve its unique resources, whether natural, architectural, or cultural, the more tourists it will attract. On the other hand, the more a community comes to resemble "Anyplace, U.S.A.," the less reason there is to visit. Make a destination more appealing, and people will stay longer — and spend more.

The following are six recommendations that communities might want to consider:

Focus on authenticity. Communities should make every effort to preserve the authentic aspects of local heritage and culture, including food, handicrafts, art, music, language, architecture, landscape, traditions, and history. Sustainable tourism emphasizes the real over the artificial. It recognizes that the true story of an area is worth telling, even if it is painful or disturbing.

In Birmingham, Alabama, for example, the Civil Rights Museum and Historic District tell the story of the city's turbulent history during the civil rights era. The authentic representation of the city's past adds value and appeal to Birmingham as a destination and the museum and adjacent historic district have proved popular with visitors from all over the world.

By contrast, many tourist attractions near the Smoky Mountains National Park portray Cherokee Indians as using teepees and totem poles and wearing feather war bonnets, even though this was never a part of their culture. This commercialized stereotype of a Native American has caused anger toward the tourism industry and devalued the area as a destination.

Ensure that tourism-support facilities — hotels, motels, restaurants, and shops — are architecturally and environmentally compatible with their surroundings. Tourists need places to eat and sleep. They also appreciate the dependable level of service and accommodation usually found in American hotels and motels. But tourists also crave integrity of place wherever they go — and homogeneous, "off-the-shelf" corporate chain and franchise architecture works against integrity of place. Freeport, Maine, home of the L.L. Bean Company, for example, is a draw for shoppers seeking bargains at the town's many outlets, but the town has also protected its character by ensuring that the likes of McDonald's, Taco Bell, Arby's, and other chains either reuse historic structures or erect one-of-a-kind buildings rather than the cookie-cutter, anywhere-in-the-U.S.A. type of buildings.

Every tourist development should have a harmonious relationship with its setting. Tourism-support facilities should reflect the broader environmental context of the community and should respect the specific size, character, and functional factors of their site within the surrounding landscape. A community's food and lodging establishments are part of the total tourism package. Hotels should reflect a city and not each other. Hotels in Maine, for instance, should be different in style than those in Maryland or Montana. It is this search for something different that has given rise to the booming bed-and-breakfast, adventure travel, and heritage tourism industries.

Interpret the resource. Education and interpretation are keys to sustainable tourism — visitors want information about what they are seeing. Interpretation can also be a powerful storytelling tool that can make an attraction, even an entire community, come alive. It can also result in better-managed resources by explaining why they are important. Interpretation instills respect and fosters stewardship in both visitors and residents. Education about natural and cultural resources can instill community pride and strengthen sense of place. The town of Gettysburg, Pennsylvania, for example, developed a community-wide interpretation program that involves public art, wayside exhibits, and interpretive markers that tell the story of the town and its role in the battle of Gettysburg. Since the program was developed, the number of visitors spending time and money in the town has drastically increased.

Consider aesthetics and ecology. Clean air and water and healthy natural systems are fundamentally important to sustainable tourism, but so is community appearance. Many cities have gotten used to ugliness, accepting it as inevitable to progress. However, other more enlightened communities recognize that the way a community looks affects its image and its economic well-being. Protecting scenic views and vistas, planting trees, landscaping parking lots, and controlling signs are all fundamentally important to the economic health of a community.

For example, Vermont's tourism office touts the fact that it is one of four states that completely prohibits billboards. Likewise, Oregon's marketing slogan is "Oregon, things look different here." Imagine a marketing campaign that touts billboards as an attraction or urges tourists to visit by bragging, "Things look the same here."

Enhance the journey as well as the destination. Tourism is the sum total of the travel experience. It is not just what happens at the destination. It involves everything that people see — and do — from the time they leave home until the vacation is over. Getting there can be half the fun, but frequently it is not.

There are many truly noteworthy destinations in America; however, there are very few truly noteworthy journeys left, which is why it is in the interest of the tourism industry to encourage the development of heritage corridors, bike paths, hiking trails, and other forms of alternative transportation. This is also why local and state governments should designate scenic byways and protect roads with unique scenic or historic character.

Recognize that tourism has limits. Savvy communities always ask how many tourists are too many. Tourism development that exceeds the carrying capacity of the ecosystem or fails to respect a community's sense of place will result in resentment and the eventual destruction of the very attributes that tourists have come to enjoy. Too many cars, boats, tour buses, condominiums — or people — can overwhelm a community and harm fragile resources.

A few communities have managed to balance nature and commerce in ways that benefit both. A popular Gulf Coast resort, Sanibel Island in Florida, is one of the world's premier places to collect seashells and see subtropical birds. To protect its abundant wildlife, white sand beaches, and quiet charm, Sanibel built an extensive network of off-road bike paths and developed a master plan based on an analysis of what was needed to protect the island's natural systems. The plan set a limit on the island population consistent with its drinking water supply, the habitat needs of wildlife, the need to evacuate the island before hurricanes, and other considerations. By establishing development standards based on ecological constants, Sanibel has managed to preserve one of America's most exceptional subtropical environments, while also accommodating a high level of visitation.

In recent years, American tourism has had steadily less to do with America and more to do with mass marketing. As the amount of open land decreases, advertising dollars increase. As historic buildings disappear, theme parks proliferate. Unless the tourism industry thinks it can continue to sell trips to communities clogged with traffic, look-a-like motels, overcrowded beaches, and cluttered commercial strips, it needs to create a plan to protect the natural, cultural, and scenic resources on which it relies. Citizens, elected officials, and developers alike can take a leadership role in promoting — through community education and comprehensive plan policies — a sustainable tourism agenda that will strengthen the local economy by protecting and enhancing the community's tourism assets.

CHAPTER 28

Memphis Focuses on Housing to Save Its Downtown

Ellen Perlman

From the chrome and vinyl bar stools upstairs at Ernestine & Hazel's, an old brothel-turned-singles bar in downtown Memphis, Phil Woodard can look out across the street and contemplate the Hotel Grand, a red-brick railroad hotel at 508 South Main Street. The building was constructed in 1913 and ruined by fire during the riots that followed the 1968 assassination of Dr. Martin Luther King Jr., which happened just a few block away.

The Grand is open again, if anything a little grander than it its working-class heyday. But it isn't a hotel. Woodard owns it now, and he has turned it into an artist's studio on the ground floor, and two-bedroom apartments above. They rent for as much as $1,400 a month, a pretty steep price for the Bluff City, but all the units are occupied. Woodard kept the sunny top-floor loft for himself.

Across the street, Woodard has just about finished renovating his second building, an old brake-shoe warehouse at 509 South Main. It, too, contains apartments and a street-level artist's studio. Meanwhile, he's purchased a third building, down the block at 505, and he's getting ready to renovate that.

Unlikely as it may seem to many who know the city, South Main in Memphis is a hot residential district. Drab and nearly empty for years after King was killed at the nearby Lorraine Motel, it reverberates every day now with hammering and drilling and the sound of the refurbished trolley cars that run down the middle of the street.

But it's not just South Main. Housing is hot in other parts of downtown Memphis — in the central business district, on the bluff overlooking the Mississippi River, and on Mud Island, which sits in the river just a few minutes away by bridge. "Everything's being worked on," says Woodard. "All of a sudden there's a renaissance." Edmond Armentrout, president of the Center City Commission, a local development group, estimates that downtown Memphis could add 1,000 new residents a year for the foreseeable future.

All of this needs to be put in perspective. There are 1.2 million people in the Memphis metropolitan area, and only about 6,300 live downtown in market-rate housing. Even if the market stays hot for the next decade, it's hard to imagine downtown becoming home to more than a tiny fraction of residents of the region. But that fraction might be sufficient to guarantee downtown Memphis a bright future, as a safe and lively community with enough people

Originally published as "Downtown: The Live-In Solution," by Ellen Perlman, *Governing*, Vol. 11, No. 9, June 1998. Published by the Congressional Quarterly Inc., Washington, D.C. Reprinted with permission of the publisher.

in residence to attract a diverse commercial sector interested in serving them.

Other cities are coming to just the same conclusion. It has been an article of faith among urbanists for more than a decade that a true downtown revival requires a healthy residential component. But only recently have local governments begun taking it to heart, and acting on it. "Downtowns until the last five years were either housing for the very rich or the very poor," says Betsy Jackson, president of the International Downtown Association. "What's happening now is filling in the gap. I don't know how it can't be good."

"I've been in the downtown redevelopment business for 15 years," says Jim Norton, who heads a group called Downtown Tulsa Unlimited. "Unless you have people living here, the process doesn't work. When people go home at night, when downtown closes up at night, it doesn't create a very viable central business district."

The revival is being stimulated not only by New Urbanist ideas but also, as in Memphis, by a surprising demand for almost anything in decent condition. "I have not run into a constituent involved in housing that doesn't see more demand than supply," says Jackson.

The trend does not appear to be regional, and it doesn't seem to be a matter of size or history. The downtown population is growing in places that have always had significant central-city housing, such as Philadelphia, and in places such as Denver, where there is no such tradition, but where the number of downtown residents is at 4,000 and growing fast. It is happening in larger cities such as Atlanta, where there are now 5,000 units of market-rate housing downtown; in Dallas, which has 10,750; and in smaller communities such as Richmond, Virginia, which is up to 2,500.

Nor is the phenomenon limited to a particular style or economic niche. Downtown housing is going up in the affordable and luxury categories, for rent and for purchase. Developers are working on high-rise apartment buildings, townhouse developments, loft conversions, units above stores, condos and restored mansions. "They can build any housing," says Betsy Jackson, "and have a waiting list."

And developers are showing interest in sites that at first glance look rather unpromising. A generation ago in Milwaukee, three legs of an elevated expressway loop were built around that city's central business district. The point was to move people downtown for work in the morning and speed them out of town at night toward suburban homes. The last leg, a lakefront expressway proposed in 1958, was never built.

But the land for that last segment was cleared of buildings, and after being vacant for many years, it has recently sprouted new townhouses and apartments. Now the city is hoping to tear down other portions of the freeway with the intention of attracting more residential development on the land underneath, which is currently used for parking lots. "It would add enormous value to downtown Milwaukee," says Mayor John O. Norquist.

More frequently, however, the downtown housing revival does not depend on new construction, but on finding new uses for buildings that have lost their traditional function. Nearly every big city has a large stock of office buildings, built in the 1920s or earlier, that no longer can attract commercial tenants. Most companies want large, square floor spaces where they can put many employees together. Older buildings tend to offer funky, oddly shaped smaller spaces. Perhaps more important, retrofitting these buildings for present-day office use involves wiring and garage construction whose costs are prohibitive. Remodeling them as apartments — even luxury apartments — is much more practical.

Tulsa has started to take advantage of its abandoned office buildings to create downtown housing for the first time in nearly three decades. One of the first projects is the *Tribune* building, which used to house the offices of the daily newspaper and is listed on the National Register of Historic Places. It will be turned into 33 lofts. The plans await final approval from the state, but there are already 15 names on the waiting list. Meanwhile, developers have broken ground on a 159-unit apartment complex on a vacant downtown site nearby.

In Baltimore's loft district, a stone's throw from the Camden Yards baseball stadium, buildings that once held manufacturers of shoes, sleepwear, straw hats and sailcloth were turned into residences several years ago. Now the city has ambitious plans for a dozen more such projects.

All along Charles Street, one of the major north-south streets running through the center of Baltimore, are venerable buildings whose only practical future appears to be in residential conversion. Last year, the city created a downtown housing council that provides property tax relief, established a loan fund and created the position of downtown housing coordinator, whose job it is to walk developers, investors and lenders through the development process. Meanwhile, the state has increased a tax credit and created new financial incentives to build downtown housing.

After Mayor Kurt L. Schmoke announced the city housing initiative last June, 12 redevelopment projects got under way, even before the downtown partnership could knock on doors to promote it. Developers are about to begin work on the Abell Building, a six-story Victorian Gothic on south Eutaw Street, built in 1870. Others are attracting similar interest, among them the Women's Industrial Exchange Building and the former YMCA, built in 1890.

Where the downtown housing comeback is strongest, local government is usually involved in a significant way. Memphis, through its Center City Revenue Finance Corp., offers developers tax abatements for 10 to 25 years, depending on the project. Its Center City Development Corp. also offers 3 percent loans ranging from $10,000 to $60,000 to fix up older buildings.

In addition, the development corpora-tion is using partnerships with developers as a way of pushing the movement along. In one case, the corporation is buying the first floor and basement vacated by an old jewelry store and reserving it for future retail, while providing funding for a developer to turn the top four stories into condominiums. "It's a shot of capital from us," says Edmund Armentrout of the Center City Commission. "We're taking the risk on retail. If they couldn't lease up the first floor, they might be in dire straits."

Baltimore and several other cities have tried a property tax freeze on historic renovation. Until recently in Baltimore, that freeze applied only to projects up to $3.5 million, but under the new housing initiative, the law has been changed so that any size development now can qualify for a graduated freeze.

Tulsa is contributing sales tax money to the downtown housing effort. Residents voted in 1996 to extend a one-penny sales tax for capital improvements that expires automatically every five years. Some $4 million of this money was earmarked for downtown housing development. It wasn't a huge pool of money, but it had the desired effect. "Once the sales tax was approved, developers were crawling all over us," says Jim Norton.

Such local tax incentives can be vital for downtown residential development because federal tax changes in 1986 had the effect of reducing the credits that developers had been using to rehabilitate historic housing. Between 1981 and 1986, more private funds went into restoring historic buildings than during the rest of American history combined. For eight years after the 1986 tax law went into effect — reducing the amount of the credit, barring high-income taxpayers from using it and creating a "passive loss" provision that sharply limited how much of the credit is available to a taxpayer — investment in rehabilitation projects was off by about 80 percent.

For much of the past decade, developers have been largely uninterested in using the federal tax credit provisions that remain. In 1993, Congress made tax law changes that exempted full-time real estate developers from the strict rules that limited how much in tax credits could be used each year. "Now there's probably 10 requests for every credit they've got," says Jay Hollingsworth of Capital Development, a Memphis development company. "They're as good as gold now." The current federal rehabilitation tax credit is equal to 20 percent of the cost of rehabilitating building officially designated as historic, or 10 percent of the cost of rehabilitating non-historic buildings that were built before 1936.

Memphis is one of those cities that is benefiting from the rehabilitation tax credit. Such credits have helped renovate crumbling Victorian townhomes and turn the old National Biscuit Co. distribution site, the Gayoso Hotel and the former Memphis Cotton Exchange into luxury apartment units. Some of these projects have been able to use both rehabilitation credits and low-income tax credits by renting a percentage of units to low-income tenants.

In many places, changing the zoning code is equally important. During the 1950s and '60s, cities all over the country wrote segregated-use codes that marked off downtown districts for commercial development and actively discouraged, or even prohibited, market-rate housing downtown. To draw maximum advantage from the renewed interest in central-city living, some cities have rewritten their codes from scratch, codifying the principle of mixed use — stores, offices and apartments coexisting with each other, even in the densest part of the downtown corridor. Others are taking the less cumbersome step of creating special mixed-use overlay districts, or simply making it clear that the city council is prepared to grant variances for downtown residential purposes.

Dayton, Ohio, for example, has massaged its zoning code to create "PUDs"— project unit developments. These are special mini-zones with their own criteria for which uses are allowed and how much parking is required. Two residential projects slated for the edge of downtown in a warehouse district zoned for commercial and industrial development, but not housing, have been designated as PUDs.

Zoning isn't the only factor that can interfere with residential downtown development. Developers in Memphis want the city to condemn buildings more aggressively so they can assemble property and begin their work. Mayor Willie Herenton agrees with them. "They're absolutely right," he says. "If we use our condemnation powers more, we can create more opportunities."

Condemnation proved essential when Memphis began amassing land for a new minor league baseball stadium diagonally across from the Peabody Hotel, one of the city's earliest restoration projects. Memphis condemned more than just the ground that the stadium was to be built on. Additional land surrounding the field now is under contract for the development of high-density market-rate housing.

Memphis lay fallow for so long, due to the wholesale abandonment of downtown in the decades after King's death, that historic buildings were not torn down to make room for shiny new office towers. That provides many opportunities for using the rehabilitation tax credits. "Memphis has everything left," says developer Jay Hollingsworth.

"There wasn't any incentive to build anything. The banks believed downtown was going down the hole and at some point would fall into the Mississippi. We have all the old buildings that can be redone, and are being redone. We've become fortunate because of our previous misfortune."

Hollingsworth himself lives in the old Exchange Building right in the middle of downtown, once the headquarters of the Memphis Cotton Exchange: His two-level loft has mosaic tile floors and 23-foot ceilings in the living and dining area. The building was vacant from 1979 until renovation began in March 1995. Now it has 202 apartments and an occupancy rate of about 93 percent.

Who are the new residents of downtown

Memphis? There's no simple answer to that question. Even within the Exchange Building, there are low-income tenants, whose rents start at $425 a month, and wealthier residents such as Hollingsworth, who pay closer to $1,800 for the choicest units.

The best guess, though, is that about three-quarters of those living in downtown Memphis are professionals who either work there or commute outward. Some of them are "empty-nest" gentrifiers, middle-aged married couples who don't want the big house in the suburbs anymore. Phil Woodard, the Hotel Grand developer, is one of those. "I got bored sitting down on the couch and eating pizza on a Friday afternoon," says Woodard, whose youngest child will be out of high school soon.

But there's also a significant "pre-nest" population — students, singled adults and young couples with no children, who want the excitement and the buzz of downtown. There are also some elderly people who might have preferred a downtown apartment years ago, if a supply of comfortable ones had existed.

The one group that's not highly represented in most cities' market-rate housing is families with young children. But in Memphis, there are even some of those. Mud Island, the suburban-like enclave in the middle of the river, is home to lots of them. A new city school is planned for Memphis to accommodate all the children living on Mud Island and in some of the other new projects downtown.

CHAPTER 29

Minneapolis, Other Cities, Redevelop Contaminated Land Areas

Charles Bartsch

With as many as 600,000 potential sites nationwide, brownfields continue to be an important issue for local governments of all sizes. Brownfields come in all shapes and sizes, including defunct or partially operating manufacturing plants, abandoned gas stations, dying or dead strip shopping and commercial centers, agricultural operations, and even residential areas. They are found in urban, suburban, and rural locations. The cleanup and reuse of these sites has become the subject of considerable government and political attention, with broad interagency and bipartisan support for such initiatives. More and more, the public and private sectors are forming partnerships to realize the economic and environmental benefits of brownfield redevelopment.

The realm of brownfield finance is rapidly evolving. To solve the brownfield financing puzzle, local leaders and agencies need to make imaginative use of the various public and private financing tools, identifying new funding combinations and approaches that make projects work. This article identifies the financing barriers to brownfield reuse, discusses public-sector approaches for facilitating brownfield redevelopment, and summarizes the litany of available brownfield financing resources.

Barriers to Brownfield Reuse

Lack of adequate and affordable financing is the most significant barrier to reusing contaminated sites. Lender liability concerns, investor expectations for return on investment, and the creditworthiness of borrowers must all be addressed within the context of the nature of the contamination, the costs of site preparation, the impact of contamination on collateral value, and marketable reuse of the site. Site remediation and related preparation costs make many sites economically uncompetitive, placing too much pressure on the bottom line — at least initially. Private parties often are not able or willing on their own to invest the resources needed to take a brownfield through its full redevelopment cycle.

Originally published as "Financing Brownfield Cleanup and Redevelopment," *Government Finance Review*, Vol. 18, No. 1, February 2002. Reprinted with permission of the Government Finance Officers Association, publisher of *Government Finance Review*, 203 N. LaSalle St., Suite 2700, Chicago, IL 60601–1210. (312/977-9700; fax: 312/977-4806; email: GFR@gfoa@org: Web: www.gfoa.org.) Annual subscriptions: $35.

Developers often have trouble putting together a complete financing package for brownfields. Specifically, developers have difficulty acquiring the capital to pay for three activities unique to brownfield redevelopment: the site assessment, the site remediation plan, and the actual site cleanup. The purpose of the site assessment is to determine the type and level of contamination by means of both primary (e.g., on-site sampling) and secondary (e.g., maps, historical records, etc.) research by technical experts. The site remediation plan is required for participation in a state voluntary cleanup program, which can streamline the cleanup process and help clarify the liability of prospective purchasers, lenders, property owners, and others with regard to the site.

Other factors make brownfield remediation a financial twilight zone for prospective developers. For starters, they will likely have to pledge a higher rate of return to their investors or lenders to persuade them to take on a project with greater perceived risk. This so-called "brownfield premium" may translate into an extra 10 to 20 percent return on investment, or one or two additional interest points on a loan rate. Project underwriting needs are inherently more extensive and, consequently, more expensive. Before assuming the risks of such a project, many lenders require environmental data collection and analysis, additional testing, and independent corroboration of collateral value. These requirements complicate loan processing and review procedures and increase transaction costs. Some banking analysts have estimated that these transaction costs have tripled since the emergence of the brownfield issue 10 years ago.

Finally, lenders tend to impose a number of conditions on the financing that they provide for contaminated properties. For example, they usually require developers to have at least 25 percent equity in the project to make sure that the borrower has sufficient capital at risk—a seriousness threshold, so to speak. Most banks also adhere to an informal rule of thumb in evaluating the viability of a project—cleanup costs should not exceed 25 percent of the fair market value of the property once it is clean. All of the foregoing considerations make brownfield redevelopment a thorny undertaking for private developers.

The Public Sector: Catalyst for Brownfield Redevelopment

Clearly, many brownfield projects simply do not work without some kind of public-sector involvement—especially at the local level. Hundreds of successful brownfield reuse projects have demonstrated that the public sector must make the first move to get these projects off the ground. Indeed, some form of local, state, or federal financial participation—even at seemingly miniscule levels of just a few thousand dollars—is often needed to jump start a brownfield reuse project and to reduce the risk thereof to a level that the private sector will accept. Public financing initiatives typically employ one or more of the following four strategies:

1. *Reducing the lender's risks* can make capital more available. Incentives such as loan guarantees or companion loans can ensure a minimum return by limiting the borrower's exposure to unforeseen problems that can affect the value of collateral or the borrower's ability to pay.

2. *Reducing the borrower's financing costs* can make capital more affordable. To this end, local officials have subsidized interest costs through tax-exempt financing and low-inter-

---

Defining Brownfields

The Environmental Protection Agency defines brownfields as abandoned, idled, or underused facilities where expansion or redevelopment is complicated by real or perceived contamination. A brownfield site typically has active redevelopment potential for commercial, residential, or recreational uses.

Exhibit 1
Low- or No-Cost Local Support of Brownfield Financing Efforts

- Facilitate site assembly and title clearance
- Connect site owners with state brownfield voluntary cleanup programs and help them negotiate a remediation strategy
- Direct site owners to information on federal and state programs and other incentives
- Offer local tax incentives or access to tax-exempt financing
- Assist site owners in initiating institutional or engineering controls and land covenants, and monitoring these controls over time
- Help prospective site reusers secure private financing by facilitating loan packaging
- Separate the environmental risk from the economic value of the property through mechanisms such as land leases, indemnities, and environmental insurance

---

est loans, and have reduced loan underwriting and documentation costs through loan packaging assistance and technical support.

3. *Improving the borrower's financial situation* through tax credits, tax abatements, or repayment grace periods can improve the project's cash flow and make it easier for the project numbers to pencil out. Similarly, training and technical assistance can offset a user's start-up costs and allow available cash to be devoted to meeting brownfield needs.

4. *Providing direct financial assistance* for site assessment and cleanup in the form of grants and forgivable loans is an increasingly popular strategy among local governments.

Because competition for public monies is increasingly fierce, local officials need to recognize that resources devoted to brownfield reuse represent an investment that often is recoverable from either the sale of the site or from new tax revenues. Public investment in brownfield reuse also can be used to leverage private investment by legitimizing the economic viability of an area. In essence, this is simply putting a brownfield spin on the public sector's classic role in economic development finance — that of catalyst.

Some cities have overcome the financing barriers by simply paying for site assessment, cleanup, and preparation themselves and then delivering a clean, "shovel ready" parcel to a private developer for reuse. The City of Minneapolis, for example, advanced its own goal of commercial development of brownfield sites by assembling and cleaning up what is now known as the Quarry Retail Center and then turning it over to a developer for $1. The site, which now has nearly 100,000 square feet of retail space, has created 1,170 jobs and generates more than $3 million per year in new tax revenues — more than justifying the initial public outlay. Trenton, Portland, Chicago, and several other cities have pursued similar strategies.

Other localities have taken similar steps to promote brownfield reuse in their communities. Ocanto, Wisconsin, is facilitating practical reuse of a small site common to all cities — an abandoned gas station. Working with the state's voluntary cleanup program, Ocanto has converted the blighted site into a small landscaped parking lot serving main street retail. Another city — Moline, Illinois — has assumed a brownfields brokering role. Recently, Moline coordinated the funding and technical assistance efforts of federal, state, and non-profit development partners to redevelop a mostly abandoned riverfront industrial site into a residential and commercial complex complete with recreational facilities.

The bottom line is that many brownfield projects do not work without some kind of local government involvement. As such, cities or development authorities are uniquely positioned to jump start the reuse process and move it through the critical make-or-break early phases. Creativity in meeting project needs is paramount. Exhibit 1 lists a variety of low- or no-cost initiatives local officials can take to enhance the financing equation and thereby attract private investment. These can be just as effective as writing a check or providing a grant.

Brownfield Financing Resources

More and more communities are devising creative solutions to the brownfield financing conundrum by leveraging a combination of available federal, state, and local resources. Unfortunately, many local officials are unaware of the breadth of these resources. This section is intended to provide a useful summary of federal, state, and local sources of brownfield funding.

Federal Programs

The numerous federal programs that can be used for the purpose of brownfield financing are summarized in Exhibit 2. The challenge for local officials is to translate their funding needs into activities that meet the eligibility criteria of these programs, many of which are intended to be used in conjunction with private funding sources. Federal resources for brownfield financing are discussed below.

Department of Housing and Urban Development. HUD programs offer the most resources and the most flexibility. The agency awards community development block grants to jurisdictions of all sizes, which can use the funds for any activity that meets one of three broad national objectives: (1) benefit persons of low and moderate income, (2) aid in the prevention or elimination of slums or blight, or (3) meet other community development needs of particular urgency. As of 1997, coping with contamination has been defined as an eligible block grant activity. Since then, more than 50 cities have used CDBG resources specifically for this purpose. Cities ranging in size from Chicago to Somerville, Massachusetts, have used CDBG funds to clean up brownfields for reuse. Other cities have used the money to capitalize local revolving loan funds for brownfield purposes. Youngstown, Ohio, is using CDBG funds to pay first-year loan costs incurred by a new manufacturing plant located on a brownfield site.

HUD's Section 108 loan guarantee program is linked to the block grant program. Section 108 was authorized to help cities finance site clearance, property acquisition, infrastructure, rehabilitation, or related activities that are too large for single year block grant funding. An increasing number of cities are using Section 108 to fund brownfield projects. For example, Denver is using 108 for short-term construction loans on downtown projects, with the developers repaying the notes upon the sale of the properties. Mid-sized cities such as Yonkers, New York, have used Section 108 proceeds to establish brownfield revolving loan funds. And San Luis Obisbo, California, is using $1.5 million of Section 108 funds to build senior housing.

For the last three years, Congress has provided HUD with $25 million for its Brownfield Economic Development Initiative, one of only three programs specifically authorized for brownfield financing. These funds are awarded competitively. Buffalo is using $240,000 in BEDI funds for site preparation and remediation at the Union Ship Canal commercial and office project. Provo, Utah, is using $1 million in BEDI funds to complete environmental site work and demolition at a former steel plant, which will be converted into a multipurpose facility that will include office and retail space, a warehousing and distribution operation, and a minor league baseball stadium. Phillipsburg, New Jersey, is using $500,000 in BEDI funds to acquire 100 acres of the Ingersoll Rand site, which it plans to redevelop as a modern industrial park.

Department of Transportation. Some communities have made creative use of Department of Transportation funds for brownfield purposes. As a growing number of case studies demonstrate, there are three specific ways that transportation projects can be connected to brownfield projects. First, the brownfield site itself be a transportation facility (typically roads or railyards) in need of

---

Exhibit 2
Federal Programs Applicable to
Brownfield Financing

Equity Capital
- SBA's Small Business Investment Companies

Grants
- EDA Title I (public works) and Title IX (economic adjustment)
- EPA assessment pilot grants
- DOT (various system construction and rehabilitation programs)
- DOT's transportation and community system preservation (TCSP) pilot grants
- HUD's Brownfield Economic Development Initiative (BEDI)
- HUD's Community Development Block Grants (for projects locally determined)
- Army Corps of Engineers (cost-shared services)

Loans
- EDA's Title IX (capital for local revolving loan funds)
- EPA capitalized brownfield revolving loan funds
- EPA capitalized clean water revolving loan funds (priorities set/programs run by each state)
- HUD funds for locally determined CDBG loans and "floats"
- SBA's microloans
- SBA's Section 504 development company debentures

Loan Guarantees
- HUD's Section 108 loan guarantees
- SBA's Section 7(a) and Low-Doc programs

Tax-Advantaged Zones
- HUD/USDA Empowerment Zones (various incentives)
- HUD/USDA Enterprise Communities (various incentives)

Tax Incentives and Tax-Exempt Financing
- Targeted expensing of cleanup costs (through December 31, 2003)
- Historic rehabilitation tax credits
- Low-income housing tax credits
- Industrial development bonds

For a complete description of all these programs and how they can meet specific brownfield needs, click on "brownfields" at nemw.org.

---

upgrading. Second, transportation system improvements may be needed to make a brownfield site more marketable, usually by expanding access for vehicles, freight, or passengers. And third, the transportation solution may contribute to the environmental solution, particularly where roads, parking lots, and other transportation structures are used as caps to limit exposure to hazardous materials.

Emeryville, California, has connected various sources of transportation funding to its brownfield reuse strategies. The city successfully marketed an old Chevron tank facility to Amtrak for its new Bay Area main station, beating out Oakland and San Francisco.

Emeryville is promoting redevelopment of adjoining brownfields into office and residential uses, using roadways as contamination caps to facilitate reuse. The city also used federal transportation dollars to construct a pedestrian network linking all of these sites together.

Economic Development Administration. EDA provides grants to communities in support of public works activities. During the past three years, EDA has made brownfield redevelopment one of its funding priorities, spending nearly 20 percent of its project resources on brownfield-related activities. EDA's public works program supports industrial development activities, while its economic adjustment and defense economic adjustment programs capitalize locally run revolving loan funds to enhance business development activities in distressed areas. Uniontown, Pennsylvania, used $923,000 in public works funding to renovate an old factory into a multi-tenant facility. Rome, New York, used $2.5 million in defense adjustment assistance for a business park expansion. These are just two recent examples of brownfield-related EDA projects.

Environmental Protection Agency. Three key EPA programs have helped finance various aspects of brownfield reuse. EPA's assessment pilot program provides $200,000 grants to cities, towns, and other governmental entities to cover site assessment and predevelopment costs. To date, EPA has made nearly 400 such pilot awards. Because of its public-sector focus, prospective site owners wishing to use this program need to work closely with their communities.

EPA provides capital to local revolving loan funds for the purpose of financing site cleanup. Revolving loan fund resources must be used at sites that are owned by government agencies or quasi-public entities like industrial development authorities. Still, private parties may tap into these funds as long as they did not contribute to or cause the contamination. The program has not been used much to date, but recent changes make it much more attractive. The agency now provides capitalization grants of up to $1 million to state and local governments—double the former ceiling—and allows a five-year time-frame for obligating the funds. Eligibility requirements have been liberalized so that recipients need only demonstrate that they have an established brownfield program to qualify for funding. The new policies also give state and local governments greater flexibility in how they use their revolving loan fund capital.

A third program has great potential but has been little used to date. Each state has been given capital to operate clean water revolving fund programs, which are used to make low- or no-interest loans of up to 20 years for projects with water quality impacts, including those that deal with petroleum contamination. State revolving funds can be used for the excavation and disposal of underground storage tanks; the capping of wells; the excavation, removal, and disposal of contaminated soil or sediments; well abandonment; and Phase I, II, or III assessments. Subject to broad EPA guidelines, each state determines who may use its revolving fund resources. EPA specifically allows local governments, citizen groups, non-profit organizations, and individuals to participate in these programs.

Brownfield projects with a water component can access these clean water revolving loan funds. To date, however, only a few states—notably New Mexico, New York, and Ohio—have encouraged the use of these funds for brownfield-related projects. Ohio-based Grant Realty Company used one of these loans to remedy contaminated groundwater and soil at a 20-acre industrial site in Cleveland and to prepare it for commercial development.

Tax Incentives. Two federal tax incentives can be used to make brownfield projects more attractive and less risky to developers, lenders, and investors. The first—low-income housing tax credits—capitalizes on the growing interest in reusing brownfield properties for residential purposes. All states receive an allocation of federal low-income housing tax credits that can be used to attract financing for these projects. Milwaukee, Portland, and a growing number of other cities are linking brownfields and housing projects with these tax credits.

Trenton, New Jersey, provides a good example of the use of low-income housing tax credits in brownfield redevelopment. In that city, the Circle F housing project was developed on a contaminated manufacturing site dating back to 1886. Working with a local neighborhood organization, the city subdivided the site and targeted the older front half of the parcel for senior citizen housing. Officials selected an established local non-profit developer to undertake the housing project. The developer fronted the $500,000 for site cleanup and preparation, and applied for and received $8 million in federal low-income housing tax credits through the state. These credits attracted a private lender, which helped finance the project. The lender assumed the role of a limited partner to benefit from the tax credits, which made the rate of return on the investment acceptable. Circle F is now the core of a reviving neighborhood in Trenton.

The brownfield tax expensing incentive is directly targeted at contaminated sites. Developers can deduct environmental cleanup costs for the year in which they are incurred instead of capitalizing them over time. Eligible costs include site assessment and cleanup, operations and maintenance, and state voluntary cleanup program oversight fees. In December 2000, Congress eliminated several restrictions from the original 1997 legislation, making it possible for virtually any owner of a brownfield to take advantage of the incentive. The signature example of the application of this incentive to brownfield redevelopment is Pacific Bell Park in downtown San Francisco. Quick recovery of the considerable cleanup costs at this site had an impact of several million dollars on the project.

State Programs

States continue to be at the forefront of creative brownfield financing efforts. Almost half of the states have developed programs that have proven effective in overcoming brownfield reuse barriers. The programs, which are summarized in Exhibit 3, fall into four broad categories: tax incentives, targeted financial assistance, direct financial assistance, and other brownfield financing initiatives. Each of these categories is briefly discussed below.

Nearly half the states offer some kind of tax incentives for brownfield projects, most often in the form of either credits or abatements. Most of these incentives are targeted to offset cleanup costs. Tax incentives enhance a project's cash flow by redirecting revenues from state coffers back into the project itself. This, in turn, enhances a project's financial viability in the eyes of potential lenders. Historically, tax initiatives have been used to channel capital investment and to promote economic development. Brownfield redevelopment is a natural evolution of this tool.

Targeted financial assistance programs, which typically involve revolving loan funds or loan guarantees, accomplish several objectives. They help reassure lenders by limiting the risk of potential losses. They also can improve the borrower's cash flow by plugging financing holes or offsetting the up-front costs of site cleanup. During 2001 state legislative sessions, lawmakers focused more on this category of brownfield financing than any other.

Nearly one-third of the states have dedicated resources to directly finance brownfield activities that the private sector avoids, such as site assessment and cleanup. Most often, direct financial assistance comes from bond proceeds or dedicated state revenues.

Exhibit 3
State Innovations in
Brownfield Financing

Direct financial assistance: 13 states, including:
- Brownfield/environmental general obligation bond issues in Michigan ($255 million), New York ($200 million), and Ohio ($200 million)
- Low-interest cleanup loans in Delaware, Minnesota, and New Jersey
- Wisconsin's $40 million package of grant and loan programs

Targeted financial assistance: 19 states, including:
- Florida's loan guarantees/loan loss reserves
- Indiana's RLF remediation loans (up to 20 percent forgivable)
- Illinois' Redevelopment Loan Program for private parties
- Massachusetts' Reclamation Payback Fund guarantees
- Wisconsin's earmarking of state CDBG funds

Tax incentives: 22 states, including:
- Colorado's sliding-scale remediation tax credit
- Illinois' transferable 25 percent remediation tax credit
- Michigan's 100 percent single business tax abatement
- New Jersey's Environmental Opportunity Zone property tax abatement/rebate
- Ohio's 10 percent/$500,000 assessment and cleanup cost tax credit
- Minnesota's hazardous waste sub-district TIFs

Other brownfield financing initiatives: 10 states, including:
- Michigan's "brownfield redevelopment authorities"
- Wisconsin's Brownfield Environmental Assessment Program and back-tax forgiveness
- Pennsylvania's Key Sites Initiative, which provides funding for contractors to do site assessments and prepare cleanup plans
- Massachusetts' Access to Capital Program, which includes $15 million to cover environmental insurance premiums on state-negotiated policies with AIG insurance company

For more information on each state's programs, click on "brownfields" at www.nemw.org

---

A handful of states have developed other brownfield financing initiatives that are intended to level the economic playing field between greenfield and brownfield sites by limiting risk or offsetting critical costs. Most of these programs were enacted as a way to leverage private investment while limiting public spending.

Local Programs

The state initiatives described in this article provide a solid foundation upon which local governments can build their own brownfield financing strategies. In general, local governments could better position themselves to support brownfield reuse projects by putting a new twist on existing economic development finance programs. This could involve something as simple as recognizing site assessment and remediation needs as legitimate project development activities within the scope of such programs. The most common forms of local government involvement in brownfield financing are discussed below.

Tax Increment Financing. Tax increment financing uses the anticipated growth in property taxes from a development project to finance public-sector investment therein. Traditionally, TIF has been used for a variety of economic revitalization efforts, usually in economically distressed or abandoned areas. Tax increment financing is the most common form of local support for brownfield reuse, and it can be easily packaged with other funding sources. Jurisdictions of all sizes have successfully used tax increment financing for the purpose of brownfield redevelopment. Tiny Frankfort, Michigan (population 1,500), for example, is working with a county-wide brownfield redevelopment authority to link TIF bond financing to cleanup efforts at an abandoned lumber mill and at decades-old orchards contaminated by pesticides.

Tax Abatements. Abatements are reductions of or forgiveness from tax liabilities. Tax abatements usually take one of two forms: (1) a reduction in rates for a specific period of time, usually 5 or 10 years, or (2) the freezing of property values, usually at a pre-improvement stage. The key advantage of tax abatement programs is that they give local governments a workable, flexible incentive that helps influence private investment decisions — a useful tool for promoting brownfield reuse. However, tax abatements must be carefully designed to target intended beneficiaries without offering unnecessary subsidies, a feat that can be difficult to accomplish. As a result, tax abatement programs have numerous critics.

Some abatement programs feature sliding scales that offer full abatements initially, when business cash needs are the greatest. Several states allow their political subdivisions this option, including Connecticut, Idaho, Maryland, Ohio, and Texas. Local governments in these states address the issue of remediated brownfield property re-valuation by allowing several years to lapse before the property is fully assessed at the value of its new use. This type of abatement provided the necessary cash flow to allow the owner of the 26-acre Vinson Street site in Dallas to pay for the cleanup himself. He later invested $1.2 million into a new wood pallet recycling operation.

Locally Capitalized, Locally Operated Revolving Loan Funds. Several cities have established local revolving loan funds for brownfield redevelopment, including Rochester and Yonkers, New York, Los Angeles, and Baltimore. Initially funded in 1997 with $2.5 million in empowerment zone funds, Baltimore's Brownfield Loan Fund has enjoyed tremendous success thus far. To date, the fund has made $2.4 million in loans to seven different brownfield projects, creating 233 jobs. Already, $475,000 has been repaid and is available for new projects. This amount includes $340,000 from the Lancaster Square mixed-use office and residential project in the city's Fells Point neighborhood, where the loan paid for the cleanup and removal of several underground tanks. The loan was retired using historic tax credit receipts.

General Obligation Bonds. Economic development practitioners can make a strong case for using general obligation bond proceeds to support brownfield cleanup and reuse projects. Brownfield redevelopment, which creates jobs and enhances the local tax base, is an appropriate use of public resources. For the purpose of brownfield redevelopment, cities typically issue general obligation bonds for ac-

---

H.R. 2869: Small Business Liability Relief and Brownfields Revitalization Act

On December 20, 2001, Congress approved a brownfields bill that will strengthen local efforts to facilitate the redevelopment of contaminated sites by providing more regulatory finality and project resources. The bill, highlights of which are summarized below, was passed more than eight years after Congress first considered brownfield proposals.

Title I: Brownfield Revitalization Funding
* Provides for $200 million per year (through 2006) in grants to states, local and tribal governments, and quasi-public redevelopment agencies and authorities.
* Funding is to be used for (1) site assessment grants of up to $200,000 (EPA has discretion to increase this amount to $350,000 under some circumstances) and (2) cleanup grants of up to $200,000 for direct remediation (up to $1 million for revolving loan fund capital).
* Funding criteria include the extent to which the money will be used to protect human health and the environment; spur redevelopment and create jobs; and preserve open space and parks. Projects also should be distributed fairly between urban and rural areas and involve the local communities.
$50 million (or 25 percent of appropriation if less than $200 million) may be used for sites with petroleum contamination.
* Insurance premiums are an eligible use of funds.
* Authorizes EPA to operate a brownfield program that includes training, research, and technical assistance activities.

Title II: Liability Clarifications
H.R. 2869 provides Superfund liability relief to:
* Contiguous property owners who provide cooperation and access for the cleanup.
* Prospective purchasers who are not responsible for contamination at the site and who do not impede its cleanup (the bill includes windfall lien provisions for sites where the government pays for cleanup, thus enhancing the fair market value of the property).
* Innocent landowners.

Title III: State Response Programs
* Authorizes $50 million per year (through 2006) in grants to states and tribal governments to establish and enhance state VCPs and response programs.
* Requires states to maintain — and to update annually — a "public record of sites" addressed through their programs.
* Establishes "finality" — sites addressed through state programs are protected from EPA enforcement and cost recovery actions under CERCLA, with a few narrow exceptions.

---

quiring land, preparing sites, and making infrastructure improvements. Many cities have used general obligation debt to support some aspect of their brownfield redevelopment strategies. Chicago used bonds to pay for assessment and cleanup at several key industrial park sites. Bridgeport, Connecticut, used bond proceeds to finance a minor league baseball stadium on a contaminated site, using its share of gate and concession receipts to service the debt.

Conclusion

Underused or abandoned industrial facilities remain a national concern. Confronting the environmental and economic issues affecting site reuse require a deliberate, multidimensional approach that does not always conform to the rules and procedures of federal, state, and local economic development or environmental programs. The lack of adequate and affordable financing has emerged as the most significant barrier to brownfield redevelopment. Site assessment and cleanup requires financial resources that many private firms either lack or cannot easily secure. The public sector can act as an important catalyst for brownfield redevelopment by leveraging the programs and resources identified in this article to encourage private investment.

CHAPTER 30

Nashua Takes Measures to Reduce Global Warming

Jennifer Schroeder

There has been increased attention recently to the roles local communities can play in the effort to halt global warming. From the big-picture, public benefit point of view, urban planning, community ordinances and public-private partnerships can help create a new energy future and protect air quality—and these are vital roles. Yet from a pragmatic, paying-the-bills-and-keeping-the-lights-on/buses-running/snowplows-moving perspective, energy costs and even energy capacity and infrastructure are increasingly sticky issues for local government. Officials from two Granite State cities, Concord and Nashua, recently had the opportunity to learn more about—and witness firsthand—energy alternatives and local leadership on curbing global warming.

It's one thing to hear about "global warming solutions"—it's quite another to understand what those solutions might look like in your community, how to get started, and how these solutions improve the community and its bottom line. Nashua city planner Angela Vincent and Concord Community Development Director Roger Hawk were part of a U.S. delegation of municipal representatives who traveled to Toronto's 6th annual "Smog Summit" in June. They participated with five other Northeast cities (Boston, New York City, Portland, Montpelier and Pittsburg) in a cross-border knowledge exchange hosted by Clean Air–Cool Planet, a nonprofit organization helping communities, businesses and campuses reduce greenhouse gas emissions.

The three-day tour was packed with firsthand, working examples of innovative energy systems along with illustrations of partnerships and processes that make the systems work. Toronto is a prime demonstration ground because the Canadian city has managed to aggressively pursue greenhouse gas reductions (greenhouses gases are the heat-trapping pollutants that result from the burning of fossil fuels and contribute to human-induced global warming) while also securing additional energy supplies that fit with the city's short-term needs and long-range vision of planning.

Angela Vincent, a city planner from Nashua stated, "Being in a non-attainment zone that includes the Boston metro area is affecting Nashua's air quality. This program will work to offset that by choosing palatable

Originally published as "Toronto's Renewable Energy Solutions," *New Hampshire Town and City*, Vol. XLIX, No. 9, October 2006. Published by the New Hampshire Local Government Center, Concord, NH. Reprinted with permission of the publisher.

options to reduce greenhouse gas emissions by increasing energy efficiency and ultimately, best of all, saving money on energy costs. We see this as a win–win–win situation for city government, citizens and the business community. We are looking forward to this program getting very big, very soon!"

Hawke, Vincent and the group first heard presentations from municipal officials about Toronto's overall energy picture. Toronto is working hard to address what is projected to be an energy supply shortage within five to seven years without the addition of substantial new sources. The city is focusing first on conservation and then on distributed generation options to avoid the logistical nightmare of siting a very large fossil fuel plant in the greater Toronto area. Having received this contextual information, the U.S. city representatives then got up close and personal tours of Toronto's wind turbine — the first urban wind turbine in North America — as well as a hydrogen refueling station servicing several municipal hydrogen vehicles and an innovative "district cooling plant."

The wind turbine is a prominent feature on the drive along the downtown Toronto lake shore, sited on the grounds of Exhibition Place, a large and historic public park on the Lake Ontario waterfront. The turbine serves not only as a working energy generator but also as an educational exhibit for which there is completely open public access. It was erected in 2002 in a partnership between a local utility (Toronto Hydro) and a citizen's cooperative. The emissions free turbine produces enough energy to power 250 households. The annual greenhouse gas reductions associated with the turbine are 1,180 a year. Hawk and Vincent learned from Toronto officials that the wind turbine is silent; is less lethal to birds than the high-rise buildings scattered throughout the downtown area (hundreds of bird killed per year, versus one documented dead bird for the wind turbine); and has never posed any problems with ice.

On the same site as the turbine is the hy-drogen refueling station, built as a test station and now serving fleet vehicles for the city. Plans are to introduce more hydrogen fleet vehicles. Another innovative project, a district heating and cooling plant that pulls cold water from deep in Lake Ontario, is serving the needs of downtown Toronto's business district, providing emissions-free heating and cooling at a fixed cost for business and commercial customers. The deep-water cooling plant was funded largely by a group of private investors already seeing higher-than-projected returns from the very large (and very capital intensive) initiative.

The value in getting up-close-and-personal looks at these projects was not just in offering models of specific technologies, but in providing insight into the creative problem-solving processes and collaborative partnerships that allowed them to happen. One such example, vital in moving projects like the wind turbine and district cooling station forward, is the Toronto Atmospheric Fund (TAF). Hawke, Vincent and the others got an inside view into this mechanism from TAF Executive Director Phil Jessup. The fund offers low-interest loans to finance capital projects that will lead to greenhouse gas reductions. The loans are then repaid from efficiency-related cost savings or other project revenues. This has proved to be a very effective investment mechanism for the City of Toronto, and projects funded by the TAF have resulted in cumulative greenhouse gas reductions of 225,000 tons and saved the city over $2.7 million annually in energy and maintenance costs.

Another example of an effective facilitation and management measure is the Clean Air Partnership, a regional group with representatives from communities across the greater Toronto area who work together on developing region-wide policies and programs to fight air pollution. The Clean Air Partnership organizes the Toronto Smog Summit every year, providing a forum for informational presentations on best practices. Hawke, Vincent and the rest of the Clean Air–Cool Planet (CA–CP) cross-border contingent took part in the summit, where CA–CP presented some of its successes with US cities, and Canadian officials shared successful projects in their communities as well. Examples presented at the summit of initiatives that achieved greenhouse gas reductions, cost savings and more livable communities included LED traffic light switchouts; building retrofits; recycling; fuel switching; public transit projects; hybrid and alternative-fuel fleets; and residential and commercial public education programs targeting energy efficiency.

One of the most useful aspects of the CA–CP cross-border exchange was that it offered an opportunity for Vincent and Hawke to network and socialize informally with professionals from other Northeast communities also taking part in the trip.

"Clean Air–Cool Planet's role," explains Koehler, "is to facilitate leadership, and to convene people so the leaders and champions who've learned about this — sometimes the hard way — can help mentor others. Whether it's [Portland Solid Waste Director] Troy Moon sharing his city's plans for developing a climate action plan or [Pittsburg businesswoman and Green Building Partnership president] Rebecca Flores explaining green building work, resources are being leveraged. Intellectual capital is being leveraged. And that's something a local government can always benefit from."

As vice-president of the New Hampshire Planner's Association and former city planner for the City of Keene, Koehler has some firsthand experience of the needs of local governments. Keene has been a leader in climate protection initiatives by completing a long-term climate action plan and implementing many of the recommendations. Keene has switched the entire public fleet to biodiesel, captures methane from the recycling center to generate power, and installed a geothermal pump in the public works building. The city also administers many public education campaigns including an aggressive anti-idle program. The city found that these changes were good not only from an environmental perspective but for its bottom line, resulting in less equipment failure, fewer employee health problems, and more reliable power supplies at fixed costs. Koehler now works to share these Keene success stories as well as CA–CP's additional successes in other Northeast communities, with local government staff and officials who can use the information day-to-day to steer their communities toward a lower global warming "footprint."

Koehler, along with Steve Whitman from Jeffrey Taylor and Associates, recently presented a session at the Northern New England Chapter of the American Planning Association (NNECAPA) conference that was held in September on different projects communities have implemented in order to address climate change at the local level. "Communities are increasingly feeling the impacts of a changing climate," explains Koehler, "and those communities play vital roles in solving this problem because so many decisions determining individual and collective energy options are made at the local level."

Concord's Roger Hawke puts it this way. "Good government means we have to act to reduce our climate change footprint, diversify our energy supply, and make our community more sustainable — economically and ecologically. Seeing and hearing what our peers are doing is exciting and it moves us closer to understanding how we can meet these needs ourselves."

CHAPTER 31

Oakland, Other Cities, Use Technology to Guide Urban Growth

Ken Snyder

Some of the challenges facing communities today involve dealing with a rapid growth in population and an even more rapid growth in land area because of low-density development patterns. Low density development, often referred to as sprawl, comes in many forms, and its impacts include the loss of open space and prime agricultural land, as well as a transportation infrastructure that is predominantly car-dependent, with too little population density to support public transit.

In their efforts to create healthy communities, how can localities be helped to understand the costs and benefits of different development patterns and thus make more informed decisions? This is the underlying question of this article. Making informed decisions also is an important way to approach the issue of growth management for public agencies. It's about enabling communities to help themselves, rather than trying to regulate solutions.

In the United States in particular, the federal government is limited in how much it can tell local communities about methods of managing their land. But the federal government can play an important role in directing localities to a variety of tools and resources helpful to them in understanding their choices and making informed decisions. The result of the U.S. Department of Energy's (DOE) efforts on Tools for Community Design and Decision, hopefully, will be healthier, more efficient, and more effective communities.

Many city and county managers are asking for tools and resources that improve community participation and input and that promote better decisions on land use and resource use. Local officials are frequently asked to make decisions without adequate information on the broader impacts of a proposed project or new development.

How will a given project affect the community in terms of taxes, demand placed on the transportation network, increased demands on schools and other services, air quality, energy use, water quality, and the like? There is a need for "decision support systems" that can help community leaders understand these costs and benefits more readily.

Originally published as "Decision Support Tools for Community Planning," *Public Management*, Vol. 83, No. 10, November 2001. Published by the International City/County Management Association, Washington, D.C. Reprinted with permission of the publisher.

Decision Support Systems: What Are They?

A bridge over a river is a useful metaphor for a decision support system. The water flowing below represents information, and in many ways, people are swimming in this information. After all, we live in the information age, and there is so much out there that it often is hard to know how to use it all.

But within this sea of data are pearls of wisdom: case studies of what works and what doesn't work; tried-and-true approaches to sustainable development; urban revitalization strategies that succeed; environmental preservation techniques linked with economic development; and methods for effective community participation.

Even when these pearls of wisdom have been located, managers may continue to feel stuck and at a loss for how to apply them. A colleague at DOE calls this syndrome "stranded inspiration," which occurs when communities inundated with good examples of other people's activities are left confounded as to how to use similar ideas in their own communities.

To help with this dilemma, decision support systems integrate information, tools, and participatory-process techniques to enable localities to move away from hit-and-miss development patterns toward more informed and vision-based decision making.

Tools and processes are the pillars of a bridge that can help us get across this sea. While tools are technological resources that help make sense of information, processes are ways in which people can apply information to make decisions, including techniques that increase pubic involvement and improve stakeholder input. Each pillar is critical; we may have the best tools in the world, but if they are not integrated into the right process, we are not going to get where we want to go. And without the right tools, a process can hit a dead end.

Technology is dramatically changing the art and science of planning. John Fregonese, a planning consultant based in Portland, Oregon, points out that the changes we are seeing in the area of planning tools are analogous to the changes we have seen in the field of medicine. Early technique like blood-letting were hit-or-miss attempts to attack symptoms, with little understanding of the causes behind them.

The CAT scan is an example of how we can now look at the body as a system, see under the skin, and locate and understand problems on a much more sophisticated level. More and more often, planners now have access to diagnostic tools that can help them reach more sophisticated, systems-level decisions.

The best example may be the ways in which geographical information system (GIS) technologies can assist planners in decision making. GIS tools give city and county managers the power to do computer mapping, tie data to places and processes, and understand development impacts in a spatial framework. These tools make it possible to see how the natural and built environments, plus the social and economic systems, of a community relate to each other on different scales and at different times.

Specific Tools for Community Design and Decision Making

So what's out there in terms of approaches to rural and urban design and to the decision-making process? A wide array of tools has emerged over the years, falling into many categories, including visualization, impact analysis, integrated GIS, predictive modeling, and community process tools. Here is a sampling of a few tools that planners might find useful.[1]

Box City.[2] The Box City planning method is a great example of a low-tech, highly effective, visual decision support tool. The low-tech aspect of Box City is one of the reasons it works so well. It uses kindergarten art supplies like box, paper, scissors, paste, and markers so that 4-years-olds, 40-year-olds, and 80-year-olds all know how to participate.

These material are used to build a 3-D replica of one's neighborhood, highlighting the treasures and precious elements that people want to preserve, as well as the things people want to change. It becomes a platform on which people can discuss where they are today and where they want to go in the future.

In Kansas City, Missouri, Box City was used by roughly 100 Washington-Wheatley neighborhood residents, who used cardboard and paper to construct tiny buildings, parks, and playgrounds. They built a miniature model of how they would like Prospect Avenue to look in the future. The Box City project then was photographed, documented, and translated into a plan for the city to implement.

Photomontage. Another visual technique is the photomontage, which is fancy lingo for doctoring up digital photos. For example, two images of East 14th Street in Oakland, California, show several ethnic neighborhoods. The first image shows present conditions: basically; strip-retail uses built along what used to be a main street. Through photomontaging, the existing image can be given a facelift and a possible vision for the future.

When communities can see "dreaded density" as a specific realistic image, they often say, "Well, that might not be too bad. I could live there." Even more important, a photomontage helps people see the relationship among different design elements. Adding a mixed-use development with combined retail and housing units, for instance, can make other elements fall into place. Now that there are more people living in this particular location, with more jobs to fill, a light-rail line has become viable.

With an increase in housing and jobs, a street market also becomes more viable. When people see that they are going to get nice shops and places to "hang out" in with neighbors,

they realize that there is a trade-off between density and amenities. In essence, the discussion topic switches from density to design.

3-D renderings on computers also have become more sophisticated and affordable. This technique can show the visual impacts of adding light rail to a street median, for example, or the change in neighborhood appearance with a new bridge or other transportation project where this might otherwise be hard to imagine.

CommunityViz. On the more sophisticated end of the spectrum of tools, CommunityViz software[3] is a set of GIS-based planning and decision support tools designed to empower people at different skill levels. It integrates GIS mapping and impact analysis information, 3-D visualization, and policy simulation technologies, which can be applied to a variety of planning and design issues in communities and towns. CommunityViz provides an interactive, 3-D real-time environment in which citizens and professionals can analyze proposed plans for their communities.

Users can propose policies and suggest design alternatives, seeing the aesthetic and cost impacts immediately. They can then visualize how different ideas might affect their environment in physical, economic, and social ways. This interactive process enables citizens, planners, designers, and public officials to make informed choices and to build consensus on proposed designs and public policies.

In Lyons, Colorado, the planning commission is using CommunityViz to develop a list of indicators of community values. Next, it will transform the permitting process from a first-come, first-served system into a system whereby proposed developments are tested against these indicators, and those projects that perform the best will get approved. This process effectively puts community values ahead of development interests.

UrbanSim. Designed to assist communities in integrating their land use, transportation, and environmental planning efforts, UrbanSim is a simulation system that models the real estate development process and the locations of households and jobs based on scenarios of transportation, land use, and environmental policies.[4] It is meant to support a community-visioning process by allowing communities to explore the potential consequences of alternative policy scenarios, such as light rail or highway expansion, and the use of urban growth boundaries and land-use plans to guide development.

By subdividing a metropolitan area into a grid system of 150-meter cells, the model is able to evaluate both neighborhood-scale and regional-scale issues. The UrbanSim system, now operational in several major metropolitan areas, is available from the Internet and has been developed as an Open Source project, meaning that the software and its source code is free and available for modification and redistribution.

Community Process Tools

Community process is a concept well embedded in U.S. history, involving ideas as basic as Jeffersonian democracy and civic engagement. Emerging technologies can help improve this process. Community process technologies include meetingware and keypad voting, which give stakeholders a more effective voice in decision making.

In 1999, for example, Mayor Anthony Williams used these technologies in Washington, D.C., to host a citywide town meeting on the city's strategic plan. Some 3,000 citizens participated in the exercise, which involved 300 tables with computers on them and 3,000 keypads to let everyone vote. On a level rarely seen, the organizers were able to collect an impressive amount of feedback from citizens. The important thing was that these tools helped the organizers to aggregate the comments by neighborhoods and stakeholder groups and thus to write a comprehensive plan to address different needs and concerns.

And, with Web-based meeting services, citizens don't have to be in the same room to participate in town meetings. Don't however, underestimate the value of meeting and talking face to face for building an effective community process.

A major challenge facing managers and planners is finding ways to integrate these tools into community decision making most effectively. It is important not to let the tool dictate the process. Instead, managers should identify the process needed to get the job done and then decide what sort(s) of tools are needed to make it happen.

PLACE³S. PLACE³S is an example of a process that uses a variety of these tools to generate success. PLACE³S — which stand for PLAnning for Community Energy and Economic and Environmental Sustainability — is a methodology for community-based planning that was developed by the state energy offices in Washington, Oregon, and California.

It uses a five-step, community-directed process. Through a visioning procedure that engages stakeholders, participants develop and evaluate alternatives that will improve upon business-as-usual conditions. One possible alternative would focus on maximizing resource efficiency. This is called the "advanced alternative," in which PLACE³S compares energy use, resource use, and their links to issues like cost and air quality.

The participants then work to hybridize the prior alternatives into a "community-preferred alternative." In the process, the community makes informed choices about trade-offs (lower-density transit means about $200 more per household in gasoline costs, e.g., and these dollars will leave the local economy). The ultimate objective is a well-understood and widely supported plan, with a mechanism to implement it.

Regional Resource Centers

The best systems for decision support bring diverse people together in one place.

Face-to-face interaction, mediated through the skilled use of decision-making tools, can help dissolve differences and fashion a unified vision of the future of the community.

Through a series of national workshops, the concept of setting up regional resource centers around the country has emerged. Chattanooga, Tennessee, has been at the forefront of making this concept a reality and is in the process of building a resource center as part of its trade center. The center will serve as an institutional knowledge base on the topic of Chattanooga's past (how the city got to where it is today), as well as a resource for determining the city's future.

Dramatic Changes Possible

The tools reviewed in this article have proved useful on multiple fronts. They have helped communities visualize where they are today and where they want to go in the future; they have helped decisionmakers quantify the impacts of their choices in terms of energy use, resource use, and other economic and social indicators; and they have aided city and county managers in improving public process, increasing public participation, and building a broad-based consensus on projects.

Advances in technologies hold the potential to change dramatically how communities shape their future. They can help shift decision making from a regulatory approach that mainly tries to prevent bad things from happening by telling people what they can't do, to a more proactive approach whereby decision making is optimized through rapid feedback on the impacts of different choices.

In essence, good tools, correctly applied, make the costs and benefits of choices more apparent and empower people to act more intelligently.

REFERENCES

1. The tools described here represent just a sample of the tools available to communities. Reference to any specific commercial product, process, or service by trade name, trademark, manufacturers' name, or otherwise does not necessarily imply its endorsement, recommendation, or favoring by the United States government or any agency thereof. Reproducing or reprinting of this material may require the explicit consent of the copyright owners.
2. For more information on Box City, visit the Web site at http://www.cubekc.org.
3. CommunityViz represents a suite of tools being developed by the Orton Family Foundation in partnership with several developers, including Green Mountain GeoGraphics, Ltd.; Fore Site Consulting, Inc.; MultiGen Paradigm, Inc.; and PricewaterhouseCoopers. For more information, visit http://www.communityviz.org.
4. UrbanSim is a software program developed by the University of Washington with funding from the National Science Foundation and state and metropolitan agencies. For more information on UrbanSim and to download the model, visit its Web site at http://www.urban.sim.org.

NOTE

Information on DOE's work on "Tools for Community Design and Decision Making" is available through a visit to the toolkit section of the Web site http://www.sustainable.doe.gov. For a broad overview of "Tools for Community Design and Decision Making," visit http://www.sustainable.doe.gov/toolkit/toolkit.shtml, or contact the U.S. Department of Energy to obtain a PowerPoint presentation on the subject.

CHAPTER 32

Parkville Approves Mixed Land Uses to Revitalize Its Main Street

Bill Quitmeier, Pat Hawver, *and* Barbara Lance

The beauty and resources of the area that came to be Parkville were discovered first by our Native American forebears, particularly the Sac and Fox tribes. Claude Alloe, a French fur trapper, called White Alloe by Indian Chief Narva, was the first European to come upon this riverside treasure, followed somewhat later by the English brothers, who built a warehouse and trading post here. Subsequently, its potential was realized by George S. Park, who made it into a village and gave it his name.

This unique small town on the banks of the Missouri River, located between downtown Kansas City and Kansas City International Airport, has been around for almost 200 years, but has been little known in this century except to residents, students, antique lovers and theater enthusiasts. Now it has been discovered anew, this time by developers.

Brothers David and Stephen English purchased the land now constituting downtown Parkville in 1839, after the Platte Purchase was consummated. (Missouri is the only state that added land after it came into the Union, when it had a straight vertical western boundary. The Platte Purchase added land west to the Missouri River.) In 1840, David English leased land to the City's founder, George S. Park, who also acquired adjacent properties. The original plat of the City, filed by Park in 1849 as part of the first of four incorporations, now comprises our downtown. In 1875 "Colonel" Park, who acknowledged but never used the honorary title, and the Rev. John A. McAfee, a Presbyterian minister from Kansas, founded Park College, now Park University.

In 1869, railroad service augmented the river commerce, and Parkville grew to a population of about 500 persons.

Residential Development

By 1990, Parkville had grown to a population of about 2,500. The growth expected when KCI Airport opened in 1972 took more than 20 years to really materialize. The first evidence of substantial growth was in the late 1980s with the residential development of Riss Lake; it is expected to build out in the next few years with a total of 800 homes, yielding 2,000 new residents.

An earlier subdivision, The Bluffs, begun in the 1970s and still building in small phases, has been recognized by the Missouri Depart-

Originally published as "Parkville Discovered ... Again," *Missouri Municipal Review*, Vol. 65, No. 10, December 2000. Published by the Missouri Municipal League, Jefferson City, MO. Reprinted with permission of the publisher.

ment of Conservation as a perfect example of how to build housing into the natural environment with minimum negative impact on the land, and with a very positive residential experience. This development overlooks the Missouri River and is a casual walk from downtown Parkville.

The National, a community being built around golfer Tom Watson's first signature golf course and a second semi-private course, also designed by Watson, has already gained a reputation as the premier place to live in greater Kansas City area's northland. Thirty-six holes of challenging golf built on the rolling hills of the Missouri River valley have spawned nearby homes as expensive as $1.8 million. The National has been the catalyst for a second and larger wave of growth. Parkville also has attracted other recent quality developments above the river. River Hills Estates and Riverchase offer quality country living within ten minutes of our downtown.

With all the expensive new homes, Parkville remains a diverse community, with modest and larger stately homes mingled together in the older parts of town, and an inviting and well-managed village for low-income senior citizens.

Main Street

Parkville's Main Street exemplifies the goals of the new urbanism movement, blending single-family, multi-family, retail and office property uses into one extremely livable and workable community. The homes are older, but most have been remodeled to accommodate modern living.

Reinvestment can be seen throughout the older areas of town.

Our historic downtown has evolved from crafts and antiques to a restaurant district. Like acorns that survive a forest fire, 14 refreshing new retail businesses arose after the Great Flood of 1993. These new artsy stores are fun for browsing and buying, especially while awaiting a dinner table at the sports/pizza bar, microbrewery, Mediterranean, Mexican, French or Argentinean restaurants. And the American Legion serves a fine breakfast on Sunday mornings — it's a great place to meet people.

Our service industry is thriving as well. Downtown also boasts a bank, post office, a publisher, accountants, attorneys, dentists, beauty shops and day spas, and a real estate office.

Near the park, the university and downtown sits our 1889 train depot, almost destroyed in the 1993 flood, newly rehabilitated and recently rededicated. After its first life as a train depot, it was our City Hall for almost two decades, and will now serve as the Main Street office, a railroad museum and a visitors center. The Parkville Spirit Fountain, dedicated in 1998 to the spirit of the City's pioneers, decorates the side yard on property that once housed Park's hotel and the college's first building.

Our new City Hall, built after the flood, is on a high and dry site overlooking the Park University soccer field.

Our other multi-use commercial area also is experiencing significant economic change. The developers of the National Golf Clubs have a contract to purchase a strip center near their golf courses. They plan to redevelop and modernize that center to fit with current shopping trends and local demographics. Recognizing that driving and walking must co-exist in any shopping center, they are committed to making this center more pedestrian friendly.

Parks

Parkville easily could be named for our commitment to parks as well as for our founder. Our 68-acre English Landing Park adjoins the Missouri River, and has a trail 2½ miles long for walkers, joggers and cyclists. Soccer and baseball fields, picnic shelters, a gazebo that is a popular setting for weddings, a Farmers Market, festivals and the river trail attract thousands of park visitors annually.

One of the world's first non-suspension train bridges spans the confluence of the White Alloe Creek and Rush Creek in English Landing Park. The Waddell A Truss Bridge joins two separate areas of the park. Labor and materials involved in the massive job of transporting and reassembling the parts of an old railroad bridge into a footbridge would have cost $200,000 in 1988, when the job was done. With donations of professional expertise, manual labor and/or materials from Howard Needles Tammen and Bergendoff, the Engineering Department at the University of Missouri in Kansas City, the Bratton Corporation, other large and small companies and hundreds of individuals, the total expense incurred by the City of Parkville was under $2,000. The bridge is listed on the National Register of Historic Places, as much for its astonishing reconstruction as for its original construction.

Operated in partnership with the Missouri Department of Conservation's urban wildlife program, Parkville's Nature Sanctuary has built trails through 110 acres of hilly wilderness. Even a short walk along the trail transports you to quiet solitude, waterfalls, beaver dams and ponds, a rebuilt Girl Scout cabin and nature left alone. Pocket parks are spotted throughout the city.

Park University

The quality of life in Parkville is, like elsewhere, created by its people. Before the Civil War, townsfolk helped black Americans escape slavery by hiding them and transporting them to Kansas. No one has been able to document the underground railroad, though its existence has been accepted as fact for many years, but, as a local professor pointed out, "it was *supposed* to be a secret." In World War II, Park College students blocked efforts to intern Japanese Americans.

We are fortunate at this point in our history to have a great many creative, committed and enthusiastic people from the City and beyond, who delight in helping with events and historic celebrations. Much of this creativity stems from the existence of Park University, whose students often have opted to stay and raise their families here.

Park graciously invites the community to watch collegiate and high school soccer, basketball, volleyball, baseball, softball, and track games at the university stadiums, to attend its theater, and to use the university library. The theater offers performances not only by the college theater department, but also by the Bell Road Barn Players, a community theater group that originated in Parkville many years ago.

While the university beautifully adorns the bluff overlooking the river basin with buildings a century and more old, it is also vigorously expanding its education and commercial facilities into the underground caves it is mining. It's another unique Parkville experience to see how elegantly the school has developed this underground into classrooms, a board room, book store and the library. The school also leases underground space for commercial use.

Annual Festivals

Our annual festivals wrap us in community spirit by bringing everyone together for a Jazzfest in the spring, a traditional All-American 4th of July, Parkville Days in the early fall, the Park University Art Festival in October, and Christmas on the River the week after Thanksgiving.

To avoid becoming concentrically surrounded by Kansas City, and to reap tax benefits from the inevitable commercialization of the interstate highway corridor that connects the new NASCAR track in Kansas city, Kansas, with KCI Airport in Kansas City, Missouri, Parkville is pursuing annexation of nearly ten square miles along the I-435 corridor. The annexation will more than double our current size.

This current era of discovery has accelerated our growth from slow and steady to a brisk trot, so our immediate priority is to guide the growth in the best possible ways, keeping what's best about small town life in the midst of all the change. We accept the challenge.

CHAPTER 33

Riverside, Other Cities, Improve Their Development Review Process

Gerald Newfarmer, Amy Cohen Paul, *and* Rebekka Hosken

"I've been getting complaints about our development review process," the city manager states, looking around the table at the appropriate department heads. "It takes too long, uses too many resources, and needs an overhaul. I want to cut our processing time by one-third. I know about a process resulting in such improvements in other jurisdictions, and I want to try it."

The department heads are skeptical. Aren't you? You've been through this drill before. When some folks complain, you bring in a consultant to tell you what's wrong (as if this were news), then lead your overworked teammates in implementing some of the recommendations.

Flash forward. It now is a few years later. The economy begins to slacken, and the complaints start in again. Then you reconvene the staff, redo your diagnosis, and, with a sigh that reflects the frustration of having to revisit an old problem, try again to do the fix.

Curing this common local-government business problem requires getting beyond mere changes for appearances' sake, to effect improvements that are both immediate and lasting. In this chapter, we will explain how to fix the development review process more deeply.

Defining the Development Review Process in Your Locality

Each city or county has special characteristics to its development review process, including its own political setting, history, legal requirements, relationships with the development community, degrees of neighborhood activism, and internal organizational structure. The approach described here, however, can be used to accurately analyze, diagnose, define, and implement meaningful enhancements to the development review processes in any organization — large or small — without compromising the quality or stringency of the review.

For purposes of this chapter, the term

Originally published as "Really Fixing Your Development Review Process: Going Beyond Cosmetic Improvements," *Public Management*, Vol. 85, No. 6, July 2003. Published by the International City/County Management Association, Washington, D.C. Reprinted with permission of the publisher.

"development review" is used broadly to comprise all planning and building processes related to the construction of a project. These include the review of plans (design review, site planning, historic preservation); the work of advisory boards (neighborhood commissions, zoning boards, planning commissions); building reviews (plan check); inspections; standalone permits associated with a project (grading, encroachment); and all enforcement actions done before the project has been completed and a certificate of occupancy has been issued. The big picture entails enormous complexity, multiple technical specialties, and (usually) divided management responsibility.

But, as shown in Figure 1, from the customer's point of view the process seems quite a lot simpler. Everything inside the center box is your responsibility, in all of its complex glory, as far as the customer is concerned. And you'd really like to fix what goes on in this box.

Elements of the Fix

The reform initiative should be managed like any project, with its steps defined from the start according to an adopted plan of action that contains a schedule for completion. To be precise, in completing such a project, three elements must be addressed:

1. Diagnosis and analysis of quality problems.
2. Focused decision making about the improvements to be made.
3. Timely execution of an implementation action plan.

To be effective, the accomplishment of these elements must be supported by strong leadership and by the full involvement of staff members who do the relevant work every day. According to Liz Miller, assistant city manager of Tucson, Arizona, "The manager has to be the catalyst to help engaged workers make the changes that are needed and to override the institutional roadblocks."

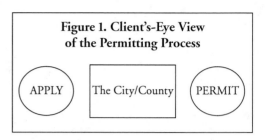

Figure 1. Client's-Eye View of the Permitting Process

APPLY   The City/County   PERMIT

Most reform efforts focus on diagnosis, usually done through an outside consultant's recommendations as to the improvements needed. And while good diagnosis is the necessary starting point, too often the consultant's report with recommendations still is sitting on the shelf five years later, only partially implemented. Indeed, as of this writing, one manager could recall five studies that had been done in his city over the past 20 years ... and users still were complaining about their slow processing time!

Mere diagnosis doesn't get the overhaul done. There must be an equal commitment to making decisions about which changes to make and about implementing these changes.

Leadership and employee engagement are essential for simple, but different, reasons. The local government administrator is the only person having the full scope of the locality within his or her province. Because responsibility for development review always is shared among departments (planning, building, fire, attorney, public works, water/sewer, finance), strong corporate leadership is essential to transcend internal organizational boundaries.

Similarly, the full involvement of the working staff is crucial in reforming the process. Staff members do the work and know what has to get done. And they will be the ones on the hook to carry out the reformed process and to deal with customers face-to-face.

Getting Improvements Made

The first step in untangling the problems of development review is to understand how things currently work, both from a staff and from a user perspective. This is done by interviewing key managers and staff in all involved departments and by thoroughly reviewing policies and procedures, previous studies, flowcharts, performance data, job definitions, and the like. The outcome of this analysis should be a clear list of the various processes falling under the development review umbrella and a general sense of why they are done and how they work.

Following initial interviews, it is essential to create detailed process maps or flowcharts of each specific process (e.g., design review, building-plan check) to understand the way the work currently flows and to gain a factual basis for designing lasting improvements. For each step on the map, employees should be asked to provide estimates both for elapsed, or cycle, time (when something comes into an office and when it leaves) and for true task time (actual time spent completing the assignment), as these estimates will clearly show where bottlenecks and idle waiting periods are occurring (see Figure 2).

While process maps are time-consuming to create, they hold the key to unlocking the mystery of the development review process. Process maps help both employees and users to pinpoint problems in process flow, and serve to depersonalize problems by focusing on tasks and not people.

Another key step in understanding development review in your organization is to interview knowledgeable users of the process for their impressions and thoughts about the way the process works and their suggestions for improvement. While some users are whiners and some have particular axes to grind, among them

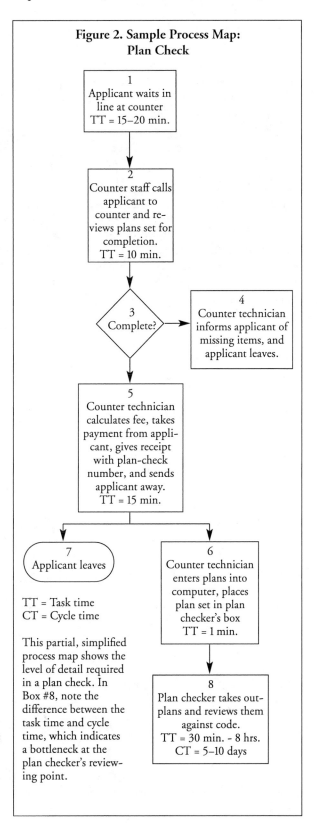

Figure 2. Sample Process Map: Plan Check

1 Applicant waits in line at counter TT = 15–20 min.

2 Counter staff calls applicant to counter and reviews plans set for completion. TT = 10 min.

3 Complete?

4 Counter technician informs applicant of missing items, and applicant leaves.

5 Counter technician calculates fee, takes payment from applicant, gives receipt with plan-check number, and sends applicant away. TT = 15 min.

7 Applicant leaves

6 Counter technician enters plans into computer, places plan set in plan checker's box TT = 1 min.

TT = Task time
CT = Cycle time

This partial, simplified process map shows the level of detail required in a plan check. In Box #8, note the difference between the task time and cycle time, which indicates a bottleneck at the plan checker's reviewing point.

8 Plan checker takes out plans and reviews them against code. TT = 30 min. - 8 hrs. CT = 5–10 days there are always thoughtful folks whose observations are worth listening to.

Staff members can compile a representative list of persons in the categories of architect, developer/planner, engineer, contractor, and homebuilder, or they can generate a random list from the computer database of recent recipients of permits and approvals. Many times, users will be hesitant to open up and feel that, if they are critical of the process, employees will retaliate by denying permits or putting up roadblocks to their projects. In this situation, it often is helpful to have a knowledgeable third party interview the users on a confidential basis. As part of a planned improvement initiative, this step should be good public relations for staff.

Once the process has been analyzed, management can set such quantifiable improvement goals as reducing processing time by a certain percentage or increasing customer satisfaction ratings on surveys by a certain percentage. In my opinion, the best way to realize these goals is to ask staff to help decide how to achieve them, using a facilitated process called the GE Work-Out™, which is based on a technique developed by the General Electric Corporation to "work steps out" in a business process.

In the Work-Out, the staff team figures out the specific actions the city or county must do to reform the process. These ideas are presented to managers for approval at the end of the Work-Out session. The purpose of the presentation session is to decide, then and there, what will be done, based on the focused knowledge of the staff.

Walking the Walk

So now you've done something more than analysis. You've gone beyond the paralysis-by-analysis syndrome and actu-

---

The GE Work-Out™ as a Tool for Improvement

In the late 1980s, General Electric Chairman Jack Welch was seeking a way to bring positive change to a large multinational corporation and to move away from traditional bureaucratic gridlock. He wanted to empower line employees with the ability to solve problems quickly and give managers a fast, efficient means to authorize and approve changes.

He hoped to bring back an entrepreneurial style of doing business — informal communication across job classes and department boundaries — to get things moving again. After working with both internal and external consultants over some years to achieve these goals, the result was a process now known as the GE Work-Out.

Quite simply, the Work-Out is a facilitated retreat with a particular methodology. Before the retreat starts, management sets specific improvement goals. In the case of development review, an example might be decreasing review processing time for building permits or site plans by 33 percent. A cross-section of staff having day-to-day working responsibility in the process, encompassing all involved departments, are invited to serve on the Work-Out team, whose members meet in a retreat setting. There, management begins by defining the improvement goals and setting forth the expectations for results by the end of the retreat.

Management then leaves, and employees are engaged in a facilitated, structured decision-making process to determine the actions required to accomplish the improvement goals. Participants identify key problems and agree upon detailed recommendations for fixing them, including how to simplify or improve the process flow. They prepare presentations outlining their recommendations, the justifications for making the changes, and the anticipated benefits. At the end of the retreat, management returns, and the employees present their recommendations. Management is expected at that time to approve the changes to be implemented, as well as the elements of the action plan for execution.

The Work-Out process is applicable to virtually any type of organization and any problem or issue. It is excellent as a tool for improving the development review process because it brings people together as a team across department boundaries to work together to improve a process in which they all share. The Work-Out is a valuable way to show your employees the big picture of how the process works, to improve teamwork, and to build "buy-in" for process improvement efforts. And also, not insignificantly, it empowers working staff to make decisions about ways in which their process can be changed for the better.

For more information, see *The GE Work-Out™. How to Implement GE's Revolutionary Method for Busting Bureaucracy and Attacking Organizational Problems — Fast!* by Dave Ulrich, Steve Kerr, and Ron Ashkenas.

ally decided something, which won't amount to a hill of beans unless you execute, or implement, what you've decided.

To execute the decisions made, it is important to prepare a written report and action plan documenting the agreements. The action plan should identify the specific improvement recommendations to be executed, with milestones and timelines for completion, as well as the name of the individual who will be held accountable for execution in each case. Everyone, including the manager, can then use this action plan to monitor improvement efforts and to ensure that things are moving forward.

According to Mark Pentz, city manager of Rockville, Maryland, "It is really important to get beyond the diagnosis stage, to actually make decisions about the improvements to be implemented, and then to have an action plan to guide the execution of implementation. That's the most effective way to realize improvements."

Because many of the recommendations should be implemented in the near term, a useful checkpoint is a Work-Out reunion, to be held about four or five months after the original was completed. Knowing that the session is coming up provides focus for involved staff, and the event itself serves as a useful opportunity to refine and update the action plan, as well as to celebrate the actual changes that have been executed.

"By involving our people in the GE Work-Out and staying focused on execution of our action plan, we improved the quality of our work for applicants and decreased cycle time by over a third," said Chris Cherches, city manager of Wichita, Kansas.

Executing a carefully crafted action plan, prepared by engaged working staff, is the sure way to get beyond cosmetic changes and to realize permanent service improvement to those who bring development to your city or county.

CHAPTER 34

Rochester Uses Citizen Stakeholders to Revitalize Inner-City Neighborhoods

Jarle Crocker

In the overlapping circles of professional worlds that collectively constitute the field of community building, the last ten years have seen a revitalization of grassroots democracy in the towns, cities, and counties of America. This movement has a variety of sources, including new federal efforts such as the Empowerment Zone/Enterprise Community Initiative, a renewed emphasis on neighborhood-level collaboration in major foundation programs such as Annie E. Casey's new Making Connections Initiative, and the national shift toward devolution of decision making to the local level across numerous policy arenas. In addition to such "external" influences, the majority of these new community-building projects have grown from the hard work of neighborhood groups, faith-based organizations, nonprofits, local businesses, and similar grassroots stakeholders.

Indeed, it is difficult to visit any community and not find several innovative efforts to convene diverse local stakeholders to build consensus on complex public policy decisions. Ask for a list of places with promising practices that use inclusive and collaborative methods to make shared community decisions, and the list could run on for pages. However, ask for a list of places that have moved beyond reforming discrete pieces of their deliberative processes to transforming their whole system of decision making, and the list suddenly shrinks to a very small and select number of communities. This is the question that is now being asked by community builders of all kinds: what does it take to "turn the corner," to move from modest efforts at reforming community to fundamentally transforming grassroots democracy?

Ironically, the small number of communities that have made this latter list looks much the same now as it did ten years ago. Such cities as Chattanooga, Tennessee — which is often lauded for its groundbreaking work with community visioning and strategic planning — have been cited as success stories for the better part of twenty years. After the last ten years of innovation at the local level, where are the new Chattanoogas and what do they have to teach us about what it takes to move

Originally published as "The Neighbors Building Neighborhoods Initiative in Rochester, New York," *National Civic Review*, Vol. 89, No.3, Fall 2000. Published by the National Civic League, Denver, CO. Reprinted with permission of the publisher.

from innovative yet often isolated reforms to truly transformative community-building work?

Of all the success stories that could be cited from the last decade of community-building work, few have come so far or so fast as Rochester, New York. A city of about 230,000, located on the shores of Lake Ontario, in Western New York, Rochester is known, among other things, for its scenic countryside and as the home of Eastman Kodak. Like many other communities, however, the city started the 1990s with its fair share of concerns. Outward migration from the city was on the rise, complicating efforts at urban revitalization. Typical of many communities, trust between citizens and the local government was strained. Perhaps most disappointingly, efforts fell through to go to scale (that is, to achieve expected impact) on a grant for the Annie E. Casey Foundation's New Futures Initiative, a project many in the community had hoped would revitalize work to improve outcomes for Rochester's families and children.

In addition to these challenges, it was becoming apparent that the city's Comprehensive Plan, which was prepared more than three decades ago, in 1964, was showing its age. Led by newly elected mayor William A. Johnson, Rochester embarked on an ambitious effort to virtually reinvent, from the ground up, its community planning process. Initiated in March 1994, the Neighbors Building Neighborhoods (NBN) process started as an effort to get citizens involved in envisioning the future of their community. After only six years, the results are remarkable. In August 1994, the NBN won the American Planning Association's Upstate Chapter Award for its Significant Comprehensive Planning Project. In March 1996, the NBN was recognized by the National Black Caucus of Local Elected Officials as one of the premier "local efforts to promote, honor, and celebrate diversity" In July 1997, the U.S. Department of Housing and Urban Development recognized the NBN

with the John. J. Gunther Blue Ribbon Best Practices in Community Development Award for Consolidated Planning. In 1998, Rochester won the highly coveted All-America City Award, the oldest award in the country that recognizes civic excellence.

How did Rochester and the NBN achieve so much success so quickly? What are the lessons learned that can be applied to other communities? The rest of this article chronicles the development of the NBN and concludes by drawing out several key principles for community-building efforts that seek to revitalize grassroots democracy.

Unlike many similar initiatives and efforts that began life as pilot projects with a limited geographic or programmatic scope, the NBN was conceived from the outset as a truly comprehensive planning process. To start the process, all of Rochester's thirty-seven neighborhoods were organized into ten neighborhood planning sectors. Even though the individual neighborhoods were recognized as important entities in their own right, this approach created an organizational framework with a workable scale (ten as opposed to thirty-seven sets of plans) and built-in incentives for neighborhood-to-neighborhood collaboration.

With support from the local government, each sector formed a committee that consisted of such diverse local stakeholders as citizens, grassroots groups, nonprofits, neighborhood associations, local businesses, faith-based organizations, and schools. In all, over two thousand citizens participated during the initial eighteen months. Each sector committee was provided with a trained professional facilitator and a city staff person to help it over the course of the initiative. It is important to note that assistance from the local government was concentrated on capacity-building efforts such as training fifty citizens in facilitation skills rather than attempts to manage the entire process from city hall. In turn, each sector committee developed its own broad based action plan that included concrete steps that covered issues including housing, land use, economic development, human services, youth, neighborhood image, public safety, the environment, and public infrastructure.

In addition, each sector developed its own asset resource maps, along with their action plans. These maps served to identify a broad range of resources in the sector neighborhoods that included schools, businesses, police stations, cultural and entertainment sites, service providers, and other such assets. These maps became important sources of support throughout the NBN process, helping the sectors identify sources of support for their action plans as well as new stakeholders to engage in the planning process. By emphasizing the existing assets in each sector, this approach also illustrated in a very tangible way that, in spite of their challenges, even the toughest neighborhoods had resources upon which to draw.

Over the initial eighteen months of the planning process, the ten sectors developed 1,420 action steps to improve their neighborhoods and the city as a whole. However, unlike similar planning efforts in other communities that struggled to take their good ideas off the blueprints and into the streets, the city and citizens had focused throughout the process on the need for accountability and sustainability. To begin with, an electronic reporting system and database was established in each sector to track the results of each action plan. Volunteers recorded their sector's action steps, as well as who was responsible for their implementation and the results achieved. From this beginning, the sector databases have grown into a system now used to create annual status reports on the action plans, track how the city is spending money, forecast volunteer needs, and monitor coordinated services. Currently, the city and sectors are working on a benchmark evaluation system to measure progress on different neighborhood indicators and track the success of the NBN process.

At the same time, the local government took several steps to ensure that the organizational framework created by the NBN would continue to drive planning in Rochester. Initially, the sector action plans were fed into the city administration's annual budget process to reflect the citizens' agenda. As the process gained momentum, it steadily became the decision-making "hub" that integrated a variety of other planning processes. Currently, the NBN framework and sector action plans are used to set priorities for the city's operating, capital improvement, and community development block grant budgets. Also notable has been the use of the NBN by other community stakeholders. For instance, the Arts and Cultural Council for Greater Rochester has engaged the ten sectors in the development of its strategic plan, the Rochester Catholic Diocese has relied significantly on the sectors in the development of a new community plan, and the local United Way uses the sector plans in setting its own funding priorities. Most recently, the sector plans are being used as the foundation for Rochester's comprehensive plan update.

A variety of other supports have been created over the last six years to ensure that the NBN initiative will be sustainable over the tong term. An NBN Priority Council was created to manage coordination among city departments and to act as liaison with the sectors. Consisting of representatives from each city department, the council works directly with sector leaders to manage implementation of the action plans and it oversees interdepartmental coordination of ongoing work.

To continue building the capacity of the community, each sector has been provided with a NeighborLink computer site. Building on the original system for reporting and tracking results of the sector action plans, NeighborLink also allows interactive discussion and information sharing among sectors and city departments, the use of geographic information system technology to map neighborhood resources and other important information, and access to the Internet. Recognizing that most citizens do not have advanced degrees in community planning, the city has also started the NBN Institute to further educate residents about how local government works. Offering workshops and seminars chosen by citizens, the institute plays an important role in ensuring that neighborhoods have the capacity to participate as true partners with local government.

Perhaps the most significant innovation to emerge from the NBN Initiative is the Neighborhood Empowerment Teams, or NETs. As Rochester began to realize the benefits of its new approach to community planning, it became apparent that the business-as-usual responses to neighborhood problems also needed an overhaul. In an effort to better coordinate city services and work more directly with the neighborhoods and their residents, the city began to decentralize the way it conducted public business. The Neighborhood Empowerment Teams work out of six neighborhood-based offices, each office serving one or two of the ten sectors. Consisting of an administrator from a city department, a police lieutenant, and several other city staff members, each team helps support communication between citizens and the city and responds to resident concerns on code complaints, public safety concerns, and other quality-of-life issues. The NET offices are in turn linked to the Priority Council, an arrangement that supports direct communication between citizens and top-level decision makers while retaining flexibility and autonomy for residents and departments alike.

Lessons Learned

The preceding summary of the NBN and Rochester's accomplishments over the last six years only skims the surface of the profound changes and many successes enjoyed by the city. What is most remarkable is how relatively quickly Rochester has been able to change on a large scale the way in which it makes a whole range of important community decisions.

Though by no means exhaustive, the following lessons learned stand out as general principles for other towns, cities, and counties engaged in the hard but important work of community building.

Transformative Change Works Best When You Dive in Head First. Rapid and significant change can be frightening. As a result, many communities hope to achieve truly transformative results through a series of more incremental reforms. This seems both practical and intuitive, but communities such as Rochester tell a different story. The problem with piecemeal reform is that it becomes extremely difficult to create the critical mass necessary to turn the corner. New initiatives and programs, however innovative, have to compete for resources with more established initiatives and departments of the local bureaucracy. Managers and frontline workers alike are often left in the frustrating circumstance of having one toe in the new paradigm and the other nine in the world of business as usual. Finally, more modest initiatives and programs are easy prey in times of funding shortfalls and the inevitable change in administrations.

One key to Rochester's success was the early decision to reinvent its entire community planning process from the ground up. To be sure, it was riskier politically than a more incremental approach, but this opening move was important for several reasons. First, it sent a clear message to citizens that the city was serious about changing the way it did business, given the scale of the initiative. Second, involving a significant number of departments and such a diversity of community stakeholders ensured the financial, human, and related resources necessary for success. Third, the size of the initiative ensured the buy-in of diverse stakeholders, since it was clear that no single set of players could accomplish the task on their own.

Transformative Change Requires New Approaches to Community Governance. One of the most remarkable aspects of the NBN is its approach to community governance — the processes, structures, and relationships that support the making of community decisions. Many recent community-building initiatives are in part a reaction to the problems caused by the existence of rigid "silos" that surround programs and funding streams and create piecemeal approaches to solving community problems, encourage turf battles, and inhibit collaboration. However, much the same criticism can be leveled at the similar silos that separate processes and forums for making community decisions.

What stands out about the NBN Initiative is the fundamentally new approach to community governance it has created in Rochester. Decision making has been decentralized in a variety of ways; it has been pushed down to the neighborhoods as organized lay sectors and pushed out into the streets by innovations such as the Neighborhood Empowerment Teams. At the same time, the process is far more collaborative despite this decentralization. Neighborhoods work together within and across sectors, citizens work with local government on teams and sector committees, and city departments work closely with one another through the Priority Council. Finally, the framework of the NBN acts as the hub to coordinate planning processes — setting priorities for the comprehensive plan and operating budget, capital improvement budget, and community development block grant funds.

Transformative Change Requires a Paradigm Shift in the Civic Culture. A remarkable aspect of Rochester's success has been the extent to which the entire community's civic culture has changed. Within local government, support for the NBN can be found at all levels. Instead of the usual credit taking and one-upmanship, the mayor and city department heads are quick to play the role of facilitative leaders, spreading the credit — and the responsibility — evenly among all the stakeholders involved. In one instance that only sounds apocryphal, the city engineer decided to push back a major new transportation project for one year to allow for more extensive consensus building and collaboration with the affected neighborhoods. What becomes apparent in talking with those working in Rochester's local government is that the NBN process marks a much deeper shift in the city's philosophy and approach to working with the community.

Talk to residents of Rochester's neighborhoods and you'll hear a similar story. During the NBN, each sector developed a stronger sense of neighborhood identity through the development of their asset maps and sector plans, and even their bumper stickers and logos. Citizens are participating in civic life at an unprecedented level of sophistication — for example, using geographic information system software at their NeighborLink centers to map demographic information, chart progress on action steps, and plan new projects. Perhaps most hopefully, many citizens report that feelings of mistrust between residents and local government have been replaced by a new sense of collaboration and partnership.

A Decision-Making Umbrella

This list of lessons learned is partial, but it does highlight several of the key factors that have led to Rochester's civic renaissance. It also points to an important challenge for communities and community builders alike. The last ten years have seen innovations such as the use of multi-stakeholder community collaboratives and citizen-driven planning develop from isolated experiments to commonplace activities. However, in too many cases, even well-established community-building efforts remain isolated from one another or are the exception to the rule. What makes Rochester remarkable is its success in using the NBN structure and process as an umbrella under which to coordinate multiple decision-making processes in a way that has truly transformed how the city conducts its public business. How to move from reforming individual pieces of our communities to transforming whole systems of governance remains one of our greatest challenges. It is our hope that highlighting communities engaged in making such a leap will provide a vital source of inspiration and new ideas alike for this important task.

CHAPTER 35

St. Louis, Other Cities, Use Citizen Input to Guide Urban Growth

David Rusk

A new association of business leadership groups in Pennsylvania, the Coalition of Mid-Sized Cities, has targeted enactment of a "Smart Growth," anti-sprawl law as its top priority. In Missouri a coalition of 80 churches — Protestant and Catholic, black and white, city and inner suburb — is lobbying for a new state growth management law for Greater St. Louis.

In Ohio, the just-formed First Suburbs Consortium, a dozen mayors from communities around Cleveland, told the Governor's Task Force on Agricultural Preservation that a strong state land-use law would be desirable to save farmland, but it is essential for the survival of older suburban communities.

Growth management is rapidly emerging as the top regional issue of the next decade. New recruits to the legislative struggle — business leaders, church coalitions, inner suburban mayors, and township supervisors — are joining forces with environmentalists and farmland preservationists, growth management's more traditional advocates.

"If regionalism isn't dealing with land use, fiscal disparities, housing, and education, regionalism isn't dealing with the issues that really matter," states Don Hutchinson, president of the Greater Baltimore Committee, the regional chamber of commerce.

Land use is the key, especially in the East and much of the Middle West where sprawling development patterns overlay a political map of thousands of cities, villages, and townships with fixed jurisdictional boundaries.

Fiscal disparities, inequitable housing, and educational opportunities — laced with racial and class segregation — all flow from skewed development patterns.

"Since the late 1940s, policies have consistently encouraged the abandonment of boroughs and cities in Pennsylvania, and discouraged the redevelopment of existing neighborhoods and established commercial and industrial sites," explains Tom Wolf, president of Better York, owner of a multi-state chain of builders-supply stores, and a leader of the Coalition of Mid-Sized Cities. In addition to Better York, the coalition includes a dozen business groups like the Lehigh Valley Partnership, the Lancaster Alliance, and the

Originally published as "Growth Management: Regionalism's Core Issue," *The Regionalist*, Vol. 2, No. 4, Winter 1997. Published by the National Association of Regional Councils, Washington, D.C. and the University of Baltimore, Baltimore, MD. Reprinted with permission of the publisher.

Erie Conference on Community Development.

"In the end, no one wins in a system that makes prosperity a temporary and fleeting phenomenon," Wolf continues. "No one wins in a system that has already condemned our cities and older boroughs to economic stagnation and decline. And no one wins in a system that ultimately threatens to do the same thing to our townships. The point is that public policies that encourage sprawl are neither smart nor right.

New Rules Needed

"We need to change the rules of the game," Wolf concludes. "Most of all we need to change the rules governing land-use planning."

That conclusion is seconded by the Rev. Sylvester Laudermill, chair of Metropolitan Congregations United for St. Louis. "St. Louis has been devastated by a growth machine that empties out our communities. In recent decades developers have consumed land at seven times the rate of our population growth. They've built twice as many new homes as there were new households for them.

"That's a guaranteed formula for abandonment. In just 20 years St. Louis city lost 70,000 housing units." Laudermill explains. "But the decline doesn't stop with St. Louis. Many of our older suburbs are also declining.

"For years our congregations have fought to stabilize and redevelop our communities. But every month more homes are boarded up, more local stores have closed. We've concluded that we cannot win the battle for our neighborhoods — the 'inside game' — unless we fight and win the 'outside game' as well."

This past February, the Metropolitan Congregations United extracted a pledge from St. Louis area legislators to back their anti-sprawl agenda. The immediate result: a new Legislative Interim Committee on Urban Growth The hotly debated hearings this fall

were headline news in the St. Louis media. Now the church coalition has crafted a bill to vest regional land-use planning power in a new commission under the East-West Gateway Coordinating Council, the region's council of governments. The regional commission would have the power to draw an urban growth boundary for the Missouri side of Greater St. Louis.

The St. Louis coalition is merely the spearhead of an anti-sprawl crusade mounted by interfaith coalitions in Gary-Hammond, Detroit, Cleveland, Chicago, and a dozen other Midwestern regions. The effort is coordinated by the Chicago-based Gamaliel Foundation. "Yesterday's winners are today's losers," might be the theme of Cleveland's First Suburbs Consortium. Barely two decades ago, inner suburbs such as Euclid, Lakewood, and Maple Heights boasted above average household incomes. Now they've sunk 10 to 20 percentage points below the regional average as higher-end households move out into new subdivisions in farther out Geauga, Lake, and Portage Counties.

"Many older suburbs are more vulnerable to sprawl-driven disinvestment than Cleveland itself. They're left with an aging housing stock, older strip shopping centers and first-generation malls that find it hard to compete with new regional malls and new higher end housing developments," explains Dr. Tom Bier, head of housing research at Cleveland State University.

"Many older suburbs generally don't have the legacy of charming old neighborhoods, fine parks, museums, or big centers of high-quality jobs found in central business districts, hospitals, and universities historically located in central cities. East Cleveland, for example, is in much tougher shape than Cleveland itself," Bier notes. New York, St. Louis, and Cleveland share one characteristic — highly-fragmented local government. With 72 municipal governments in York County, 105 local governments in metro Cleveland, and 134 local governments just in the Missouri portion of Greater St. Louis, purely voluntary co-operation won't produce a meaningful regional plan. As York's Tom Wolf says, changing the rules of the game for land-use planning is essential, and only state legislatures can change those rules.

Different Rules Used

Across the continent, business and civic delegations, state and local politicians, and professional planners are flocking to Portland to see the practical results of nearly 25 years of operating under different rules of the game. In 1973 the Oregon legislature enacted the Statewide Land Use Law. It required that urban growth boundaries be drawn around cities throughout the state. Portland Metro, the nation's only directly elected regional government, is responsible for land use and transportation planning in the 1.5 million-person metropolitan area.

Anticipating a 50 percent growth of population over the next 45 years, last November the Portland Metro Council voted 5–2 to add less than 8 square miles to Portland's existing 342-square-mile urban growth boundary. (The two dissenting voters believed the expansion was too little.) Opposition to greater ex-pansion was led by many local officials like Mayor Gussie McRobert of suburban Gresham, as well as many environmentally concerned citizens.

Portland's urban growth boundary has succeeded in protecting farmland in Oregon's rich Willamette Valley. If the Metro Council sticks to its plans, over the next 45 years, only about four square miles of current farmland will be urbanized — as much farmland as is subdivided in the state of Michigan every 10 days!

A big bonus is that shutting down sub-urban sprawl has turned new private investment back inward into existing neighborhoods and retail areas. Mayor McRoberts' Gresham, Milwaukie, Oregon City, and other older suburbs are booming. Property values in Albina, Portland's poorest neighborhood, have doubled in just five years. As Metro Councilor Ed Washington, whose District 6 includes Albina, explained his vote for the small boundary expansion. "We are having redevelopment in my district for the first time in 40 years; we don't want to lose it."

You cannot win the "inside game" without playing the "outside game" as well. That lesson is bringing many new recruits into the swelling ranks of growth management advocates across the country.

CHAPTER 36

St. Maries Takes Steps to Preserve Its Forest Land

Mark Matthews

Even if you don't spot the lumber and plywood mills on the banks of the St. Joe River in St. Maries, Idaho, there are unmistakable clues that this is a logging town: the 40-foot-tall statue of Paul Bunyan hefting his ax on the front lawn of the high school, the fading signs stenciled on barroom doors warning that no caulk logging boots are allowed inside, the 3 a.m. opening of the Handi Corner Diner, so loggers can fuel up before heading into the woods.

"By 5 a.m. the amount of activity around town is just phenomenal," says Norm Linton, forest manager for Potlatch Corporation. Potlatch owns the mills along the river, employs 2,500 woods workers and millworkers, and is the largest private landowner in the state.

St. Maries started from a single 19th-century sawmill at the junction of the St. Maries and St. Joe Rivers. Timber and good river transportation for getting the timber to market were the reasons for choosing the location, and timber has remained central to the town's reason for being.

Timber keeps St. Maries alive, says Larry Haskell, owner of the St. Maries Boot Corral on Main Street, where Haskell sells more logging boots than any other style. "I don't think anything would be here if it weren't for the logging." Across Idaho, the timber industry generates approximately $1.4 billion in revenues each year and provides more than 14,500 jobs.

But the private forests around St. Maries provide much more than logging jobs. "Forested private land offers local communities many nontimber benefits," says John Robison of the Idaho Conservation League. "These include watershed protection, wildlife habitat, and recreation opportunities."

The interwoven complex of public and private forests in the Idaho Panhandle offers a 2.2-million-acre forested landscape — critical habitat of sufficient size to support endangered and threatened species, such as Canadian lynx, gray wolf, and big game species, such as elk, deer, moose, and bear. Where streams run clear and cold through forested lands, they support world-class fisheries for native westslope cutthroat trout and habitat for federally threatened bull trout.

These ecosystem values also translate into economic benefits for towns like St. Maries. World-class outdoor recreation attracts residents, retirees, and tourists who help fuel the local economy and contribute to Idaho's

Originally published as "Out of the Woods," *Land & People*, Spring 2004, reprinted with permission from the Trust for Public Land. To learn more about TPL, please visit www.tpl.org.

$167 million in annual tourism-related tax receipts.

"Fishing and hunting have always been a strong component of the economics for this state," says Alex Irby, who works in the Idaho timber industry and is also a commissioner with the Idaho Department of Fish and Game. In addition to trophy trout and salmon fishing and hunting for elk and other big game, superb hiking and horseback riding attract many visitors. A network of backcountry logging roads accommodate all-terrain vehicles, mountain bikes, and snow machines.

Changes Endanger Communities and Forests

But timber towns like St. Maries and the forests that support them face looming changes that could damage both economies and ecosystems. Timber industry mechanization is reducing the number of timber jobs, and less harvestable timber is available from public forests. At the same time, some private landowners are selling timberland for development of cabins or second homes, removing the land forever from the timber supply and dramatically decreasing its value for wildlife.

Development of the forests becomes an increasing threat as land values rise, the timber economy falters, and timber company stockholders look to real estate as a way to increase revenues. In St. Maries, Potlatch has lost money in each of the last two years, and the $1.3 billion company is looking for other ways to turn a profit.

"Revenues from traditional sources will not be enough to compete in the world of forest products and landownership," says Mark Benson, Potlatch director of public affairs in Idaho. "We see increasing emphasis by forest-owning companies on converting lands to nonforest uses that derive higher monetary value from the land."

The same is true across the nation. According to a 2001 report by the Pinchot Institute for Conservation, as many as 12 million to 15 million acres of industrial timberland — an area nearly the size of West Virginia — will be transferred out of industry ownership over the next decade. According to the U.S. Natural Resources Conservation Service, more than a million acres of forestland is developed each year.

The trend worries residents across the political and social spectrum in St. Maries and similar forest-based communities nationwide. People in the timber industry worry that land sold for development cannot support logging. Hunters, anglers, off-road enthusiasts, and snowmobilers — and the businesses that cater to them — worry that development will inevitably bring with it "No Trespassing" signs and a loss of traditional forest access. And environmentalists worry that inappropriate development will disrupt wildlife corridors and damage watersheds — and that efforts by logging companies to maximize profits will lead to overcutting and threaten the health of the forests, rivers, and streams.

Easements Protect Forests and Communities

But there is hope for a brighter future for timber towns and their forests thanks to the adaptation and increasing use by forest landowners of a traditional conservation tool — the conservation easement.

Conservation easements have been used for years to protect scenic open space, wildlife habitat, and working agricultural land. Easements are now being used to protect working forestland and the many conservation values associated with these lands. Nationwide, the use of this specialized kind of conservation easement — commonly referred to as a working forest conservation easement — has helped protect more than two million acres of forestland from development over the past two decades.

While every easement is unique, a timber company that sells a working forest conservation easement agrees to certain restrictions on how the land can be used. Development generally is not allowed, and the easement may also stipulate how and where timber may be harvested, how much can be harvested, and whether public access is permitted. In return for giving up development rights associated with the land and agreeing to other restrictions that may limit the land's value, the timber company receives compensation through the sale of an easement.

Increased use of the tool has been prompted not only by the rising threat of development, but also by the availability of federal funds from the U.S. Forest Service's Forest Legacy Program, specifically targeted to prevent the conversion of forests to nonforest uses. To be eligible for the funding, states must officially establish a Forest Legacy Program, produce an Assessment of Need that establishes program goals and priority areas, and provide at least a 25 percent match with money raised through state, local, and private funds. All transactions are voluntarily agreed to by landowners, and while a few projects involve acquiring outright title to the land, most protection is done through easements.

"All the projects are in some sense working forests," says Rick Cooksey, who oversees the Forest Legacy Program for the U.S. Forest Service. "And every project — whether it's land belonging to a timber investment management association or a family-owned forest — sub-

mits a stewardship management plan." Such plans include forest management recommendations that are geared to the soil, water, recreation, timber, fish, wildlife, forest health, wetlands, and threatened and endangered species.

Each state tailors its program to its own individual needs, adds Kathy DeCoster, who tracks federal projects for TPL. "In New Jersey the program may be geared to preventing development and protecting drinking water. In Maine the goal may be to sustain the economic benefits of recreation and timber harvesting. In Utah it may be to preserve forested watersheds."

Using Forest Legacy funds, state matching funds, and other support, various partnerships are helping states and the Forest Service protect hundreds of thousands of acres of forestland across the nation. Under the Forest Legacy Program, more than 600,000 acres of forested properties have been protected through easements. TPL alone has recently completed or is working on forestry easements in Idaho, Montana, New Hampshire, Vermont, Maine, Utah, Washington, and New Mexico.

Broad Support for Easements

The concept of working forest easements has been met with considerable enthusiasm, even in states where private landowners traditionally have been wary of, or even outright opposed to, publicly funded easement programs, says Brenda Brown, a TPL project manager who has worked on the forest-protection effort around St. Maries. "Working forest easements are attractive to states like Idaho and Montana because they keep the land in private ownership, help maintain the regional timber economy, and protect important resource values such as water quality and wildlife habitat," Brown says.

In Idaho, Potlatch hopes to sell conservation easements on much of its 600,000 acres of timberland between Lake Coeur d'Alene,

> **By the Numbers:**
> **TPL Working Forest Highlights**
>
> NORTHERN IDAHO FOREST CONSERVATION INITIATIVE
> *Protected 2,700 acres as part of an ongoing effort to conserve 80,000 acres in the Idaho Panhandle*
>
> THOMPSON AND FISHER RIVER VALLEYS, MONTANA
> *Protected 140,000 acres northwest of Missoula*
>
> CONNECTICUT LAKES, NEW HAMPSHIRE
> *Conserved 171,000 acres south of the Canadian border*
>
> MT. BLUE/TUMBLEDOWN MOUNTAIN CONSERVATION PROJECT
> *Protected 12,000 acres as part of an ongoing effort to conserve timberland in western Maine*
>
> NICATOUS LAKE, MAINE
> *Conserved 20,000 acres northeast of Bangor*
>
> POND OF SAFETY, NEW HAMPSHIRE
> *Protected 10,000 acres west of Berlin*

the St. Joe River, and the Clearwater River. This land supplies timber to Potlatch's own seven wood and paper product mills in central Idaho and also keeps a dozen smaller mills in operation.

Potlatch asked TPL to coordinate and build support for the complicated conservation transaction and helped protect the first 80,000 acres. The first phase of the project, now known as the Northern Idaho Forest Conservation Initiative, was completed in 2003 and protected 2,710 acres along the St. Joe River. Funding for this component came from private donations, a Potlatch donation, and the Forest Legacy Program. The Idaho Department of Lands will hold the easements acquired and will be responsible for monitoring and stewarding them.

By keeping out development and preventing fragmentation of the forest, the easements will enhance wildlife habitat, protect water quality, and make it easier and less costly to fight wildfires. Potlatch agreed, among other restrictions, not to clear-cut any areas visible from within the St. Joe River corridor scenic view shed. Future negotiations on other parcels could generate additional conservation restrictions, such as expanded streamside buffer zones, where no logging would be allowed, and reduced cutting in areas of old growth, critical wildlife habitat, or rare species of plants.

"This is a great opportunity to protect jobs and conserve all the values associated with healthy forestlands," noted Idaho Governor Dirk Kempthorne when the first phase of the project was accomplished last year. "This is exactly the sort of win-win outcome we envisioned in establishing the Idaho Forest Legacy Program."

Senator Larry Craig, whose support was crucial in securing the Forest Legacy funding, agreed. "I have seen these working forest projects keep land in private, productive ownership while assuring the many public values, including access, are retained. I will continue to support this model program and secure funding to successfully implement this project."

Conservation groups also voiced support for the Northern Idaho Forest Conservation Initiative. "Wildlife, fisheries, habitat protection, and public recreation all benefit from this type of conservation approach on private lands," said Craig Gehrke of The Wilderness Society. Ken Retallic, of the Idaho Council of Trout Unlimited, cited benefits for fisheries. "The easements will provide phenomenal benefits to native fisheries, especially westslope cutthroat trout and bull trout populations," Retallic said. Other support came from the Idaho Conservation League and Idaho Rivers United.

"It's the greatest thing for the critters and the people who have played on timber company land for years," says lumberman and

Idaho Fish and Game commissioner Alex Irby, adding that the easement projects are "the worst thing for urban sprawl and backwoods cabins. We in the industry understand the significance of a long-term strategy. It gives a good balance to the area."

Joe Empler, supervisor for a local logging company, put it this way: "I like to see timberland growing timber and not turning into urban sprawl. I think conservation easements are a win-win situation for all parties and the public."

CHAPTER 37

St. Paul Officials Work with Citizens to Create an Inner-City Park

Vicki Monks

Carol Carey admits that not everybody could see beauty in the abandoned railyard on the east side of downtown Saint Paul, Minnesota, before volunteer and redevelopment groups in nearby neighborhoods joined forces to reclaim the land. One of the biggest challenges was to convince others that this long-neglected property near the Mississippi River was worth protecting.

"The area was a toxic mess," says Carey, who was active in the effort and now leads Historic Saint Paul, a heritage preservation organization. Oily patches contaminated the soil, and heaps of junked appliances, garbage, and moldy mattresses littered the yard. Graffiti marred the tall sandstone bluffs at the edge of the site, and thickets of spiny buckthorn made walking treacherous.

As a former industrial property, already contaminated, the 27-acre railyard had been eyed for an asphalt recycling plant or a transfer station for concrete trucks. But Carey and others believed that the land would make a great park site. A park on the land would link up four recreation trails that now end at its boundaries, protect bluff-top views down the

Mississippi, and provide a natural refuge within an easy walk of Lowertown and downtown. A park would aid restoration of migratory waterfowl and songbird habitat along the Mississippi flyway.

A park also would promote the ongoing revitalization of two neighborhoods: the blue-collar East Side and Lowertown, a former warehouse district. The railyard blocked these neighborhoods from each other, from downtown, and from the Mississippi River corridor, while a cleaned-up park with bike trails would link them to downtown and its vitality. An asphalt plant or concrete station would have only reinforced an existing perception that the site and its adjoining neighborhoods were a wasteland. "It would have solidified an impression that there was no hope for a better community." Carey says.

So Carey and other neighborhood activists organized a partnership, the Lowe Phalen Creek Project, to take on the quixotic, complicated task of convincing the city of Saint Paul to purchase the land for conversion to a nature sanctuary. They battled for years to turn their vision into reality, eventually assem-

Originally published as "Off the Track," *Land & People*, Spring 2006. Reprinted with permission from the Trust for Public land. To learn more about TPL, please visit www.tpl.org.

bling a broad coalition of supporters, including members of Congress, the city, the state, the county, the National Park Service (whose Mississippi National River and Recreation Area works with partners to protect lands along the river in the Twin Cities area), and nonprofits. The Trust for Public Land joined the effort to help navigate the project through a maze of legal, political, and financial obstacles and persuade the Burlington Northern and Santa Fe Railway Company to sell the land.

"We walked around, pushed through, leaped over obstacles — any way we could to keep it moving forward," Carey recalls. "So many partners worked hard for years to protect his diamond in the rough; we all saw its potential through the trash and grit. Getting each key partner to succeed took patience and years of community commitment."

A Sacred History

Neighbors knew that the old railyard's history ran long and deep, spanning many cultural groups — from the region's indigenous Dakota inhabitants to successive waves of European settlers to the most recent Hmong and other Southeast Asian immigrants who have settled in nearby neighborhoods.

Thousands of years ago, the prehistoric Hopewell culture thrived along the junction of the Mississippi and Minnesota Rivers at the edge of the Great Plains. These people built burial mounds on the high bluffs overlooking the Mississippi, at the point where the river makes a sharp curve southward toward the Gulf of Mexico.

Dakota people, descendants of the Hopewell, still revere a cave near the brow of the bluffs that they call Wakan Tipi — dwelling place of the spirits. Located near a historic Dakota village and below burial sites on the bluffs, the cave probably served as a ceremonial site and later as a landmark for other tribes like the Ho-Chunk and Anishanabeg. Some Dakota believed it to be the source of their

origin and the home of Unktehi, a water spirit who brings forth new life each spring and protects the water. (White settlers later called it Carver's Cave, for British explorer Jonathan Carver, who described petroglyph images of snakes and buffalo he found etched inside and near the cave opening during his first encounter with the Dakota in 1767.)

In 1862, the year the railroad began laying tracks below the bluffs, almost all of the Dakota in Minnesota were forced into exile, and many were killed. The Dakota had gone to war because the federal government had not honored its 1858 treaty obligations, and they were starving. Fur traders, settlers, Ojibwe, and the Dakota themselves had hunted out most of the game; crops failed; and the federal government delayed sending promised payment and annuities for land the Dakota had given up under the treaty.

During the years of European settlement, the damp, low-lying land below the bluffs and along the river became home to recent immigrants, the working poor, and the industries that employed them. Sawmills and one of the city's first breweries tapped the power of Phalen Creek — which then threaded the property but now runs in an underground culvert — and the brewery carved out cool caverns below the bluffs to store beer. Gradually, the railroad expanded its tracks to create one of the busiest rail maintenance yards in the Midwest, blasting away some of the bluffs to make more room. On the scenic bluff tops, developers leveled all but six of the ancient sacred burial mounds to improve the views for mansions that sprouted there as the economy thrived. (Those six mounds would later be protected in the city's nearby Indian Mounds Park.)

Early in this period of development, rubble from rockslides filled the entrance to Wakan Tipi. Over the next two centuries, the cave was periodically opened, covered, and ignored. In 1913 it was opened as a tourist attraction, and in the Depression, people lived in the cave. In 1977 the city cleared the entrance with the intention of reviving the tourist trade.

But when Native Americans protested that the plan would desecrate a sacred site, the city agreed to install steel doors over the cave entrance to keep tourists and vandals out. At about the same time, the railway removed its maintenance yard and later its rails. By the 1980s, the former railyard degenerated into a dumping ground, and the cave's steel doors were almost obscured by more fallen rocks.

The Greening of a Brownfield

By the time neighborhood groups began eyeing it for a park, the railyard had become what is technically known as a brownfield — an underutilized or abandoned and often contaminated former industrial property. On the face of it, brownfields might not seem like good candidates for parks. But many are located near urban downtowns and major waterways, making them ideal for conversion to parks and open space.

In Saint Paul, the soil at the railyard had been tainted by years of train maintenance with carcinogenic petrochemicals and toxic metals. Remnants of a nearby coal gasification plant and a petrochemical storage facility added to the mess. Because the Burlington Northern and Santa Fe Railway was potentially liable for cleaning up the contamination, the company was more inclined to sell the land to another industrial user who would pave it over and be done with it, says Cordelia Pierson, TPL's project manager in Saint Paul. And the city was wary about accepting land where contamination and liability might be issues. The area was zoned for industry, Pierson notes, "so that was always out there as a threat to us in trying to create the nature sanctuary."

But the community rallied behind the idea, and the Lower Phalen Creek Project grew to include more than 25 partner organizations. On the strength of that support, TPL opened negotiations with the railroad and, over three years, devised and executed a plan to clean up the contamination with private and public money, reducing that potential expense to the railroad and city and further protecting them by purchasing insurance against costs from unforeseen environmental problems.

A wide variety of nonprofits, foundations, and government agencies contributed to the cost of cleaning up the land — more than $3.4 million — and its acquisition for a city park, with TPL taking the lead on fundraising. One early and important commitment came from the Minnesota Department of Natural Resources' recently established Metro Greenways program, which recognized the site's significance as a natural resource in the heart of a city.

Because the site would also become part of the Mississippi National River and Recreation Area, Minnesota congressman Martin Olav Sabo secured federal funding from the National Park Service to purchase the land for the new nature sanctuary, which was named after Congressman Bruce Vento, who served 12 terms in the House and died in 2000 from asbestos-related cancer. Vento was an ardent supporter of parks, and Congress agreed that creating one in his home district would be a fitting tribute. Even after he became ill, Vento took a keen interest in the project — for example, joining neighbors to plant lily pads in a nearby pond. Vento's successor, Congresswoman Betty McCollum, has also lent important support to the project.

Building Community

Creating the Bruce Vento Nature Sanctuary has done more to draw local communities and the Dakota Nation together than any civic project in recent memory. Many residents have been motivated to help improve the site because their own immigrant relatives originally put down roots nearby, while neighborhood leaders have been excited by the project's potential to revitalize communities and economies and to honor the site's spiritual significance for the Dakota.

By the Numbers:
VOLUNTEER FOR VENTO

Estimated number of volunteer hours contributed by residents of Saint Paul's East Side and Lowertown neighborhoods to promote, plan for, and create the Bruce Vento Nature Sanctuary: **13,000**

Number of volunteers in 2003 who helped prepare the former railyard along the Mississippi River to become a park: **150**

Number of hours put in by these volunteers: **800**

Amount of surface debris they helped remove, in tons: **50**

High school interns from the East Side Youth Conservation Corps who helped prepare the site: **17**

Total hours contributed by these interns in 2005: **2,000**

Number of wetland plantings by the interns during this time: **9,000**

Trees and shrubs planted by volunteers from the 3M corporation in the new park: **320**

Total number of trees planted by all volunteers during the project: **700**

Local elementary schools students who volunteered on two days in 2005: **130**

Satisfaction felt by volunteers as a result of all this work: **immeasurable**

"This is a place where people can find rest, be regenerated, and then go back to the urban center," says Weiming Lu, president of the Lowertown Redevelopment corporation. Lu sees the sanctuary as essential to the economic success of the former warehouse district, which is close to downtown and only a short walk from the new sanctuary. The neighborhood's redevelopment has attracted artists and high-tech enterprises with a mix of affordable and upscale housing and work space. Had the railyard become an asphalt plant rather than a park, Lu believes that traffic and pollution might have spun Lowertown into another decline. "We are building community, rather than just building projects," he says.

Neighbors, particularly minority and immigrant residents, contributed thousands of volunteer hours to sanctuary projects, helping city workers haul away 50 tons of debris.

Recently, teenage interns from the East Side Hmong community helped rid the sanctuary of buckthorn. "It's hard work," 16-year-old Keng Lee told a visitor. "Buckthorn is a really tough plant to get rid of. It takes a lot out of you, and the thorns — they're huge." Another young worker, 15-year-old Pakou Thao, discovered a side of herself and a side of nature she hadn't known existed. "I'd never really seen what nature has for me until I worked here," she said. "I didn't think it could be possible for this to be a park, but it is possible. I'm proud because I made it happen — I'm part of it."

In recognition of this land's importance to their heritage, American Indians have been deeply involved in its rehabilitation. Federally recognized Dakota tribes joined the coalition to reclaim and restore the railyard. Young students from the city's American Indian magnet school are growing native plants for the sanctuary, and learning their own history in the process.

At the request of local Dakota people, the steel doors to the cave remain in place. But the cave's immediate environment is now more in keeping with its spiritual nature. The debris that once degraded the site is replaced by a small lake, wetland, trail, and trees. Jacob, an 11-year-old Ojibwe student at the Indian magnet school, says that he's happy park planners let the Indians decide whether to reopen Carver's Cave. "People were very careless with that cave," he says. "The government doesn't really let Indians make choices a lot, so I think that's good for the Indians to get to choose if they want it closed or if they want it open."

At a ceremony to dedicate the sanctuary last spring, in a drenching rain, Jim Rock — a Dakota math and science teacher — offered tobacco, sweetgrass, strawberries, and prayers — a ritual for healing and the wiping away of tears. Growing up, Rock heard stories of Wakan Tipi and wandered through the former railyard's trashed landscape. Later he too joined the coalition.

"We are here today for good feelings," he

Vento Sanctuary Acquisition and Cleanup

National Park Service

Minnesota Department of Natural Resources —
Metro Greenways Program

Minnesota Pollution Control Agency/
U.S. EPA Environmental Assessment Grant

City of Saint Paul

Burlington Northern and Santa Fe Railway Company

U.S. Environmental Protection Agency —
Brownfield Cleanup Grant

The Saint Paul Foundation

Butler Family Foundation

F. R. Bigelow Foundation

St. Paul Travelers Foundation

Ecolab Foundation

McKnight Foundation

McNeely Foundation

Wildwood Fund of Fidelity Investments
Charity Gift Fund

Minnesota Environmental Initiative

Individual donors to the Trust for Public Land

told all of those who had worked to make the project happen. "We hope what has happened in these 140 years, the pain, can be in the past. There is history that needs to be taught, to be acknowledged, to begin the healing. May it never happen again, and please, when you're on these sites, treat them with reverence and teach your children what reverence means — the meaning of respect for the ancestors and for the earth."

Three months later, in July 2005, the campaign that created the Bruce Vento Nature Sanctuary won a national award from Take Pride in America, a partnership established by the U.S. Department of the Interior to engage, support, and recognize volunteers who work to improve our public parks and public lands. The award stressed the partnership of 25 public and private organizations that "turned a community eyesore into a unique urban open space, with recreational, cultural and natural benefits."

"Creating this nature sanctuary has been a true cooperative effort and a labor of love for a huge and diverse group of people," says TPL's Cordelia Pierson. "The neighbors are the heroes here. They saw what this place could be and rallied all of us to make it happen. Now we all can find sanctuary in this place that has been so important for so many cultures over so many generations."

CHAPTER 38

San Diego Revises Its General Plan to Guide Future Urban Growth

Nancy Bragado

The last time the City of San Diego up-dated its general plan, charting the future of thousands of acres of then-undeveloped land was the city's primary concern. Twenty-five years later, the city is more than 90 percent developed, growth projections show a contin-ued demand for new housing, and the city is shaping its future using a strategy based on infill and redevelopment.

"Our challenge for the new general plan was how to handle projected new growth while maintaining the qualities of San Diego that people value," explained Planning Direc-tor Gail Goldberg.

The City of Villages

After a two-year public process, the city council adopted the City of Villages strategy as the recommended course of action. The strategy calls for new growth to be targeted in mixed-use village centers in order to create lively activity hubs, provide housing, improve walkability and help support a state-of-the-art transit system. In addition to this strategy, the council adopted a slate of policies to pro-tect the natural environment, increase housing affordability, enhance neighborhoods, improve mobility, create economic prosperity and pro-vide for equitable development and public fa-cilities.

The City of Villages growth strategy — and San Diego's new citywide policies — be-came the strategic framework element of the general plan, which provided direction to planning staff on how to update the rest of the general plan. The citywide policy areas were expanded and refined as nine elements of a new general plan. Central themes of the gen-eral plan include:

- Transit-land use connection;
- Housing;
- Community planning; and
- Infrastructure.

Transit-Land Use Connection

Planning Commission Chairperson Barry J. Schultz calls "transit and land use coordination ... an integral part of the general plan and a fundamental component of a smart growth strategy."

The city's highest density residential and employment uses are to be located in village centers and corridors along the regional transit system. Equally important, lower density uses are to be located away from transit-served areas, and all parks, open spaces and residential neighborhoods are to be preserved. Additional policies further delineate where development is prohibited or limited, such as lands in the multi-habitat planning area, steep slopes and flood hazard areas.

Urban design element policies further strengthen the commitment to transit, neighborhoods and the natural environment through transit-oriented, distinctive neighborhoods and landform preservation design guidelines.

Housing

The village strategy seeks to provide opportunities for developing higher density and diverse housing types, largely through infill and redevelopment of aging commercial centers. By focusing the city's highest density housing and employment uses in transit-served areas, more opportunities are provided to improve jobs/housing balance within communities and to improve the linkages between jobs and housing citywide. However, the plan does not contain recommended density goals; actual designation of sites and implementation of the plan is deferred to the community planning program.

Community Planning

San Diego's 330 square miles are divided into more than 50 community planning areas. These areas are monitored by community planning groups comprising volunteers who serve as advisors to the planning commission and city council. The community plans provide detailed community and neighborhood-based planning recommendations that supplement the general plan's citywide focus, and are officially recognized as a part of the general plan land use element.

A drawback to the program is that community plans take several years to update, and staffing levels cannot keep pace with the need to keep community plans up-to-date. The general plan recognizes the critical role of the community planning program and seeks to help streamline the preparation of community plans so that they can be updated more frequently. Streamlining would occur in part by clearly documenting the role of the general and community plans. Rather than having each community plan function as a mini general plan covering the full range of general plan topics, community plans would focus on providing site-specific guidance to tailor the application of citywide policies.

In deference to the community planning program, no land use amendments or rezonings will take place concurrently with general plan adoption. General plan implementation will occur as community plans are updated or amended over time. Despite this linkage to the community plans, some community planning groups are opposed to the new general plan because they believe it will result in unwanted new growth in their communities.

Planning for Infrastructure

According to Council Member Toni Atkins, "For older urban communities, the primary challenge has always been to make sure that infrastructure improvements, including much needed public facilities and services, are adequately provided for in the implementation plan."

Infrastructure in the city's urban neighborhoods has not kept pace with growth. Given the city's longstanding status as a low-revenue city and a current budget crisis resulting in part from pension underfunding, the short-term outlook for making up the facilities shortfall is grim. Under these conditions, some of the neighborhood opposition to increased density is more of a logical response to funding shortfalls, rather than a NIMBY ("Not in my back yard") attitude. To address this issue, the general plan proposes that new broad-based funding sources be considered and that discretionary projects provide their fair share of infrastructure and public facilities. An individual project may not be able to solve all of a community's facilities problems, but it can certainly not compound existing deficiencies.

The Regional Connection

Regional initiatives underway are adding momentum and resources to implementing San Diego's strategy. The Regional Comprehensive Plan, prepared by the San Diego Association of Governments (SANDAG), outlines a complementary smart growth strategy for the region along with a competitive grants program designed to reward smart growth planning with regional transportation funds. SANDAG also oversees the implementation of the Regional Transit Vision, which outlines a plan to greatly improve transit service throughout the region.

The new general plan is intended to proactively address the challenges of growth and development through better linkage between transit and land use planning, preserving important open spaces, strengthening our existing communities and creating new neighborhood centers. It focuses on what residents love most about San Diego — its distinctive neighborhoods and natural environment — while addressing its most pressing infrastructure and housing challenges.

Ideally, the plan would be linked to concurrent community plan amendments that would bring the City of Villages closer to fruition. However, the incremental approach of going from the strategic framework element, to a comprehensive general plan update, to a series of community plan amendments, allows San Diego to gain faith with the public and build upon its successes over time.

CHAPTER 39

Santa Rosa Goes "Green" to Enhance Its Environment

Dell Tredinnick

Growth and environmental protection are often at odds, but not in the City of Santa Rosa, where city leaders decided three years ago to bring the two into balance. The result was the voluntary Santa Rosa Build It Green (SR BIG) program.

At present, SR BIG has certified as "green" more than 75 dwelling units, and 850-plus additional dwelling units have applied for green status under the program.

What Is SR BIG?

A voluntary program, SR BIG promotes building and remodeling homes in a way that reduces energy demands, releases far fewer pollutants into the atmosphere, conserves water and reduces construction waste. The resulting structures are easier to maintain, less expensive to operate, produce less air pollution and are healthier to occupy. This may seem impossible or impossibly expensive for most people, but it is neither.

The program follows a set of simple but comprehensive Green Building Guidelines that provide a roadmap for building design

and construction. These guidelines were hammered out by developers, environmentalists, bankers, planners, educators, architects, engineers, maintenance personnel, designers, government officials and city staff. The result is a consistent and flexible tool that can deliver significantly better results and a better bottom line than the conventional building process. The guidelines SR BIG uses are adaptable to any geographic/climatic region or distinctive culture.

What Does a SR BIG Home Look Like?

The short answer is "like any other home." The SR BIG program has certified large custom homes, production subdivision homes, affordable homes (built by Habitat for Humanity) and municipal remodeled dwellings, such as the Santa Rosa Samuel Jones Hall Homeless Shelter.

SR BIG also embraces the very active remodeling market by reaching out to the public in workshops and educating local home improvement suppliers. Remodelers can gain

SR BIG certification by adding more insulation, installing low-flow and energy efficient fixtures and appliances, using paints and coating that emit low or no volatile organic compounds, and basically following the same guidelines, where possible, that exist for new construction.

How Are SR BIG Homes Evaluated?

Green homes differ from most conventional dwellings in how they perform in four rated categories. These categories and the required minimum points needed in each are:

1. Energy Efficiency — 11 points (107 possible);
2. Resource Conservation — 6 points (64 possible);
3. Indoor Air Quality — 5 points (45 possible); and
4. Water Efficiency — 3 points (31 possible).

An SR BIG home must achieve a total score of at least 50 points, which includes the minimum number of points in each of these four categories. A dwelling or project can get additional points to bring it up to the total minimum requirement of 50 points if it qualifies for community and/or innovation points.

How Does SR BIG Work?

The SR BIG program's success is attributed to several key elements:

- **It is voluntary.** Mandatory programs can work but typically result in construction that achieves only the minimum requirements. A voluntary program allows the market to drive the standard, achieving better and better buildings as time goes by and builders find more efficient ways to do things. The competition to be "greener" is already manifesting in the city's building culture.

- **It has a strong marketing component.** Santa Rosa actively educates the public, suppliers, designers, contractors and everyone involved in the building process. This creates an informed public that demands greater performance from their homes.

- **The program uses trained personnel.** Independent third party inspectors, who must pass a rigorous exam at Sonoma State University, perform the inspections. Currently, about 50 SR BIG inspectors have been trained and certified. Developers and builders hire the SR BIG inspectors to help them achieve and verify their project's green status. The city recommends that the inspector is involved in a project as early as possible so that green scores can be maximized by better design and early integration of green elements.

- **The program provides certification.** Once the project has been "scored" by the inspector, the SR BIG Executive Committee reviews each application, verifies the points gathered and awards the certificate, which is a source of pride to homeowners and can be used to enhance resale.

- **The program is dynamic and flexible.** Santa Rosa is constantly looking for ways to improve the process and program. Currently, it's focusing on ways to bring "green" to affordable housing projects. Green homes cost much less to operate and maintain and are healthier living environments. Individuals with low or fixed incomes have the greatest need for such savings.

- **Information is readily shared.** SR BIG owes much of its success to regional and national partners and shared knowledge. An example is the shared product data base, an online tool developed by the regional green partners that helps a supplier or do-it-yourselfer find locally available "green" products to meet their project needs (online at *www.ciwmb.ca.gov/Green Building/Materials*).

How Does SR BIG Relate to LEED?

Leadership in Energy and Environmental Design (LEED) standards were originally established for commercial and municipal buildings. LEED is an international rating mechanism that requires significantly more attention and inspections. LEED is in the process of developing standards for homes. Once those standards are complete, they will complement the SR BIG program. The upfront costs are typically much more for LEED than SR BIG.

Putting It in Perspective

Homes in California account for 31 percent of the state's energy use. New homes built in California must meet Title 24 energy efficiency standards. SR BIG homes must ex-

ceed the Title 24 standards and get 1 point for every percentage point by which they exceed the required energy efficiency standards. An SR BIG home is at least 11 percent more energy efficient than a conventional new home and is commensurately less expensive to heat, cool and operate. That also means that the environmental impact of the home is reduced, which benefits everybody.

Water conservation is another area included in the SR BIG integrated approach. Choosing landscaping plants that are drought tolerant and installing high-efficiency irrigation systems can greatly reduce water use and create a beautiful space even during a drought. Highly efficient water devices inside the home are also important. Low-flow fixtures and Energy Star appliances are vital in saving water and reducing overall energy demands.

The initial cost of going green can be minimal, and the long-term savings can be significant. While there are many types and levels of green homes, research shows that for every $1 invested in a "green" home, a return of $10 is realized after the first year or two and thereafter for the life of the structure. Building green is building smart.

CHAPTER 40

Sarasota Improves Safety in Its Neighborhoods through Enhanced Urban Design Practices

Sherry Plaster Carter

The idea of smart growth is to reverse what we regard as the undesirable impacts of suburban sprawl, such as inner-city neglect, heavy traffic, and the loss of our natural environment. While various groups differ somewhat in their particular concerns and in their definitions and use of the term "smart growth," we can all agree that the improvement of safety and the perception of it in existing downtowns and residential areas is paramount to achieving common start growth initiatives — particularly those that seek to redevelop inner-city areas and that encourage people to walk and use public transit. All smart growth initiatives require environments where people feel and are safe.

Not coincidentally, "safe" areas tend to be places with the greatest sense of a cohesive community: areas that are active, attractive, and functional and that support the needs of residents, businesses, and visitors. Design fulfills a critical function, and designing for safety means designing for community.

How is this kind of design achieved? Many people have heard of *crime prevention through environmental design*, commonly referred to as CPTED, but now many CPTED practitioners have gone beyond the basic principles. Their goal is to craft a framework on which to build safer places by creating more visible neighborhoods.

Safe and Unsafe

Where to begin? First, it's important to understand the answer to the question "What makes people feel unsafe?" Over the past 10 years, my partner, Stan Carter, and I have conducted CPTED training throughout the United States. We ask participants this very question, and typical responses have included:

- Dark and isolated areas.
- Areas that are hidden from view or that allow for concealment.
- Vacant, abandoned, and unkept properties.
- The perception of being lost.
- Crowding and congestion.
- Restricted spaces.

Originally published as "Community Safety: Beyond the Basics," *Public Management*, Vol. 84, No. 5, June 2002. Published by the International City/County Management Association, Washington, D.C. Reprinted with permission of the publisher.

- Overgrowth of vegetation
- Signs of vandalism.
- Illegal activities.
- Loitering and panhandling.
- Lack of access to assistance.

Conversely, "safe" areas are clean, orderly, and well-lit places where people follow the rules, buildings are occupied and actively used, and ownership is demonstrated through well-kept grounds, gardens, artwork, and preserved historic features. Other noted factors include the presence of authority or access to assistance.

Basic CPTED

Many undesirable environmental conditions, and even disorderly behavior, can be reversed through fairly simple design, maintenance, and management strategies, commonly referred to as CPTED practices. This concept was introduced by Professor C. Ray Jeffery in his book of the same title. In present-day use, the CPTED concept incorporates both Jeffery's contention that the physical environment is as important as the social environment and Oscar Newman's precept that people care for what they believe is theirs — giving rise to the importance of territoriality.

Both Newman and Jeffery have been influenced in part by Jane Jacobs's famous book *The Death and Life of Great American Cities*. Since Jacobs's book was published in 1961, a variety of theories, concepts, and strategies have developed that seek to minimize the chances for crime and to maximize the opportunities for positive social interaction.

Timothy D. Crowe, criminologist, in his book *Crime Prevention Through Environmental Design*, expands upon the assumption that "the proper design and effective use of the built environment can lead to a reduction in the fear of crime and the incidence of crime, and to an improvement in the quality of life." Crowe promotes the use of three basic concepts: natural surveillance, natural access control, and territorial reinforcement.

Natural surveillance. The placement of physical features, activities, and people in such a way as to maximize visibility [includes] the lighting of public spaces and walkways at night.

We feel and are safer when our activities and those of others can be monitored. Creating opportunities for casual surveillance can be accomplished with design features and the placement of activities.

Natural access control. The physical guidance of people coming to and going from a space, by the judicious placement of signs, entrances, exists, fencing, landscaping, and lighting.

Barriers can be real or symbolic. The goal is to clarify acceptable routes. Clarified access assists the first-time user by providing direction, raising comfort levels, and reducing the vulnerability associated with feeling lost. At the same time, trespassing and unacceptable entry are more easily recognized.

Territorial reinforcement. The use of physical attributes that express ownership, such as fences, pavement, treatments, are signage, landscaping, and the placement of buildings.

The idea is to define clearly the private, semiprivate, and public spaces. Good border definition provides visual cues as to ownership and acceptable behavior. Property that is enhanced is perceived as cared for and therefore looked after. Likewise, ownership or a sense of proprietorship can be increased by the participation and physical representation of a target population. Examples include displays of student art in schools, historic preservation projects, community gardens, and cultural themes in transit stations.

In addition to these three basic CPTED strategies, consideration must be given to maintenance, which often is included as a fourth principle.

Maintenance. Allows for the continued use of a space for its intended purpose and serves as an additional expression of ownership.

Beyond the Basics

The design, use, and maintenance of a space can reduce opportunities for crime, enhance comfort, and have an overall positive impact upon quality of life. Design alone, however, cannot resolve all public safety issues associated with declining neighborhoods and downtowns.

A successful program must consider social and economic factors and their relationships with disorderly and criminal behavior. Efforts to do this have resulted in an expansion upon the basic CPTED principles discussed above.

Community CPTED

This author, working with another company on a financial sustainability study for the city of Sarasota, Florida, has developed a model by which selected physical, social, and economic factors can be examined in relationship to one another. These relationships then can be used both to predict a pattern of increasing disorder and criminal behavior and to form the basis for specific countering strategies appropriate to the target area. I call this model community CPTED. It's a process that can be applied to a small or a large area and is particularly useful for residential neighborhoods.

The process begins with a review of basic demographic data for households: educational attainment, income, composition, and housing type and value. This review is followed by an examination of land use mix and spatial distribution of assessed values. Calls for law enforcement services and code violations are plotted, and traffic patterns and volume are determined. These steps begin the identification of problem areas.

Next comes the field survey. The following circumstances are noted on maps: the condition of public and private facilities; the condition of transitions between land uses, particularly residential and business; transportation patterns; and social patterns. Physical conditions that support order and community and those that disrupt them are identified.

The physical data are compared with the demographic and public service data compiled earlier. Finally, public opinion is sought and used in developing customized recommendations for combined strategies to address the physical, social, and economic issues.

Here are two examples of problems described in the Sarasota study, with related recommendations:

Negative traffic impacts. In all residential areas, a notable factor relating to neighborhood cohesion, homeownership, and physical deterioration was the manner in which roads were widened, along with the amount and speed of traffic moving through, next to, or around residential areas. Routine road improvements had destroyed the residential quality of many older neighborhoods.

Left were fragmented, dysfunctional residential sections with ill-defined boundaries and with little hope of improving on their own. Two key recommendations, which would require the involvement of the affected citizens, working with planning and design assistance, included:

- Creating identity and a sense of pride by improving and defining boundaries; enhancing the public space with signage, landscaping, and historic or cultural connections; and involving local children and artists in these efforts.
- Streetscape improvements to mitigate the impacts of roads and traffic. Might include traffic-calming neighborhood entry features and suitable buffers along heavily traveled roads.

In general, both strategies reinforce the sense of community by fashioning a more orderly and secure environment that promotes positive social interaction. These improvements make a neighborhood more attractive to newcomers and enhance the quality of life for existing residents.

Low educational attainment. The level of household educational attainment was a factor consistently found to be related to income, the physical deterioration of both personal and public property, and disorderly and criminal behavior. Low levels of education and skills were directly related to people's ability to provide for themselves, their families, and their neighborhoods.

Improving the appearance and function of the neighborhood could have a positive effect by bringing in better role models and raising the personal self-esteem of residents. But a successful program also would include youth development and adult education opportunities. Also, given an aging housing stock, shortages in the construction industry, and limited job opportunities for non-college-bound youth, training in the construction fields was specifically recommended.

Overall, implementation for such programs requires a trained staff, collaboration between and among governmental departments, and meaningful public participation. Benefits include the enhancements of physical, social, and economic conditions that support smart growth initiatives.

CHAPTER 41

Seattle, Other Cities, Take Steps to Improve Their Air Quality and Environment

Josh Goodman

When it comes to climate change initiatives, states and localities are up front and out there. Consider one 90-day period last year:

In late September, New Mexico became the first state to join the Chicago Climate Exchange, a market where businesses and governments pledge either to reduce their greenhouse-gas emissions or buy credits from other participants who have.

In early November, Seattle City Light announced that it had become the first major U.S. utility to reduce its net greenhouse-gas emissions to zero.

On December 20, seven Northeastern states that make up the Regional Greenhouse Gas Initiative — known as RGGI — announced a mandatory multistate agreement to reduce carbon dioxide emissions from power plants.

Just as this dizzying array of activity highlights interest in staving off global warming, it also reflects federal inaction. Since the Bush administration and the U.S. Congress refused to ratify the Kyoto Protocol — the international agreement to reduce greenhouse gases — many state and local officials have stepped up their efforts to fill the void. As a result, the climate-change issue is testing the ability of state and municipal governments to create political consensus, drive technological innovation and influence federal policy.

Most efforts at reducing global warming focus on limiting man-made emissions of carbon dioxide, a greenhouse gas produced by the burning of fossil fuels such as oil, natural gas and coal. The action options range from greater reliance on renewable energy to increased investment in mass transit to new regulations on industry. If there's a reasonable approach out there, some state or local government is probably thinking of trying it. "The states have been the leaders in climate change and will continue to be the leaders," says Joanne Morin, a New Hampshire environmental administrator involved in RGGI.

Three of the efforts stand out for their ambition and the attention they have garnered. The first, and perhaps most controversial, dates back to 2004. That's when California developed rules to place limits on carbon dioxide emissions from new cars and light trucks. These standards haven't been implemented yet and are currently being challenged

Originally published as "Greenhouse Gumption," *Governing*, Vol. 19, No. 8, May 2006. Published by Congressional Quarterly Inc., Washington, D.C. Reprinted with permission of the publisher.

in court. But they have proved to be politically viable in other places: Ten states have said they will meet the California standards if the state's rules go forward.

Then there's the call to arms from a group of mayors led by Seattle's Greg Nickels to participate in the Kyoto Protocol, with or without the blessing of a federal signature on the treaty. Under the Kyoto standards, the United States is supposed to reduce its greenhouse-gas production to 7 percent less than 1990 levels by 2012. Nickels reaffirmed that Seattle would be taking steps to meet the 7 percent goal and then began to persuade others to join him — an effort that has landed the support of more than 200 mayors. If these promises are met, 45 million Americans — 15 percent of the U.S. population — will be living in places abiding by Kyoto.

Most recently, the regional greenhouse-gas group took a major step to reduce CO_2 emissions from power plants. The states involved — Connecticut, Delaware, Maine, New Hampshire, New Jersey, New York, Vermont and, as of April, Maryland — promised a 10 percent reduction in power plant emissions by 2019.

On the Ramparts

It's one thing to write a slogan or make a pledge. It's another to reach lofty goals, and that won't be easy — technologically or politically. Some business groups are especially concerned because many of the tools needed to reduce carbon dioxide emissions are not yet available. When it comes to meeting the California auto emission rules, "there are only a handful of models that would currently meet the standards," says Charles Territo, a spokesman for the Alliance of Automobile Manufacturers. Similarly, Franz Litz, a New York state environmental official who chairs a RGGI working group, admits that the technology to scrub CO_2 from power plant emissions does not currently exist.

The officials promulgating these rules are banking on regulation to forge the technological innovations needed to meet the standards. Although that might sound confrontational, it tells only part of the story. While the battle over California's auto emission standards is a classic struggle between environmentalists and industry, both Nickels with his 200 mayors and the Northeast compact of eight states are working with the business community to develop a workable road map.

To generate a plan in Seattle to meet the Kyoto standards, Nickels appointed a "Green Ribbon Commission" that included a former Starbucks CEO, the chairman of REI Inc. and a local cement plant manager, as well as the founder of Earth Day. In March, the commission produced its recommendations, which called for investing in more mass transit, bike trails and energy-efficient buildings as well as — and more controversially — imposing congestion pricing on roads and passing a parking tax.

Although the local business community might have been expected to oppose at least some of these ideas, in reality it is teetering somewhere between cautious optimism and ambivalence. "We see this as a good step forward," says Charles Knutson, vice president for public affairs for the Greater Seattle Chamber of Commerce, adding, "We currently don't have a position." That statement may speak to a cultural difference between Seattle's business community and the U.S. Chamber of Commerce, which has actively opposed greenhouse-gas regulation, but it also suggests that compromise between environmentally oriented public officials and cost-conscious industry isn't impossible. While he expects the business sector to oppose some of his proposals, Nickels is recruiting major Seattle employers to voluntarily pursue measures to reduce emissions, much as he recruited mayors.

The Regional Greenhouse Gas Initiative is also seeking a business-friendly track, notably with a trading system where power plants can sell emissions allowances to those that fail to meet the standards. This type of cap-and-trade program is generally regarded as a way to keep down costs. It is especially appropriate for carbon dioxide because transferring pollution from one place to another is not harmful — all that matters is the total amount of pollution generated. "In some ways, carbon is the perfect pollutant to control with cap and trade because you're not worried about short-term local concentrations," Litz says.

This concept has also led RGGI to include "offsets." With offsets, emitters are allowed to spend money on curtailing greenhouse gases elsewhere, in place of meeting their emissions targets. For example, under the initiative's tentative rules, power plants will be able to meet the standards by doing such things as planting trees rather than simply producing cleaner emissions. When the pollution allowances reach certain price thresholds, emitters are allowed to rely more heavily on offsets — a measure intended to control costs.

The danger in making concessions to business is that they may come at the cost of support from environmentalists. For example, both Dan Lashof of the Natural Resources Defense Council and Daniel Sosland, executive director of Environment Northeast, support RGGI. Yet they view offsets with some skepticism, worrying that, if broadly utilized or poorly designed, they could fail to produce meaningful emissions reductions. This balancing act underscores the guinea-pig role state and local governments play, both in terms of overcoming technical obstacles and forging political coalitions. Surprisingly, that's not something that worries Litz, who says his group of eight states is concerned only with establishing a model for others to follow.

Political Influence

Nickels' mayoral partnership and the RGGI group aren't the only state or local climate-change compacts. There is also, among others, the West Coast Governors' Global Warming Initiative and the Southwest Climate Change Initiative. Nickels links this impulse to collaborate to the global scope of climate change. "None of us as individuals or even individual communities feel we have the power to change it," he says. "If I were simply to say Seattle is going to do what it can in a vacuum, it would be a very frustrating exercise."

There are also frustrations inherent in working with one's peers. Although Nickels found mayors eager to join him, the tough part may come as city leaders have to take concrete steps to reduce emissions. RGGI went through this process last year: Massachusetts and Rhode Island, two states that had been part of the initiative's discussions, refused to join, citing fears of increased energy costs.

Not everyone sees the compacts and their regulations as an appropriate solution. Marlo Lewis Jr., a senior fellow at the Competitive Enterprise Institute, argues that regulations on CO_2 emissions could cost hundreds of billions of dollars without significantly affecting global warming. He also says that the current state and local efforts are intended to create a web of regulatory requirements aimed at compelling business leaders to do something they wouldn't otherwise do: Ask Congress to adopt national regulations for CO_2 emissions. The state and local groups, he says, "want to confront Congress, but especially the Bush administration, with a patchwork quilt that will drive the business community up the wall. They see this as a political campaign."

Those pursuing climate change efforts make no secret of their desire to influence federal policy. That's because there are substantial limitations on what states or localities can achieve on their own. Nickels has no legal authority to punish mayors who do not keep their word to him. Proponents of RGGI face a number of obstacles to getting their trading system operational, but, even if they do, they have no power to compel other states to join. And, besides facing challenges in court, California must get permission from the U.S. Environmental Protection Agency before it can enforce its auto emissions regulations. Furthermore, environmentalists fear that state and local rules will fail to chip away at emissions nationally or globally because polluters will simply shift their activities to unregulated locales.

As a result, state and local governments may make their most significant impact on greenhouse-gas emissions by driving federal action, either in the coercive way that Lewis describes or in the way supporters of the initiatives say they plan: by proving that the programs can work. In particular, they say that if their efforts demonstrate that progress can be made against global warming without adverse economic impacts, then they will have neutralized the strongest argument against federal action. "There's a lot of hope that state activity will end up driving federal action," says Sosland. "There's a lot of governors of both parties who believe that is inevitable."

Inevitable or not, it remains a goal. "All of the states involved in RGGI would love to see a national model," says Litz. "We would love to see an international program. You have to start somewhere."

CHAPTER 42

Silver Spring, Other Communities, Take Steps to Improve Their Inner-Ring Suburbs

Mary Ann Barton

Neglected inner-ring suburbs finally receive the attention they need to thrive.

Like a family with three kids, city and county officials have their hands full with three types of communities, all clamoring for attention: downtown, the loud and brassy firstborn; the newborn outer suburbs, wailing in the crib; and the inner-ring suburbs, the quiet middle-child. Traditionally, the two demanding the most attention — downtowns and outer suburbs — have been local governments' first priorities. Local officials focus on building roads and schools in the newer outlying suburbs; in the urban areas, they try to create a mix of development, including renovating office buildings and arts and convention centers.

Overlooked in the equation are the long-suffering inner-ring suburbs, literally trapped between the urban center and outer-ring suburbs. Decaying from lack of attention, they have grown tired and worn. Partly as a result, some inner-ring suburb residents have moved to newer suburbs, often leaving their lower-income neighbors behind.

"[The inner-ring suburbs] all are suffering from common problems: the aging process and losing their tax base," says William Hudnut, former mayor of Indianapolis, current senior fellow at the Urban Land Institute in Washington, D.C., and author of "Halfway to Everywhere: A Portrait of America's First-Tier Suburbs."

"First-tier is not a connotation of elite status," says Hudnut, who also serves as a member of the Chevy Chase, Md., Town Council. First-tier suburbs "were the first ones founded after the central city —first in time, first in place."

In addition to losing people and increasing poverty, the older suburbs are experiencing a deteriorating infrastructure, rapid ethnic change, a decreasing retail presence and poor school performance, Hudnut points out. To reverse those trends, some communities are focusing redevelopment efforts in inner-ring suburbs in an effort to reestablish their cultural, social and economic viability.

Blaming the Throw-away Society

Once seen as an answer to life in the city, inner suburbs have suffered from the Ameri-

Originally published as "A New Lease on Life," *American City & County*, Vol. 119, No. 3, March 2004. Published by Prism Business Media, Overland Park, KS. Reprinted with permission of the publisher.

can cultural attitude of "use it up and throw it away," Hudnut says. "Move up and move out. You make it in the first suburb, and then you move on. These places become jumping-off communities for people."

But across the country, Hudnut says, local officials in places like Emeryville, Calif., and Chelsea, Mass., are renewing their acquaintance with inner-ring suburbs, forging public-private partnerships to bring them back to life and allowing them to age gracefully.

Emeryville, which is adjacent to Oakland on the east side of San Francisco Bay, began losing businesses in the 1960s because of a high cost of living. It soon found itself littered with abandoned buildings and land, and pollution and brownfields, according to City Manager John Flores.

After Flores was hired in the 1980s, vacant warehouses were converted to artists' lofts, and a 33-story condominium building was built along the waterfront. His job included adding trees and parks to the community, and attracting more service and technology companies to an area that once housed heavy industry. The city brought in big-box retail and started building new housing.

Developers and businesses were drawn to Emeryville for several reasons, including the city's central location at the nexus of four Bay Area freeways and the availability of large parcels of land, which gave it an edge over neighboring cities, according to "Behind the Boomtown," a report by the East Bay Alliance for a Sustainable Economy. City government's orientation toward business, low tax rates and desire to provide a smooth development process made locating in Emeryville attractive, the report says.

Extensive capital improvements provided the necessary infrastructure for new, high-intensity land uses. The city's willingness to allow large-scale developments that changed the shape and character of the landscape provided developers with opportunities rarely found in the densely built urban environment of the East Bay, according to the report.

The city also made extensive use of state-granted redevelopment powers to take land for private development and to fund large-scale redevelopment efforts, according to the report. With 95 percent of the city under the jurisdiction of the redevelopment agency, the scope of the powers extended to nearly every parcel of land.

Like Emeryville, other communities are attracting new retailers to places once home to crabgrass and boarded-up strip malls. New residents, tired of long commutes, are giving inner-ring suburbs a second look. For example, parts of Arlington County, Va., such as the Clarendon neighborhood, have become revitalized after a new grocery store, new shopping center and new housing were built. "In one generation, Arlington has gone from a declining inner-ring suburb to a vibrant urban community by successfully pairing transit with good urban design based on a mix of uses and 'walkability,'" says Chris Zimmerman, Arlington County board member.

Location, Location, Location

Several communities have found that retailers provide the platform for developing inner-ring suburbs. To attract business growth, they are playing up the strengths of inner suburbs, such as a close-in location and unique neighborhoods.

Silver Spring, Md., once was written off as a tired inner-suburb in Montgomery County, but, today, it has seen a rebirth through a $400 million redevelopment effort. The project follows one of Hudnut's pieces of advice: build near transportation. Silver Spring is one of the busiest subway stops on the Washington, D.C., area's Metro system.

Redevelopment first caught the attention of Montgomery County Executive Doug Duncan 10 years ago in his first term. As part of an aggressive smart-growth program, Duncan made inner-suburbs a priority. "He had a vision from day one for what Silver Spring could be, and he's gotten the right people to come to the table and share his vision, and it's happening right now," says Bonnie Ayers, Montgomery County spokesperson.

The county bought 22 acres in the Silver Spring area and hired The Peterson Co. in Fairfax, Va., to help make it more livable. The area was not attractive to residents because they had to travel out of it to find a large grocery store, hardware store, movie theater or book store — the kinds of amenities residents expect in a community.

County officials thought that new retail would revitalize the core and spread out from there. At first, attracting new tenants was not easy. The demographics were good, but retailers only would be convinced if other tenants were making the move with them. After considerable effort by the city and developer, stores began moving in, and, more importantly, they were successful. The county attracted a Whole Foods supermarket and cultural attractions such as the American Film Institute Silver Theatre and Cultural Center. Cable TV giant Discovery Communications also moved its headquarters there from Bethesda, Md. Now, the Silver Spring Whole Foods store is ranked number three in sales among the company's 180 stores.

Like Silver Spring predicted, the success of the first few businesses bred further success. Today, the city's retail space is 69 percent leased, and letters of intent to lease an additional 11 percent of the space have been signed. Borders will open a bookstore there this spring.

Strength in Numbers

Some cities have banded together to renew their inner suburbs. For example, the Michigan Suburbs Alliance (MSA), which is composed of 24 cities with a combined population of 1 million people, formed in 2002. The Michigan cities banded together initially because "there was a growing sense among city officials that the issues confronting them were beyond their control," says alliance Executive Director Jim Townsend. "As a group, they can possibly influence public policies that contribute to or subsidize sprawl."

The MSA is implementing a Redevelopment-Ready Communities Project. The group is identifying what successful inner suburbs are doing to attract and keep businesses and residents, and then developing a set of redevelopment process standards for its members.

Once the standards are in place, the MSA will invite an independent third party to review its members' redevelopment processes and certify that they meet the standards. Certification will demonstrate that the cities have favorable environments for development, and it will give cities a marketing tool that can be used to attract developers. "We [try to stop] the cycle of build-and-abandon, and encourage rebuilding these older communities," Townsend says. "One way we do that is to get communities to work together on redevelopment strategies, to 'brand' themselves as 'redevelopment-ready.'"

"We have to succeed in people demanding to live in older suburbs," says Townsend, whose nonprofit corporation makes its home in Ferndale, an older inner-ring suburb. "The chief advantage of the inner suburbs is their central location within a region, between the central city and the newly developed exurbs. They feature lots of access to transportation links and a region's major job centers and other destinations, so you can get lower commute times and generally have more options for things to do."

The alliance also promotes inner suburbs as more "walkable" because many were developed initially as stops on trolley or train lines. Many also feature older "they don't make them like they used to" housing stock and a decent amount of density to support stimulating nightlife.

Looking to the future, the main challenge facing inner suburbs, according to Townsend, is "to realize they must grow to survive. Costs in these communities are going up rapidly, so they have to figure out how to generate more tax revenue without taxing their populations into oblivion. That means building up, getting more dense — not things that most suburbanites have traditionally embraced."

"In short, the Ozzy [*sic*] and Harriet model, nuclear family-centered, segregated land-uses version of suburbia does not work, especially in older suburbs," Townsend says. "We need to engage in a dialogue that will help residents come up with a new vision of their communities that is sustainable."

CHAPTER 43

Sitka, Other Cities, Work with Nonprofits to Promote Conservation

Rebecca Bryant

From Ecotrust's office in a renovated red-brick building on the banks of the Willamette River in Portland, there is a view of Broadway Bridge and Union Station. The office is an open, high-ceiling room decorated with plants, photos, maps, even a moose head, full rack and all. It could be any professional office, but "we're not," jokes communications director Ted Wolf. "We're a demolition company."

Wolf is referring to the organization's penchant for demolishing existing paradigms, especially when it comes to the relationship between conservation, rural economic development, and community decision making. Ecotrust was founded in March 1991 by Spencer Beebe, an advocate of tropical rain forest conservation, who hoped to further the credibility of international efforts by demonstrating at home — in the Pacific Northwest — what he and others were preaching abroad. Drawn by the visionary Beebe, the fourteen-member staff of paradigm-busters are an eclectic group. What they share, says Wolf, is a belief that things can be done differently.

Ecotrust has a working board of directors that meets three times a year. Like the staff, it is diverse. Unified by a core commitment to conservation, board members have achieved success in different areas. Board chair Jack Hood Vaughn is a former director of the Peace Corps; others come from private consulting, nonprofits, and banking. Ecotrust also has a large advisory council to call upon when further expertise is needed.

The overriding mission or civic agenda is to conserve and restore ecosystems by helping local communities develop their capacity to fulfill human needs and maintain ecological integrity. Most of the work is decentralized. Within the bioregion of temperate coastal rain forests, Ecotrust has local partnerships (each distinctive in character) at Columbia Pacific, Oregon; Willapa Bay, Washington; Clayoquot Sound, British Columbia; Kitlope River, British Columbia; Sitka, Alaska; and Prince William Sound/Copper River, Alaska.

To support its local partnerships, Ecotrust has also been building bioregional institutions. Interrain Pacific, an effort supported

Originally published as "Conservation, Community, and Rural Economic Development," *National Civic Review*, Vol. 86, No. 2, Summer 1997. Published by the National Civic League, Denver, CO. Reprinted with permission of the publisher.

by Intel and other corporate and university participants, uses geographic information system (GIS) and other computer technologies to understand large-scale patterns of change. Mapping aerial and satellite images into computer databases provides a baseline for monitoring social, economic, and ecological changes in local ecosystems.

In its initial scoping for the Willapa Bay project, Ecotrust noticed that people didn't lack creativity or business ideas. In short supply were business skills, marketing know-how, and risk capital for business ventures. To address those problems, Ecotrust persuaded Chicago's Shorebank Corporation (parent company to South Shore Bank, noted for its success in revitalizing housing in a blighted Chicago neighborhood) to collaborate on the Willapa Bay project. The progeny of Ecotrust and Shorebank is ShoreBank, Pacific: The First Environmental Bancorporation.

ShoreBank, Pacific will evolve into a system of wholesale banks and branches (both urban and rural), making loans primarily to businesses that do conservation-based work. ShoreBank, Pacific is already capitalized by $7 million in EcoDeposits made by foundations, individuals, and nongovernmental organizations; these insured deposits link investors to environmentally sensitive projects. The goal is to raise $12 million in equity for the bank holding company by the planned August, 1997 opening of ShoreBank, Pacific headquarters in Ilwaco, Washington.

A nonprofit affiliate, called Shore Trust Trading Group (STTG), provides business development and marketing assistance to entrepreneurs. STTG also manages a $2.5 million revolving loan fund (financed largely by Meyer Memorial Trust, the MacArthur and Northwest Area Foundations, and Weyerhaeuser Company) that has approved over $1.5 million to date for timber, seafood, real estate, and farming projects.

The Conundrum

Ecotrust operates in two worlds — rural economic development and environmental advocacy — that have often been at odds with one another. To me the word *rural* has always evoked images of small, quaint American towns nestled in cotton fields or wheat farms, among cattle ranches or wilderness. We tend to think of rural America as a scenic landscape occupied by people whose lifestyles, values, and livelihoods are anchored to the land. Perhaps this is because rural America has long served as a psychic antidote for the relentless pressure of urban expansion and physical growth. Our image of rural America is pastoral, a place or space that is out there waiting when people need it.

That image, however, changed for me when I began to interview rural community leaders throughout the United States to write their economic development success stories for a report to the U.S. Department of Agriculture. It wasn't so much the stories about industrial parks and Mercedes plants and tourist corridors that changed my view. It was the statistics, the business sector analyses. These little communities in the boondocks of South Carolina, West Virginia, Minnesota, and New Mexico didn't have an economic base of farming, fishing, and forestry. Natural resources, in most cases, were a tiny portion of their economic base. Typically, the mainstays were manufacturing, wholesale and retail trade, professional and related services — just like cities. Slice open many a rural town and you find an urban spore.

To my astonishment, I learned that what rural really means these days is how far a community is from an urban area and how its population size compares to an urban area. On road trips, the images I'd been blocking from sheer psychic preservation began to pour in: telephone wires criss-crossing the countryside, sign clutter, sprawl, traffic congestion, Wal-Marts, parking lots. That open land — it wasn't farms or ranches — it was real estate in a holding pattern for development.

How did this happen? How did we lose Arcadia, our domesticated Garden of Eden? This is how: through expansion to support our ever-increasing population and traditional models of rural economic development. In a recent essay, "Soul Searching: At What Cost Rural Economic Development?" William Falk, Professor of Sociology at the University of Maryland, concludes:

> So will the soul of a rural community be lost inevitably, one way (population out-migration) or the other (outside economic development)? If the answer seems to be yes, how can rural communities secure new economic opportunities yet maintain the desirable traits that made them what they were or what they are imagined to be by potential new residents? A conundrum indeed.[1]

It is a conundrum I observe now, working with a group of small towns south of Ft. Smith, Arkansas. Residents there don't know whether to fear more the growth spilling over from Ft. Smith or the crumbling of downtown buildings. According to Ecotrust, conservation-based development is the answer to this riddle and others. Conservation-based development is, in short, both a reconciliation of economics and environment and a departure from each of these roots; it's a form of economic development that produces an environmental return. Since 1991, Ecotrust and its philanthropic muses have staked $10 million on this approach.

The Rural Development Context

Traditional models of rural development emphasize the creation of wealth by importing urban job generators into rural areas. Ecotrust has a different approach. If the demand for high-quality forest products, organic food, fish, wild areas, clean air, and unpolluted water is increasing while supply is decreasing, then it is possible to capitalize on the supply-demand gap, create wealth, and improve the quality of life by restoring natural ecological processes. Shorebank president Mary Hough-

ton adds that the idea is to "support measurable increases in the amount of local small business activity in the belief that you can get a synergistic effect." She cites examples where networks or clusters of firms have succeeded in Northern Italy, Denmark, and Germany by virtue of such synergy. Importantly, conservation-based development puts the "rural," with all its Arcadian connotations, back in rural development. In theory, at least, the conundrum is solved.

The Environmental Context

While Ecotrust is to its core an environmental organization, it does not send out appeals to save whales or indigenous tribes of Bolivia. It does not lobby Congress to enact regulations. It does not stockpile wilderness. It does not battle the U.S. Forest Service or local planning commissions.

What Ecotrust does, again, is economic development that produces an environmental return. In its early search for bearings, Ecotrust vice president Arthur Dye says, "We came to the conclusion that the environmental movement was headed in the wrong direction. We needed to build community capacity rather than regulations or legislation." In its strategic vision report, Ecotrust contends, "No amount of outside intervention can substitute for the tenacity and commitment of those who live in a place and who have most at stake in its future." Moreover, stockpiling wilderness to protect it from human threats and pressures is what Ecotrust calls the "museum-science" approach to conservation. Separating humans from their traditional habitat is not the solution. The better answer is to build the capacity of local communities to steward their natural capital. Recognizing that the goal of communities — long-term economic prosperity — is inextricably bound to the goal of environmental organizations — the conservation and restoration of ecosystems — shifts the paradigm into a more constructive mode, wherein the forces of economic development and conservation are no longer enemies but allies.

Ecotrust, repudiating models and maps, has developed instead a compass, suggesting directions in which its local partners might move. Like all compasses, it has four cardinal directions:

1. *Understanding through ecosystem research, monitoring, and education.* While Ecotrust may deplore the excesses of science that have contributed to human alienation from the natural world, it also believes that we must regain an understanding of our local environment. Extensive application of GIS databases, locally and bioregionally, is a case of using science to serve nature. Additionally, Ecotrust and its partners have published books, CD-ROMs, and journals like *Rain: A Journal of the Clayoquot Biosphere Project* that link science and nature. Biologist E. O. Wilson, speaking at a lecture sponsored by Portland Arts and Lectures in May 1996, said, "By applying GIS to conservation problem-solving, Ecotrust and Interrain Pacific are helping to lead a national trend — I hope a global trend — toward win-win political solutions that will allow us to do a vastly better job of conservation."[2]

2. *Conservation through protection, stewardship, and restoration.* The Willapa Fisheries Recovery Strategy, a two-hundred-page document, has driven $1.2 million in salmon-habitat restoration projects along the Willapa and Bear Rivers in southwestern Washington. Ecotrust has also worked with nonprofit Sea Resources and the Chinook Indian tribe in the Columbia Pacific region of northwestern Oregon to develop a watershed restoration training program. At Kitlope River, Haisla Rediscovery has conducted five summer camps to revive Haisla culture and its ethic of stewardship.

3. *Economic development that supports ecological businesses.*

4. *Policy reform, using local experience and needs, to inform regulation.* Based on research at Kitlope and Clayoquot Sound, the Haisla First Nation and Province of British Columbia adopted a joint management agreement that assures permanent protection of Kitlope Valley. At Willapa Bay, pollution caused by chemical control of spartina, an invasive aquatic weed, led to an education and lobbying effort that resulted in the state legislature enacting a new permitting process to regulate control activities.

The Nonprofit Context

Many community activists say that there hasn't been as much organizing for change at the grassroots level as there used to be in the sixties and seventies. Conservation organizations in particular haven't a strong tradition of community-based efforts. According to Ecotrust policy director Erin Kellogg, this trend seems to be shifting because people are recognizing that not all solutions can come from government. Kellogg says there aren't enough resources at the federal and state levels and, besides, those often aren't the appropriate agents for change. Now, she points out, there is more movement to do things from both the bottom-up and top-down. Communities are taking responsibility for coming up with their own solutions; federal and state entities are partnering more with local communities instead of regulating them. This retooling of the public sector — trading partnerships for regulations — has its genesis in the Clinton administration's desire to reinvent government.

If the first-generation approach among nonprofits engaged in community development (economic development and conservation) was, "Stand back; we'll do it for you," the second generation is a construct of public involvement and self-empowerment. In devising local solutions, community activists are putting more stress on collaborative decision making amongst stakeholders and less on adversarial politics. This new dogma of collaboration between stakeholders at the community level in a consensual process troubles Sierra Club chairman Michael McCloskey.

In an article in *High Country News*, McCloskey contends that local solutions disenfranchise urban and national constituencies, which are valid, if absentee, stakeholders. Additionally, he fears that local development interests will more frequently outmuscle grassroots opposition, if they haven't the benefit of financial assistance and expertise from national groups.[3]

For an organization that isn't local or civic and, as a consequence, might he viewed with wariness, Ecotrust has found that the most effective mode of operation is to forge local partnerships and operate in the capacity of catalyst and broker. Ecotrust gets things started. For example, in 1991 Ecotrust sent Orville Tice, an environmental mediator, to assess the situation at Willapa Bay and determine whether people were interested in a partnership solution to the problems of rural poverty and environmental preservation. When the answer came back affirmative, Ecotrust brokered $600,000 from the Northwest Area Foundation to launch the Willapa Bay project. Ecotrust then initiated capacity building by recruiting residents interested in conservation-based development. These individuals became the founding board of the Willapa Alliance, which now has a budget of $500,000 and a staff of seven. Their mission: to enhance the diversity, productivity, and health of Willapa's unique environment; to promote sustainable economic development; and to expand the choices available to the people who live there.

Ecotrust incorporates collaborative decision making while also laying groundwork for a third-generation approach that is characterized by sophisticated use of technology, a role trimmed to catalyst and broker, careful selection of projects, and the extensive use of partnerships. Additionally, Ecotrust is mediating between its internally defined public interest mandate (conservation) and an increasingly intense external pressure on nonprofits to become market-oriented. It has done this by building its own obsolescence into local partnerships. When local capacity comes online, Ecotrust can fade into the background, as it has at Willapa Bay where the Willapa Alliance, STTG, and others now occupy center stage.

Conclusion

Ecotrust, as you see, is writing a new story in which humans are one with nature again. This time, we've learned our lesson. We're serious about this stewardship job. Ecotrust is writing this story on the coastal landscape of the Pacific Northwest from Northern California to Alaska so that people can see and hear a different way of doing things.

Mostly the reviews of Ecotrust are positive, but there have been criticisms as well. Some environmentalists feel Ecotrust has sold out. Partnering with Weyerhaeuser on projects hasn't helped set the minds of purists at rest. Jim Sayce, who grew up in the Willapa Bay area and is now executive director of the Pacific County Council of Governments, feels that Ecotrust has been very successful in seeding the Willapa Alliance and moving financial resources into the resource service area with stream restoration and spartina control. However, he believes that the mobility of the labor force undermines Ecotrust's approach because it severs local commitment to place. The less commitment to place, the less capacity for stewardship there is to build.

At the University of Arkansas, professor of rural sociology Donald E. Voth has studied Shorebank's rural initiatives in Arkansas. He sees the Ecotrust-Shorebank effort as "courageous" and commends the organizations for their focus on local capacity building. However, in Voth's opinion, "it's risky to rebuild local communities on the natural resource base because the potential for generating income is limited." Voth also suggests that a model capitalized in the multimillions is not a widely reproducible model.

Stewart Brand, founder of *Whole Earth Catalogue* and member of Ecotrust's advisory council, counters, "If Ecotrust tries to be a model, it fails. If it tries to save the rain forest and succeeds, it becomes a model. Successes are models. Attempts to be models are not models."

Aside from potential design flaws in Ecotrust's compass, a more formidable obstacle (a societal design flaw) may be the short-term perspectives that drive decision making. Arthur Dye says, "Everything is geared toward the short term, whether it's state or federal government. All the energy in local government goes to getting money for the community; like compensation for salmon fishermen. But short-term solutions don't get to the basic problem of why fish have declined. We're trying to build a longer-term effort — ten to twenty years — that will change the way government people look at these issues." Dan'l Markham, executive director of Willapa Alliance, admits long-term strategies are "tough because the culture has short-term expectations and funders do too."

Futurist Stewart Brand (now noted for his scenario-planning firm Global Business Network) would not advise Ecotrust to change its timetable. He learned from ecology long ago that the slowest moving parts are the most powerful. "The organization that takes the long view will succeed. Ecotrust is operating on the same time frame as forests — many generations. That's where the power is."

NOTES

1. Falk, W. W. "Soul Searching: At What Cost Rural Economic Development?" *Economic Development Quarterly*, 1996, *10*, 104–109.

2. Wilson, E. O. Address to Portland Arts and Lectures, Portland, Oreg., May 15, 1996.

3. McCloskey, M. "The Skeptic: Collaboration Has Its Limits." *High Country News,* May 13, 1996.

CHAPTER 44

South Amboy Improves Its Waterfront to Revitalize Its Aging Downtown

Allan Hope

South Amboy gets it. The city is transforming itself from a dying urban center with a run down waterfront that literally exploded in flames in the 1950's into a forward looking, exciting community. This Middlesex county city is the new benchmark for what smart growth, smart change and urban living can be and, indeed, should be.

The success of South Amboy's revitalization has been so dramatic, that it has even caught the eye of Professor Mario Gandelsonas from the Princeton University School of Architecture, who is using the South Amboy model as a classroom for the students who will build and design the cities of tomorrow.

According to Gandelsonas, "The city of South Amboy occupies a special place in New Jersey, a state that enters the 21 century with renewed energy. South Amboy as a future transportation node within the proximity of Manhattan, presents a unique opportunity to create a new type of city that takes advantage of unique conditions: a solid and stable community, a waterfront with exceptional views, unspoiled natural preserves and large but dormant industrial structures that offer an excit-

ing potential for jumpstarting future development. In the last few years, ambitious plans of a scale that very few large cities would envision have materialized in the form of a new neighborhood and the beginning of a new waterfront that starts to create a new image for South Amboy."

But make no mistake about it, the South Amboy phoenix is not the result of a massive urban renewal effort where city blocks are destroyed and residents are displaced. It is instead, a moderated, well thought-out, carefully planned and finely executed integration of the old and the new. In one area the reclaimed waterfront is dotted with new homes; in another part older neighborhoods have received the coveted national "Main Street USA" designation for their beauty.

In South Amboy, the infrastructure has been carefully rebuilt without destroying the bends in the roads and the bumps in the sidewalks that give a community its sense of character and maturity. The city's planners have given as much thought to new bridges' aesthetics as they do to traffic. Elsewhere in South Amboy, quality builders are creating commer-

Originally published as "How to Succeed: South Amboy Gets It!" *New Jersey Municipalities*, Vol. 83, No. 4, April 2006. Published by the New Jersey State League of Municipalities. Reprinted with permission of the publisher.

cial ratables that will increase tax revenues without quality of life disruption.

The city's location, nestled on the water but literally within walking distance of many of New Jersey's major roadways, makes it an ideal location for what will become one of New Jersey's major data centers. "South Amboy is uniquely suited to positively and proactively take advantage of the major transportation improvements in which NJDOT is engaged," said NJDOT spokesperson Erin Phalon.

But how did they do it? And where do they plan to go next?

It all starts with a vision, which grew out of long-time Mayor Jack O'Leary's love of his hometown and dreams for what it can become. O'Leary has never wavered from achieving the goals he set for himself and his city.

Today, South Amboy's renaissance continues under his leadership. Now in his 18th year as mayor, O'Leary's smart growth, smart change plan is paying huge dividends after nearly a decade of planning, analysis and management. The new South Amboy is a blend of family-oriented neighborhoods thriving side by side with a modern transportation village, new waterfront residences, and business and professional enterprise zones. In South Amboy smart change works hand in hand with family values, civic responsibility and fiscal conservatism.

Jack O'Leary knew when he began the South Amboy rebirth that it would take years to achieve his vision. But he never wavered. "It was clear to me that the city needed to undergo not only smart growth but smart change. We had to adapt to the changing times in New Jersey," O'Leary said. But he is quick to add, "I was absolutely committed to insuring that our city did not lose its special character and that it remained affordable for the diverse and vibrant family-based community that we are."

In order to succeed, O'Leary knew that South Amboy needed a redevelopment partner

qualified to resolve significant up-front infrastructure and cleanup problems long before the development phase began. Faced with this unique redevelopment challenge, the city turned to Joseph Jingoli and Son to perform as the Master Developer for the Northern Waterfront Redevelopment Area. The location of the city and its assets dictated the selection of a partner with the expertise in engineering, infrastructure, power plants, technology and environmental cleanup. Jingoli has proven to be a crucial element in tackling the first commercial phase of the city's plan.

Joseph P. Baumann, Jr., of McManimon and Scotland LLC has been watching the redevelopment process evolve in South Amboy and had this to say: "Redevelopment is not for the faint of heart or the shortsighted. It requires vision, long range planning, leadership, diligence, and patience. It requires a leader willing to work hard and make hard decisions — decisions that may not bear fruit for many years. As such, redevelopment does not work well with many political cycles where instant gratification is often the real goal."

Inevitable Change

As a life long South Amboyan, O'Leary had seen his beloved city decline as so many others in New Jersey. "I intuitively understood that change was inevitable," O'Leary said. "However, I was going to commit myself to insuring that the change in South Amboy evolved in a positive direction, away from the darkness of decay and blight and toward the light of a future designed around combining the best of all worlds into a working city that served the needs of both its residents and its businesses."

New Homes

Today, the signature piece of O'Leary's dream is the transforming of the once underutilized waterfront of South Amboy into a beautiful environment of upscale homes, a bayfront brick paver walkway, surf fishing beach, marina, gorgeous waterfront park along with water ferry transportation, new public library, Community School and a state-of-the-art 600-plus seat Community Theater.

But long before these homes and amenities became a reality, O'Leary and his team needed to provide tens of millions of dollars in infrastructure repairs and rebuilding of the city's core business sector. Said O'Leary, "Broadway has always been the gathering spot for our community. Without that we've lost our heart."

Business

A walk through South Amboy's downtown shows the old and the new happily blend together in a vibrant business community.

Jim Moutsadatos, the owner of Jimmy's Broadway Diner, agrees "It's great to watch the changes that are taking place on Broadway. It took years of hard work and planning to bring it about and now there is definitely a difference."

The city has already been the beneficiary of well more than $100 million in re-development funds that the Mayor and the City Council have been directly responsible for bringing into our city.

Just ask Bob Dato, an attorney in town, who had a choice of where he wanted to locate his business, why he came to the city. He says, "Locating my business in South Amboy was an easy decision. The town is growing, the business potential is increasing and it is all due to the smart growth tools being used by the Mayor and Council."

The local government team is also committed to its Neighborhood Preservation Program, which provides grant money to improve the visual appearances of older homes in a targeted area of a community, and the surrounding entranceways including sidewalks and landscape plantings.

Community gatherings and festivals also enrich life in South Amboy. The annual St. Patrick's Day Parade fills the streets with on-lookers as the city celebrates its Irish heritage. Each year, the highlight of the parade is the city's volunteer fire department, which has won the top honors in the statewide parade competition in Wildwood three times in a row. The city also hosts the Annual Raritan Bay Seafood Festival which draws anywhere from 8,000 to 12,000. And at its Annual Tree Lighting in December, South Amboy's youngest citizens are treated to a visit from Santa Claus who arrives on his own fire truck accompanied by other decorated fire equipment.

In South Amboy, no one is left behind. The city's elderly population, many of whom have lived and worked here for a lifetime, are well cared for and housed in the senior citizen complex, known as McCarthy Towers. Under O'Leary's leadership, that facility has also enjoyed more than $1 million in renovations and upgrades in just the last year. The city and the South Amboy Housing Authority are poised to add another tower to its Senior Citizen housing inventory.

O'Leary believes that the community life of the city is a tribute to the strength and character of its citizens. He says the culture of the city attracts people who want to live and work together, sharing their common interests and protecting the middle class life style and unique quality of life that South Amboy provides.

According to Phil Green, a South Amboy native who has recently returned to the city, "South Amboy is not only the best kept secret in Middlesex County, it's the best kept secret in the state."

Redevelopment Tools

Mayor O'Leary and the South Amboy City Council have consistently used redevelopment tools made available by the State of New Jersey to reinvigorate their city. The positive impact of successful redevelopment can be seen readily in this mile square city. And nowhere is this more visible than where the city meets the bay. Here you will find residents strolling the waterfront walkway, and families enjoying the Karitan Bay waterfront park's panoramic views.

"The Raritan Bay Environmental Education Center and Nature Preserve in South Amboy is one of the region's most exciting and publicly beneficial new projects," noted Greg Remaud, the Preservation Director and NY/NJ Baykeeper for the Bi-State Harbor Estuary Program. "It combines natural land preservation, ecosystem restoration and environmental education in an urban setting. It also serves as a key component of South Amboy's model community redevelopment that links environmental preservation with mass transportation, main street revitalization and economic growth. The Nature Center and Preserve located along Raritan Bay at the mouth of the Raritan River will provide hands on research opportunities and nature education to school children and residents throughout the area."

The resurgence of Broadway, and jobs that will be produced by Raritan Landings, the planned Hotel, Conference and Office Park and Data Center are all positives that have resulted from the careful implementation of the city redevelopment plans.

A Transportation Village

Key to the overall business success of South Amboy has been its embracing and understanding of the benefits of its location and working with the major transportation players in the state.

For example, NJ TRANSIT has worked closely with the city for a number of years to both improve its rail station and implement transit-oriented development according to Jack M. Kanarek, NJ TRANSIT's Senior Di-

rector of Project Development. NJ TRANSIT assisted South Amboy in the development of a vision plan for transit-oriented redevelopment and new development using the rail station as the focal point. With the vision in place, South Amboy was among the first five Transit Villages designated under the State of New Jersey's Transit Village Program. This has enabled South Amboy to receive assistance from several state agencies. The result is that the rail station is being improved, roadway access is being upgraded, ferry service to Manhattan is operating and the city's Broadway area is being revitalized. In addition, new transit-oriented development is also planned along South Amboy's waterfront.

South Amboy can provide bus, rail, commuter and ferry service from within its borders for those that need it. Few, if any, other cities can compete with that convenience. For South Amboyans to have the lifestyle we provide without having to significantly extend their daily commute makes all the difference in the world to our residents. And finally, the design of our transportation village is such that we do not adversely impact our residential areas while maximizing opportunities for our commercial enterprises. That planning forethought makes a huge difference in the character and feel of South Amboy.

And for those that do not live in the city but want to take advantage of the transportation village, the direct benefits to the downtown business community are readily visible. Where once there were vacant storefronts and empty buildings, there are now few, if any, "for rent" signs.

In just the last three years, O'Leary's South Amboy has also seen the reclamation of its waterfront, the creation of beautiful new housing, the rise of an intermodal transportation village and business center and a new office park along with additional acreage for his open space inventory and so much more.

Mayor O'Leary wants to see the completion of the Community Recreation Center/YMCA for his residents and their children.

There are road improvement projects on the horizon and he pledges to continue the search for quality businesses that enhance the city while simultaneously providing the critical tax ratables that are the economic engine of the South Amboy miracle.

Asked about his success, O'Leary takes a moment or two to reflect before answering.

"We are a great city," he says, "and our people are our greatest asset. Because of that, I believe together we have a great future."

CHAPTER 45

Stamford, Other Cities, Use Land Trusts to Preserve Their Open Spaces

Christine Woodside

"Everywhere across America we're losing our rural environment," says Larry Power, a former public relations executive with a booming voice. Power lives with his Tibetan terrier, Bandit, in a house overlooking a pond, woods, and a meadow in the town of Sharon in northwestern Connecticut. As president of the Sharon Land Trust, he has been preoccupied with the loss of his own rural environment in recent years — the loss of what he calls his region's "unique combination of wild open spaces and quintessential New England scenery."

Northwestern Connecticut's beauty is on a humble scale: the forested foothills of the Berkshire Mountains, threaded by the Housatonic River and its tributaries, small farms, ponds, low ledges, clapboard houses, and downtowns marked by white Colonial churches. Three hundred years ago, settlers from Europe cleared its forests to grow crops, raise animals, and mine iron. With the gradual decline of these enterprises, the forests have returned while the region has remained pastoral and sparsely populated. Tourism and service industries form the backbone of the economy.

Telecommuters and weekend residents from New York are common and have included such celebrities as Henry Kissinger, Meryl Streep, Placido Domingo, and Skitch Henderson.

In towns like Sharon and nearby Kent, which borders Sharon on the south, community land trusts formed in the 1980s to preserve the rural landscapes people love. The Sharon and Kent Land Trusts were originally established to accept small gifts of land or easements, but their work has accelerated recently as land values have risen and development pressure has grown. Together the two groups have protected more than 3,000 acres, most of this in the last five years.

But despite their accumulating experience, the two land trusts found themselves at a loss when, in 2001, residents raised the alarm about a plan to develop land on Skiff Mountain, straddling the towns' border. While development can benefit a community if sited in the right place, to the land trusts and local conservationists this clearly seemed like the wrong place: 200 acres in the midst of a potential 5,800-acre open space corridor where

Originally published as "Partners in Trust," by Christine Woodside, *Land & People*, Vol. 16, No. 2, Fall 2004, reprinted with permission from the Trust for Public Land. To learn more about TPL, please visit www.tpl.org.

the Appalachian Trail meanders through the state.

Much of this open space was already protected by the National Park Service, the land trusts, and Macedonia Brook State Park. The land scheduled for development includes meadows, a young hardwood forest, and a rare black spruce bog. It provides important habitat for bears, bobcats, golden-winged warblers, blue-winged warblers, and wood thrushes, and it is crossed by many cross-country skiing and hiking trails.

Skiff Mountain neighbors, local conservationists, and the land trusts organized themselves as the Friends of Skiff Mountain, and for two years they faithfully attended more than 60 public hearings, trying to hold off the development. What upset many of them was that the land was owned by the private Kent School, the town of Kent's largest employer, and was under contract for sale to a development group of Kent School alumni. The battle over development would soon assume all the bitterness and sense of betrayal of a family fight.

"This was a classic David-and-Goliath battle," says resident Dennis De Paul, whose wife's family has lived on Skiff Mountain for generations. De Paul and local lawyer Theresa D'Alton were the first residents to appeal to the Kent town commissioners to stop the plan.

For its part, the school — which had been trying to sell the land for many years — believed it had a contract with the development group, says Arthur Collins, Sr., chairman of the Real Estate Committee for the Kent School Board of Trustees. And so a stalemate developed, with the school beginning to look for options that would resurrect its relationship with the townfolk and the developers pushing the town to approve the project. "It was chaos for a while," Collins says. "A lot of people weren't talking to a lot of other people around this town."

The Kent Land Trust's Harmon Smith recalls a meeting in which conservation-minded residents got together to raise money for legal funds and consider next steps. "My opinion was that the project was too complicated, too large, and the issues were too difficult for local land trusts to deal with successfully," Smith says. "I thought we needed the expertise and advice of an organization like the Trust for Public Land."

Partnership Drives Projects

Local land trusts across the nation frequently call in the Trust for Public Land when trying to accomplish a difficult project. Land trusts are community groups organized to protect open space by holding land or easements, which restrict development. Some employ a part-time director or a small staff. Many more are all-volunteer groups, meeting in their spare time in members' homes. This is the case with the Sharon and Kent Land Trusts.

The Trust for Public Land, despite its name, is not a land trust at all but rather a national nonprofit that helps agencies, communities, and local land trusts plan, raise funds for, and complete conservation projects. But TPL has long recognized the importance of local land trusts as partners. In the 1970s, TPL helped found or train several hundred such groups. As the number grew and it became clear that they needed their own support organization, TPL helped found the Land Trust Alliance (LTA), a national umbrella group that today provides training, publications, and lobbying services for the nation's approximately 1,300 local land trusts.

Current LTA president Rand Wentworth, previously director of TPL–Georgia, has had ample opportunity to see how local land trusts and TPL work together to conserve land. "What land trusts bring to the table is a keen knowledge about local lands that are currently threatened," Wentworth says. "They know the politics; they know the people. But they may not have the professional experience to negotiate with a multinational paper company or a sophisticated real estate developer. This is es-

---

Partnering with Local Land Trusts

TPL often partners with local land trusts to plan for open space conservation and complete complicated conservation projects. Depending on the partnership, TPL may offer:

- National experience and computerized GIS mapping to help identify lands for protection
- Help from TPL's conservation finance program with the planning and mounting of conservation ballot measures
- Help in identifying and securing public and private funds that might be available for a conservation project
- Lobbying for conservation funding at the state and national level
- Temporary "bridge" financing to protect land while funding for permanent protection is secured
- Help in completing complicated transactions, including those involving multiple landowners, multiple funding sources, title disputes, site contamination, complicated negotiations, and/or the need to transfer the land to multiple land trusts or agencies for protection
- Publications and Web resources on conservation planning, funding strategies, and the management of strategic conservation programs

---

pecially true if the land trust has a small staff or is made up entirely of volunteers. The members just don't have the time to do the work."

TPL can come into a community and inject energy into a project that may be stalled, or step in as a neutral party in negotiations that have become polarized. In addition, TPL may be aware of funding from state, federal, or other sources that could help protect a particular parcel — or may be able to help a community raise funds for a project.

As a national organization, TPL also works with LTA and other organizations to create an infrastructure that assists local land trusts in their work. TPL works actively to promote conservation funding at the local, state, and national levels. TPL publications highlight conservation strategies that are often of interest to local land trusts. And TPL often has the knowledge to solve a local problem, because it knows about solutions that have worked elsewhere.

In Connecticut, partnering with community land trusts has become a mainstay of

TPL's work, says Alicia Betty, a TPL project manager who works out of TPL-Connecticut's New Haven office. In part this is because the state has so many land trusts: more than 100, second only to Massachusetts. Also, with public conservation funds on the decline in Connecticut, land trusts and private donations are becoming more and more important to conservation. Finally, notes Betty, "the development pressure is just phenomenal in this state. Land trusts are finding that they have to be proactive to protect priority properties."

In only the last few years, TPL and local land trusts have protected significant properties across Connecticut. Typically, TPL will negotiate a transaction and then work with local land trusts to raise private and government funds to protect the property.

- In Southbury, TPL and Southbury Land Trust helped protect 97-acre Phillips Farm, whose hiking trails and views figure heavily in books by Gladys Taber, a well-known mid-twentieth-century writer who lived nearby.
- In New Milford, TPL worked with Weantinoge Heritage, a local land trust, to raise more than a quarter of the $823,000 required to conserve a much-loved farm.
- In Fairfield County, TPL worked with the Darien Land Trust to protect a nine-acre field near the former home of Steven Mather, founder of the National Park Service.
- In Goshen, in the northwest hills not far from Kent and Sharon, TPL purchased 16.5 acres along the Bantam River, while the Goshen Land Trust raised part of the money needed to add this land to a 156-acre preserve.
- In Greenwich and Stamford, TPL worked with the Stamford and Greenwich Land Trusts to protect the 94-acre Treetops estate on the Mianus River.

Saving Skiff Mountain

Despite successful partnerships elsewhere in Connecticut, TPL State Director Tim Northrop didn't hold out much hope when the Sharon and Kent Land Trusts first came to him about helping to protect Skiff Mountain. For one thing, he believed it unlikely that Kent School's contract with the development group could be changed. "I told them we probably had a 5 or 10 percent chance of being successful, but that it was worth giving it a shot," Northrop says.

The ensuing effort took long enough that Northrop left TPL on sabbatical to attend the Yale School of Forestry and Environmental Studies, then returned to work on the project with a newly minted master's degree in hand. In the interim, Badge Blackett, a TPL project manager from Boston, drove down to Kent a half-dozen times to strategize with the land trusts and negotiate with Kent School and the development group.

When Blackett finally got to sit down with the Kent School, the project suddenly doubled in size and complexity as the school asked TPL to acquire an additional 250 acres — a contingency for its breaking off negotiations with the development group. The final, painfully negotiated transaction reimbursed Kent School for the value of its land and reimbursed the developers for their expenses, while leaving them with a 17-acre lot on which to build a single home.

Even the school and the developer credit Blackett with structuring the deal that led to the land's protection. "TPL was a catalyst in this whole thing," says Kent School trustee Arthur Collins. "Everyone understood what they stood for — that the land would be protected. Badge Blackett did an incredible job of putting this thing together, and it wouldn't have happened without him."

In the meantime, the land trusts, with their local connections, pitched in to help raise nearly $1.5 million in private donations to help fund the acquisition. The Kent and Sharon Land Trusts will end up owning the land and protecting it for community benefit.

For its part, the state helped propel the transaction forward, as it has with similar transactions, by granting $1.25 million for the protection effort from the Connecticut Open Space and Watershed Land Acquisition Grant Program. The grants were among the highest in the program's history, says Connecticut Department of Environmental Protection Deputy Commissioner David K. Leff, because the two parcels adjoined other conservation lands. "This kind of project shows a lot of vision in trying to quilt together a contiguous band of open space," Leff says. "This has a great deal of value for recreation and for wildlife, and requires long-term commitment to eventually piece the entire thing together."

Saving Skiff Mountain seemed impossible at the start, and those who fought for it look back in glad amazement. They believe that the housing development would be under construction now if not for all the partners who joined hands in the project.

Another important outcome is that those partnerships continue, with residents even more energized than before to conserve land. Even now, TPL's Tim Northrop is working with residents to preserve an additional 1,000 acres on Skiff Mountain.

"It's great to be able to come in and help a community protect a landscape that is important to them," Northrop says. "And it's wonderful to see that work promote a conservation ethic that will survive after we are gone."

CHAPTER 46

Taos Uses Nonprofit Organization to Restore and Preserve Native Lands

Richard Mahler

To early settlers from Europe, America seemed like unexplored territory waiting to be taken. But to the people who were already here, the land seemed, very simply, like home.

Native people had developed land-based cultures in every corner of the Americas by the time the newcomers arrived, and when they ultimately lost most of that land, they lost much more than places to hunt, fish, farm, and dwell. They lost spiritual sustenance, sacred burial grounds, and knowledge based on specific places, along with the kind of soul connection to a familiar environment that cannot be summarized in words.

"There was virtually no pristine wilderness by the time Europeans arrived, because we'd already been there," says Alvin Warren, the first Land Claims/Rights Protection Coordinator for New Mexico's Santa Clara Pueblo. "Only today are non-Native people starting to appreciate the intimate relationship between our ancestors and their homeland."

Hundreds of years after the land was lost, Alvin Warren and other Native Americans are teaming up with the Trust for Public Land to recover at least some of that former territory for tribal use or ownership — melding Native American knowledge with TPL's expertise in real estate, finance, conservation, and the law to create the only program of its kind at a U.S. conservation organization. Through 2003, TPL's Tribal Lands Program has helped 17 tribes secure more than 43,000 acres in 12 states. "This program epitomizes TPL's mission of conserving land for people," says TPL Senior Vice President Bowen Blair, who helped launch the effort in 1999. "And, more important, TPL's experience, skills, and mission are a perfect match for the needs we see in Native communities across the country — communities that traditionally had and, to a large extent, today have an intimate relationship with the land."

Alvin Warren serves as chairman of the TPL program's ten-member Tribal Lands Advisory Council. "Fundamental issues of justice and empowerment are involved in the reacquisition of ancestral land," Warren says. "TPL's Tribal Lands Program recognizes the crucial value of land within Native American societies and the careful stewardship of natural resources that result from that life-

Originally published as "Restoring Homelands," by Richard Mahler, *Land & People*, Vol. 16, No. 1, Spring 2004, reprinted with permission from the Trust for Public Land. To learn more about TPL, please visit www.tpl.org.

sustaining relationship. The program also demonstrates how unifying and expanding ancestral land bases can help tribes deal with ongoing economic issues."

A History of Dispossession

Restoring Native lands is a task much complicated by history. Virtually from the moment of their arrival, immigrants began displacing indigenous people. One culminating insult was the 1887 Dawes Act, an effort to turn Native peoples into farmers and private landowners that ultimately resulted in more than 90 million acres of Native land passing into non–Native hands.

Today much of the land that was once most important to Native peoples is thoroughly developed and irretrievably lost to tribal ownership. But other traditional lands are available, and tribes are more committed than ever to recovering at least some of that property. Owning or managing traditional land strengthens Native communities and expands opportunities for tribal groups, while conserving natural resources. It also reduces such illegal activities as the looting of artifacts and desecration of graves.

Take, for example, the traditional homeland of the Nez Perce Tribe in the Wallowa Valley of northeastern Oregon. In 1805, the tribe had offered assistance to explorers Lewis and Clark as they crossed Nez Perce territory. But by 1877, the Nez Perce under their charismatic leader, Chief Joseph, were defeated in their last attempt to hold onto that land and were relocated to reservations in other states.

But some tribal members never gave up hope that they would recapture at least a foothold in their Oregon homeland. They petitioned the government to no avail, and they tried to buy land from the descendents of the settlers who had displaced them. Finally, in 1997, after years of intricate negotiations, TPL forged a deal for the Nez Perce to acquire a former 10,000-acre cattle ranch to manage as

a wildlife refuge. Support for the $2.5 million project came from TPL donors and from the Bonneville Power Administration, which needed to protect habitat as replacement for land lost to wildlife by dams on the Columbia River.

"Those of us working with the Tribal Lands Program care deeply about our mission," says Jaime Pinkham, a former Nez Perce council member who has gone on to help TPL's Tribal Lands Program protect land for other Native peoples. "We are absolutely unique in what we do: successfully carrying out real estate negotiations, locating money, working with state and federal funding sources, and making legal agreements that return land to tribes."

Any transaction involving tribal land is likely to be complex. Participants tiptoe through a daunting minefield of federal treaties, Supreme Court decisions, judicial authorities, ownership claims, tax codes, and multiagency regulations. Potential funding is often hidden in obscure programs, while transfers may demand in-depth knowledge of public landownership. It's no surprise that many tribal governments, with limited financial and legal resources of their own, frequently find it hard to respond even to overtures from willing sellers.

Land for Pueblo People

"I think that 100 percent of tribes in this country are eager to reacquire at least some of their lands," declares Everett Chávez, governor of New Mexico's Santo Domingo Pueblo, which has partnered twice with the Tribal Lands Program to obtain more than 8,500 acres.

While each of New Mexico's 19 pueblos kept at least some of their ancestral land during Spanish and Mexican rule, they lost much of that — tens of thousands of acres — following the U.S. takeover in 1846.

"Our legal position was weak," explains

Chávez, "since our people never felt compelled to put up fences or to build permanent structures on much of their land. We didn't occupy it, though we all shared in our use of it." Chávez estimates that Santo Domingo retains only 90,000 acres of its original 277,000 acres of homeland. The pueblo continues to negotiate for more land, not "simply for monetary reasons," Chávez stresses, "but mainly because of the land's cultural significance.

"It's great that there are groups out there, like TPL, that can help us do this," says Chávez. "Creative partnering can be challenging, and we appreciate the expertise that others provide."

How complicated can such deals be? In 2001 TPL helped San Felipe Pueblo — a next-door neighbor to Santo Domingo — add 9,000 acres to its tribal land base. These lands were not simply purchased by San Felipe Pueblo but were gained through a TPL-assisted land exchange. Pueblo funds were used to help acquire spectacular lands along the Rio Grande River just south of Taos, New Mexico, for the public ownership by the Bureau of Land Management. The property, known as the Taos Valley Overlook, offers one of the most sweeping and best-known views in the Rio Grande Valley. In return for this land, the BLM exchanged ancestral lands of an equal market value to San Felipe Pueblo.

Protecting Traditional Uses

Other projects focus on creating Native access to lands of historic, spiritual, and cultural importance. Farther south in New Mexico, the Tribal Lands Program is working with the Ácoma and Zuni Pueblos in an effort to acquire ranchland threaded with ceremonial trade routes and dotted with cultural sites and sacred petroglyphs that have been visited by Native people for centuries.

"Today the Zuni must cross private property in order to collect mud, cattails, and other materials that are used for sacred purposes,"

Tribal Lands Project Highlights

CHIEF JOSEPH RANCH
Wallowa County, Oregon
Restored a portion of ancestral homeland to the Nez Perce Tribe

SABO FARM
Clearwater County, Minnesota
Helped acquire a wild rice farm for the Red Lake Band of Chippewa Indians

LYLE POINT
Klickitat County, Washington
Protected a traditional fishing site of four Columbia River treaty tribes

YOWKWALA PRESERVE
Tacoma, Washington
Conserved baylands salmon habitat for the Puyallup Tribe

TRAIL OF TEARS
Georgia and Tennessee
Helped protect multiple sites associated with the removal of Southeast tribes to Oklahoma

---

says Deb Love, director of TPL's New Mexico office. "We're trying to change that." She adds that such agreements often yield win-win situations for all parties: honoring Native American traditions, compensating sellers, and conserving precious natural resources.

In the Pacific Northwest, analogous struggles are opening access to lands where that region's tribes traditionally have hunted, fished, and obtained culturally important materials. On the rainy Olympic Peninsula of Washington, for instance, a series of events, including a fraudulent 19th-century survey, has long restricted the Quinault Indian Nation's use of old-growth forests, including the harvesting of large trees for ceremonial canoes.

Now TPL is working to secure a $50 million conservation easement over 4,000 acres of old growth, allowing the tribe to protect the land forever while opening it to traditional use. "Our tribe will be able to use that land, while the habitats of sensitive species are protected," says Pearl Capoeman-Baller, president of the Quinault Indian Nation Business Committee. Such species include the threatened marbled murrelet, northern spotted owl, and bull trout.

Farther inland in Washington, the Tribal Lands Program has spearheaded a campaign to protect Lyle Point at the confluence of the Klickitat and Columbia Rivers in the eastern Columbia Gorge. For generations, members of the Klickitat Band of the Yakama Nation have come to Lyle Point to net salmon from wooden perches high above the river, and the land has great meaning to the band.

In 1998, after a plan to build 33 vacation homes at Lyle Point had been approved, TPL stepped in to purchase the land for $2.5 million, even before a source of funding for permanent protection became obvious. Thanks to the generosity of its donors, TPL has been able to hold the land ever since, all the while working toward permanent funding and a protection plan that includes Native American access and use.

Honoring Forebears

"When your spirit goes, it should be sent off properly or you wander," tribal elder Patty Timbimboo-Madsen of the Northwestern Band of the Shoshone Nation told an interviewer last year. "Those people who passed on could never tell their story. They're calling out for someone to help them, to send them on their way."

"Those people" were 300 of Timbimboo-Madsen's own ancestors — men, women, and children gunned down in 1863 by U.S. volunteer soldiers along the Bear River in southeastern Idaho. Last year, TPL and its partners raised funds to purchase the Bear River massacre site, most recently a cattle pasture, and donate it to the band. Following the acquisition, the band held a sacred ceremony honoring the people brutally murdered more than 140 years ago. The spirit of her ancestors, says Patty Timbimboo-Madsen said, were finally at rest.

Despite their relatively small acreage, the potential educational and human impact of such projects is enormous, says Tribal Lands Program field representative Laura Baxter, a member of the Pit River Tribe in California. "Our goal is not simply the pragmatic one of returning lands to tribal hands," she concludes, "but of bringing understanding to others about the relationship between Native American people and the land."

CHAPTER 47

Tulare, Other Cities, Use Redevelopment to Enhance Community Safety

John F. Shirey

Redevelopment is more than just making physical improvements and aesthetic enhancements in a community. By using redevelopment's tools, a city can expand its housing stock, increase job opportunities, improve business viability and attract resources for the community. But equally important are the ways that redevelopment affects quality of life issues — the factors that make neighborhoods and cities places we like to call home. Public safety is one of these factors.

Tulare Builds Police/ Community Center

"Most redevelopment projects deal with public safety in one way or another," said Howard Edson, development services director for the City of Tulare. Redevelopment's ability to leverage other resources positively impacts all aspects of community life, including public safety. In addition to helping build police and fire facilities, redevelopment enables a local government to free up resources for code enforcement, sidewalk and street improvements, better traffic signaling at busy intersections, graffiti removal and facade enhancement programs that include seismic upgrades. Homeownership programs available to police officers and firefighters also make it easier for them to live in neighborhoods close to work.

In Tulare, the city leveraged federal Community Development Block Grant funds with redevelopment dollars to build a police/ community center in the Alpine Redevelopment Project Area. This center is used by police to offer Neighborhood Watch, seatbelt safety, health screening and other programs.

Communities throughout California are utilizing redevelopment to help address public safety issues as they fight blight — both physical and social.

Turning Around North Richmond

Beleaguered for years by crime and abandoned unsafe buildings, North Richmond residents have been actively reclaiming their community. They have worked with the Contra Costa County Redevelopment Agency and other stakeholders during the past 10 years to achieve that goal and to improve the quality of life for themselves and their neighbors.

"It is a misconception that the people living in a high-crime area such as North Richmond are the problem. In this case, the criminals came from outside the area," explained Lt. Donny Gordon of the Contra Costa County Sheriff's Department. "The North Richmond community members didn't want this to continue. They were all for change. What we — law enforcement personnel, redevelopment officials and residents — manage to do as a collective effort is improve the community aesthetics and services, and reduce the crime occurring here."

The Sheriff Department's Crime Analysis Unit data show that criminal activity has decreased nearly 11 percent over the past five years in North Richmond.

In March 2005, the California Redevelopment Association (CRA) awarded its annual Award of Excellence for Mixed-Use Development to the North Richmond Town Center. This 52-unit apartment complex for low-income seniors included provisions for a sheriff's substation. The county Sheriff's Department and California Highway Patrol both use the center's police substation, and a new resident deputy sheriff exclusively dedicated to the North Richmond area was hired July 1, 2005. The project also incorporated traffic calming streetscape improvements, lighting and pedestrian features.

In addition to the senior housing and substation, the project includes a center for health, education and social services offered through the county's Services Integration Team. Plans call for a local mini-market as well as a produce stand to be added to the center.

In order to complete this project, the local redevelopment agency put together a finance package of $13.8 million. The agency financed $1.6 million for the commercial center and leveraged the additional $12.2 million from a variety of local, state and federal sources.

One benefit of the senior housing and the presence of the resident deputy sheriff is that it has spurred private redevelopment in the surrounding neighborhoods. Another result is the removal of a blighted building across the street by its owner — one sign of a changed attitude about this area.

Brentwood Residents Applaud New Police Facility

Located in the City of Brentwood's downtown core and redevelopment project area, the existing Police Department facilities were inadequate to meet the department's public safety responsibilities. City leaders knew this inadequacy would only worsen as the population grew and the project area's renewal continued. The citizens of Brentwood voted overwhelmingly to support a general obligation bond to build a new police facility.

While the local redevelopment agency was developing strategies to implement the redevelopment plan, a site in the redevelopment project area was identified for a new police facility, and the city subsequently purchased it for this purpose. However, once the off-site improvement phase of the new police facility was under way, an opportunity arose that would not only resolve a number of issues for the project area and the city, but also provide revitalization opportunities in the downtown area.

In 2003, a company called U.S. Print filed for bankruptcy and abandoned its 10-acre property located within the downtown redevelopment project area. The property went into foreclosure. The company removed its personal property and equipment, lowering the parcel's assessed value by $11 million in one year.

The city purchased the property to provide space for the current and future needs of the Police Department, and rehabilitated the vacant facility that would otherwise be unattractive to private commercial investment. This purchase opened up two new sites for private investment in the redevelopment project area. These two sites are well situated to stimulate economic development in downtown Brentwood.

"In this location, the new police facility would help Brentwood improve the shortcomings of existing facilities while reusing a vacant property in our redevelopment area," said Gina Rozenski, redevelopment manager for the City of Brentwood. "The increase in our public safety personnel has strained current quarters, making it harder for them to do their jobs properly. With this new facility, the city will be better prepared to respond to emergencies, which means a safer community as well. And the availability of two redevelopment sites within the downtown project area is an added benefit that will help revitalization efforts."

The redevelopment agency staff expects that private investment in new housing, retail, commercial and transit uses at these two high-profile sites will move their plans forward for revitalizing the downtown core and act as a catalyst to realizing the aims of the city's Downtown Specific Plan. The old police station site will provide redevelopment opportunities suitable for a historic downtown district with restaurants and retail. The first construction site purchased during this process is ideally located for transit-oriented development, including a Bay Area Rapid Transit (BART) station and mixed uses. The city has embarked on a ridership development plan and feasibility study to accomplish this objective.

The total project costs are $16.3 million. Brentwood funded the project with $8.31 million in community facility fees collected from residential and commercial development projects throughout the city and $6 million from the voter-approved general obligation bond proceeds. The resulting $2 million gap was bridged with the redevelopment agency's 2001 tax allocation bond proceeds, which it will repay with future tax increment revenue.

The plan for the police facility was to construct new tenant improvements and seismically retrofit the existing structures to accommodate a 45,000-square foot police facility, which was completed in July 2005. The new police facility includes an emergency operations center and a dispatch center as well as exterior improvements such as a plaza area and attractive landscaping. Redevelopment Manager Rozenski added that another objective is to improve traffic circulation and reduce existing parking constraints, thereby increasing the attractiveness of downtown as a destination spot.

Lt. Kevin King, co-project manager, observed, "The new police facility site is one that will serve the local area and the City of Brentwood through the city's build-out, and the city was fortunate to be able to take advantage of the value of an existing building." There will be many benefits to the downtown Brentwood project area, including heightened security for the community as a whole.

Poway Redevelopment Agency's Civic Center Drive Extension

Using resources available through its redevelopment agency, the City of Poway is constructing a number of improvements related to public safety.

The city wanted to improve response times for police, fire and emergency services. Building a critical roadway connection that got sheriffs and firefighters to the scene of a call more quickly was a top priority.

Before Poway's Civic Center Drive extension was completed, the city's Fire Station #1 engine responded to emergency calls by navigating multiple turns and intersections through a heavily traveled area with more than 73,000 vehicles per day. It was difficult for fire equipment and law enforcement vehicles to maneuver through this busy corridor. In an effort to improve emergency response time and traffic circulation through this area, the city determined that there was a significant benefit to extending Civic Center Drive north to Poway Road.

To realize safer access to Poway's west side, the redevelopment agency acquired a 0.4-acre parcel to create a new street. The property was the site of a former gas station, which presented site contamination problems requiring environmental remediation to meet human health and safety standards. Redevelopment staff found funds for the property cleanup and negotiated a willing sale of the property to the agency under California's redevelopment agency rights and protections provided by the Polanco Act (for more about the Polanco Act, visit www.westerncity.com/polanco).

"Not only were we able to improve the fire station's and sheriff's response times, clean up a dirty site and better serve the community, this project fills a vital need for the other public facilities in the redevelopment area — Valley Elementary School, Parkview Terrace and Poway Villas affordable housing communities and the county library," said Deborah Johnson, redevelopment services director for the City of Poway. "Redevelopment frequently works behind the scenes to assist with some of the less glamorous but equally critical aspects of community improvement, ensuring that the lives and homes of the community members are protected."

Poway's main commercial corridor is now directly linked via a new extension to Civic Center Drive, establishing easy access between its community park, community library, city hall, the Boys and Girls Club, a public school, affordable housing complexes, Fire Station #1 and the Poway Sheriff Department's substation.

Public Safety Is a Quality of Life Issue

When asked about the value of integrating a sheriff's substation with a low-income senior housing redevelopment project, Lt. Gordon of the Contra Costa County Sheriff's Department said, "We hope that this entire project serves as a catalyst for building a new identity for the community. Our city had some of the highest crime statistics in the nation. We regard the North Richmond Town Center as the key for turning this around. We can build attractive houses and streetscapes, but if people don't feel safe and secure in their homes, then we really haven't improved the quality of life in a community."

The efforts of Tulare, North Richmond, Brentwood and Poway are good examples of the resources and tools that redevelopment offers local governments in California to improve public safety for their residents. When these resources are available, local government can help residents feel safe in their homes and neighborhoods, enhancing the impact of the improvements that redevelopment can bring to the quality of life. Many California communities use redevelopment to help improve public safety and build better communities in the process.

CHAPTER 48

Vancouver Promotes Inner-City Housing to Create a Vibrant Downtown

Alan Ehrenhalt

From a distance, especially from the air, downtown Vancouver looks like most downtowns: a pack of modern skyscrapers nesting in a dense and confined central area. Only when you hit the ground do you realize that it is different. The skyscrapers are virtually all condominium towers. This is an overwhelmingly residential high-rise downtown. Some 560,000 people live in Vancouver, Canada's third-largest city, and nearly 100,000 of them reside in tall, slender towers on the less than five square miles of the downtown peninsula.

There is nothing quite like this in North America, not in San Francisco, Chicago or even New York. When it comes to downtown housing density, the closed comparisons are to places such as Rio or Hong Kong. And virtually the entire change has happened in the past 15 years. Since 1991, when Vancouver rewrote its zoning laws to attract downtown residents, launching a self-described "Living First" policy, the physical character of the central city has been so thoroughly transformed that a visitor returning after two decades would have trouble even recognizing the place.

While cities in the United States struggle to lure as many as 5 percent of their residents into downtown living—and some are glad to have 2 or 3 percent—Vancouver is at nearly 20 percent and gaining. What's most remarkable, though, is that the downtown residential boom in Vancouver includes not just singles, couples and empty-nesters but a significant number of families with young children.

There is a brand-new public school in the downtown megaproject called Concord Pacific Place, at the southern tip of the peninsula, and another one under construction at Coal Harbour, the other huge cluster of condo towers at the northern end. In the words of Lance Berelowitz, a local architect and author of "Dream City," an urban history of Vancouver, "we are seeing the first break in the single family house paradigm. We've discovered that far more families with kids would live in downtown than anyone expected."

Vancouver, in short, has what every city wants these days: a vibrant, safe, glamorous downtown, full of residents who have money to spend and who enjoy themselves spending it at all hours of the day, everyday of the week. Promotions for one of the newest condo proj-

Originally published as "Extreme Makeover," *Governing*, Vol. 19, No. 9, June 2006. Published by Congressional Quarterly Inc., Washington, DC. Reprinted with permission of the publisher.

ects, now under construction, proudly advertise it as "life without compromise."

In fact, though, there is a compromise. Vancouver has begun to realize that its downtown is such a magnet for urban condo dwellers that it runs the risk of ceasing to serve the other purposes downtowns have traditionally served — as centers of commerce, corporate employment, jobs and overall economic life. It's not that business has fled central Vancouver: The downtown peninsula still ranks first as an employment center within the metropolitan area, with about 77,000 jobs. But the percentage keeps going down, there have been virtually no major office building projects launched in this century, the amount of land available for new commercial development is almost non-existent, and given the still-explosive demand for high-rise urban living, it doesn't take too much imagination to see what downtown Vancouver could become in a decade or two: a place where huge numbers of people live but not many work.

"The city we are shaping in the current boom," says local architecture critic Trevor Boddy, "is something quite different from any notion of what a downtown is, was or will be — more of a resort than a conventional downtown."

Planners and elected officials in Vancouver, intensely proud of Living First and the revival it has created, take pains to disagree with sentiments like that. "This isn't a resort strip in Hawaii," says senior planning official Michael Gordon. "This is still the financial and corporate center of a whole province's economy." But then he adds, "we really have to be careful ... we could very easily see the entire downtown snapped up for residential."

Downtown Demographics

How relevant is this situation to cities in the United States? Well, almost all of them would love to be in the position Vancouver is in now and worry about the consequences

later. But, in fact, quite a few American cities are about to face their own variant of the same problem: downtowns that are increasingly attractive to residents and increasingly problematical for businesses.

The 2000 Census confirmed that during the decade of the 1990s, downtown population in major U.S. cities increased by about 10 percent, after several decades of steady decline. Hard data for the past five years are difficult to come by, but the numbers that do exist point to a much more rapid acceleration.

In Philadelphia, which keeps good statistics, the Center City population jumped 11 percent between 2000 and 2005, with predictions of a 25 percent increase for the decade, bringing the total downtown population to more than 100,000. At the end of last year, there were 97 residential projects on the drawing board for Center City, millions of square feet of space for 18,000 new residents, stimulated in part by a 10-year tax abatement program for new residential construction, enacted in 2000. Meanwhile, the amount of office space in Center City was no higher than it had been in 1990, the share of the regional office market was down substantially, and the number of office and professional jobs in the city had declined by nearly 10,000 in 15 years.

In New York, after September 11, 2001, the city's primary commitment was to rebuild the office towers at the World Trade Center site and restore the commercial and office presence that was lost when the towers went down. Nearly five years later, no new office buildings on the site have even started construction.

Meanwhile, all over Manhattan, older commercial space has been going condo at a rapid rate — an estimated 8 million square feet of it in five years. The number of people living in the area below the World Trade Center was about 15,000 in 2001; now it is more than 30,000; by the end of next year, there are projections of more than 40,000. Thirty floors of the Woolworth Building are being turned into condominiums, and the House of Morgan building at Broad and Wall streets, recently reopened with 326 new condo units.

This isn't happening only among the elite in coastal cities. Officials in St. Louis discovered a few months ago that the downtown office vacancy rate had fallen to less than 15 percent — the lowest number in many years. This wasn't because of an increase in the number of office tenants looking for space. It was because of the amount of office space that had turned residential — more than 1.3 million square feet in the past several years. Perhaps the most conspicuous move involves the vacant 22-story Union Pacific building, a downtown landmark that employed more than 1,000 workers before the company moved those jobs to Omaha last year. When it is renovated, the building will contain a token number of office suites, but it will essentially be a residential tower, with 153 condominiums and 30 rental apartments.

A Fiscal Spiral

These are all striking changes, but are they really problems? After all, cities have changed their function repeatedly over time. If, 20 years from now, historic downtowns are mostly placed to live, with diverse entertainment choices and a vibrant street life, and the offices and jobs exist somewhere else, who will really suffer?

This is just the question that is preoccupying Vancouver these days. There is a fair amount of evidence that, if nothing else, the municipal budget suffers in the long run. Commercial properties account for about 40 percent of Vancouver's current tax base, and they pay taxes at a higher rate than residential properties do, while costing less in services. As the balance tilts toward the condos, the burden on business goes up even more, potentially driving commercial tenants out of the central city and creating a dangerous fiscal spiral.

One of those who worries publicly about

this is Vancouver's mayor, Sam Sullivan, elected last November on a generally pro-business platform. "Business per assessed value is now paying six times as much in taxes," Sullivan says. "We're making extra effort to nurture industry, but it's constantly under threat."

Most academics who have studied the issue agree that it's a genuine problem. "If we went totally residential, there would be some very significant tax consequences," says geographer Tom Hutton, who heads the Centre for Human Settlement at the University of British Columbia. "You can't be a purely residential consumption-based urban economy."

Hutton raises larger questions as well, about the mixture of uses and people that has defined downtowns for the past century: daytime office workers, retail shoppers, out-of-town visitors — and in some places, a modest number of residents. That combination, in varying proportions, has created the sense of energy and vitality that characterized the very best downtowns. If the office and commercial element goes away, or even shrinks by a significant margin, will the energy still be there? Hutton doubts it. "It would be a funny place if it were purely residential," he says. "You'd have a weird mix of people who weren't tied to the city in any way." Indeed, Vancouver already has a substantial "reverse commuter" population that leaves the downtown condos in the morning to work in the suburbs. Some demographers think that by 2020, more people could be commuting out of downtown each day than into it.

All those points are echoed, not surprisingly, by the commercial real estate industry, which feels it has largely been left out of the boom that has come to Vancouver in the 21st century. "There's a reason New York or London has that financial power," says Wendy Waters, research director at Avison Young, one of Canada's largest commercial firms. "The reason you have downtown is for the synergies of businesses working together." Waters thinks her city is losing much of its global economic importance even as it wins consistent praise for its planning achievements.

One oddity of this situation is that, by common agreement, there is no shortage of commercial tenants who would willingly move in to new office space downtown. But there's little incentive to build it, and very few places to put it. The return on investment for condominiums is five times as high as the return on office space. Moreover, the sites are virtually all taken. Five years ago, there were a handful of sites on the downtown peninsula viewed as favorable for projects that would bring renewed commercial life to the heart of the city. One by one, they have gone condo.

Density and Demand

All these consequences, the exciting ones and the more worrisome ones, trace back to a decision that the city government made, without a great deal of fanfare or expectation, in the summer of 1991: to increase the allowable density for new residential units downtown, thus giving landlords the option of building condominiums on sites previously reserved for commercial use. If one event can be said to mark the beginning of the downtown revival that is moving across North America, it is the rezoning in Vancouver.

It was a painless decision, because the office market was flat and few commercial buildings would have been constructed in the early 1990s anyway. The city council and planning department thought it made sense to ease up on the rules and see if the market might respond. It did — with a deluge. "Overnight, we got these huge condo towers," says Gordon Price, who was on the council at the time. Within a relatively short time, 8 million square feet of downtown space had been converted to residential use.

This was in part the result of some strictly local demand factors. Vancouver's downtown has a magnificent setting, with blue water and snow-capped mountains visible in nearly every direction. Almost as important in the early 1990s was the arrival of thousands of affluent Asians who were used to high-rise urban living in Hong Kong and other distant places. Living First made perfect sense to them.

Still, its success was a revelation even to its creator, Larry Beasley, who had recently taken over as Vancouver's co-director of planning. "It worked well beyond what we dared to dream," Beasley was to say many years later.

On the other hand, he will tell you, "it isn't something that happened by accident." Beasley knew what sort of city he wanted. Raised in Las Vegas in the 1950s, he became a planner with a vision of someday creating an urban place that was everything Las Vegas wasn't. A disciple of Jan Jacobs and a student of early New Urbanist literature, he set a goal of creating "an urban lifestyle that will bring people back from their 50-year romance with the suburbs."

Beasley was also a remarkably good politician. As the condos began to sprout up all over the peninsula, generating enormous profits for an emerging corps of residential developers, he saw that the city was in a position to extract substantial concessions from those eager to erect the next tower. In exchange for a building permit — controlled much more tightly by government in Canadian cities than in America — developers could be asked to provide all sorts of amenities: parks, waterfront walkways, community centers, child care centers. This was the political core of Living First, a collaborative policy that brought huge profit to the residential real estate industry even as it brought tangible public benefits to those who lived downtown.

Living First didn't just change the appearance of Vancouver — it changed the structure of community power. Bob Rennie, a real estate marketing entrepreneur who became sales agent for most of the big new projects, began to play a role somewhat akin to the role Michael Milken played on Wall Street in the 1980s: If Rennie gave the word that a project would fly, it flew. The units usually sold out on the first day they became available, long before the buildings were even built. "He's the king of the condo market," says urban geographer David Ley, of the University of British Columbia. "He's the king of downtown." In 2005, *Vancouver Magazine* voted Rennie the most powerful man in the city. In that year's election, he bankrolled the campaigns of both mayoral candidates.

Urban Choreography

By 2000, Beasley had begun to articulate the principles of Living First in published articles and speeches throughout North America. He painted the portrait of a downtown that stressed walking and bicycling over automobiles, one in which moderate levels of congestion were accepted and even encouraged but where green space could be required by law in any new development, and developers could be forced to provide subsidized housing along with the luxury units. "You don't have to wait for lightning to strike," he told audiences in other cities. "You can choreograph this."

Of course, they couldn't choreograph the mountains and the ocean that give downtown Vancouver a spectacular natural setting. But Beasley is convinced that something like Living First can work in places that don't have his city's advantages. "The determinants for housing choice are not all that different," he says. "Households are looking for the same thing. It's that we haven't designed communities in America for families at high densities."

It's a safe bet, however, that no American city is going to look much like Vancouver anytime soon. Walking south across the downtown peninsula, one traverses what feels like forest of green glass towers, hundreds of them, tall and slender to avoid spoiling the view from the upper floors. At the base of most of the towers, extending to the sidewalk, is a podium-like row of two- and three-story townhouses.

The towers have to be set back at least 12 feet from the sidewalk, so if you walk along the street and avoid looking up too far, you almost feel as if you're passing a row of medium-sized single family homes.

It's these townhouses, aimed at attracting families with children, that Beasley seems proudest of. There were exactly six of them in downtown Vancouver a decade ago; now there are more than 1,000. "It's the way we get domesticity and urbanism to the street," he says. He calls it "a humane domestic building form for high-density housing."

Not everyone likes the way downtown Vancouver looks. A local architect once called it a "sterile row of glassy towers marching down the street." A recent visiting critic chose to describe them as "cliffs of slivery ice on cloudy days." But it is undeniably original, attracts visitors from all over the world and wins awards every year for planning and architecture. When Beasley retires from his planning post later this year, to preach the Living First gospel in other places, he will arguably have staked a claim as one of the most important urban planners anywhere in the past half-century. And most of the city's residents seem comfortable with the dramatic change that has taken place.

Or, at least, they were until recently. Over the past year, they have begun to worry out loud that the blessing of Living First might be too good to be true. In particular, they have begun the use the "R" word — R for resort, the one thing nobody wants downtown Vancouver to become. "Resort," says the geographer Tom Hutton, "is a metaphor for a non-serious city."

The issue came up repeatedly one evening in May, at a public hearing convened to discuss the qualities citizens are looking for in the successors to Beasley and his co-director of planning, Ann McAfee, who also is retiring this summer. One panelist after another expressed concern for the future. "We've become victims of our own success," warned Leonie Sandercock, a prominent author and community planning scholar. Ray Spaxman, who preceded Beasley as city planner and in many ways set the stage for Living First, conceded that "cities get to the point where they are full of something. We're full of residential now."

These people might have reached their conclusion independently, but there's no question that the catalyst for Vancouver's present discontents is Trevor Boddy, the iconoclastic architect, journalist and critic who has made a virtual career out of debunking the Vancouver miracle.

In a series of newspaper columns, in architecture journals and in public speeches, Boddy has challenged almost every aspect of the Living First orthodoxy. He has warned American cities not to copy it. But the arrow that made a direct hit was his "Fool's Paradise" article in the *Vancouver Sun* in August 2005. "We may once have dreamed of taking our place in the list of the world's great cities," Boddy wrote, "but unless something is changed soon, to preserve and promote our downtown as a place to work, we will instead join Waikiki and Miami Beach on the list of resorts filling up with aging baby boomers lounging around their over-priced condos."

Nearly everyone in the city's planning and development circles insists that Trevor Boddy is a little over the top, but they are also starting to accept some of his ideas, which were considered little more than eccentric when he began expressing them a few years ago.

He has certainly gotten the city government's attention. The planning department has imposed what amounts to a moratorium on new residential construction is key areas of the downtown peninsula, while it conducts a 15-month study of the city's future prospects and needs. "We've drawn a line in the sand for commerce," Mayor Sullivan says, "and we aren't allowing condos within there." Sullivan realizes a flat-like prohibition on condos can't work forever, but he's hopeful that in a cooler atmosphere, the city might be able to design incentives for more of the mixed-use residential and office projects that few developers have been willing to take on so far. Bob Rennie, the Condo King, says flatly that this is the answer. "If you mix uses," Rennie proclaims, "it works."

Boddy derides the moratorium idea as "closing the barn door after the office horses had long departed." Beasley insists that it is the right approach at the right time. "We dealt with this issue before it became a crisis," he says. "Five years from now, it might have been a crisis." But timing aside, the new policy does seem to mark the beginning of a rough consensus among most of the major players involved: Vancouver's experiment has been a success, but it couldn't go on unchecked without doing serious damage.

No American city is close to where Vancouver is on the downtown-living front. But if you plot the changes in demographics over the past few years — not only in New York and Philadelphia but also in the less trendy big cities — it isn't hard to believe that the "Vancouver question" will be at the center of policy and planning debates. "I don't know if you could replicate this in Cleveland," says Tom Hutton. "But it could happen. It might take a Larry Beasley. But it could happen eventually."

CHAPTER 49

West Des Moines, Other Cities, Create Mixed-Use Town Centers to Preserve Their Downtowns

Mike Sheridan

In the once-sleepy bedroom community of Sugar Land some 20 miles west of Houston, developers are constructing the Sugar Land Town Square, which will feature high-rise buildings with residential lofts, as well as office, retail, and restaurant components, all anchored by the new Sugar Land City Hall. "We are seeing a number of municipal buildings, such as a city hall, now being included in new town center projects," says David Lewis, president of Houston-based Lewis Realty Advisors, a valuation and advisory services firm. "When you are trying to create a main street feel in suburban America, there's nothing like the presence of an authentic city hall, the heartbeat of a community. People crave the feeling of community that many small towns have given us in the past, with the county courthouse being the center of town and social life."

About a thousand miles to the north, in West Des Moines, Iowa, General Growth Properties's Jordan Creek Town Center has introduced a broad selection of shopping and entertainment activities to central Iowa. The 2 million-square-foot master-planned development includes a two-level enclosed shopping center, plus a 3.5-acre lake surrounded by bike trails, pedestrian walkways, and a boardwalk. The development also has a collection of large and specialty retailers in an open-air lifestyle center design. "Shopping centers are evolving into more than just retail," says John Bucksbaum, chief executive of General Growth Properties. "We are creating experiences at our centers. Jordan Creek Town Center is the blueprint for our new developments and redevelopments moving forward."

In Miramar, Florida, city officials have approved construction of a town center that will include municipal uses such as a new city hall, a public library, a cultural center arts park, and an educational facility, all surrounded by residential, retail, office, and entertainment space. A joint venture of Rockefeller Group Development Corporation and Kimco Developers, Inc., is slated to purchase the land earmarked for the mixed-use retail, office, and residential components of the project. The new development will be a "genuine town center with arts, commerce, social, civic, and government activity," says Mayor Lori Moseley.

Originally published as "Centering Towns," by Mike Sheridan, *Urban Land*, Vol. 64, No. 4, April 2005. Published by the Urban Land Institute, Washington, DC. Reprinted with permission of the publisher.

The town center concept is changing, developers say. Consumers now demand places offering more urban, walkable facilities that serve as gathering spots for individuals and provide a sense of community through a well-thought-out, cohesive design. Called town centers, transit-oriented developments, urban villages, or main street developments, these new offerings seek to create unique places with lasting value. Already such developments have challenged conventional wisdom about consumers, retailing practices, building design, parking arrangements, and housing types. The desire of Americans to live in neighborhoods that provide a higher quality of life is expected to result in the creation of even more town centers in the years ahead that integrate housing, office, retail, and entertainment space.

John Torti, president of Torti Gallas and Partners, an architecture, planning, and urban design firm based in Silver Spring, Maryland, says his firm is working on a half dozen town center developments in several areas. Each development is unique to the area, he explains, and developments include what he characterized as the "true" town center, the "fill the hole in the doughnut" town center, and the "build it and they will come" town center.

A true town center — an area that is, in fact, the governmental and civic core of a municipality — is being built in south Florida's Miramar community, whose new city hall is the centerpiece of its town center. "Miramar does not enjoy the beaches of a Fort Lauderdale or a Palm Beach, but it had profitable tax generators such as big-box and industrial users," says Torti. "Because the city was running out of space in its present city hall, it decided to build a new mixed-use town center neighborhood and purchased a parcel in the geographic middle of the town for its new city hall and a new performing arts center to make the once-moribund area a desirable live/work/play environment." The city is selling the surrounding parcels to private developers for office, housing, and retail uses to animate the center and to help defray some of the costs of buying the land and building the city hall, he says. "It's very unusual and very exciting. Miramar is a real, honest-to-goodness town center."

In contrast, at Orlando's bustling Baldwin Park is an example of another type of town center — an effort to "fill the hole in the doughnut." The developers of Baldwin Park have transformed a 1,000-acre set of neighborhoods, once the Orlando Naval Training Center, into residential, office, and retail space. "The surrounding area has existing infrastructure and people are already living there. The development, however, is in search of a central place — a civic heart, if you will — in the midst of the new neighborhoods," says Torti. "In this case, the town center is in an area where a full-size Publix supermarket is located on a new main street of shops and restaurants with housing above. It is essentially a fourth neighborhood with a main street used as a town center."

The Twinbrook development in Rockville, Maryland, is a similar infill town center. "Its generator is the existing transit station surrounded by well-established residential, employment, and retail neighborhoods," says Torti. "This transit-oriented development creates a new town center of 2.5 million square feet of mixed-use new urbanism where old, underutilized warehouses once existed along the tracks."

Torti says a third category of town center is greenfields development, in which a new town center is used as the generator or marker of the development. An example is Disney's Celebration community in Florida, he says, where developers built the town center first "as a stake in the ground" to identify the place, and it, in turn, became the generator for housing development. "They built the town center upfront and it became an identifiable symbol of the town: a very handsome place that operates on the same set of principles as a town center with wonderful mixed uses — a place where you could live, work, shop, and enjoy. The town center was used as a generator for the residential development that followed."

The keys to a successful town center, Torti explains, are numerous high-density mixed uses and an appealing public realm designed especially for pedestrians and their activities. It needs to have good connections to neighborhoods and the region so that people can come and enjoy it, and it must have a mix of activities so it is full of life not only in the day, but also during evenings and weekends. "Thus, today's new town center becomes a place people want to go to as a reflection of their lifestyle," says Torti. "We are basically remaking suburbs that were built over the past five decades to create more intimate, interconnected areas."

The town center concept can be expanded to encompass plans to relieve traffic congestion as well, notes John Ellis, principal at WRT/Solomon E.T.C. of San Francisco. Transit-oriented developments (TODs) as well as town centers are popular in many cities and towns on the West Coast because municipalities are realizing that they need to offer an opportunity for growth without necessarily increasing traffic congestion or continuing sprawl into greenfield sites.

"Transit-oriented development is a hot-button issue today because people realize that as our communities get bigger and our highways become increasingly congested, it makes sense to build higher-density developments around transit networks," says Ellis. In the San Francisco Bay area, for instance, transit-oriented development is being planned along several of the region's transit corridors, including the 72-mile Bay Area Rapid Transit (BART) network, the Caltrain system, and Amtrak's Capitol Corridor. "At many of those stations, the huge surface parking lots that have been destructive to the life of the surrounding community have been rebuilt as mixed-use developments," he says.

Recognizing that marrying mass transit and real estate development could be a smart move, forward-thinking California communities such as Hercules, Hayward, and Mountain View are embracing TOD to revitalize neighborhoods.

"Several communities have turned surface parking lots into structured parking areas and then built high-density multifamily developments," says Ellis. "Recent examples include the Fruitvale BART mixed-use development and downtown Hayward, where, as master planners, we proposed the new city hall, multifamily housing, and new retail next to the BART station." In Mountain View, WRT/Solomon E.T.C. designed a TOD/residential infill project that demonstrates how development can occur successfully in an upscale suburb while responding to the local context and the needs of the community. "A big part of this plan is obtaining community acceptance," emphasizes Ellis.

One of WRT/Solomon E.T.C.'s most recent projects was a study that reimagined the Hacienda Business Park in Dublin, about 30 miles east of Oakland. The business park consisted of a huge arterial road network with acres of surface parking surrounded by isolated low-density office buildings. Originally planned in 1985 and adjacent to a new BART station, Hacendia Business Park is a good candidate for a mixed-use community rather than one with a single use. "We worked within the constraints of the existing infrastructure to create a new network of streets and blocks," says Ellis. "Since some 65 percent of the land in the business park was surface parking, we suggested creating a parking district and building parking structures. In addition, we proposed reducing the width of some of the roadways and liberated land for development."

Such reconstruction is occurring all over the United States. "We must continually come up with new ideas for places that have reached the end of their natural economic cycle, such as dead shopping malls, empty business parks, or defunct brownfield sites, and create more compact, mixed-use communities that are smarter and more sustainable," says Ellis.

Near the Fruitvale BART station in Oakland, for example, San Francisco's Patri Merker Architects is designing a mixed-use development that consists of residential condominiums and retail lease space. Piero Patri, a principal at Patri Merker, says the idea is to be as flexible as possible with new TOD developments. "Many cities are grappling with similar problems, so it's an interesting challenge," he says. "Our key idea is to offer flexible space in a development that will evolve over time."

As a result of the increasing popularity of public transit and the importance of smart growth initiatives, the land surrounding transportation hubs has grown significantly more valuable, continues Nate Cherry, a vice president in the Los Angeles office of Baltimore, Maryland–based RTKL Associates's planning/urban design group. Consequently, developers and municipalities are looking to increase the density and to diversify the uses around these hubs. "What used to be just retail is now retail, office, and residential," says Cherry. "For example, in Anaheim, California, the downtown redevelopment project that began 20 years ago has evolved to accommodate a changing economic climate. As traffic woes have heightened in the region, development has demanded more than an office base. Today, residential is a major component in Anaheim's town center redevelopment plan."

Cherry says he is also seeing changes in how TOD projects are being created. "There's significantly more diversity in the kinds of developers getting involved in a single project, and public agencies are playing a far more proactive role in assembling a good development team," he explains. "In California's San Gabriel Valley around Pasadena, developers are scrambling to get involved in these transit projects because they want to take advantage of the high-density options. It took the market ten to 15 years to realize that transit is a plus, and now these are some of the best projects to be involved in."

This kind of development has a promising future, Cherry emphasized, adding that businesses are beginning to support transit routes, which suggests a heightened awareness of the financial benefits of transit. "Consecutive federal transportation laws are increasingly broadening funds to support transit projects," he says. "And, with every success, developers and planners are growing more knowledgeable on how to successfully implement this crucial new type of development."

A number of other developers throughout the country have latched on to the new development concepts. Simon Property Group of Indianapolis and Atlanta's Ben Carter Properties recently opened St. Johns Town Center in Jacksonville, Florida, a mixed-use town center development that will include 225 townhouses, 225 luxury apartments, two hotels, and 1.5 million square feet of retail, restaurant, and entertainment space.

Lewis notes that developers will continue to create town centers, transit-oriented developments, and other new developments designed to transform suburbs from satellite communities into more self-sufficient areas that have urban complexity without urban concentration.

"Town centers and transit-oriented developments are a way for developers and municipalities to create their own center, their own identity," says Lewis. "It is an attempt to make a development stand out, while at the same time give residents a main street feeling. The concepts will continue for some time to come."

CHAPTER 50

Cities, Change, and Growth

Roger L. Kemp

Citizens throughout the world face the challenges of the twenty-first century, the dawn of our civilization's third millennium. Dynamic changes are taking place in society that will have a profound impact on our cities in the future. Evolving societal conditions and public perceptions have created trends that require communities to change in order to meet the public's expectation of effective and equitable governance. The milestone changes examined in this chapter are based on established and predictable trends. They will have a measurable impact on municipalities across the nation during the coming years. Adapting to these changes will test the abilities of public officials as they strive to represent the citizens they serve.

Gone are the traditional and predictable days for local government. When revenues were plentiful, public officials could merely adjust tax rates to balance budgets. The outside environment was relatively tranquil, and it did not pose many significant challenges, impending threats, or even available opportunities. Public programs were merely increased in response to citizen demands for more services. In the future, both the scale and mix of public services, as well as how they are financed, will be critically examined in response to changes taking place in our society. Our traditional electoral practices have long formed the basis of local democracy. Minority and ethnic groups now demand greater representation in the governance processes of their community.

The traditional municipal planning practices of the past were designed during periods of steady growth and routine change. They are now being questioned and replaced by modern and more relevant planning practices. Practicing strategic planning, developing alternative scenarios, and using issues management techniques — long common in the private sector — have been at the forefront of this planning trend. The traditional planning practices of the past, characterized by merely projecting previous trends into the future, will increasingly be found to be lacking in reliability and credibility. In the future, more sophisticated, technically accurate, and politically acceptable planning practices will be developed to adapt a municipal organization to its changing environment.

The Forces of Change

The changes currently taking place in society will have a profound impact on our cities in the future, as well as on how they are governed and managed. How public officials adapt to these evolving conditions directly reflects on their ability to adapt municipal institutions in the future. Today's public officials are typically preoccupied with the present and reactive to change. Most of the time government officials, at all levels, respond to change after the fact. Municipal officials are no exception to this common practice. External circumstances and public attitudes are changing so rapidly that the practice of the past is quickly becoming obsolete. The process of community governance and type of service provided to citizens are in a state of transition.

The magnitude and momentum of these changes will directly influence public services during the coming years, as well as how they are financed and the extent to which they meet the needs of citizens. By purposely adapting local democratic institutions to citizens's expectations, and by productively planning for the future of municipal organizations, public officials will be able to create a smooth transition for their local governments in future years. If this does not happen, then throughout the United States, city hall will increasingly become a vocal forum for debating citizen demands for greater government accountability, citizen responsiveness, and organizational change.

To illustrate the extent of these changing societal trends, and to make them easier to understand, I present them using six categories:

1. Readily predictable demographic shifts
2. Major economic factors
3. Escalating environmental concerns
4. Evolving political considerations
5. State-of-the-art technological trends
6. Changing urban patterns and shapes

The next sections describe those changes taking place in our society, as well as how they are influencing the very fabric of life in our communities and how they affect local government.

Demographic Shifts

Thanks to emigration from South and Central America, Hispanics will soon become the largest minority group in America. Their political impact will be felt in city halls in many communities, especially in cities located in the Southwest and Southeast.

A growing number of senior citizens will, because of their increasing life span and available leisure time, become more politically active, particularly at the local level, where access to local democratic institutions and processes is readily available to all. These senior citizens will demand more specialized public services, such as those provided by recreational, cultural, library, health, and social programs. Large-print books, health clinics, nutrition workshops, and exercise classes are but a few examples of services of this type.

The growing number of small households will require more high-density residential developments, such as condominiums, townhouses, and apartments. This type of development will place greater demands on existing public services in these residential areas.

There will be a larger percentage of women in the workforce, and they will become more politically active there. Such issues as equal opportunity, comparable worth, sexual harassment, and family leave policies will increase in importance.

A greater number of minority and immigrant groups will create new demands for specialized public services, such as the need to hire bilingual employees, implement cultural diversity programs, and enhance equity in delivery of existing public services to citizens.

More minority and immigrant groups will become involved in the political process. This will create greater demand for equitable election practices, resulting in more minorities and immigrants in the political arena, and demands that a municipal workforce reflect a community's ethnicity.

Because of the increase in families with a female head of household, community issues such as provision of affordable health care, after-school child care centers, community policing programs, and specialized programs for young people, such as teen centers, will be high on the municipal agenda.

Immigrant groups will continue to enter the United States, expanding existing ethnic centers and creating new ethnic neighborhoods in these highly urbanized metropolitan areas.

The second generation of American immigrants will increasingly relocate to other states surrounding these centers; but unlike their parents, they will move to the suburbs as they have families and assimilate into the mainstream of American society.

Economic Factors

Because of limited discretionary money at the federal level, new grant-funded programs will be limited and earmarked for local services that help achieve national goals, such as providing affordable housing, alleviating unemployment, making shelters available for the homeless, improving urban planning practices, and lowering health care costs.

Public officials increasingly will focus on economic development as a vehicles to raise revenue without increasing property taxes. Cities in highly urbanized areas will have to resort to intense redevelopment of brownfield areas for their very economic survival.

Job retention programs that prevent employment opportunities from migrating to other cities will be high on the municipal agenda. The focus of economic development will shift, as land becomes scarce, from incentives that favor job creation to those that enhance job-retention programs.

Since virtually every community finances and provides the essential "hard" services (such as police, fire, and public works programs), there will be greater emphasis on how to pay for the quality-of-life, or so-called soft, services (such as recreation, museums, libraries, and cultural programs). User fees and charges will become more common.

The public's aversion to escalating property taxes will continue, forcing local officials to look for other revenue sources not related to property taxes, such as new user charges, increases in existing fees, and improvement in tax collection from already approved revenue sources.

A greater number of taxpayers will acknowledge that it is the legitimate role of government to extend safety-net services to truly needy citizens. Taxpayers will not mind paying taxes for these necessary and important services, on a temporary basis.

Millions of American will continue to move to the city to chase their dreams. Sociologists call this the "bright-lights effect." Increased international trade, superior infrastructure, and greater access to technology will make cities responsible for a growing proportion of the nation's economic production.

The public will recognize the value of the social cohesion that only a city can produce. The vitality, excitement, and sense of community that a city can create and foster will increasingly be recognized and appreciated for its economic value. This trend, coupled with Americans' moving to cities, will serve to limit suburbanization and urban sprawl in the future.

Public officials will increasingly focus on economic development as a vehicle to raise revenue without increasing taxes. Highly urbanized cities will have to resort to redevelopment for their financial survival. Municipal tax abatement will increase in popularity.

Citizens do not mind paying for those services they use, but they will increasingly demand that other taxpayers pay their fair share of taxes for the cost of those "other" services that they do not use. This will pose a political problem, since everyone uses selected services but no one uses every public service.

Environmental Concerns

The need to create sustainable communities will enjoy new emphasis. Citizens will recognize that human population must be concentrated in cities to preserve America's agricultural and wilderness areas. Circular rather than linear urban systems will become necessary if we are to recapture our nation's natural resources.

Both planners and developers will become aware of the need for newly designed communities to foster balanced quality of life within a traditional neighborhood setting. This trend will concentrate development, with commercial and high-density residential mixed land use in the center, along with adjacent single-family residential areas surrounded by common open spaces.

Greater urbanization, coupled with renewed appreciation of our natural environment, will result in new planning models that permit multijurisdictional stewardship of those important natural amenities that transcend our traditional political boundaries.

A new planning discipline, called "horizon-line management," will emerge, whereby communities and their public planners will take responsibility for managing scenic areas and corridors for such natural amenities as ridge tops, mountains, and plateaus, as well as man-made urban skyline in densely populated metropolitan areas.

Quality-of-life issues such as air and water purity, availability of parks and open spaces, and preservation of natural amenities will increase in importance as citizens come to understand the positive relationship between the natural environment and the economic health of their community.

Older and more politically sensitive land use (such as aging and outdated commercial buildings and industrial plants) will be upgraded or retrofitted with new improvements and amenities to make them more attractive to the public for both employment and shopping.

The public will increasingly embrace comprehensive code enforcement as a vehicle to improve the condition of aging residential neighborhoods. Department managers will be held accountable for enforcing these municipal codes to improve the housing stock within the community.

Citizens will acknowledge the need to plan properly for such local natural amenities as coastlines, rivers, streams, lakes, wetlands, and other natural wonders, designated for all citizens to enjoy. Citizens of all income groups will increasingly embrace these environmental issues, which once were the concern of individuals only in high-income communities.

Citizens are starting to appreciate the main attributes of nature — the sky, the land, and the water — and will increasingly demand that their public officials, especially elected officials and professional planners, properly plan for the stewardship of these natural resources to make them available for future generations to enjoy.

More multicity, city-county, multicounty, multistate, and national-state agreements will emerge for managing those unique natural amenities that spill over artificial political boundaries. Public-private partnerships will also be developed to enhance the stewardship of these natural resources. Citizens will come to recognize the finite quality of our natural resources.

Political Considerations

Minority and immigrant groups will increasingly demand change to existing democratic institutions, such as traditional election methods and voting options. There will be greater pressure to move toward district elections and alternative voting practices.

More federal and state laws, and court decisions of all types, will greatly usurp the home-rule powers of locally elected officials, central administrators, and functional managers, serving to limit their municipal discretion in many ways as to how these services are provided to citizens in the future.

Although special-interest groups typically pursue their own narrow goals, these groups will increasingly form broad coalitions around major issues of mutual interest at the local, state, and national levels. This will create a turbulent political environment in public meeting halls throughout the country.

Brought about by limited revenues, many political issues will have no simple or clear-cut response, as in evolving debate concerning which services to reduce, options for holding down property taxes, which taxes to increase, and whether to increase program user fees and charges.

Citizens will demand public services but not want increased taxation, making it more difficult for public officials and administrators to set program priorities, determine appropriate service levels, and balance the annual municipal budget.

General responsibility for services will continue to shift from the federal and state governments to cities, forcing communities to solve their own problems. Because of the mismatch between available revenues and existing problems, communities with a low tax base may have to resort to service reduction to balance the budget.

As they become more involved in the political arena, minority group representatives (including immigrants) and women will demand specialized and diversified public services. These individuals will advocate for neighborhood services tailored to meet the needs of the citizens they serve.

The NIMBY (not in my back yard) movement will continue to grow in size at the neighborhood and community levels. It will be ever more difficult to locate or relocate within a community undesirable public facilities such as jails, wastewater treatment plants, and waste disposal facilities.

More political coalitions and partnerships involving business, government, education, and the nonprofit sector will emerge to address a community's social and economic problems of mutual concern. A greater number of nonprofit organizations will be formed to address these emerging problems in the coming years.

Current public officials, both elected and appointed, will feel the increasing political influence of these new special-interest groups (seniors, women, immigrants, and minorities). When service reductions must be made in the future, it will be difficult to cut the services intended for these new constituent groups.

Technology Trends

There will be increased use of microcomputers in the workplace, brought about by more sophisticated hardware systems, advanced user-friendly software applications, and lower cost for both. In the not-too-distant future, nearly every municipal workstation will have a microcomputer with state-of-the-art software.

Microcomputer systems will increasingly incorporate and combine such existing pieces of office technology as facsimile machines, photographic copiers, document scanners, specialized printers, and telecommunication devices.

All municipal organizations will standardize their computer hardware systems and software applications in the near future. This will create uniformity for these technological applications, facilitating the trend to conduct generic hardware and software training for all employees.

Expensive organization-wide, stand-alone computer systems will become a thing of the past, primarily because of the development of improved and inexpensive mainframe computer systems and networking techniques, as well as ever more inexpensive and sophisticated microcomputers.

Information management will become necessary as advanced computer hardware systems and software applications facilitate generating all types of information. The emphasis will switch from merely receiving information to acquiring quality information in a timely manner.

As utility costs escalate, computerized energy monitoring and management systems will grow popular and become less expensive, facilitating widespread use of these systems to limit energy consumption in city hall and other public buildings.

Advanced videotaping equipment and municipal-owned public-access cable television stations will broadcast more public meetings to citizens. This medium will be used to educate citizens about available public services, as well as major issues facing the community.

Greater energy costs will continue to shape our personal values, lifestyle preferences, and future technological developments. Smaller automobiles, less spacious offices, new energy-saving devices, and more sophisticated building techniques are examples of this phenomenon.

More advanced telecommunication systems with video capability will make conference calling commonplace. This will limit the number of face-to-face business meetings and reduce travel expenses. More and more personal computers will feature this as standard equipment in the future.

Every municipal government will have an interactive Web site, which can be accessed by citizens and used to contact public officials in local government twenty-four hours a day, seven days a week. Virtual city halls will emerge, where citizens can make applications, receive permits, download public announcements, and view videos about the community, all on line. On line voting will also become commonplace in the future.

Also, sophisticated Geographic Information Systems (GIS), while slow to enter the public sector, are becoming increasing popular as a vehicle for urban planning. The databases for GIS systems have been expanded in recent years to include population factors, the age of residents, urban density, prevailing zoning patterns, land uses, street patterns, and other criteria. The use of such GIS is becoming commonplace. This information assists urban planners, appointed officials such as planning commissioners, and elected officials such as mayors and city councils, when making important land-use decisions. This significant trend will continue in future years.

Urban Patterns

Urban sprawl will grow but be primarily located along major vehicular transportation corridors, such as highways and freeways, and contiguous to public mass-transit routes in suburban transportation rings with hubs located outside the nation's inner-city areas.

Citizens will witness greater in-fill development in already highly urbanized areas. Land areas that were once considered marginal for development will be purchased and improved to meet increasing community demands for commercial and industrial development.

In our country's central-city areas, escalating land values will lead to increased gentrification of inner-city neighborhoods, further exacerbating the need for affordable housing for low- to moderate-income families in the poorer metropolitan areas.

New ethnic centers will emerge and evolve in major metropolitan areas. First-generation residents will stress maintaining their cultural traditions and personal values, as well as the unique customs brought to this country from their homeland.

Higher energy costs and greater traffic congestion will create political pressure for public mass-transit systems. Emphasis will be placed on multimodal systems that offer transportation options to citizens. Expensive construction costs will lead to more routes in densely populated urban areas. Light-rail systems will become commonplace for longer routes connecting cities with their suburbs.

Those inner-city public services provided by many urban cities will migrate to the suburbs. Since so many people have moved to the suburbs during the past few decades, and public problems are more prevalent in densely populated areas, suburban communities will have to provide this type of service in the future.

As young people age and gain employment, they will increasingly use e-commerce to purchase consumer goods. This will limit the need for new regional shopping malls and strip-mall commercial centers. Warehousing and distribution centers will feel increased pressure to meet the new demand created by e-commerce.

Population shifts away from the Northeast and Midwest will exacerbate the decline of the existing corporate tax base in these locations, possibly forcing public service reductions or property tax increases in the future. Statewide economic development incentives will be used to counteract this negative economic trend.

Gentrification will continue as young single people, childless couples, well-to-do empty-nesters, and active retirees continue to move from the suburbs to inner-city metropolitan areas. This movement will be fueled by less expensive housing, lower energy costs, and a desire to be closer to available commercial and cultural amenities.

Our nation will witness a dramatic shift in the nature of public attitudes toward cities. These changing attitudes stem from the realization that the social problems of our cities cannot be geographically contained. Wherever people move and wherever the population spreads, these problems will follow.

The Future

All of these changes — demographic shifts, shifting economic factors, evolving environmental concerns, political considerations, the latest technology trends, and new urban patterns — will have a dramatic impact on the field of urban planning in general, and growth management practices in particular. Also, these changes, for a number of reasons, will likely increase during the coming decades.

Several new movements are at the forefront of urban planning. These relate to the facilitated trends related to the creation of healthy cities (which focuses on the relationship of buildings to their environment), the concept of new urbanism (which focuses on the design of neighborhood, their housing, and how they impact people), and the new emphasis on cities and sustainability (which focuses on the relationship of entire cities to their broader environment).

All of the major urban planning and development *movements*, which are and will continue to have a profound influence on our society, are all alive and well and will continue, even increase, in importance in future years. These trends, no doubt, will be significantly impacted by new technologies, both hardware and software, that will facilitate the codification of knowledge in these fields, as well as the cross-pollination of this knowledge to professional planners, developers, elected officials, and citizens in general.

CHAPTER 51

Cities and Their Infrastructure

Roger L. Kemp

The term "infrastructure" refers to the basic facilities and installations necessary for society to operate. These include transportation and communication systems (e.g., highways, airports, bridges, telephone lines, cellular telephone towers, post offices, etc.); educational and health facilities, water, gas, and electrical systems (e.g., dams, power-lines, power plants, aqueducts, etc.); and miscellaneous facilities such as prisons, asylums, national park structures, and other improvements to real property owned by government. In the United States, the infrastructure is divided into private and public sectors (in the latter case, divided again between facilities owned by municipal, county, state, and federal governments, as well as many special district authorities such as the Port Authority of New York and the Los Angeles Department of Water and Power, to name a few).

According to the American Society of Civil Engineers (ASCE), the only professional membership organization in the nation that has graded our nation's public infrastructure, there are fifteen major categories of government infrastructure. These infrastructure categories include:

- Aviation,
- Bridges,
- Dams,
- Drinking Water,
- Energy,
- Hazardous Waste,
- Navigable Waterways,
- Parks and Recreation,
- Rail,
- Roads,
- Schools,
- Security,
- Solid Waste,
- Transit, and
- Wastewater.

Fiscal Crisis

All levels of government in the U.S. are facing a new era of capital financing and infrastructure management. Revenues that once were available for capital construction, restoration, and maintenance have either diminished or evaporated entirely in recent years. Portions of the public infrastructure that were once adequate are now experiencing signs of distress, even decay, with no end in sight to the ongoing deterioration of America's infrastructure.

Local, state, as well as the federal government are now subjected to unprecedented fiscal demands for public services in an environment of limited taxation and dwindling financial resources. Throughout the nation, many state government deficits loom ominously on the horizon. At the same time, the federal deficit is at an all-time high, exacerbated by the fact that our nation is financing an undeclared war in the Middle East. These negative fiscal circumstances, experts believe, are likely to continue for many years to come.

Congested highways, overflowing sewers, and corroding bridges are constant reminders of the looming crisis that jeopardizes our nation's prosperity and the quality of life for our citizens. With new grades for the first time since 2001, the condition of our nation's infrastructure has shown little to no improvement since receiving a collective grade of D+ in 1998, with some areas sliding toward failing grades. The American Society of Civil Engineers' *2005 Report Card for America's Infrastructure* assesses the same 12 categories as in 2001, and added three new categories. The grade comparison of America's infrastructure between the ASCE's most recent 2005 survey and its original survey in 1988 are highlighted below.

- Aviation — Received a grade of B- in 1988, and a grade of D+ in 2005.
- Bridges — Received a grade of C+ in 1988, and a grade of C in 2005.
- Dams — While not graded in 1988, they received a grade of D in 2005.
- Drinking Water — Received a grade of B- in 1988, and a grade of D- in 2005.
- Energy — While not graded in 1988, this category received a grade of D in 2005.
- Hazardous Waste — This category received a grade of D in 1988 and in 2005.
- Navigable Waters — While not graded in 1988, they received a grade of D- in 2005.
- Parks & Recreation — While not graded in 1988, they received a grade of C- in 2005.
- Rail — While not graded in 1988, this category received a grade of C- in 2005.
- Roads — Received a grade of C+ in 1988, and a grade of D in 2005.
- Schools — While not graded in 1988, this category received a grade of D in 2005.
- Security — This category did not exist in 1988, and insufficient data is available to properly evaluate this category (i.e., this is a new category since 9/11/01).
- Solid Waste — Received a grade of C- in 1988, and a grade of C+ in 2005. This is the only infrastructure category to increase its grade since the original graded evaluation some 17 years ago.
- Transit — Received a grade of C- in 1988, and a grade of D+ in 2005.
- Wastewater — Received a grade of C in 1988, and a grade of D- in 2005.

In short, U.S. roads, bridges, sewers, and dams are crumbling and need a $1.6 trillion overhaul, but prospects for improvement are grim. This is the amount of money necessary over the next five years to restore and rebuild major components of our nation's public infrastructure. The nation's drinking water system alone needs a public investment of $11 billion a year to replace facilities, as well as comply with regulations, to meet our future drinking water needs. Federal grant funding, in 2005, is only 10% of this amount. As a result, aging wastewater systems are discharging billions of gallons of untreated sewage into surface waters each year, according to the ASCE's report.

And the signs of our deteriorating infrastructure go on! Poor roads costs motorists $54 billion a year in repairs and operating costs, while American's spent 3.5 billion hours a year stuck in traffic jams. The country's power transmission system also needs to be modernized, the report said. While demand continues to rise, transmission capacity failed to keep pace and actually fell by 2 percent in 2001. As of 2003, 27 percent of the nation's bridges were structurally deficient or obsolete, a slight improvement from the 28.5 percent in 2000. It is alarming to note, but since 1998, the number of unsafe dams in the country rose by 33 percent to more than 3,500.

Several national professional associations have officially endorsed the ASCE's *2005 Report Card for America's Infrastructure.* They include the American Public Works Association; the National Stone, Sand and Gravel Association; the U.S. Conference of Mayors; the National Heavy and Highway Alliance; the American Road and Transportation Builders Association; and the Association of State Dam Safety Officials. These endorsements are listed in Table 1.

Economic Development

It should be emphasized that the improvement and maintenance of our nation's public infrastructure, at all levels of government, is critically linked to economic development in all regions of the country. Economic development programs, as most people are aware, bring in additional private-sector investment, add much-needed jobs to the local economy, as well as provide additional tax revenues to fund future public services (for all levels of government). An adequate infrastructure makes a city, county, state, and nation more desirable from an economic development perspective. Without an adequate infrastructure, the financial plight of all levels of government is likely to deteriorate even further in the future. Hence, finding solutions to the country's infrastructure problems is an important issue facing public officials (and citizens) in every level of government.

If the public officials continue to let these critical infrastructure issues remain unresolved, the next generation of political leaders at each level of government will either have to raise massive taxes to repair and maintain their government's respective portion of the infrastructure, or be forced to close many public facilities due to their disrepair, deterioration, or decay. In short, major portions of our public infrastructure will become unsafe for the public to use. Economic development programs will also diminish if these infrastructure issues are not properly addressed and resolved, creating lost opportunities for private sector investment, the jobs they would bring, as well as the much needed revenues that could be used

to maintain essential public services at all levels of government.

National Leadership Is Needed

While the views expressed by many experts who research and write on infrastructure issues throughout the nation point to a general agreement on the magnitude and complexity of this problem, little agreement exists on a consensus on how to achieve a comprehensive nation-wide solution to restoring and maintaining America's public infrastructure. Although there is disagreement as to an acceptable solution, one point seems obviously clear: *the necessary leadership and policy direction required to properly address this national issue must come from the highest level of government.* Is only within a national policy framework that states, counties, and cities can work together to improve the current condition of our public works facilities. Local and state governments alone, because of their many diverse policies, multiple budget demands, and varied fiscal constraints, cannot be relied upon to achieve the comprehensive solution required to solve this national problem.

The current philosophy of our national government has been to let the lower levels of government (states, counties, and cities) solve their own problems, regardless of the nature of their complexity or the magnitude of funds needed. The political posture of our national government needs to become more positive and proactive if a solution is to be forthcoming. For these reasons, it is obvious that assertive leadership is needed from the federal government to make the difficult policy decisions, as well as to approve the funding requirements necessary to solve our country's infrastructure problem. Fundamental changes are needed to redirect national priorities about how public capital investments are made. Public officials, at all levels of government, can no longer merely build public facilities without adequately maintaining them in future years.

Table 1

**Endorsements of the Report Card for America's Infrastructure
by the American Society of Civil Engineers**

American Public Works Association
National Stone, Sand and Gravel Association
The U. S. Conference of Mayors
National Heavy and Highway Alliance
American Road and Transportation Builders Association
Association of State Dam Safety Officials

Source: American Society of Civil Engineers, Infrastructure Report Card for 2005,
Website (http://www.asce.org/reportcard/2005), March 13, 2005.

Table 2

Infrastructure Internet Resources

American Association of State Highway & Transportation Officials
(http://www.transportation.org)
American Public Transportation Association (http://www.apta.com)
American Public Works Association (http://www.apwa.net)
American Society of Civil Engineers (http://www.asce.org)
Global Security (http://www.globalsecurity.org)
Infrastructure Security for the Built Environment (http://www.tisp.org/isbe)
International City/County Management Association (http://www.icma.org)
National Association of Counties (http://www.naco.org)
National Civic League (http://www.ncl.org)
National Infrastructure Protection Center (http://www.nipc.gov)
National League of Cities (http://www.nlc.org)
The Council of State Governments (http://www.csg.org)
The Infrastructure Security Partnership (http://www.tisp.org)
U. S. Department of Homeland Security (http://www.dhs.gov)
U. S. Department of Housing & Urban Development (http://www.hud.gov)
U. S. Department of Transportation (http://www.dot.gov)
U. S. Economic Development Administration (http://www.eda.gov)

The Future

As the severity of this issue escalates, and citizens become more aware of the increased costs of postponing a decision on this pressing issue, taxpayers may be more willing to become politically involved in solving this issue in the future. Taxpayers cannot be expected, however, to foot the entire bill for a solution, since the majority of our country's capital assets have been constructed over the past several decades, some over a century ago, and frequently with the assistance of grant funds from our federal government. This bullet is "too big to bite" by other levels of government alone.

Also, cities, counties, and states have relative degrees of wealth based on their taxing capacity, bonding levels and ratings, and budgetary reserves. Because of this, many lower levels of government do not have the financial capability, even with increased taxation, to adequately address those issues related to restoring and maintaining America's infrastructure. It is safe to say that most citizens throughout the country already feel overtaxed by all levels of government. Even thought citizens may be willing to assist financially, a major redirection of federal government funds will be required for a truly comprehensive and coordinated nation-wide response to our country's outstanding infrastructure problems and issues.

Even with some additional taxes and user fees, funding will be limited at all levels of government. For this reason, argue those who deal with infrastructure issues, national priorities must be established for the replacement and restoration of capital facilities at all levels of government, starting with those projects that are necessary to ensure the public's security, health, and safety. Funds from the national government must be targeted for infrastructure projects from less important operational programs with limited, or only special interest, constituencies. Within the framework of national policies, existing federal grant programs must be redirected to provide the necessary funds to assist in the financing of those capital projects necessary to restore America's public works infrastructure to ensure the security, as well as the health and safety, of all our citizens throughout the country. See Table 2 for a list of Infrastructure Internet resources.

Our nation is not "on the road to ruin," as some experts explain, but merely going through the transition period required to properly sort out and arrive at politically acceptable long-term solution to this critical and complex policy issue that plagues all levels of government — federal, state, county, and city alike. If our nation's infrastructure is allowed to deteriorate even further in the future, possibly to the point of decay, the cost of resolving this issue will escalate significantly in future years, for all taxpayers. If this happens, economic development programs will also continue to suffer, and the revenues they could generate will not be available to assist in restoring our public infrastructure.

This lack of investment in America's infrastructure will also restrict urban growth as well as compound urban problems such as roadway traffic, mass-transit facilities, the provision of drinking water, and the elimination of sewage in towns and cities throughout the country. New developments are being located adjacent to public transit facilities. The new phrase for these types of residential projects is Transit Oriented Development (TOD). This type of development promotes a lifestyle for those folks who do not want cars, but would like to be close and have access to public mass-transit. If a public investment is not made in public transit facilities, urban sprawl will continue as more new housing development are placed adjacent to our suburban and rural highways. This phenomenon will further exacerbate our nation's urban transportation, and traffic, problems.

BIBLIOGRAPHY

Bietro, David T. and Bruce Smith, "The Formation of Urban Infrastructure Through Nongovernmental Planning: The Private Places in St. Louis," *Journal of Urban History,* Vol. 16, No. 3, May 1990, SAGE Publications Ltd., London, UK.

Blackburn, Stephanie J. and David E. Dowall, *The Tools for Financing Infrastructure,* Institute of Urban and Regional Development, University of California, Berkeley, CA, 1991.

Chapman, Jeffrey I., *Long-Term Financial Planning: Creative Strategies for Local Government,* International City/County Management Association, Washington, DC, 1999.

Hudgins, Edward, *How Privatization Can Solve America's Infrastructure Crisis,* The Heritage Foundation, Washington, DC, 1992.

Johnson, Mike, *World Infrastructure 1994,* Sterling Publications Limited, London, UK, 1994.

Kemp, Roger L., *America's Infrastructure: Problems and Prospects,* The Interstate, Danville, IL, 1986.

_____, "Public Works" in *Managing America's Cities: A Handbook for Local Government Productivity,* McFarland & Company, Inc., Jefferson, NC, 1998.

_____, *Main Street Renewal: A Handbook for Citizens and Public Officials,* McFarland & Company, Inc., Jefferson, NC, 2000.

_____, *The Inner City: A Handbook for Renewal,* McFarland & Company, Inc., Jefferson, NC, 2001.

Levy, Matthys and Richard Panchyk, *Engineering the City: How Infrastructure Works: Projects and Principles for Beginners,* Chicago Review Press, Chicago, IL, 2000.

Office of Technology Assessment, Congress of the U.S., *Delivering the Goods: Public Works Technologies, Management, and Practices,* U. S. Government Printing Office, Washington, DC, 1991.

Revell, Keith D., *Building Gotham: Civic Culture and Public Policy in New York City, 1898–1938,* John Hopkins University Press, Baltimore, MD, 2002.

Rosen, Howard and Ann Durkin Keating, *Water and the City: The Next Century,* Public Works Historical Society, American Public Works Association, Chicago, IL, 1991.

Schmandt, Jurgen et al., *The New Urban Infrastructure: Cities and Telecommunications,* Praeger Press, New York, NY, 1990.

Walker, Warren E., *Policy Analysis and the Public Infrastructure.* RAND Corporation, Santa Monica, CA, 1993.

CHAPTER 52

Cities and Their Environment

Kevin Fletcher

"I want to protect our community's natural environment. I think most of our Town Board and a significant number of government staff thinks it's important ... but taking that interest beyond mere words continues to be a challenge."—Town Planner, Upstate New York

I recently spoke at a local planning association meeting on techniques for creating a more sustainable future for small cities and towns. After the talk, one of the local planners from a rural community outside Albany, New York made this statement (above) to me. Clearly frustrated, he expressed something that green champions in communities across the country are expressing—a type of green fatigue. Elected officials and professional staff in communities from New York to Florida and beyond are struggling with a passion for environmentally-focused governance, without a means to make it "the way we do things around here."

Addressing Common Elements of Failure

It's important to recognize that you and others like you are "change agents" within your local government, and your goal is to create an environmental culture within your community—starting with the local government as a role model. Where to begin? Start by addressing eight common failures for environmental organizational change (adapted from John Kotler, *Leading Change*, Harvard Business School Press, 1996):

Failing to Create a Sense of Urgency

Moving people, and entire organizations or communities, in a new direction can be a little like moving an iceberg. Effective environmental champions find ways to create a sense of urgency. Incorporating environmental stewardship into local government has to be viewed as a critical part of your community's long-term success, and a critical part of each person's job. It's also critical to secure top management support for your environmental efforts. If employees see upper management or elected leaders treating the environment as a side issue, then they will too.

Originally published as "Injecting Environmental Culture into Local Government," *New Jersey Municipalities*, Vol. 83, No. 4, April 2006. Published by the New Jersey State League of Municipalities, Trenton, NJ. Reprinted with permission of the publisher.

Not Creating a Guiding Coalition (Team)

You can't go it alone. Build a "green team," with people from all levels and departments — and ideally, include community residents who are not a part of the government structure. Be aware of who, throughout your local government, has an ability to help motivate staff and coordinate government operations. Who in your community has knowledge and technical skills to help solve environmental problems? Who has the authority and respect to help you mobilize your entire community? Answers often lead to people not directly involved in local politics.

Underestimating the Power of a Vision

People want to feel as if they are a part of something bigger than themselves. Create a bigger vision for your community — starting with your government operations. Every town and city is located in a watershed. Every facility depends upon energy, water, and other natural resources in order to function. Every person on your staff has a family. Find the connection between the day-to-day actions that people take, and the effect that those actions can have on our natural environment and everyday quality of life. Make a connection between the financial health of your community and the money wasted on eco-inefficiency (i.e., lights left on, leaking water pipes, waste that could have been recycled).

Under-Communicating the Vision

Once you've developed a "vision message," make sure that vision is communicated to staff, and to town and city residents. You may think that people have heard or read what you're saying, but most environmental messages are under-communicated. Use posters, regular departmental and public meetings, and perhaps even bonuses or other incentives to reinforce the vision and the role that each individual plays in achieving that vision.

Not Addressing Obstacles

Most environmental efforts fail in organizations — public and private alike-because they are viewed as side issues. Remove these obstacles along the way. The City of Eufaula, Alabama — the first community designated a Certified Audubon Sustainable Community — made environmental protection and sustainability the driving force for their comprehensive planning process, but only after generating a great deal of buy-in from the entire community. By the time citizens gathered to take details about the vision for their community, many of the potential obstacles had already been addressed.

Failing to Create Short-Term Wins

Keep you and your staff motivated throughout any culture-building process. Have a long-term vision, but set short-term goals. Meet them. Publicize and celebrate those shorter term successes. Then, set new goals.

Declaring Victory Too Soon

At the same time, don't settle on limited results. Remember that the longer term goal is to create an environmental culture throughout your community, starting with the local government itself. One or two recycling success stories do not lead to changed culture. Culture change takes years to accomplish. And the bigger the organization or community, the longer it takes. That's why rural and small communities have an advantage over larger communities to become more sustainable.

Not Anchoring Changes in the Culture

Use projects and performance goals to change behavior, but use management systems, rewards programs and training programs to reinforce and embed that behavior in staff. As an environmental champion, part of your job for ensuring success is managing the environmental culture that you've created.

Final Thoughts

With top management and elected officials' support, a team of staff from all levels and departments, a well-communicated vision, a set of achievable short-term goals, and mechanisms to make environmental stewardship "the way we do things around here," you will be on your way to improving the overall environmental performance of your community. Be willing to start small while thinking big. Remember that any positive environmental action you and your staff take brings us that much closer to a more sustainable world.

CHAPTER 53

Telecities and the Future

Joseph N. Pelton

Modern technological process is essentially one-way: Once major innovations occur — regardless of whether they are helpful or harmful — they cannot simply be undone. They are almost always here to stay. During the last several millennia, we have seen "progress" as a set of trends toward megacities: increased urbanization and technological development; higher capacity and faster transportation systems; concentrated and centralized infrastructure for energy, water, and sewage; and expanded police, military, and weapons systems.

In the twenty-first century, these trends will accelerate, according to some urban planners, architects, and industrialists. There will be more centralization, more urbanization, and greater concentration of people in high-rise urban structures. Models of such a future of high-tech megastructures, with dense concentrations of populations, are visible everywhere. We already see this ill-advised vision of the future in huge skyscraper megastructures in Kuala Lumpur, Shanghai, and most remarkably in the redesigned World Trade Center.

These exotic and exciting testimonials to high-rise technology and centralization are as awe-inspiring as they are wrong-minded and potentially destructive. The twenty-first century demands a new direction — a megashift in value systems and a move toward electronic decentralization. The future of human, intellectual, and economic relationships will be based not in the traditional city, but in the *telecity*— a global community whose life, direction, and functioning are shaped by telecommunications.

The End of the Megacity

Telecities will supersede megacities for several reasons, including the drive toward clean air, reducing pollution, energy conservation, more jobs based on services, and coping with the high cost of urban property. Now we must add the need to cope with terrorist threats in a high-technology world.

Western mind-sets were clearly jolted in the wake of the terrorist attack on the World Trade Center in New York City and attacks in Indonesia, Saudi Arabia, and elsewhere. But the risks posed by twentieth-century patterns of urbanization and architecture have yet to register fully with political figures and leaders of industry. The pentagon, for example, has been rebuilt in situ rather than distributed to multiple locations and connected by secure

Originally published as "The Rise of Telecities," in the Vol. 38, No. 1, January-February 2004, issue of *The Futurist*. Used with permission from the World Future Society, 7910 Woodmont Avenue, Suite 450, Bethesda, MD 20814. Telephone: 301/656-8274; Fax: 301/951-0394; http://www.wfs.org.

landlines and broadband wireless systems. Likewise, the reconstruction of the World Trade Center complex still represents a massive concentration of humanity and infrastructure. This is a remarkably shortsighted and dangerous vision of the future.

The security risks, economic expenses, and environmental hazards of overcentralization are everywhere, and they do not stop with skyscrapers and large governmental structures. There are risks also at seaports and airports, in food and water supplies, at nuclear power plants and hydroelectric turbines at major dams, in transportation systems, and in information and communications systems.

This vulnerability applies not only to terrorist threats but also to human error, such as system-wide blackouts in North America in August 2003 and in Italy in September 2003, and natural disasters such as typhoons, hurricanes, floods, and earthquakes. Leaders and planners are only slowly becoming aware that overcentralized facilities are the most vulnerable to attack or catastrophic destruction.

There is also growing awareness that new broadband electronic systems now allow governments and corporations to safeguard their key assets and people in new and innovative ways. So far, corporations have been quickest to adjust to these new realities, but some governments have begun to adjust as well.

In Japan, for example, the 1995 Kobe earthquake not only killed many people but also wiped out transportation, fiber-optic communications systems, and key infrastructure for many months. The government decided to place satellite earth terminals throughout the country at post offices to ensure communications backup in times of disaster. More than 4,000 small satellite terminals are already in place, and soon a total of 10,000 will provide the Japanese with a level of secure communications far exceeding any other country's capabilities.

The United States, Europe, and other regions should look to the Japanese model to mitigate the impacts of terrorist attacks or natural disasters. Backup data centers, distributed wireless and satellite facilities, and a new emphasis on replacing classic megacities like New York City and London with telecities will likely ultimately represent a key trend of the twenty-first century.

Today, most communications providers and satellite system operations are beginning to provide managed network services that are safer from natural disasters and terrorist attack. Basic issues to carefully consider include the following.

- **Reviewing key facilities** to ensure that they are not clumped together, built in flood zones, or built in structures that are not hurricane and earthquake proof. Verizon put much of its wireless antenna systems for Manhattan on top of the World Trade Center, for instance, and in Florida, the construction of several teleports has been allowed in flood zones.
- **Strategic planning** to place government and corporate offices in locations that are not only more decentralized, protected, and cheaper, but also where their data and communications centers will be more protected.
- **Decentralizing** all critical infrastructure wherever possible.
- **Reorganizing corporations** to allow them to work as distributed information systems so as to conserve energy, reduce commuting time, improve the environment, and sharply reduce capital and operating costs.
- **Designing better and "smarter" airports, transportation, and energy systems,** with greater attention to disaster and terrorist risks and their implications.

In short, there are many key facilities of the twenty-first century that need to be conceived in different ways and designed to be smarter, more distributed, and more resilient.

Goodbye to Commuting

The world is a much smaller place today than 40 years ago, when the age of satellites and fiber-optic networks began. These electronic systems now link billions of people via telephone, radio, television, the Internet, and so on. Everything from astrophysics to *I Love Lucy* to religious ceremonies at the Vatican are instantly available via satellite-linked modems, even in the rain forests of Brazil and the frozen shores of Antarctica. In the age of the telecity, concentrations of people, government facilities, and other infrastructure are simply not necessary and can only serve to increase risks and elevate costs and pollution.

Fiber-optic and coaxial cables, satellite networks, terrestrial wireless, and other transmission systems allow instant and broadband broadcast and electronic exchange on a planetary scale. Today, fiber-optic networks are capable of transmitting hundreds of terabits per second within the world's most advanced countries. Advanced satellites allow more than 200 countries and territories to achieve instantaneous linkage via telephone or the Internet. More than 100 million satellite terminals located everywhere serve a global cast of users. Satallite-user terminals are now interlinked via an amazing combination of broadcast, fixed, navigational, and mobile satellites. In another decade, that number of terminals will likely grow into the several hundreds of millions. In another two decades, that number might even exceed a billion and be so pervasive that we may own several satellite terminals, including one that we wear within a suit coat or on our arm like a wristwatch.

Satellite-user terminals will continue to shrink in size and cost and "disappear" within our clothing or briefcase or into handheld personal data assistants. A flip-down eye loupe will provide multimedia information from anywhere on the planet or even outer space colonies.

In such a world environment, an organization could transfer operations from the

world's most expensive (and potentially vulnerable) locations to lower cost suburbs, rural locations, or another country entirely. No need exists for mass commutes to move millions of people into massive high-rise compounds. New electronic and optical systems will be able to provide true "telepresence" anytime and anywhere at virtually no cost.

Global business via satellite and fiber is already commonplace. Electronic funds transfers worldwide were projected to approach $400 trillion during 2003. As impressive as the growth rates in information services around the work have been during the past four decades, this is nothing compared to what will soon be. Studies by Pioneer Consulting and other organizations suggest that e-business and electronic services could increase by an order of magnitude in the next five years.

Working from Home or Hawaii

Rapid, fundamental shifts in work patterns and in corporate organizations are already occurring in the United Sates and around the world. Hewlett-Packard, for example, has some 40,000 teleworkers at home or at remote work sites. In Japan, NEC continues to expand its network of remote telework centers to bring workers together electronically, since it can no longer afford to build new workspace in the heart of Tokyo. Although these efforts began through IT networking based on terrestrial cable technology, more-flexible satellites will provide the wireless networks of the future.

The Yankee Group estimates there are more than 15 million teleworkers in the United States. They and other market forecasters, such as the Gartner Group and Nielson's, expect this number to rise to more than 50 million by 2010. Similar patterns of growth are expected in Europe, Canada, Japan, and elsewhere around the world. Broadband satellite links are well positioned to fuel this trend due to their flexibility of interconnection, universal coverage, increasing ability to support Internet-protocol based local and wide area networks, and ever cheaper micro-terminals.

There are also more than a million international teleworkers worldwide. Twenty years ago, hourly labor wages were well below the cost of international tie-lines, but now the cost of international information networks is a small fraction of the cost of skilled personnel. We see a continued growth of "lone eagles"—people who decide to locate in scenic Hawaii or Switzerland. From their electronic perches, service providers can provide information or consulting services around the world via broadband connections.

People in dozens of emerging economies already telework via fiber or satellites for companies in the United States or Japan. Insurance companies in the northeastern United States have teleworkers in the Caribbean providing word processing and data entry, while Japanese companies hire low-salary computer software development engineers in India, Pakistan, or South Korea. Programmers from Bangalore to St. Petersburg are essentially providing data and IT services around the world live via satellite. The question is whether new broadband networks will beget telework and more worldwide teleservices or the other way around, with the demand for telework-based services begetting new "telepresence" systems. The most important question is whether these trends are driven by the pursuit of new economies of operation and labor markets, by envi-ronmental savings, or by the desire to protect population and critical systems against terrorist attacks.

Mobile Money

A few decades ago, the world banking community invented new electronic funds transfer (EFT) systems to move money more efficiently across countries and around the globe. The driving benefit of such systems was to reduce the float of capital that was unavailable for use while checks were being cleared through banking systems. Today, we understand that the benefits of electronic banking are far more extensive than just reducing floating cash. The entire world of banking has been revolutionized. It is not only more efficient and faster, but also more global. And now with the Internet, EFT systems are increasingly integrated with the new world of e-commerce and e-trade.

Between 1997 and 2003, EFT value soared from less than $50 trillion to nearly $400 trillion, more than the combined economic product of all the countries and territories of the entire world. These statistics along should underscore the true importance of transnational EFT. Satellite, wireless, and cable-based electronic fund transfers represent the hub of global enterprise. Such electronic cash is therefore central to the idea of an emerging "worldwide mind."

Without the satellite and fiber infrastructure to support the flow of electronic funds, the world economy would grind to a halt. A frontal assault on this system by cyberterrorists could be nearly lethal blow to global economic prosperity. Of course, such vulnerability is only the beginning: Information networks control energy grids, transportation systems, water systems, dams, and flood-control systems. The great challenge is, therefore, to provide new forms of security for all aspects of twenty-first-century telecommunications, including media redundancy, improved code and authentication systems, and enhanced cyberlocation.

Other Telecity Revolutions

More people will need education and health care in the next two generations than have ever been educated or treated since the beginning of human civilization. The technology that makes it possible to deliver health and education services more effectively across long distance and to remote areas must not be confused with the core objectives themselves. The new way of looking at governmental services is to seek ways to deliver more and better services to more people. A corollary is that one must use the most effective technology and system in order to deliver services more effectively and with the most up-to-date information.

Media can and will assist in this great challenge, but the tool must never be confused with the social need. These teleservices must reach the most remote and isolated spaces and with the most up-to-date information. In some cases, satellites and/or fiber networks can also conserve substantial amounts of energy and provide financial savings, but this should be considered a side benefit rather than the object of telecare, tele-health, and tele-education.

Bridging the Gap

For the last half of the twentieth century, there were broad concerns about economic and information gaps among the world's nations. The rise of terrorist attacks has increased awareness of the risks that such gaps entail.

There have been continuing charges of neo-colonialism and exploitation of emerging nations by multinational corporations. The advent of the World Trade Organizations, free trade coalitions, and e-commerce has tended to increase rather than ameliorate some of those concerns. On one hand, international trade originating from developing countries is increasing as a percentage of the world's total, but much of that trade can be traced to multinational organizations ("North-to-South"). Although telecommunication developments seem to offer new hope and opportunity, the concerns remain. Telenetworks can help bridge the digital divide if planned and implemented in the right way. This must be considered part of the twenty-first-century telecity conception.

The roughly 2 billion people in developing nations who lack basic services must be considered a challenge not only for the poorest countries, but also for the stability of the world's economic and political systems. What seems clear is that wireless communications and satellite networks often represent the best hope for enabling sustainable development in emerging countries.

Fiber-optic networks and high-end computers do not address the basic needs of many emerging economies. Satellites allow "South-to-South" communications and programs and facilitate tele-education, tele-health, and the growth of services in developing countries. The spread of e-commerce, Internet, and other modern services will most likely come via wireless and satellite technology to the world's poorest or most isolated nations. Certainly satellites and low-cost technologies are not a panacea, but they do represent solid ways of addressing basic needs in Africa, Asia, South and Central America, and the Middle East. It is key to recognize that the critical pathway to success in the delivery of these services relates to the educational and health content and not the delivery system.

Fundamental Shifts and Emerging Patterns

Today, information available to our global society is accelerating at exponential speeds. Electronic networks and satellites interconnect even the most remote areas. The nature of learning, communications, and social interchange is being totally transformed via distance learning, international scientific collaboration, access to the Internet, and the global reach of corporations and electronic commerce.

As the rate of speed in the circulation of information has accelerated, new ways of obtaining, storing, and sharing information have evolved. The final trends regarding the development, sharing, protection, and refinement of information in the twenty-first century are still evolving and have yet to be fully understood. One thing that is now clear is that satellites and broadband fiber-optic networks will make the world ever more visually oriented and less text-oriented. We have yet to understand the full implications of this change. But just as more and more information depreciates the value of any one intellectual item, more and visual information also likely depreciates both visual and text information.

The patterns by which information is circulated are changing, and quickly so. Many factors drive this changing pattern, including global reach, increasing speed and volume of the information being circulated, the magnitude and education level of the populations of modern countries, the ownership patterns of media by private and public entities, the interaction of news with sports and entertainment, and the falling costs of computing and communications.

Thus, information is becoming not only increasingly visual, but also almost randomly prioritized in terms of its meaning, importance, or relevance. The unexpected results include information overload, decreased vocabularies, and educational systems that create more specialization and fewer broadly educated generalists or systems analysts.

The speed and low cost of modern transmission systems appear to be major drivers in this transformation, not only in the most developed countries but also around the world. The fact that television entertainment, sports, movies, and multimedia-based games and e-commerce now dominate traditional telecommunications networks and the Internet appears to represent a fundamental shift in the world today — with much more to come tomorrow.

Making Lives Better

The digital revolution has made more information available to more people, faster, and from more varied types of media and applications. Perhaps the most important application of telecity technologies may be to save the environment.

NASA's Mission to Planet Earth and Earth Observation System provide us with air, water, land, glacier, and pollution data. Increasingly sophisticated and high-resolution multispectral sensors, side-looking and synthetic aperture radar, infrared, thermal mapping systems, and other devices allow us to collect data from all over the world. But we need communications satellite technology to transfer this data from remote sensing satellites to data analysis centers and then to users, wherever they may be.

Global information networks are now creating truly global corporations, supporting electronic immigrants (transnational telecommuters), and supporting telework and telecommuting for tens of millions of workers around the world. Tele-education, tele-health, and telegovernment are megatrends of the new millennium. These networks are essential to linking scientists together to carry out big projects and support supercomputer processing to help protect against natural disasters. The key is not only to do this effectively and at low cost, but also to provide the coverage and bandwidth to be able to do it quickly and accurately. It is also important to allow the right person or organization to obtain the right information at the right time — that requires decentralization.

Often our short-term calculations are at

odds with the interests of our children and grandchildren. There are many issues we must address.

- We must find applications and benefits of satellite system and fiber operators that go beyond merely developing networks that are faster and cheaper.
- We must create not only better electronic and photonic machinery, but also improved educational, medical, social, and cultural systems that serve the needs of future generations. We need to create economic and political systems that are wise enough to look beyond short-term material and monetary gains.
- As we move from national and regional to international and global economic, social, and cultural networks and systems, we must learn to use new technology not only to transact business faster and at higher volume, but also to improve the human condition. We must improve security, environment, world peace, prosperity, and sustainable livelihood for ourselves and for our progeny.
- Finally, we must find ways through economic, legislative, regulatory, or judicial systems for controlling the use of digital information systems to produce a higher quality of life, protect privacy, offer greater environmental protection, and sustain human life.

CHAPTER 54

Sustainable Communities and the Future

Susan F. Boyd

There has been an impressive flowering of community-oriented movements in recent years, of which the Sustainable Community movement is one of the best developed. Although the term itself may not be familiar, many of the concepts of sustainability are. Sustainable communities are analogous to living systems in that all resources — human, environmental, economic, and cultural — are interdependent and draw strength from each other. Support is growing across the country for new planning and governance processes that seek to address environmental, economic, and social issues as an integrative whole. A number of community-building initiatives are being implemented in which participants create a vision of the future to protect and restore the environment, expand economic opportunity, and promote social justice. These processes are inclusive, open, transparent, adaptive, collaborative, and participatory. Win-lose outcomes are being altered to become win-win, and diverse participants collectively and proactively develop long-term visions of the future. The greater the number of constituencies involved and the more voices heard, the greater the opportunity for success, since they all have a stake in the outcome.

Principles of Sustainable Community Development

Although each sustainability initiative self-organizes, many create a set of operating principles to guide their governance and their programs. Some develop locally relevant community indicators to measure performance, identify and communicate progress toward sustainability, and guide public policy. Others introduce collaborative, participatory approaches within their respective disciplines to design outcomes that have multiple benefits. In essence, whether implicitly or explicitly, these efforts have been guided by principles and values that demonstrate a shift to sustainability:

- Employ whole systems processes that integrate equity, environment, and economy as equals
- Support planning and decision making that is community-based, long-term, inclusive, and open, and that fosters full community participation

Originally published as "Sustainable Communities and the Future of Community Movements," *National Civic Review*, Vol. 90, No. 4, Winter 2001. Published by the National Civic League, Denver, CO. Reprinted with permission of the publisher.

- Create processes that are interdisciplinary and that involve the community, business, and government sectors
- Develop solutions that yield multiple, complementary outcomes
- Identify, support, and link existing efforts and resources
- Share information and develop open communications systems
- Recognize linkages to the regional, national, and global community

Who Is Involved?

"It takes all of us and it takes forever." This is the philosophy of residents of Chattanooga, Tennessee, where conditions were so bad — environmentally, economically, and socially — in the late 1960s that the community had to come together to address them in an unprecedented way Chattanooga has become a symbol for what can be achieved when a common vision is collectively developed by diverse members of the community. It continues to be a laboratory for sustainability design, enterprise, and innovation. It is one of many communities around the country in which sustainable community development efforts have had lasting impact.

Participants in many local initiatives have been pioneers with a vision of what was possible and a heartfelt commitment to make something happen. They tend to have broadly similar values and share a worldview that challenges traditional assumptions and recognizes the possibility of a win-win solution. They seek the opportunity to create connections and link efforts with others. In general, these champions of sustainability — community members and leaders in business and government — tend to share their lessons learned and are likely to cross traditional boundaries in their work. Irrespective of their background or held, they tend to bridge disciplines and enjoy working in a multidisciplinary, mutigenerational framework.

Opportunities for Collaboration

Many community-building efforts exist in the United States; each is making a contribution to the field as a whole. One of the values of letting a thousand flowers bloom, as is now the case with multiple strands of community movements, is the diversity of invention that it encourages and the range of opportunity for involvement. Those committed to making positive change happen in their communities may prefer an approach that reflects the culture of their place. The challenge now is to consider the benefits and drawbacks of aligning some of these efforts to leverage existing resources and enhance future outcomes. Collaboration among other movements increases the number of perspectives on an issue and thus increases the likelihood that creative solutions will be developed. Because styles and strategies are likely to differ among community efforts, working together informally on the efforts discussed here might constitute a proving ground to help decide on the desirability of future collaboration.

Principles. Principle-based organizations flourish in the sustainability field. They often draw on elements of existing documents, such as the Earth Charter, the Ahwahnee Principles, the Hannover Principles, the Natural Step, and many others. The Earth Charter, drafted by more than two hundred organizations and thousands of individuals, contains sixteen principles in four categories: respect and care for the community of life; ecological integrity; social and economic justice; and democracy, nonviolence, and peace. The Ahwahnee and Hannover Principles were drafted by members of the design community, and the Natural Step was developed by scientists in Sweden. There are numerous other examples and considerable overlap between them. Therefore a body of work exists to help with a new collaborative effort. This might be an opportunity to develop and distill a shared set of principles among the community movements. We are in a transition from one era to the next, with an enormous opportunity for entrepreneurial innovation. Principles create a framework for those in many fields to align their efforts. This first step could be the most important one that the community movements can take.

Language and Communication. Language evolves and changes in every field, and each has its own lexicon and buzzwords. Members of the various community movements could explore development of a common vocabulary and a process to communicate and work together. There is a need for a common lexicon and glossary to align thinking in the community field without detracting from the richness of the differences. Links among a distributed electronic framework and e-zines featuring ongoing efforts might supplement existing communication systems and increase understanding about the benefits of a systemic, integrative approach. Similarly, selected graphics depicting before and after images would illustrate concrete outcomes.

Regional Resource Centers. As our organization works with numerous communities, we repeatedly hear from them that they had no idea others were attempting similar processes, and that they would have benefited from what others had done and experienced. To take one instance, the Sustainable Communities Network, an electronic clearinghouse of resources, tools, and case studies on the Internet (www.sustainable.org), was conceived to meet this need. It is a valuable resource; many others like it exist, but they are not sufficient to meet the growing demand for information. Similarly, training for civic engagement, sustainability facilitation and processes, dialogue, and many other skills are needed to build capacity at the local level that furthers the goals of those involved in many aspects of community work.

Unlike graduate programs in law, medicine, engineering, and other professions, there is no degree in civic engagement. One answer might be collaborative regional resource centers that model sustainability systems and offer such training. A number of people involved in community-based decision making have already begun thinking about creating such centers. These resource centers could house representatives from agencies within a given jurisdiction, thereby increasing cross-fertilization of ideas and encouraging integrative decision making.

Strengthen the Knowledge Base. Showcasing initiatives and explicitly communicating their economic, environmental, and social benefits leverages and galvanizes development of the nascent community movement. Certainly there is demand for information about comparable initiatives, organizations, and tools in geographically defined areas. The Internet makes it possible to informally share initiatives across even greater distances. Community movement practitioners could develop shared criteria for evaluating the sustainability of programs and projects that simultaneously strengthen equity, environmental, and economic goals. These initiatives could be catalogued in a standardized format. In some localities where this has been done, individual organizations are able to better understand how their work relates to others and to determine the synergistic possibility of working together for common goals and effective results. Furthermore, this documentation could inform future funding priorities in the public and private sectors.

Change, Evaluation, and Recognition. Communities are all affected by waves of change. Some changes we can influence; others are beyond our control. The question is whether we help create the future we want or the future we get. Community building is an act of will. Political and civic will and persistence, along with willingness to think imaginatively and boldly, is essential. In any municipality there is typically resistance to change and concern about power and turf issues; there also tends to be a silo mentality that results in a piecemeal approach and discourages whole systems thinking and a cross-sector approach. Incentives systems in all sectors generally reward what one knows more than what one shares. Commitment to what is usually an unpredictable civic engagement dialogue and process is essential, but depending on the place some cultures will find this more or less tolerable than others. Engaging and valuing diverse participation continues to be a challenge for many of these efforts. Sharing early and visible results can build the foundation for future work.

It is also important to develop criteria for evaluating the success of projects and for designing and implementing recognition programs. Collaboration among community movements in this endeavor might be resource-efficient and help attract and retain those engaged in this work. The Joint Center for Sustainable Communities has a recognition program for municipal efforts. A parallel program among community organizations could be established to honor existing efforts and galvanize others.

Research. Investment in efforts that yield tangible, measurable results in one year is commonplace. Grants that support long-term, interdisciplinary efforts are scarce. There is a well-known story among sustainability advocates that Gregory Bateson used to tell about New College in Oxford, England. After 350 years, the beams in one of the buildings built in the early 1500s were rotting and in need of replacement. The faculty gathered and pondered about what to do. Purchasing new ones would be prohibitively expensive, so they called in the college forester. He said he had been thinking they never would ask; three hundred fifty years previously the architects foresaw such a need and specified that a stand of trees be planted for just such a purpose. That is sustainability thinking.

Effective programs require building trust, respect, and a sense of community. Institutions — private foundations, public agencies, and businesses — focus on short-term results. Therefore we need to introduce a common

sustainability ethic and metrics that reward a long-term approach, as well as projects that promote individual and collective steps in the right direction.

A collaborative approach with other community movements could create research and documentation supporting the merits of this perspective and thus strengthen the case for this type of anticipatory, preventive investment. A more coordinated effort to educate grant-making institutions about the value of these systemic, interdisciplinary, long-range approaches might help everyone. Presenting the benefits of interdisciplinary programs might also influence how stories are communicated within the media. More coverage of the overarching good news, rather than pieces of the bad news, might constitute compelling journalism some day.

Conclusion

In a recent sustainable community grants program, CONCERN communicated a vision: "Our vision of a local sustainability initiative is one that brings diverse participants together to draw on their collective wisdom to help create a more sustainable community. It engages representatives from nonprofit organizations, the business community, and the government sector to develop innovative and integrative approaches to help build communities that are *environmentally sound, economically vital, and socially just.* The initiative creates systemic change which will have the potential to inspire and inform similar initiatives in communities throughout the United States."

No doubt many of those involved at different levels in the various community movements share this vision. Now is an opportune time to begin to weave these strands to strengthen the fabric of our communities, businesses, and agencies. A principle-based approach could be a shared framework for achieving outcomes and thus engage all the talents of all the participants. The various community movements can benefit from an informal network of communication and cross-fertilization that reinforces, supports, and sustains those committed to this work and begins to move these approaches into the mainstream.

Appendices

Containing I. Periodicals Focusing on Planning; II. Glossary; III. Acronyms and Abbreviations; IV. Regional Resources; V. National Resources

I. Periodicals Focusing on Planning

The following list consists of periodicals that are dedicated to planning or that often address related subjects.

California Planner; monthly; subscription included with membership in the California Chapter of the American Planning Association, c/o S/G Assoc., 1333 36th St., Sacramento, CA 95865.

This is the official newsletter of the CCAPA. It contains articles on current planning activities around the state, an update on state legislation relating to planning, and information on workshops on planning.

Journal of the American Planning Association; quarterly; from the American Planning Association Planners Book Service, 122 S. Michigan Ave., Suite 1600, Chicago, IL 60603-6107, (312) 786-6344.

A collection of academic articles relating to current physical, economic, and social planning research. Recent topics include infrastructure finance, homelessness, strategic planning, and economic development. In addition, it contains detailed reviews of new literature in the field.

PAS (Planning Advisory Service) Memo; published six times a year for subscribers to the American Planning Association's Planning Advisory Service, 122 S. Michigan Ave., Suite 1600, Chicago, IL 60603-6107, (312) 786-6344.

The *PAS Memo* highlights new planning programs, identifies and examines planning trends, and analyzes escalating problems relative to land use and planning throughout the nation. It offers expert commentary on timely topics like immigration, Internet resources for planners, and using remote sensing technology for planning.

Planning; monthly; from the American Planning Association Planners Book Service, 122 S. Michigan Ave., Suite 1600, Chicago, IL 60603-6107, (312) 786-6344.

The magazine of the American Planning Association, *Planning* focuses on solutions to common planning problems, reviews new planning techniques, and highlights successful planning programs. It is written by practitioners for practitioners.

Planning and Environmental Law; monthly; from the American Planning Association Planners Book Service, 122 S. Michigan Ave., Suite 1600, Chicago, IL 60603-6107, (312) 786-6344.

This periodical summarizes recent litigation occurring in state and federal courts around the country. Other topics include recently enacted state legislation affecting planning and expert commentary on subjects relating to land use regulation.

The Commissioner; quarterly; subscription included with "planning commissioner" membership in the American Planning Association, 122 S. Michigan Ave., Suite 1600, Chicago, IL 60603-6107, (312) 786-6344.

This periodical features expanded coverage on contemporary planning issues, and land use practices, and planning commission trends throughout the country. This is a non-technical publication written for citizens who serve as planning commissioners in their community.

Urban Land; monthly; subscription included with membership in the Urban Land Institute, 1090 Vermont Ave., N.W., Washington, D.C. 20005, (202) 289-3381.

This is the magazine of the Urban Land Institute, an independent education and research organization primarily made up of developers and private sector planners. It profiles successful development projects around the country as well as discussing current planning topics such as transportation funding and mixed use development.

Western City; monthly; from the League of California Cities, 1400 "K" St., Sacramento, CA 95814, (916) 444-5790.

This is the League of California Cities' magazine. Its articles concentrate on innovative programs in city administration, funding, and other topics such as fire and police protection. Although it does not concentrate on planning, it usually contains news of local planning-related programs.

Zoning and Planning Law Report; 11 issues per year; from Clark Boardman, Co., Ltd., 435 Hudson St., New York, NY 10014.

In each issue, this report carefully examines some aspect of planning law. Recent topics have included vested rights, exaction ordinances and "takings" theory. This periodical is valuable to both those considering new land use regulations and those interested in keeping current regulations up to date.

Zoning News; monthly; from the American Planning Association Planners Book Service, 122 S. Michigan Ave., Suite 1600, Chicago, IL 60603-6107, (312) 786-6344.

This is a four-page newsletter devoted to monitoring trends in local land use controls. It discusses innovative development regulations, code amendments, development projects, development incentives, and design standards. Each issue usually concentrates on a particular subject.

II. Glossary

Acre: 43,560 square feet of area. For example, a residential parcel of land that is 52' × 100' is 5,200 square feet which is 0.12 acres. The term gross acres means all land within a given boundary. The term net acres means all land measured to remove certain features such as roads, utilities, and open space.

Blight: Physical and economic conditions within an area that cause a reduction of or lack of proper utilization of that area. A blighted area is one that has deteriorated or has been arrested in its development by physical, economic, or social forces.

Brownfield: Abandoned industrial site likely to have groundwater or soil pollution that is deterrent to redevelopment.

Buffer Zone: A strip of land created to separate and protect one type of land use from another; for example, as a screen of planting or fencing to insulate the surroundings from the noise, smoke, or visual aspects of an industrial zone or junkyard.

Building Area: The total square footage of a lot covered by a building, measured on a horizontal plane, exclusive of uncovered porches, terraces, and steps.

Building Envelope: The net cubic space that remains for placing a structure on a site after setbacks and height/bulk regulations are observed.

Bulk Regulations: Zoning or other regulations that control height, mass, density, and location of buildings. The purpose of bulk regulations is to provide proper light, air, and open space. Some bulk regulations also are intended to reflect context-sensitive design.

Carrying Capacity: The level of land use or human activity that can be permanently accommodated without an irreversible change in the quality of air, water, land, or plant and animal habitats. In human settlements, this term also refers to the upper limits beyond which the quality of life, community character, or human health, welfare, and safety will be impaired. The estimated maximum number of persons that can be served by existing and planned infrastructure systems; the maximum number of vehicles that can be accommodated on a roadway.

Cluster Development (zoning): A type of development pattern for residential, commercial, or other uses in which the uses are grouped, or clustered through density transfer, rather than spread evenly throughout a parcel. Cluster development is more efficient because it requires building fewer streets and utility lines.

Community Plan: A portion of the local general plan that focuses on a particular area or community within the city or county. Community plans supplement the policies of the general plan.

Conservation Easement: A tool for acquiring open space with less than full-fee purchase; the public agency for not-for-profit corporation buys only certain specific rights from the landowner in order to restrict the development, management or use of the land. The landowner may be allowed to continue using the property for agricultural purposes.

Context Sensitive Design: A collaborative, interdisciplinary approach that involves all stakeholders to develop a transportation facility that fits its physical setting and preserves scenic, aesthetic, historic, and environmental resources, while maintaining safety and mobility. CSD is an approach that considers the total context within which a transportation improvement project will exist.

Density: The average number of families, persons, or housing units per unit of land. Usually density is expressed "per acre." Gross density includes the area necessary for streets, schools and parks. Net density does not include land area for public facilities.

Density Bonus: An increase in the allowable number of dwelling units granted by the city or county in return for the project's providing low- or moderate-income housing.

Floor Area Ratio: Abbreviated as FAR, this is a measure of development intensity. FAR is the ratio of the amount of floor area of a building to the amount of area of its site. For instance, a one-story building that covers an entire lot has an FAR of 1. Similarly, a one-story building that covers ½ of a lot has an FAR of 0.5.

General Plan: A statement of policies, including text and diagrams setting forth objectives, principles, standards, and plan proposals, for the future physical development of the city or county.

Geographic Information System: Computer mapping system that produces multiple "layers" (coverages) of graphic information about a community or region. For example, one layer might show the parcels, another layer might show key habitat areas, another layer might show school sites, etc. Considered a tool for analysis and decision-making, it may be composed of maps, databases and point information.

Grayfield: A blighted area that is ripe for redevelopment; the distinguishing characteristic between a grayfield and a brownfield is the absence of substantial groundwater or soil pollution.

"Granny" Housing: Typically, this refers to a second dwelling attached to or separate from the main residence that houses one or more elderly persons.

Greenbelt: A wide band of countryside surrounding a city on which building is generally prohibited, usually large enough to form an adequate protection against objectionable uses of property or the intrusion of nearby development.

Gridiron Street Pattern: A pattern of streets that, from the air, looks like a gridiron (i.e., based on right-angle intersections and parallel sets of roadways). Grid street pattern usually refers to shorter, more frequent block patterns, as compared to "superblocks" or a streets system with cul-de-sacs predominant.

Historic District: An area or group of areas designated by a local agency as having aesthetic, architectural, historical, cultural, or archaeological significance that is worthy of protection and enhancement.

Imageability: The quality in a city or any of its districts that will evoke a strong image in the observer.

Improved Land: Raw land that has been improved with basic utilities such as roads, sewers, water lines, and other public infrastructure facilities. The term "developed land" usually means improved land that also has buildings.

Infill Development: The creative recycling of vacant or underutilized lands within cities and suburbs. (Congress of New Urbanism). Among the variables in the definitions of infill development are whether the property must be surrounded by existing development or just within existing urban boundaries, whether infill projects must have a higher density than surrounding properties, and whether individual infill projects must be mixed use.

Infrastructure: A general term describing public and quasi-public utilities and facilities such as roads, bridges, sewers and sewer plants, water lines, power lines, first stations, etc. necessary to the functioning of an urban area.

Intensity: The degree to which land is used. While frequently used synonymously with density, intensity has a somewhat broader, though less clear meaning, referring to levels of concentration of activity in uses such as residential, commercial, industrial, recreation, or parking. Density usually refers to residential, while intensity usually refers to non-residential uses.

Jobs-Housing Ratio: The numeric relationship between the number of jobs (employment) divided by the number of housing units. A "jobs-housing balance" is the jobs-housing ratio that has a job for every member of households participating in the labor force. For example, if a typical housing unit has 3.0 people/housing unit, and ⅔ of those residents are in the workforce, then each housing unit generates 2 workers. In a "closed system," two jobs need to be available per housing unit within that system (e.g., a region).

Leapfrog Development: Development that occurs well beyond the existing urban limits of urban development, leaving intervening vacant land. The pattern of urbanization characterized by leapfrog development is sometimes referred to as "sprawl."

Livability Space: Open space used for people, planting, and visual appeal which does not include parking and driveway areas. It is a basic element of land-use-intensity ratings.

Lot Area: The total square footage of horizontal area included within the property lines. Zoning ordinances typically set a minimum required lot area for building in a particular zoning district.

Neighborhood: Residential area within a governmental unit that has some distinct identity to its inhabitants and observers.

Neighborhood Completeness: A land use indicator that attempts to define how well a neighborhood is served by specific land uses (e.g., affordable housing, fire/police station, grocery store, parks, library, school, post office).

New Urbanism: Similar to Traditional Neighborhood Development, this design philosophy is intended to create a strong sense of community by incorporating features of traditional small towns.

Open Space: That part of the countryside which has not been developed, and which is desirable for preservation in its natural state for ecological, historical, or recreational purposes, or in its cultivated state to preserve agricultural, forest, or urban greenbelt areas.

Overlay Zone: A set of zoning requirements that is superimposed upon a base zone. Overlay zones are generally used when a particular area requires special protection (as in a historic preservation district) or has a special problem (such as steep slopes, flooding or earthquake faults). Development of land subject to overlay zoning requires compliance with the regulations of both the base and overlay zones.

Planned Unit Development: Land use zoning which allows the adoption of a set of development standards that are specific to the particular project being proposed. PUD zones usually do not contain detailed development standards; these are established during the process of considering the proposals and adopted by ordinance if the project is approved.

Quality of Life: Those aspects of the economic, social and physical environment that make a community a desirable place in which to live or do business. Quality of life factors include climate and natural features, access to schools, housing, employment opportunities, medical facilities, cultural and recreational amenities, and public services.

Rural: Areas generally characterized by agricultural, timberland, open space, and very low-density residential development (e.g., less than one dwelling unit per acre). A rural community is not generally served by community water or sewer services.

Setback: A minimum distance required by zoning to be maintained between two structures or between a structure and property lines.

Smart Growth: A contemporary phrase related to development that better serves the economic, environment and social needs of communities. The US Environmental Protection Agency identifies the following 10 principles of smart growth:

1. Mix Land Uses
2. Take Advantage of Compact Building Design
3. Create a Range of Housing Opportunities and Choices
4. Create Walkable Neighborhoods
5. Foster Distinctive, Attractive Communities with a Strong Sense of Place
6. Preserve Open Space, Farmland, Natural Beauty, and Critical Environmental Areas
7. Strengthen and Direct Development Towards Existing Communities
8. Provide a Variety of Transportation Choices
9. Make Development Decisions Predictable, Fair and Cost Effective
10. Encourage Community and Stakeholder Collaboration in Development Decisions

Specific Plan: A plan addressing land use distribution, open space availability, infrastructure, and infrastructure financing for a portion of the community. Specific plans put the provisions of the local general plan into action.

Sphere-of-Influence: A planning area usually larger than, although sometimes contiguous with, a city's municipal limits.

Sprawl: The process in which the spread of development across the landscape far outpaces population growth. The landscape sprawl creates four dimensions: a population that is widely dispersed in low-density development; rigidly separated homes, shops, and workplaces; a network of roads marked by huge blocks and poor access; and a lack of well-defined, thriving activity centers, such as downtowns and town centers. Most of the other features usually associated with sprawl — the lack of transportation choices, relative uniformity of housing options or the difficulty of walking — are a result of these conditions. (Smart Growth America)

Subdivision: The process of laying out a parcel of raw land into lots, blocks, streets, and public areas. Its purpose is the transformation of raw land into building sites.

Suburban: Areas generally characterized by low-density residential development (e.g., 1 to 5 dwelling units per acre) and limited commercial uses.

Sustainability: A strategy by which communities seek economic development approaches that also benefit the local environment and quality of life. For a community to be truly sustainable, it must adopt a three-pronged approach that considers economic, environmental and cultural resources. Communities must consider these needs in the short term as well as the long term (Smart Communities Network).

Traditional Neighborhood Design: These neighborhoods encompass many modern land use strategies into one concept. Several cities across the nation (including Sacramento) have studied these models to improve the efficiency and facilitate the use of transit, pedestrian, and other alternatives to single-occupant motor vehicles. Public transportation and pedestrian use is encouraged through compact neighborhood development, where the distance from the center to the edge of a neighborhood can be walked at an easy pace in 10 minutes. Public interaction is fostered through the development of sidewalks, trees along streets, narrow roads that slow down cars, and parks or plazas that are located close to housing.

Universal Design: Various sources list the Seven Basic Principles of Universal Design:

1. Equitable Use (design is fair)
2. Flexibility in Use (design is adjustable)
3. Simple and Intuitive Use (design is elegant)
4. Perceptible Information (design is obvious)
5. Tolerance for Error (design is safe)
6. Low Physical Effort (design is easy)
7. Size and Space for Approach and Use (design is reasonable)

Urban: Areas generally characterized by moderate and higher density residential development (e.g., 5 or more dwelling units per acre), commercial development, and industrial development.

Urban Design: The attempt to give form, in terms of both beauty and function, to entire areas or to whole cities. The focus is on the massing and organization of buildings and on the spaces between them, rather than on the design of individual structures.

Urban Service Area: The area eligible to receive urban infrastructure (sewer and/or water service) in the short term.

Valued Environment: A place that holds personal meaning for a group of people, who may act to enhance or protect it.

Visual Preference Survey: An innovative and successful technique that enable citizens to evaluate physical images of natural and built environments. The process involves asking participants to view and evaluate a wide variety of slides depicting streetscapes, land use, site designs, building types, etc. Individual scores indicate whether the participant likes what they have seen and whether they feel it is appropriate for the community.

Zoning: Local codes regulating the use and development of property. The zoning ordinance divides the city or county into land use districts of "zones," represented on zoning maps, and specifies the allowable uses within each of those zones. It establishes development standards for each zone, such as minimum lot size, maximum height of structures, building setbacks, and yard size.

III. Acronyms and Abbreviations

ACEC— area of critical environmental concern
ADT— Average Daily Traffic
APF— Adequate Public Facilities
ARPA— Archaeological Resources Protection Act
AUM— animal unit month
BA— Biological Assessment
BCC— Birds of Conservation Concern
BE— Biological Evaluation
BMP— Best Management Practices
BRT— Bus Rapid Transit
CCC— consult, cooperate, and coordinate
CEQ— Council of Environmental Quality
CIP— Capital Improvement Program
CO— carbon monoxide
CSD— Context Sensitive Design
CRD— Clustered Residential Development
CWA— Clean Water Act

DEIS— Draft Environmental Impact Statement
EA— Environmental Assessment
EIR— Environmental Impact Report
EIS— Environmental Impact Statement
EPA— Environmental Protection Agency
ESA— Endangered Species Act
FAR— Floor Area Ratio
FGT— Fixed Guideway Transit
GFA— Gross Floor Area
GIS— Geographic Information System
IGA— Intergovernmental Agreement
IMPLAN— Impact Analysis for Planning
LOS— Level of Service
LSS— Level of Service Standard
MPOT— Master Plan of Transportation
NAAQS— National Ambient Air Quality Standard
NEPA— National Environmental Policy Act
NHPA— National Historic Preservation Act
NLCS— National Landscape Conservation System
NOI— notice of intent
NOX— oxides of nitrogen
NRA— Natural Reserve Area
O3— Ozone
OHV— Off Highway Vehicle
PAB— Planning Area Boundary
PLC— Public Lands Council
PLF— Public Lands Foundation
PM— particulate matter
POD— Pedestrian-Oriented Development
PSD— prevention of significant deterioration
PUD— Planned United Development
RNAs— Research Natural Areas
SEF— Sensitive Environmental Features
SFR— Single Family Residential
SOI— Sphere of Influence
SOX— oxides of sulphur
SWL— Sustaining Working Landscapes
T&E— Threatened or Endangered
TCP— Tree Conservation Plan
TDR— Transfer of Development Rights
TIP— Transportation Improvement Program
TMP— Transit Master Plan
TNC— The Nature Conservancy
TND— Traditional Neighborhood Design
TNR— temporary, nonrenewable
TOD— Transit-Oriented Development
USC— United States Code
USFS— U.S. Forest Service
USA— Urban Service Area

USFWS— U.S. Fish and Wildlife Service
WSA— Wilderness Study Area

IV. Regional Resources

The community governments included in the case studies in this volume are listed below alphabetically by city, town, and township.

Bernards, New Jersey
(See Township of Bernards)

Cherry Hill Township, New Jersey
Office of the Mayor
City Hall
820 Mercer Street
Cherry Hill, NJ 08002
Telephone: (856) 665-6500
FAX: (856) 488-7893
Internet: http://www.cherryhill-nj.com

City and Borough of Sitka, Alaska
Office of the Administrator
City Hall
100 Lincoln Street
Sitka, AK 99835
Telephone: (907) 747-1808
FAX: (907) 747-7403
Internet: http://www.cityofsitka.com

City of Apopka, Florida
Office of the Mayor
City Hall
120 East Main Street
Apopka, FL 32704-1229
Telephone: (407) 703-1703
FAX: (407) 703-1720
Internet: http://www.apopka.net

City of Athens, Georgia
Office of the Manager
Government Building
120 Dougherty Street
Athens, GA 30603
Telephone: (706) 613-3515
FAX: (706) 613-3844
Internet: http://www.athensclarkcounty.com

City of Atlanta, Georgia
Office of the Mayor
Executive Offices
City Hall
55 Trinity Avenue
Atlanta, GA 30303
Telephone: (404) 330-6000
FAX: (404) 685-7673
Internet: http://www.ci.atlanta.ga.us/

City of Austin, Texas
Office of the City Manager
City Hall
301 West 2nd Street, 3rd Floor
Austin, TX 78701
Telephone: (512) 974-2200
FAX: (512) 974-2833
Internet: http://www.ci.austin.tx

City of Berea, Kentucky
Office of the City Manager
City Hall 212 Chestnut Street
Berea, KY 40403
Telephone: (859) 986-8258
FAX: (859) 986-7657
Internet: http://www.cityofberea.com

City of Boston, Massachusetts
Office of the Mayor
1 City Hall Plaza
Boston, MA 02201
Telephone: (617) 635-4500
FAX: (617) 635-3496
Internet: http://www.cityofboston.gov/

City of Boulder, Colorado
Office of the City Manager
Municipal Building
1777 Broadway, 2nd Floor
Boulder, CO 8306
Telephone: (303) 441-3090
FAX: (303) 441-4478
Internet: http://www.ci.boulder.co.us

City of Bozeman, Montana
Office of the City Manager
City Hall
411 East Main Street
Bozeman, MT 59771-1230
Telephone: (406) 582-2306
FAX: (406) 582-2344
Internet: http://www.bozeman.net/government

City of Cape Coral, Florida
Office of the City Manager
City Hall
P.O. Box 150027
Cape Coral, FL 33915-0027
Telephone: (239) 574-0447
FAX: (239) 574-0452
Internet: http://www.capecoral.net

City of Colorado Springs, Colorado
Office of the City Manager
City Hall
107 North Nevada Avenue
Colorado Springs, CO 80903
Telephone: (719) 385-5455
FAX: (719) 385-5488
Internet: http://www.springsgov.com

City of Concord, New Hampshire
Office of the City Manager
City Hall
41 Green Street
Concord, NH 03301
Telephone: (603) 225-8570
FAX: (603) 225-8558
Internet: http://www.ci.concord.nh.us

City of Cumming, Georgia
Office of the City Manager
City Hall
100 Main Street
Cumming, GA 30040
Telephone: (770) 781-2010
FAX: None Listed
Internet: http://www.cityof cumming.net

City of Franklin, Tennessee
Office of the City Administrator
City Hall
109 Third Avenue South
Franklin, TN 37064
Telephone: (615) 791-3217
FAX: (615) 790-0469
Internet: http://www.franklin-gov.com

City of Hartford, Connecticut
Office of the Chief Operating Officer
City Hall
550 Main Street
Hartford, CT 06103
Telephone: (860) 543-8520
FAX: (860) 722-6619
Internet: http://www.ci.hartford.ct.us/

City of Hoboken, New Jersey
Office of the Mayor
City Hall
94 Washington Street
Hoboken, NJ 07030
Telephone: (201) 420-2059
FAX: (201) 420-9513
Internet: http://www.hobokennj.org

City of Irwindale, California

Office of the City Manager
City Hall
5050 Irwindale Avenue
Irwindale, CA 91703-2133
Telephone: (626) 430-2200
FAX: (626) 962-4209
Internet: http://www.ci.irwindale.ca.us

City of Las Vegas, Nevada
Office of the City Manager
City Hall, Eighth Floor
400 Stewart Avenue
Las Vegas, NV 89101
Telephone: (702) 229-6501
FAX: (702) 388-1807
Internet: http://www.lasvegasnevada.gov

City of Lowell, Massachusetts
Office of the City Manager
City Hall
375 Merrimack Street
Lowell, MA 01852
Telephone: (978) 970-4000
FAX: (978) 970-4161
Internet: http://www.ci.lowell.ma.us/

City of Memphis, Tennessee
Office of the Chief Administrative Officer
City Hall
125 North Main Street
Room 308
Memphis, TN 38103
Telephone: (901) 576-6558
FAX: (901) 576-6555
Internet: http://www.cityofmemphis.org

City of Minneapolis, Minnesota
Office of the Mayor
City Hall
350 South 5th Street
Room 331
Minneapolis, MN 55415
Telephone: (612) 673-2100
FAX: (612) 673-2305
Internet: http://www.ci.minneapolis.mn.us/

City of Nashua, New Hampshire
Office of the Mayor
City Hall
229 Main Street
Nashua, NH 03060-2019
Telephone: (603) 589-3260
FAX: (603) 534-3450
Internet: http://www.gonashua.com

City of Oakland, California
Office of the City Manager
City Hall, 3rd Floor
250 Frank H. Ogawa Plaza
Oakland, CA 94612-1932
Telephone: (510) 238-3301
FAX: (510) 238-2223
Internet: http://www.oaklandnet.com

City of Parkville, Missouri
Office of the City Administrator
City Hall
1201 East Street
Parkville, MO 64152
Telephone: (816) 741-7676
FAX: (816) 741-0013
Internet: http://www.parkvillemo.com

City of Riverside, California
Office of the City Manager
City Hall
3900 Main Street
Riverside, CA 92522
Telephone: (951) 826-5760
FAX: (951) 826-2046
Internet: http://www.riversideca.gov

City of Rochester, New York
Office of the Mayor
City Hall
30 Church Street
Rochester, NY 14614-1265
Telephone: (585) 428-7600
FAX: (858) 428-6137
Internet: http://www.ci.rochester.ny.us

City of St. Louis, Missouri
Office of the Mayor
City Hall
1200 Market Street
St. Louis, MO 63103-2805
Telephone: (314) 622-4000
FAX: (314) 622-4310
Internet: http://.stlouis.missouri.org

City of St. Maries, Idaho
Office of the Mayor
City Hall
602 West College Avenue
St. Maries, ID 83861-1822
Telephone: (208) 245-2577
FAX: (208) 245-6579
Internet: None Listed

City of Saint Paul, Minnesota
Office of the Mayor
City Hall
Room 390
15 West Kellogg Boulevard
Saint Paul, MN 55102
Telephone: (651) 266-8510
FAX: (651) 266-8513
Internet: http://www.co.stpaul.mn.us/

City of San Diego, California
Office of the City Manager
City Administration Building
202 "C" Street, 11th Floor
San Diego, CA 92101
Telephone: (619) 236-6330
FAX: (619) 236-7153
Internet: http://www.sandiego.gov

City of Santa Rosa, California
Office of the City Manager
City Hall, Room 10
100 Santa Rosa Avenue
Santa Rosa, CA 95404
Telephone: (707) 543-3010
FAX: (707) 543-3030
Internet: http://ci.santa.rosa.ca.us

City of Sarasota, Florida
Office of the City Manager
City Hall
1694 Floyd Street
Sarasota, FL 34239-2132
Telephone: (941) 954-4109
FAX: (941) 954-4129
Internet: http://www.sarasotagov.com

City of Seattle, Washington
Office of the Mayor
City Hall
600–4th Avenue
Seattle, WA 98104
Telephone: (206) 684-4000
FAX: (206) 684-5360
Internet: http://www.ci.seattle.wa.us/

City of South Amboy, New Jersey
Office of the Mayor
City Hall
140 North Broadway
South Amboy, NJ 08879
Telephone: (732) 525-5932
FAX: None Listed
Internet: http://www.yoursouthamboy.com

City of Stamford, Connecticut
Office of the Mayor
Government Center, 10th Floor
888 Washington Boulevard
Stamford, CT 06902
Telephone: (203) 977-4150
FAX: (203) 977-5845
Internet: http://www.cityofstamford.org

City of Tulare, California
Office of the City Manager
City Hall
411 East Kern Avenue
Tulare, CA 93274-4257
Telephone: (559) 684-4200
FAX: (559) 685-2398
Internet: http://www.ci.tulare.ca.us

City of West Des Moines, Iowa
Office of the City Manager
City Hall
4200 Mills Civic Parkway
West Des Moines, IA 5265
Telephone: (515) 222-3610
FAX: (515) 222-3638
Internet: http://www.city.west-des-moines.ia.us

City of Vancouver, Canada
Office of the City Manager
City Hall
453 West 12th Avenue
Vancouver, British Columbia V5Y 1V4
Canada
Telephone: (604) 873-7626
FAX: (604) 873-7641
Internet: http://vancouver.ca

Eastville, Virginia
(See Town of Eastville)

Hanover, New Hampshire
(See Town of Hanover)

Silver Spring, Maryland
c/o Montgomery County
Department of Economic Development
101 Monroe Street, Suite 1500
Rockville, MD 20850
Telephone: (240) 777-2000
FAX: (240) 777-2001
Internet: http://www.montgomerycountymd.gov

Sitka, Alaska
(See City and Borough of Sitka)

Taos, New Mexico
(See Town of Taos)

Town of Eastville, Virginia
Office of the Mayor
P.O. Box 742
Eastville, VA 23347
Telephone: (757) 678-7523
FAX: (757) 678-5329
Internet: None Listed

Town of Hanover, New Hampshire
Office of the Town Manager
Town Hall
41 South Main Street
Hanover, NH 03755-0483
Telephone: (603) 643-0701
FAX: (603) 643-1720
Internet: http://www.hanovernh.org

Town of Taos, New Mexico
Office of the Mayor
Town Hall
400 Camino de la Placita
Taos, NM 87571
Telephone: (505) 751-2000
FAX: (505) 751-2026
Internet: http://www.taosgov.com

Township of Bernards, New Jersey
Office of the Township Administrator
Town Hall
28 Encampment Drive
Bedminster, NJ 07921-1836
Telephone: (908) 204-3011
FAX: (908) 204-3015
Internet: http://www.bernards.org

Township of Cherry Hill, New Jersey
(See Cherry Hill Township)

V. National Resources

Major national professional associations and research organizations serving local governments, as well as environmentally concerned professionals and citizens.

Advisory Council on Historic Preservation
Old Post Office Building
1100 Pennsylvania Avenue, N.W.
Suite 809
Washington, D.C. 20004
Telephone: (202) 606-8503
FAX: (202) 606-8467 or 8672
Internet: http://www.achp.gov

Alliance for National Renewal
c/o National Civic League
1319 "F" St., N.W.
Suite 204
Washington, D.C. 20004
Telephone: (202) 783-2961
FAX: (202) 347-2161
Internet: http://www.ncl.org/anr

Alliance for Redesigning Government
c/o National Academy of Public Administration
1100 New York Ave., N.W.
Suite 1090 East
Washington, D.C. 20005
Telephone: (202) 347-3190
FAX: (202) 393-0993
Internet: http://www.alliance.napawash.org

Alliance for Regional Stewardship
785 Castro St.
Suite A
Mountain View, CA 94011
Telephone: (650) 623-3082
FAX: (650) 623-0900
Internet: http://www.regionalstewardship.org

American Economic Development Council
9801 West Higgins Road
Suite 540
Rosemont, IL 60018-4726
Telephone: (847) 692-9944
FAX: (847) 696-2990
Internet: http://www.aedc.org

American Planning Association
122 S. Michigan Ave.
Suite 1600
Chicago, IL 60603-6107
Telephone: (312) 431-9100
FAX: (312) 431-9985
Internet: http://www.planning.org

American Real Estate and Urban Economics Association
Kelly School of Business
Indiana University
1309 East Tenth Street
Suite 738
Bloomington, IN 47405
Telephone: (812) 855-7794
FAX: (812) 855-8679
Internet: http://www.areuea.org

American Society for Public Administration
1120 "G" St., N.W.

Suite 700
Washington, D.C. 20005
Telephone: (202) 393-7878
FAX: (202) 638-4952
Internet: http://www.aspanet.org

American Society of Landscape Architects
636 Eye St., N.W.
Washington, D.C. 20001-3736
Telephone: (202) 898-2444
FAX: (202) 898-1185
Internet: http://www.asla.org

Asset-Based Community Development Institute
Institute for Policy Research
Northwestern University
2040 Sheridan Road
Evanston, IL 60208-4100
Telephone: (847) 491-3518
FAX: (847) 491-9916
Internet: http://www.nwu.edu/IPR/abcd.html

Association for Enterprise Opportunity
1601 North Kent Street
Suite 1120
Arlington, VA 22209
Telephone: (703) 841-7760
FAX: (703) 841-7748
Internet: http://www.microenterpriseworks.org

Brownfields Technology Support Center
U.S. Environmental Protection Agency
1200 Pennsylvania Avenue, N.W.
Washington, D.C. 20460
Telephone: (877) 838-7220 (toll free)
Internet: http://brownfieldstsc.org

Building Officials and Code Administrators International
4051 Flossmoor Road
Country Club Hills, IL 60478-5795
Telephone: (708) 799-2300
FAX: (708) 799-4981
Internet: http://www.bocai.org

Center for Compatible Economic Development
7 East Market Street
Suite 210
Leesburg, VA 20176
Telephone: (703) 779-1728
FAX: (709) 779-1746
Internet: http://www.cced.org

Center for Neighborhood Technology
2125 W. North Ave.
Chicago, IL 60647
Telephone: (773) 278-4800
FAX: (773) 278-3840
Internet: http://www.cnt.org

Center for Regional and Neighborhood Action
1009 Grant St.
Suite 203
Denver, CO 80203
Telephone: (303) 477-9985
FAX: (303) 477-9986
Internet: http://www.crna.net

Committee for Economic Development
477 Madison Avenue
New York, NY 10022
Telephone: (212) 688-2063
FAX: (212) 758-9068
Internet: http://www.ced.org

Community Associations Institute
225 Reinekers Lane
Suite 300
Alexandria, VA 22314
Telephone: (703) 548-8600
FAX: (703) 684-1581
Internet: http://www.caionline.org

Community Development Society International
1123 North Water Street
Milwaukee, WI 53202
Telephone: (414) 276-7106
FAX: (414) 276-7704
Internet: http://comm-dev.org

Congress for the New Urbanism
The Marquette Building
140 South Dearborn Avenue
Suite 310
Chicago, IL 60603
Telephone: (312) 551-7300
FAX: (312) 346-3323
Internet: http://www.cnu.org

Corporation for Enterprise Development
777 North Capitol Street, N.E.
Suite 410
Washington, D.C. 20002
Telephone: (202) 408-9788
FAX: (202) 408-9793
Internet: http://www.cfed.org

Council for Urban Economic Development
1730 "K" St., N.W.
Suite 700
Washington, D.C. 20006
Telephone: (202) 223-4735
FAX: (202) 223-4745
Internet: http://www.cued.org

Downtown Development and Research Center
215 Park Avenue South
Suite 1301
New York, NY 10003
Telephone: (212) 228-0246
FAX: (212) 228-0376
Internet: http://www.DowntownDevelopment.com

Ecological Society of America
1707 "H" Street, N.W.
Suite 400
Washington, D.C. 20006-3915
Telephone: (202) 833-8773
FAX: (202) 833-8775
Internet: http://www.esa.org

Empowerment Zones
(See U.S. Dept. of Housing and Urban Development)

Enterprise Communities Initiative
(See U.S. Dept. of Housing and Urban Development)

Environmental Assessment Association
1224 North Nakomis, N.E.
Alexandria, MN 56308
Telephone: (320) 763-4320
FAX: (320) 763-9290
Internet: http://iami.org

Habitat for Humanity International
Partner Service Center
121 Habitat Street
Americus, GA 31709
Telephone: (912) 924-6935, Ext. 2551 or 2552
FAX: (912) 924-6541
Internet: http://www.habitat.org

Interactive Economic Development Network
1730 "K" Street, N.W.
Suite 700
Washington, D.C. 20006
Telephone: (202) 223-4735

FAX: (202) 223-4745
Internet: http://www.iedn.com

International City/County Management Association
777 North Capitol Street, N.E.
Suite 500
Washington, D.C. 20002
Telephone: (202) 289-4262
FAX: (202) 962-3500
Internet: http://www.icma.org

International Conference of Building Officials
5360 South Workman Mill Road
Whittier, CA 90601-2258
Telephone: (310) 699-0541
FAX: (310) 692-3853
Internet: http://www.icbo.org

International Downtown Association
190-17th Street, N.W.
Suite 210
Washington, D.C. 20006
Telephone: (202) 293-4505
FAX: (202) 293-4509
Internet: http://ida-downtown.org

Local Government Commission
1414 "K" Street
Suite 250
Sacramento, CA 95814
Telephone: (916) 448-1198
FAX: (916) 448-8246
Internet: http://www.lgc.org

National Academy of Public Administration
1101 New York Ave.
Suite 1090 East
Washington, D.C. 20005
Telephone: (202) 347-3190
FAX: (202) 393-0993
Internet: http://www.napawash.org

National Association of Counties
Joint Center for Sustainable Communities
440 First Street, N.W.
Washington, D.C. 20001-2080
Telephone: (202) 393-6226
FAX: (202) 393-2630
Internet: http://www.naco.org

National Association of Development Organizations
444 North Capitol Street, N.W.

Suite 630
Washington, D.C. 20001
Telephone: (202) 624-7806
FAX: (202) 624-8813
Internet: http://www.nado.org

National Association of Housing and Redevelopment Officials
630 Eye Street, N.W.
Washington, D.C. 20001
Telephone: (202) 289-3500
FAX: (202) 289-8181
Internet: http://www.nahro.org

National Association of Regional Councils
1700 "K" Street, N.W.
Suite 1300
Washington, D.C. 20006
Telephone: (202) 457-0710
FAX: (202) 296-9352
Internet: http://www.narc.org/narc

National Association of State Development Agencies
750 First Street, N.E.
Suite 710
Washington, D.C. 20002
Telephone: (202) 898-1302
FAX: (202) 898-1312
Internet: http://www.ids.net/nasda

National Association for Environmental Management
1612 "K" Street, N.W.
Suite 1102
Washington, D.C. 20006
Telephone: (202) 986-6616
FAX: (202) 530-4408
Internet: http://www.naem.org

National Association of Local Governmental Environmental Professionals
1333 New Hampshire Ave., N.W.
Washington, D.C. 20036
Telephone: (202) 638-6254
FAX: (202) 393-2866
Internet: http://www.nalgep.org

National Audubon Society
700 Broadway
New York, NY 10003
Telephone: (212) 979-3000
FAX: (212) 979-3188
Internet: http://www.audubon.org

National Business Incubation Association
20 East Circle Drive
Suite 190
Athens, OH 45701-3751
Telephone: (740) 593-4331
FAX: (740) 593-1996
Internet: http://www.nbia.org

National Center for the Revitalization of Central Cities
College of Urban and Public Affairs
University of New Orleans
New Orleans, LA 70148
Telephone: (504) 280-6519
FAX: (504) 280-6272
Internet: http://www.uno-edul-cupa/ncrcc

National Civic League
1445 Market Street
Suite 300
Denver, CO 80202-1728
Telephone: (303) 571-4343
FAX: (303) 571-4404
Internet: http://www.ncl.org

National Community Development Association
522-21st St., N.W.
Suite 120
Washington, D.C. 20006
Telephone: (202) 293-7587
FAX: (202) 887-5546
Internet: http://www.ncdaonline.org

National Congress for Community Economic Development
1030-15th St., N.W.
Suite 325
Washington, D.C. 20005
Telephone: (202) 289-9020
FAX: (202) 289-7051
Internet: http://www.ncced.org

National Council for Urban Economic Development
1730 "K" Street, N.W.
Suite 700
Washington, D.C. 20006
Telephone: (202) 223-4735
FAX: (202) 223-4745
Internet: http://www.cued.org

National Endowment for the Humanities
1100 Pennsylvania Avenue, N.W.
Washington, D.C. 20506

Telephone: (202) 606-8310
FAX: (202) 606-8600
Internet: http://www.neh.gov

National Groundwater Association
601 Dempsey Road
Westerville, OH 48081-8978
Telephone: (614) 898-7791
FAX: (614) 898-7786
Internet: http://www.ngwa.org

National Housing Conference
815 Fifteenth Street, N.W.
Suite 538
Washington, D.C. 20005
Telephone: (202) 393-5772
FAX: (202) 393-5656
Internet: http://www.nhc.org

National Housing Institute
439 Main Street
Suite 311
Orange, NJ 07050
Telephone: (973) 678-9060
FAX: (973) 678-8437
Internet: http://www.nhi.org

National Humanities Alliance
21 Dupont Circle, N.W.
Suite 604
Washington, D.C. 20036
Telephone: (202) 296-4994
FAX: (202) 872-0884
Internet: http://www.nhalliance.org

National League of Cities
1301 Pennsylvania Avenue, N.W.
Washington, D.C. 20004-1763
Telephone: (202) 626-3000
FAX: (202) 626-3043
Internet: http://www.nlc.org

National Main Street Center
(See National Trust for Historic Preservation)

National Trust for Historic Preservation
1785 Massachusetts Avenue, N.W.
Washington, D.C. 20036
Telephone: (202) 588-6219
FAX: (202) 588-6050
Internet: http://www.mainst.org

Natural Resource Conservation Service
(See U.S. Department of Agriculture)

Nature Conservancy
4245 North Fairfax Dr.

Suite 100
Arlington, VA 22203-1606
Telephone: (703) 247-3678
FAX: (703) 841-1283
Internet: http://nature.org

Office of Community Development
U.S. Department of Agriculture
Whitten Building
Washington, D.C. 20250-1301
Telephone: (202) 720-3621
FAX: (202) 720-5043
Internet: http://ocdweb.sc.egov.usda.gov

Partners for Livable Communities
1429-21st Street, N.W.
Washington, D.C. 20036
Telephone: (202) 887-5990
FAX: (202) 466-4845
Internet: http://www.livable.com

Partnership for Regional Livability
2125 W. North Ave.
Chicago, IL 60647
Telephone: (773) 278-4800, Ext. 135
FAX: (773) 278-3840
Internet: http://www.pfrl.org

Rails-to-Trails Conservancy
1100 Seventeenth St., N.W.
10th Floor
Washington, D.C. 20036
Telephone: (202) 331-9696
FAX: (202) 466-3742
Internet: http://www.railtrails.org

Sierra Club
85 Second Street
2nd Floor
San Francisco, CA 94105
Telephone: (415) 977-5500
FAX: (415) 977-5799
Internet: http://www.sierraclub.org

Society of Wetland Scientists
1313 Dolly Madison
Suite 402
McLean, VA 22101
Telephone: (703) 790-1745
FAX: (703) 790-2672
Internet: http://www.sws.org

The Urban Institute
2100 "M" St., N.W.
Washington, D.C. 20037
Telephone: (202) 833-7200

FAX: (202) 331-9747
Internet: http://www.urban.org

Trust for Public Land
116 New Montgomery St.
4th Floor
San Francisco, CA 94105
Telephone: (415) 495-4014
FAX: (415) 495-4103
Internet: http://www.tpl.org

United States Conference of Mayors
1620 Eye St., N.W.
4th Floor
Washington, D.C. 20006
Telephone: (202) 293-7330
FAX: (202) 293-2352
Internet: http://www.usmayors.org

U.S. Department of Agriculture
14th and Independence Avenue, S.W.
Room 5105-A
Washington, D.C. 20250
Telephone: (202) 720-7246
FAX: (202) 720-7690
Internet: http://www.nrcs.usda.gov

U.S. Department of Housing and Urban Development
451-7th Street, S.W.
Washington, D.C. 20410
Telephone: (202) 708-1112
FAX: (202) 401-0416
Internet: http://www.hud.gov

U.S. Department of the Interior
1849 "C" Street, N.W.
Washington, D.C. 20240
Telephone: (202) 208-3100
FAX: (202) 208-4833
Internet: http://www.doi.gov

Urban and Regional Information Systems Association
1460 Renaissance Drive
Suite 305
Park Ridge, IL 60068
Telephone: (847) 824-6300
FAX: (847) 824-6363
Internet: http://www.urisa.org

Urban Land Institute
1015 Thomas Jefferson St., N.W.
Suite 500 West
Washington, D.C. 20007-5201

Telephone: (202) 624-7000
FAX: (202) 624-7140
Internet: http://www.uli.org

U.S. Environmental Protection Agency
Ariel Rios Building
1200 Pennsylvania Ave., N.W.
Washington, D.C. 20460
Telephone: (202) 272-0167
FAX: None Listed
Internet: http://www.epa.gov

U.S. Fish & Wildlife Service
1849 "C" Street, N.W.
Washington, D.C. 20240
Telephone: (202) 208-4717
FAX: (202) 208-6965
Internet: http://www.fws.gov

Water Environment Federation
601 Wythe Street
Alexandria, VA 22314-1994
Telephone: (703) 684-2452
FAX: (703) 684-2492
Internet: http://www.wef.org

About the Editor and Contributors

Editor and Contributor

Roger L. Kemp, PhD, has been the chief executive officer of cities on both the West and East coasts for over two decades. He is presently town manager for Berlin, Connecticut, which was founded in 1785. Dr. Kemp has also been an adjunct professor at leading universities during his career, including the University of California, California State University, Rutgers University, the University of Connecticut, and Golden Gate University. Roger holds BS, MPA, MBA, and PhD degrees, and is a graduate of the Program for Senior Executives in State and Local Government from the John F. Kennedy School of Government at Harvard University. Dr. Kemp is listed in *Who's Who in America, Contemporary American Authors*, and the *International Who's Who Registry of Outstanding Professionals*. Roger has been an author, editor, and contributing author to nearly 50 books dealing with America's cities, and their future. He is past-president of the Connecticut City and Town Management Association, and the Connecticut Chapter of the American Society for Public Administration.

Contributors

Affiliations are as of the times the articles were written.

Jacquelyn A. Anthony, assistant coordinator, the America Project, Atlanta, Georgia.

Tom Arrandale, freelance writer covering state and local government environmental policies, Livingston, Montana.

Mary Ann Barton, freelance writer, Arlington, Virginia.

Charles Bartsch, supervisor of Brownfield Financing Studies, Northeast-Midwest Institute, Washington, D.C.

David A. Bloom, freelance writer and former research associate, National Civic League, Denver, Colorado.

Susan F. Boyd, executive director, CONCERN, Washington, D.C.

Nancy Bragado, acting general plan program manager, Planning Department, City of San Diego, California.

Hamilton Brown, director of training and technical assistance, National Center for Small Communities, Washington, D.C.

Rebecca Bryant, freelance writer and planning consultant, Fayetteville, Arkansas.

Sherry Plaster Carter, urban planner and partner, Carter and Carter Associates, Sarasota, Florida.

Darryl Clare, program manager, Geographic Information Systems (GIS), City of Cape Coral, Florida.

Jarle Crocker, assistant director, Community

Services Program, National Civic League, Denver, Colorado.

Storm Cunningham, chief executive officer, Restor Ability Inc., Alexandria, Virginia.

Robert B. Denhardt, Messick Professor of Public Administration, School of Urban Affairs and Public Policy, University of Delaware, Newark, Delaware.

Alan Ehrenhalt, executive editor, *Governing*, Congressional Quarterly Inc., Washington, D.C.

Dennis Farney, freelance journalist and staff writer, *The Wall Street Journal*, New York, New York.

Richard C. Feiock, professor and PhD program director, Askew School of Public Administration and Policy; and program director, Local Governance, DeVoe L. Moore Center; Florida State University, Tallahassee, Florida.

Kevin Fletcher, director of programs and administration, Audubon International, Selkirk, New York.

David Gales, principal, Vantage Technology Consulting Group, Los Angeles, California, and Boston, Massachusetts.

John Goodman, staff writer, *Governing*, Congressional Quarterly Inc., Washington, D.C.

Joseph E. Gray, department manager, Office of Community Affairs, Orange County, South Apoka, Florida.

Rob Gurwitt, correspondent, *Governing*, Congressional Quarterly Inc., Washington, D.C.

Pat Hawver, city administrator, City of Parkville, Missouri.

Timothy Hayes, director of sustainable development, Northampton County, Eastville, Virginia.

Allan Hope, executive director, Main Street Program, City of South Amboy, New Jersey.

Rebekka Hosken, management advisor, Management Partners, Inc., San Jose, California.

Moon-Gi Jeong, PhD candidate and DeVoe L. Moore Graduate Fellow, Askew School of Public Administration and Policy, Florida State University, Tallahassee, Florida.

Curtis Johnson, chairman, Metropolitan Council, St. Paul, Minnesota, and long-time urban affairs writer with service in the public and nonprofit sectors.

Barbara Lance, city clerk, City of Parkville, Missouri.

Mary Lechner, director of finance, Northampton County, Eastville, Virginia.

Susan Bass Levin, commissioner, Department of Community Affairs, State of New Jersey, Trenton, New Jersey.

Richard Mahler, freelance writer specializing in Native American and environmental issues, Santa Fe, New Mexico, and Santa Cruz, California.

Emil Malizia, professor and chair, Department of City and Regional Planning, University of North Carolina, Chapel Hill, North Carolina.

Mark Matthews, freelance writer, Missoula, Montana.

Edward T. McMahon, senior resident fellow and the Charles E. Fraser Chair, Sustainable Development and Environmental Policy, Urban Land Institute, Washington, D.C.

Peter A. Messina, engineer and planner, Bernards Township, New Jersey.

Lance Metzler, county administrator, Northampton County, Eastville, Virginia.

Vicki Monks, freelance writer and broadcast journalist, Santa Fe, New Mexico.

Gerald Newfarmer, president and chief executive officer, Management Partners, Inc., Cincinnati, Ohio.

Mark A. Nuszer, president, Nuszer and Kopatz, Denver, Colorado.

Kim A. O'Connell, freelance writer, Arlington, Virginia.

John O'Looney, public service associate, Carl Vinson Institute of Government, University of Georgia, Athens, Georgia.

Amy Cohen Paul, partner, Management Partners, Inc., Cincinnati, Ohio.

Joseph N. Pelton, executive director, Arthur C. Clarke Institute; and director, Space and

Advanced Communications Research Institute; George Washington University, Washington, D.C.

Ellen Perlman, staff writer, *Governing*, Congressional Quarterly Inc., Washington, D.C.

Bernie Platt, mayor, Cherry Hill Township, New Jersey.

Bill Quitmeier, mayor, City of Parkville, Missouri.

David Rusk, international consultant, and former mayor, City of Albuquerque, Albuquerque, New Mexico.

Carleton Ryffel, former planning director, City of Cape Coral, Florida.

Jennifer Schroeder, program officer, Clean Air–Cool Planet, Portsmouth, New Hampshire.

Richard M. Sheehan, accountant, Finance Department, Arapahoe County, Littleton, Colorado.

Mike Sheridan, financial journalist, Houston, Texas.

John F. Shirey, executive cirector, California Redevelopment Association, Sacramento, California.

Ken Snyder, project specialist, Community Development Program, U. S. Department of Energy, Denver, Colorado.

Matt Stansberry, freelance writer, Needham, Massachusetts.

Nancy Stark, director of community and economic development, National Center for Small Communities, Washington, D.C.

Dan E. Sweat, director, the American Project, Atlanta, Georgia.

Stella Tarnay, principal, Tarnay & Associates, a planning and communications firm, Washington, D.C.

Dell Tredinnick, project development manager, Build It Green Program, City of Santa Rosa, California.

Paul Van Buskirk, independent planning consultant, Estero, Florida.

Alexander von Hoffman, senior research fellow, Joint Center for Housing Studies, Harvard University, Cambridge, Massachusetts.

Todd Wilkinson, freelance writer, Bozeman, Montana.

Christine Woodside, freelance writer and editor, Deep River, Connecticut.

Index